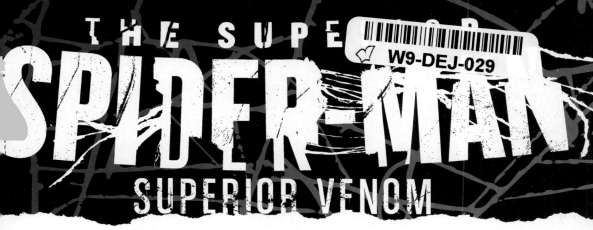

THE SUPE

SPIDER-MAN

SUPERIOR VENOM

SUPERIOR SPIDER-MAN #22-25

WRITERS
DAN SLOTT & CHRISTOS GAGE

PENCILER
HUMBERTO RAMOS

INKER
VICTOR OLAZABA

COLORISTS
EDGAR DELGADO
WITH ANTONIO FABELA
& VERONICA GANDINI (#24-25)

COVER ART
HUMBERTO RAMOS
& EDGAR DELGADO

SUPERIOR SPIDER-MAN #26

WRITER
DAN SLOTT

PENCILERS
HUMBERTO RAMOS, JAVIER RODRIGUEZ & MARCOS MARTIN

INKERS
VICTOR OLAZABA, ALVARO LOPEZ & MARCOS MARTIN

COLORISTS
EDGAR DELGADO, JAVIER RODRIGUEZ
& MARCOS MARTIN

COVER ART
RYAN STEGMAN &
JASON HOWARD

SUPERIOR SPIDER-MAN ANNUAL #1

WRITER
CHRISTOS GAGE

PENCILER & COLORIST
JAVIER RODRIGUEZ

INKER
ALVARO LOPEZ

COVER ART
J.G. JONES & LAURA MARTIN

LETTERER
VC'S CHRIS ELIOPOULOS

ASSISTANT EDITOR
ELLIE PYLE

EDITOR
STEPHEN WACKER

Collection Editor: **Jennifer Grünwald** • Associate Managing Editor: **Alex Starbuck** • Editor, Special Projects: **Mark D. Beazley**
Senior Editor, Special Projects: **Jeff Youngquist** • SVP Print, Sales & Marketing: **David Gabriel** • Book Design: **Jeff Powell**

Editor in Chief: **Axel Alonso** • Chief Creative Officer: **Joe Quesada** • Publisher: **Dan Buckley** • Executive Producer: **Alan Fine**

ERIOR SPIDER-MAN VOL. 5: THE SUPERIOR VENOM. Contains material originally published in magazine form as SUPERIOR SPIDER-MAN #22-26 and ANNUAL #1. First printing 2014. ISBN# 978-0-7851-8796-7. Published by MARVEL LDWIDE, INC., a subsidiary of MARVEL ENTERTAINMENT, LLC. OFFICE OF PUBLICATION: 135 West 50th Street, New York, NY 10020. **Printed in Canada.** ALAN FINE, EVP - Office of the President, Marvel Worldwide, Inc. and EVP & CMO Marvel Characters B.V.; DAN BUCKLEY, sher & President - Print, Animation & Digital Divisions; JOE QUESADA, Chief Creative Officer; TOM BREVOORT, SVP of Publishing; DAVID BOGART, SVP of Operations & Procurement, Publishing; C.B. CEBULSKI, SVP of Creator & Content lopment; DAVID GABRIEL, SVP Print, Sales & Marketing; JIM O'KEEFE, VP of Operations & Logistics; DAN CARR, Executive Director of Publishing Technology; SUSAN CRESPI, Editorial Operations Manager; ALEX MORALES, Publishing ations Manager; STAN LEE, Chairman Emeritus. For information regarding advertising in Marvel Comics or on Marvel.com, please contact Niza Disla, Director of Marvel Partnerships, at ndisla@marvel.com. For Marvel subscription inquiries, e call 800-217-9158. **Manufactured between 2/21/2014 and 3/31/2014 by SOLISCO PRINTERS, SCOTT, QC, CANADA.**

8 7 6 5 4 3 2 1

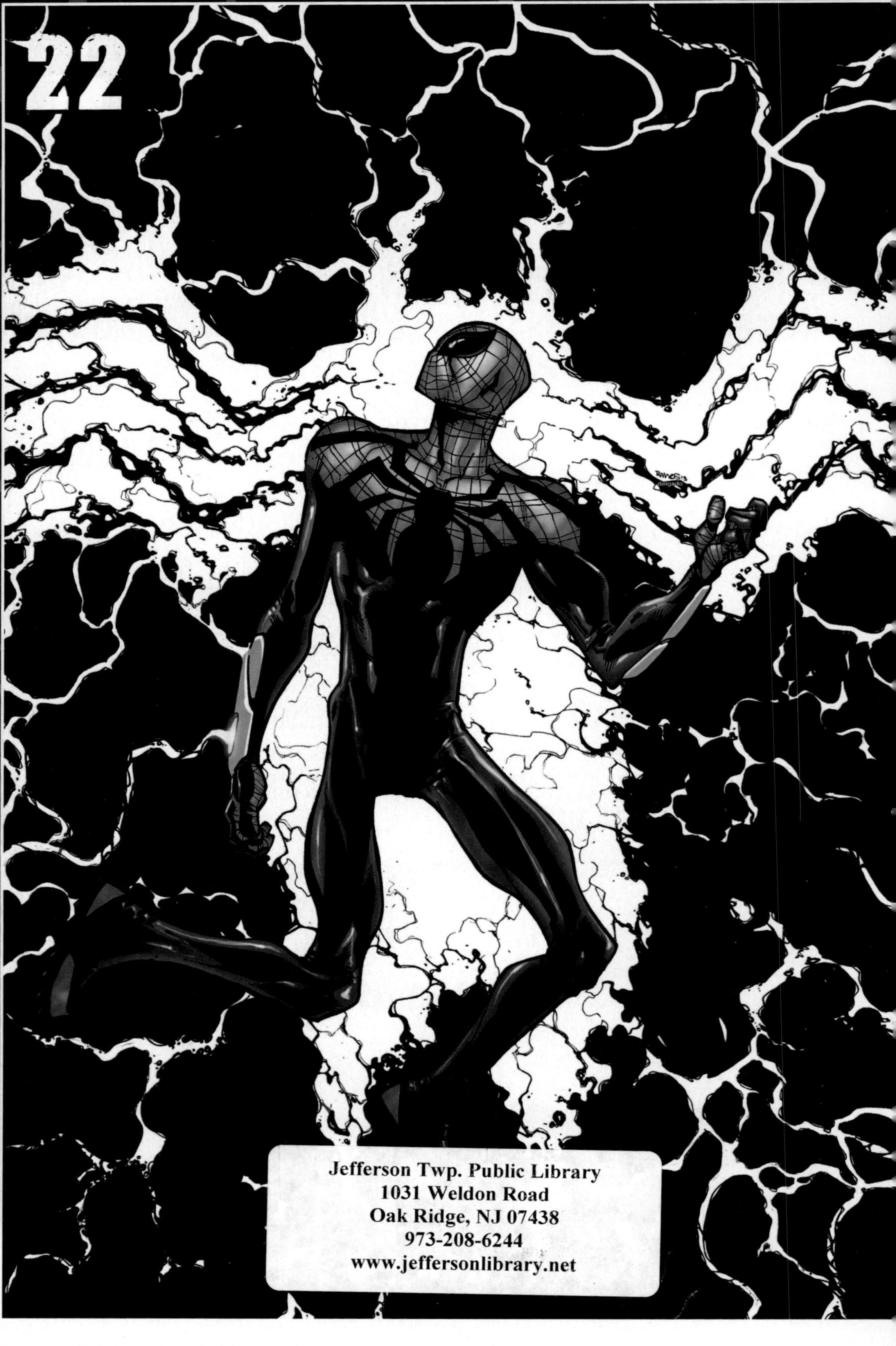
22

DARKEST HOURS PART 1: FACE TO FACE

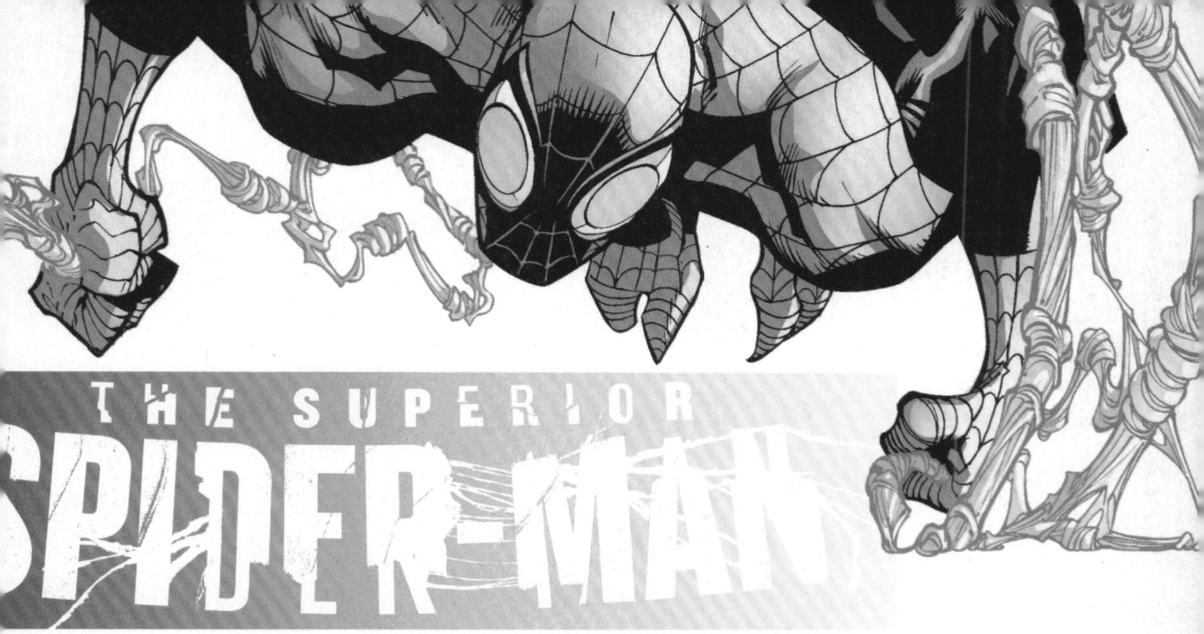
THE SUPERIOR
SPIDER-MAN

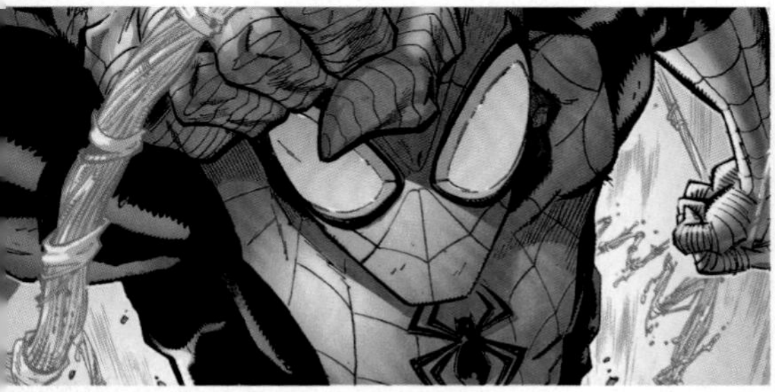

HEN **OTTO OCTAVIUS** WAS DYING, HE SAVED HIS GREATEST ICK FOR LAST: SWITCHING BODIES WITH **PETER PARKER.** TH THIS, OTTO GAINED THE AMAZING SKILLS OF SPIDER-AN, AS WELL AS ALL OF PETER'S MEMORIES, INSPIRING M TO BE A BETTER HERO THAN PARKER EVER WAS AND BECOME — THE SUPERIOR SPIDER-MAN!

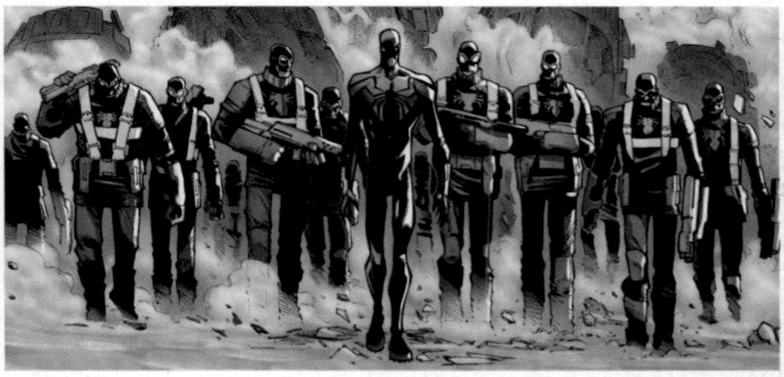

SINCE THEN, HIS REPUTATION FOR MERCILESS EFFICIENCY HAS GROWN. HE HAS HIRED HENCHMEN AND USES SPIDER-BOTS TO MONITOR THE CITY AT ALL TIMES. HE HAS EVEN HAS A BASE HE'S CALLING "SPIDER-ISLAND."

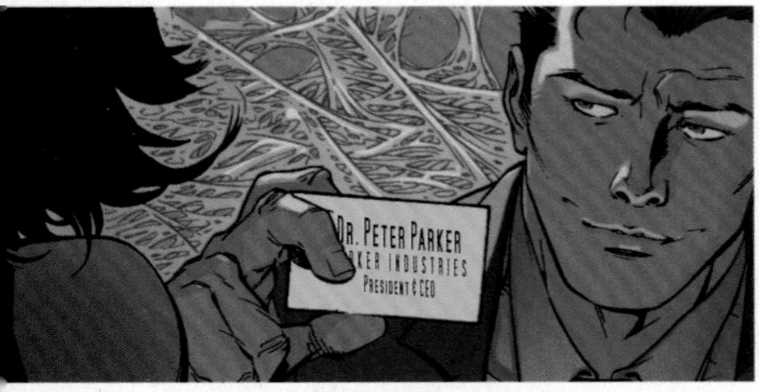
DR. PETER PARKER
PRESIDENT & CEO

EANWHILE, AFTER THE DESTRUCTION OF HORIZON BS, PETER PARKER HAS BEGUN A NEW BUSINESS NTURE WHERE HE WILL NO DOUBT CONTINUE TO ISTOMIZE HIS ARSENAL OF WEAPONS AGAINST SPIDER-MAN'S KNOWN ENEMIES.

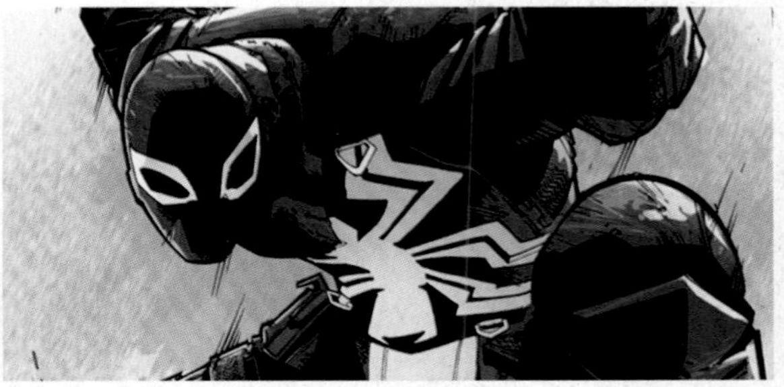

AS A TEENAGER, FLASH THOMPSON WAS THE AMAZING SPIDER-MAN'S BIGGEST FAN. NOW HE IS **AGENT VENOM,** A SUPERHERO IN AN ALIEN PARASITE SUIT THAT GRANTS ITS HOSTS SHAPE-SHIFTING ABILITIES AND POWERS SIMILAR TO SPIDER-MAN. THE VENOM SYMBIOTE HAS BEEN AN ENEMY OF SPIDER-MAN'S IN THE PAST. BUT SPIDER-MAN AND AGENT VENOM HAVE NEVER MET.

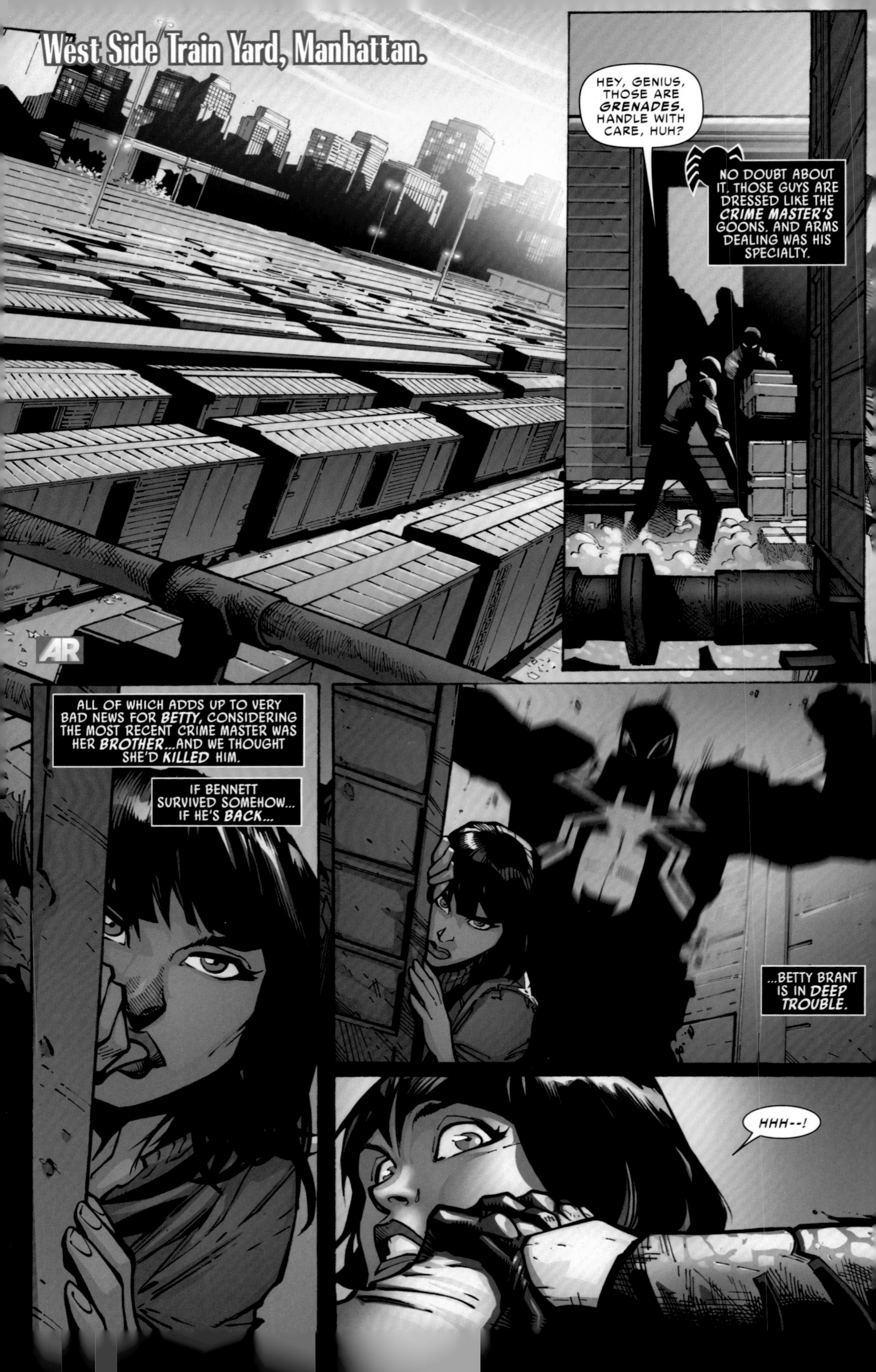

West Side Train Yard, Manhattan.
HEY, GENIUS, THOSE ARE GRENADES. HANDLE WITH CARE, HUH?
NO DOUBT ABOUT IT. THOSE GUYS ARE DRESSED LIKE THE CRIME MASTER'S GOONS. AND ARMS DEALING WAS HIS SPECIALTY.
ALL OF WHICH ADDS UP TO VERY BAD NEWS FOR BETTY, CONSIDERING THE MOST RECENT CRIME MASTER WAS HER BROTHER...AND WE THOUGHT SHE'D KILLED HIM.
IF BENNETT SURVIVED SOMEHOW... IF HE'S BACK...
...BETTY BRANT IS IN DEEP TROUBLE.
HHH--!

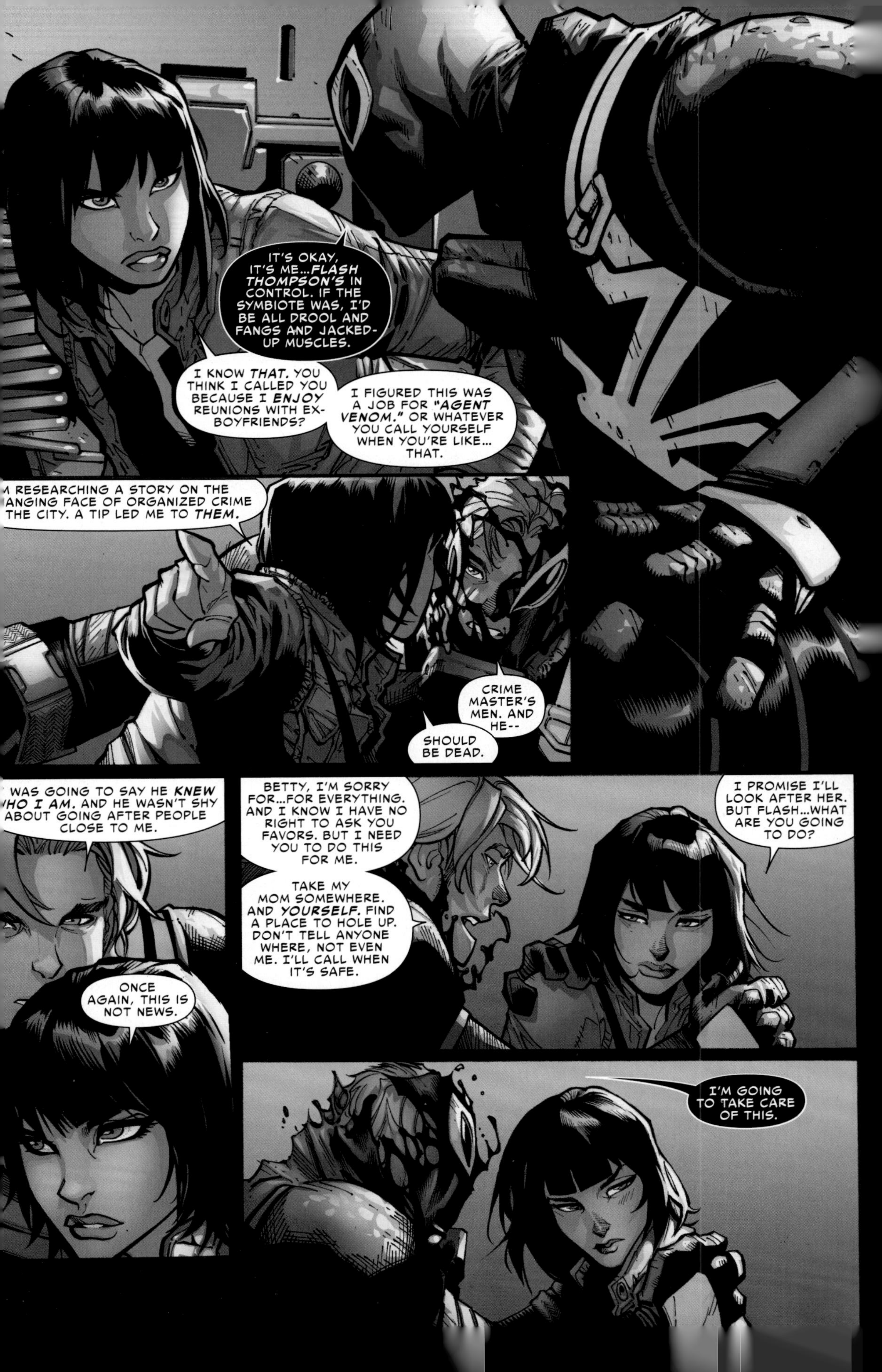
IT'S OKAY, IT'S ME...FLASH THOMPSON'S IN CONTROL. IF THE SYMBIOTE WAS, I'D BE ALL DROOL AND FANGS AND JACKED-UP MUSCLES.
I KNOW THAT. YOU THINK I CALLED YOU BECAUSE I ENJOY REUNIONS WITH EX-BOYFRIENDS?
I FIGURED THIS WAS A JOB FOR "AGENT VENOM." OR WHATEVER YOU CALL YOURSELF WHEN YOU'RE LIKE... THAT.
M RESEARCHING A STORY ON THE ANGING FACE OF ORGANIZED CRIME THE CITY. A TIP LED ME TO THEM.
CRIME MASTER'S MEN. AND HE--
SHOULD BE DEAD.
WAS GOING TO SAY HE KNEW HO I AM. AND HE WASN'T SHY ABOUT GOING AFTER PEOPLE CLOSE TO ME.
ONCE AGAIN, THIS IS NOT NEWS.
BETTY, I'M SORRY FOR...FOR EVERYTHING. AND I KNOW I HAVE NO RIGHT TO ASK YOU FAVORS. BUT I NEED YOU TO DO THIS FOR ME.
TAKE MY MOM SOMEWHERE. AND YOURSELF. FIND A PLACE TO HOLE UP. DON'T TELL ANYONE WHERE, NOT EVEN ME. I'LL CALL WHEN IT'S SAFE.
I PROMISE I'LL LOOK AFTER HER. BUT FLASH...WHAT ARE YOU GOING TO DO?
I'M GOING TO TAKE CARE OF THIS.

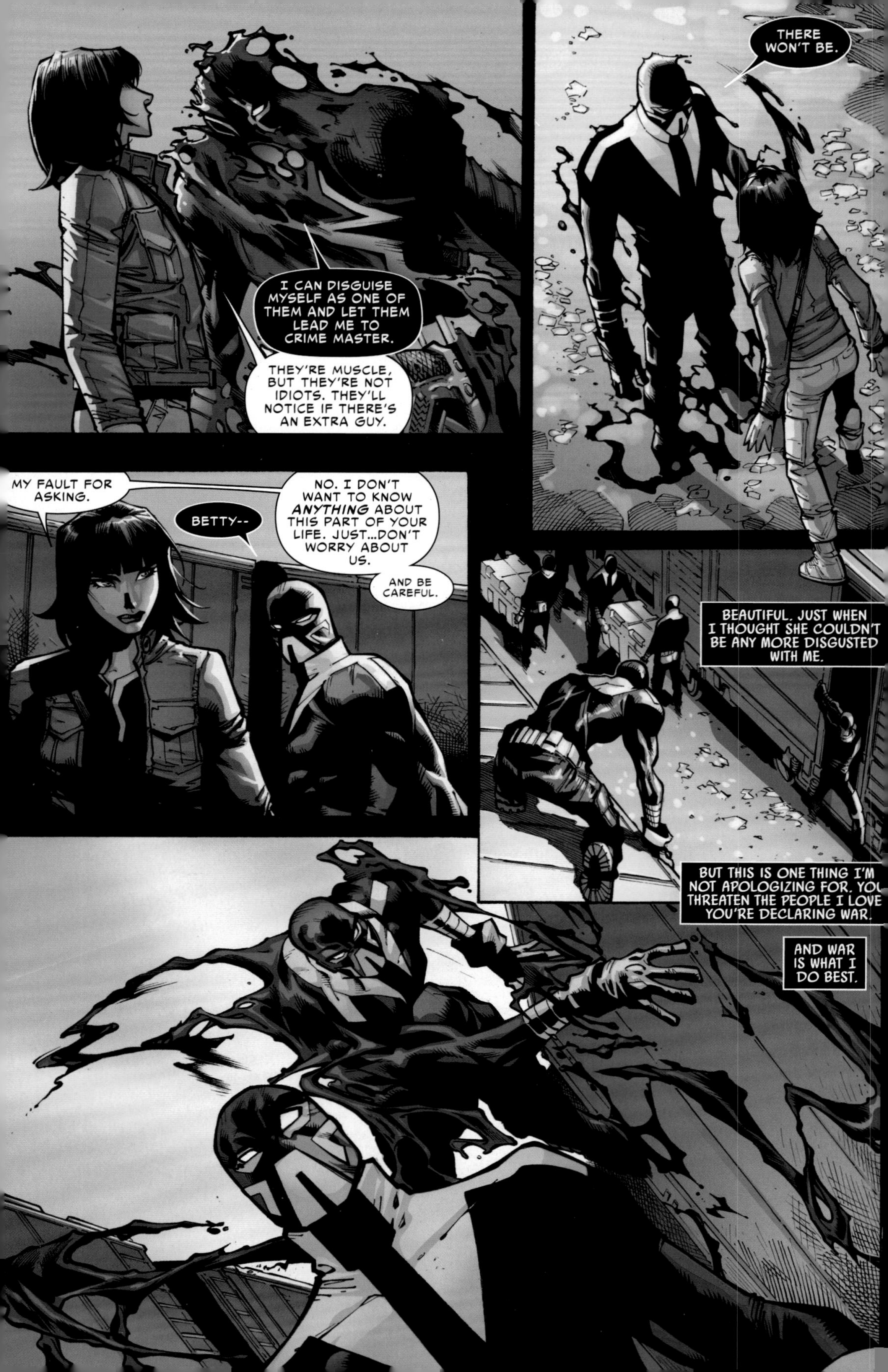
I CAN DISGUISE MYSELF AS ONE OF THEM AND LET THEM LEAD ME TO CRIME MASTER.
THEY'RE MUSCLE, BUT THEY'RE NOT IDIOTS. THEY'LL NOTICE IF THERE'S AN EXTRA GUY.
THERE WON'T BE.
MY FAULT FOR ASKING.
BETTY--
NO. I DON'T WANT TO KNOW *ANYTHING* ABOUT THIS PART OF YOUR LIFE. JUST...DON'T WORRY ABOUT US.
AND BE CAREFUL.
BEAUTIFUL. JUST WHEN I THOUGHT SHE COULDN'T BE ANY MORE DISGUSTED WITH ME.
BUT THIS IS ONE THING I'M NOT APOLOGIZING FOR. YOU THREATEN THE PEOPLE I LOVE YOU'RE DECLARING WAR.
AND WAR IS WHAT I DO BEST.

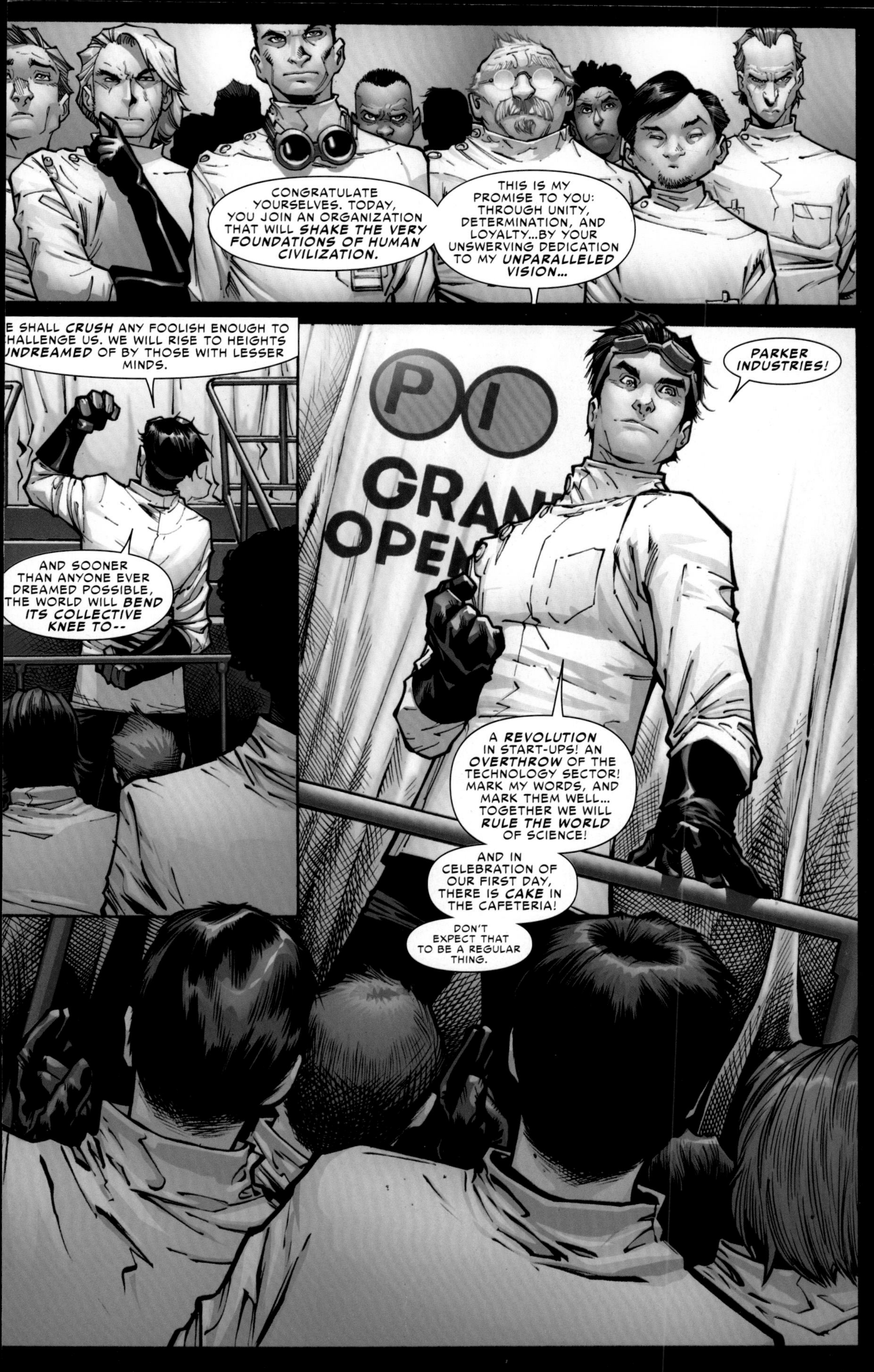

CONGRATULATE YOURSELVES. TODAY, YOU JOIN AN ORGANIZATION THAT WILL SHAKE THE VERY FOUNDATIONS OF HUMAN CIVILIZATION.
THIS IS MY PROMISE TO YOU: THROUGH UNITY, DETERMINATION, AND LOYALTY...BY YOUR UNSWERVING DEDICATION TO MY UNPARALLELED VISION...
E SHALL CRUSH ANY FOOLISH ENOUGH TO HALLENGE US. WE WILL RISE TO HEIGHTS UNDREAMED OF BY THOSE WITH LESSER MINDS.
AND SOONER THAN ANYONE EVER DREAMED POSSIBLE, THE WORLD WILL BEND ITS COLLECTIVE KNEE TO--
PARKER INDUSTRIES!
PI
GRAN
OPE
A REVOLUTION IN START-UPS! AN OVERTHROW OF THE TECHNOLOGY SECTOR! MARK MY WORDS, AND MARK THEM WELL... TOGETHER WE WILL RULE THE WORLD OF SCIENCE!
AND IN CELEBRATION OF OUR FIRST DAY, THERE IS CAKE IN THE CAFETERIA!
DON'T EXPECT THAT TO BE A REGULAR THING.

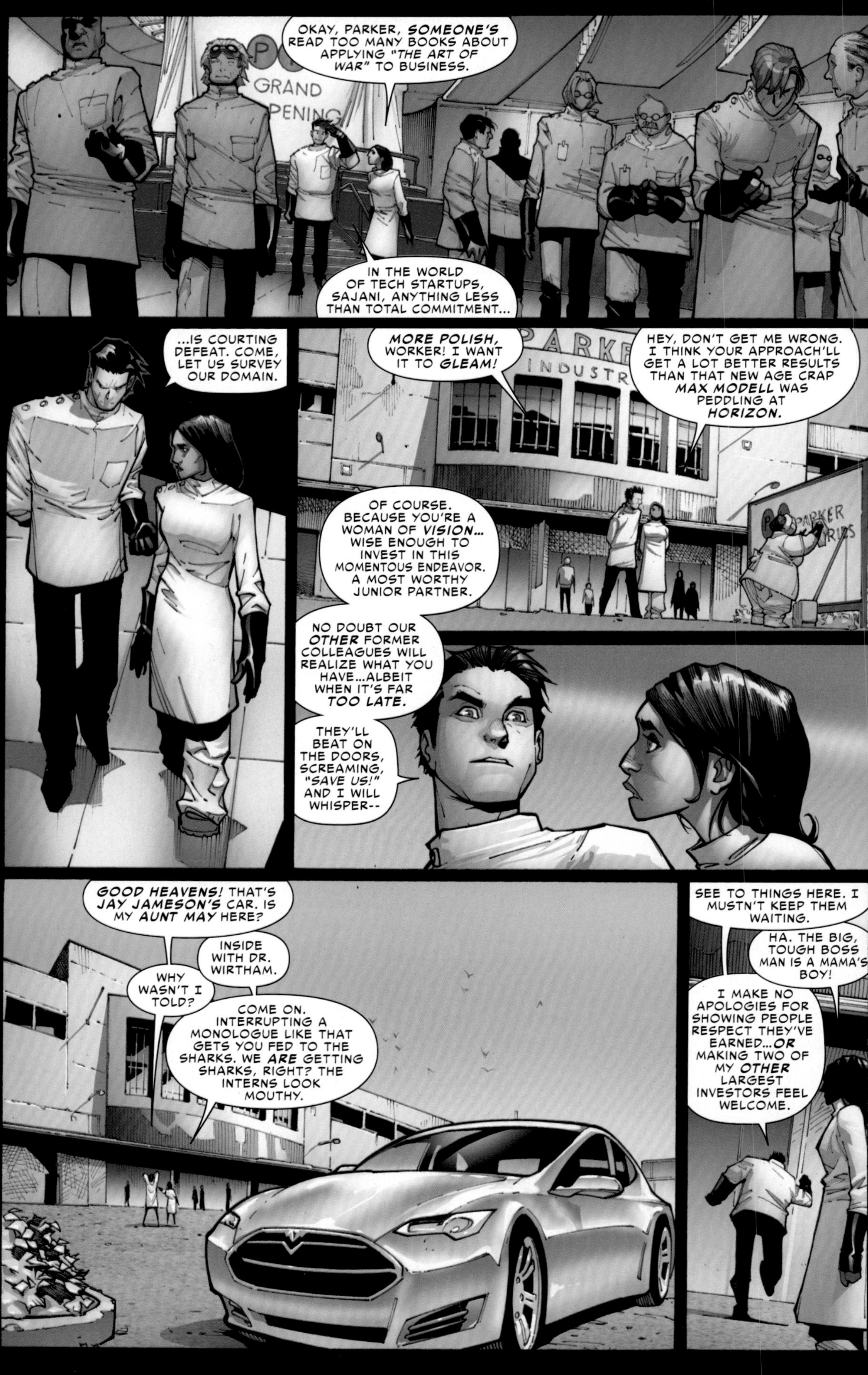
OKAY, PARKER, SOMEONE'S READ TOO MANY BOOKS ABOUT APPLYING "THE ART OF WAR" TO BUSINESS.
GRAND
PENING
IN THE WORLD OF TECH STARTUPS, SAJANI, ANYTHING LESS THAN TOTAL COMMITMENT...
...IS COURTING DEFEAT. COME, LET US SURVEY OUR DOMAIN.
MORE POLISH, WORKER! I WANT IT TO GLEAM!
HEY, DON'T GET ME WRONG. I THINK YOUR APPROACH'LL GET A LOT BETTER RESULTS THAN THAT NEW AGE CRAP MAX MODELL WAS PEDDLING AT HORIZON.
ARKE
INDUSTR
OF COURSE. BECAUSE YOU'RE A WOMAN OF VISION... WISE ENOUGH TO INVEST IN THIS MOMENTOUS ENDEAVOR. A MOST WORTHY JUNIOR PARTNER.
PARKER
NO DOUBT OUR OTHER FORMER COLLEAGUES WILL REALIZE WHAT YOU HAVE...ALBEIT WHEN IT'S FAR TOO LATE.
THEY'LL BEAT ON THE DOORS, SCREAMING, "SAVE US!" AND I WILL WHISPER--
GOOD HEAVENS! THAT'S JAY JAMESON'S CAR. IS MY AUNT MAY HERE?
INSIDE WITH DR. WIRTHAM.
WHY WASN'T I TOLD?
COME ON. INTERRUPTING A MONOLOGUE LIKE THAT GETS YOU FED TO THE SHARKS. WE ARE GETTING SHARKS, RIGHT? THE INTERNS LOOK MOUTHY.
SEE TO THINGS HERE. I MUSTN'T KEEP THEM WAITING.
HA. THE BIG, TOUGH BOSS MAN IS A MAMA'S BOY!
I MAKE NO APOLOGIES FOR SHOWING PEOPLE RESPECT THEY'VE EARNED...OR MAKING TWO OF MY OTHER LARGEST INVESTORS FEEL WELCOME.

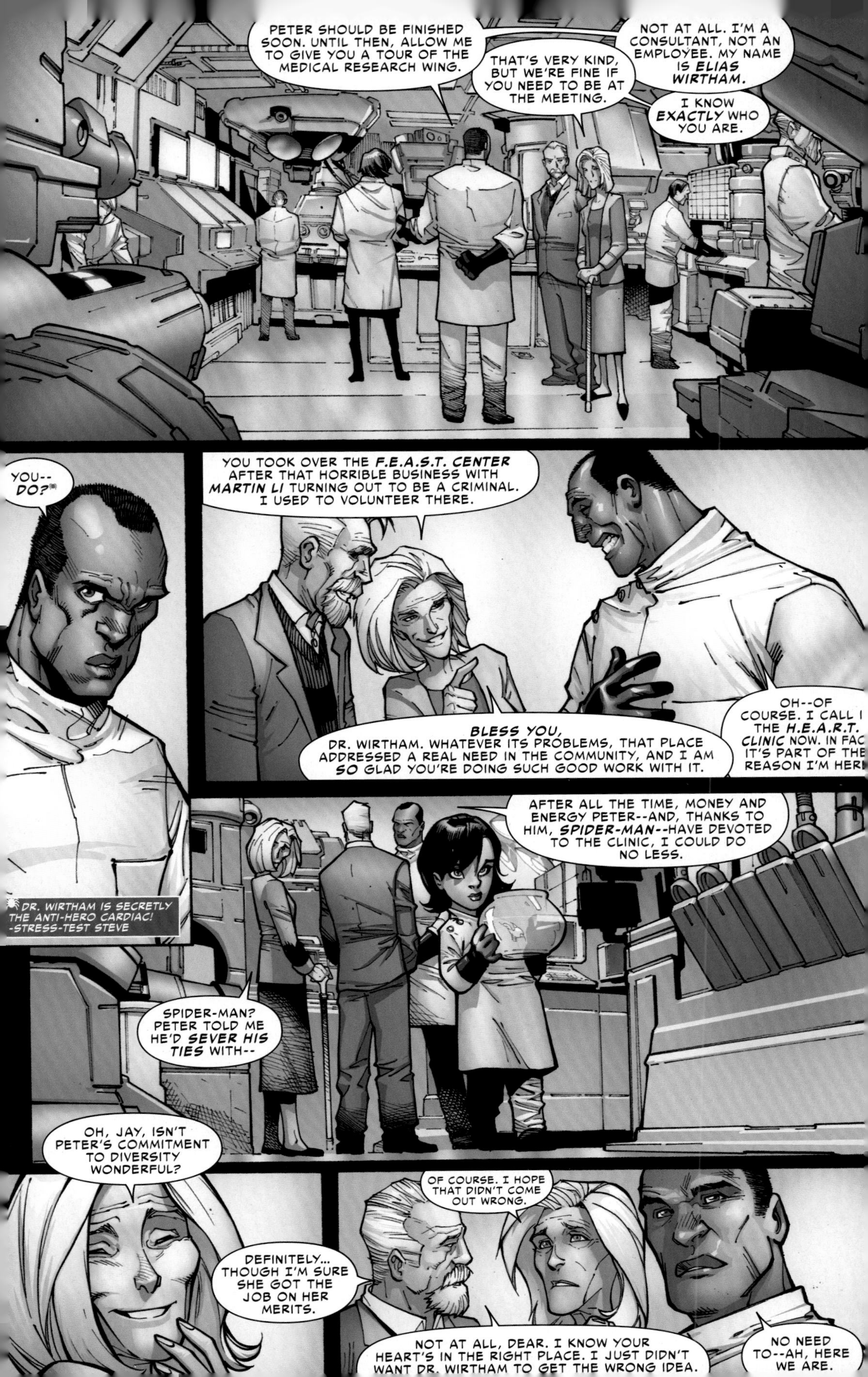

PETER SHOULD BE FINISHED SOON. UNTIL THEN, ALLOW ME TO GIVE YOU A TOUR OF THE MEDICAL RESEARCH WING.
THAT'S VERY KIND, BUT WE'RE FINE IF YOU NEED TO BE AT THE MEETING.
NOT AT ALL. I'M A CONSULTANT, NOT AN EMPLOYEE. MY NAME IS ELIAS WIRTHAM.
I KNOW EXACTLY WHO YOU ARE.
YOU--DO?
YOU TOOK OVER THE F.E.A.S.T. CENTER AFTER THAT HORRIBLE BUSINESS WITH MARTIN LI TURNING OUT TO BE A CRIMINAL. I USED TO VOLUNTEER THERE.
BLESS YOU, DR. WIRTHAM. WHATEVER ITS PROBLEMS, THAT PLACE ADDRESSED A REAL NEED IN THE COMMUNITY, AND I AM SO GLAD YOU'RE DOING SUCH GOOD WORK WITH IT.
OH--OF COURSE. I CALL I THE H.E.A.R.T. CLINIC NOW. IN FAC IT'S PART OF THE REASON I'M HER
DR. WIRTHAM IS SECRETLY THE ANTI-HERO CARDIAC! -STRESS-TEST STEVE
AFTER ALL THE TIME, MONEY AND ENERGY PETER--AND, THANKS TO HIM, SPIDER-MAN--HAVE DEVOTED TO THE CLINIC, I COULD DO NO LESS.
SPIDER-MAN? PETER TOLD ME HE'D SEVER HIS TIES WITH--
OH, JAY, ISN'T PETER'S COMMITMENT TO DIVERSITY WONDERFUL?
DEFINITELY... THOUGH I'M SURE SHE GOT THE JOB ON HER MERITS.
OF COURSE. I HOPE THAT DIDN'T COME OUT WRONG.
NOT AT ALL, DEAR. I KNOW YOUR HEART'S IN THE RIGHT PLACE. I JUST DIDN'T WANT DR. WIRTHAM TO GET THE WRONG IDEA.
NO NEED TO--AH, HERE WE ARE.

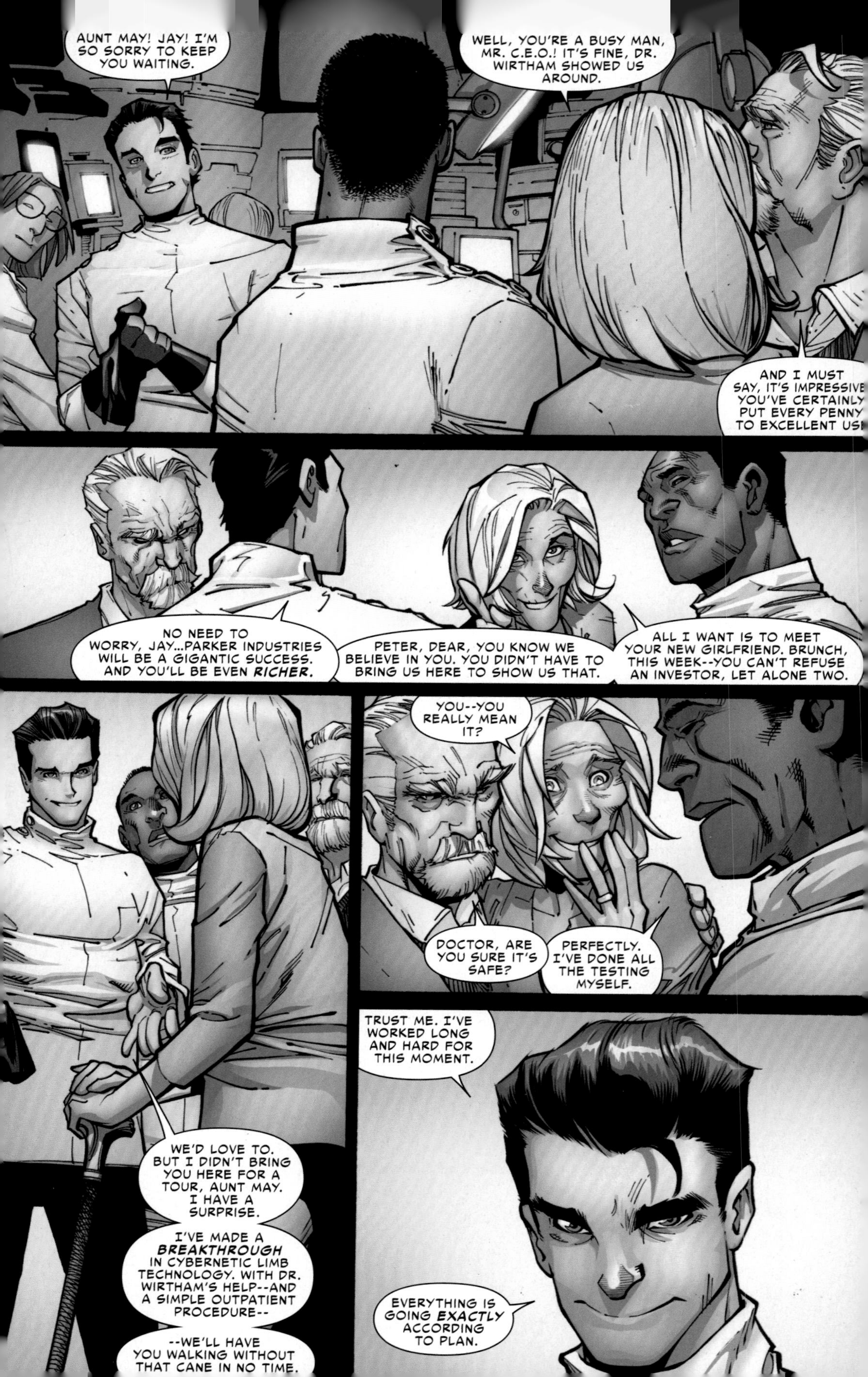
AUNT MAY! JAY! I'M SO SORRY TO KEEP YOU WAITING.
WELL, YOU'RE A BUSY MAN, MR. C.E.O.! IT'S FINE, DR. WIRTHAM SHOWED US AROUND.
AND I MUST SAY, IT'S IMPRESSIVE YOU'VE CERTAINLY PUT EVERY PENNY TO EXCELLENT US
NO NEED TO WORRY, JAY...PARKER INDUSTRIES WILL BE A GIGANTIC SUCCESS. AND YOU'LL BE EVEN *RICHER*.
PETER, DEAR, YOU KNOW WE BELIEVE IN YOU. YOU DIDN'T HAVE TO BRING US HERE TO SHOW US THAT.
ALL I WANT IS TO MEET YOUR NEW GIRLFRIEND. BRUNCH, THIS WEEK--YOU CAN'T REFUSE AN INVESTOR, LET ALONE TWO.
WE'D LOVE TO. BUT I DIDN'T BRING YOU HERE FOR A TOUR, AUNT MAY. I HAVE A SURPRISE.
I'VE MADE A *BREAKTHROUGH* IN CYBERNETIC LIMB TECHNOLOGY. WITH DR. WIRTHAM'S HELP--AND A SIMPLE OUTPATIENT PROCEDURE--
--WE'LL HAVE YOU WALKING WITHOUT THAT CANE IN NO TIME.
YOU--YOU REALLY MEAN IT?
DOCTOR, ARE YOU SURE IT'S SAFE?
PERFECTLY. I'VE DONE ALL THE TESTING MYSELF.
TRUST ME. I'VE WORKED LONG AND HARD FOR THIS MOMENT.
EVERYTHING IS GOING *EXACTLY* ACCORDING TO PLAN.

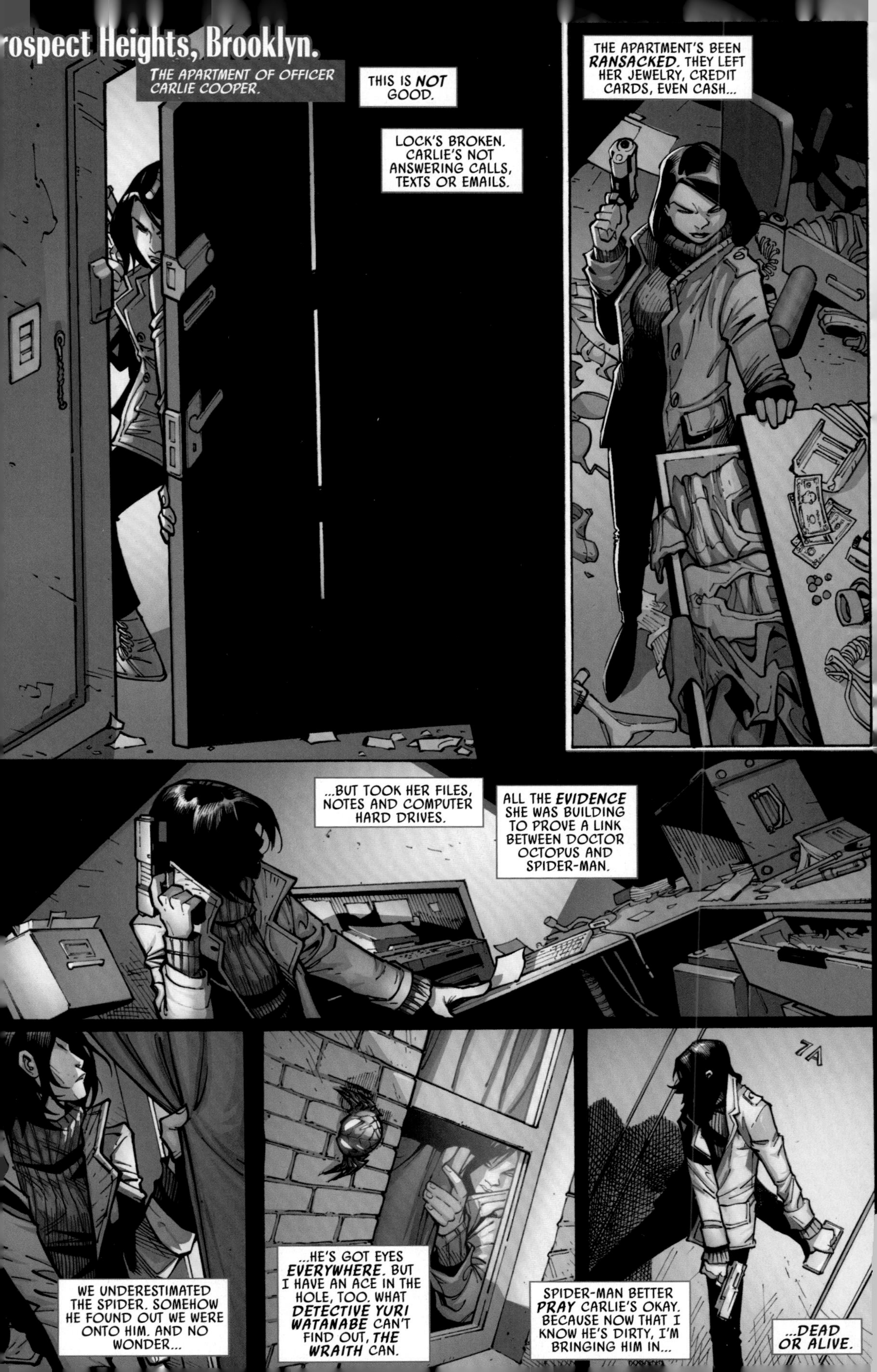

rospect Heights, Brooklyn.
THE APARTMENT OF OFFICER CARLIE COOPER.
THIS IS NOT GOOD.
LOCK'S BROKEN. CARLIE'S NOT ANSWERING CALLS, TEXTS OR EMAILS.
THE APARTMENT'S BEEN RANSACKED. THEY LEFT HER JEWELRY, CREDIT CARDS, EVEN CASH...
...BUT TOOK HER FILES, NOTES AND COMPUTER HARD DRIVES.
ALL THE EVIDENCE SHE WAS BUILDING TO PROVE A LINK BETWEEN DOCTOR OCTOPUS AND SPIDER-MAN.
WE UNDERESTIMATED THE SPIDER. SOMEHOW HE FOUND OUT WE WERE ONTO HIM. AND NO WONDER...
...HE'S GOT EYES EVERYWHERE. BUT I HAVE AN ACE IN THE HOLE, TOO. WHAT DETECTIVE YURI WATANABE CAN'T FIND OUT, THE WRAITH CAN.
7A
SPIDER-MAN BETTER PRAY CARLIE'S OKAY. BECAUSE NOW THAT I KNOW HE'S DIRTY, I'M BRINGING HIM IN...
...DEAD OR ALIVE.

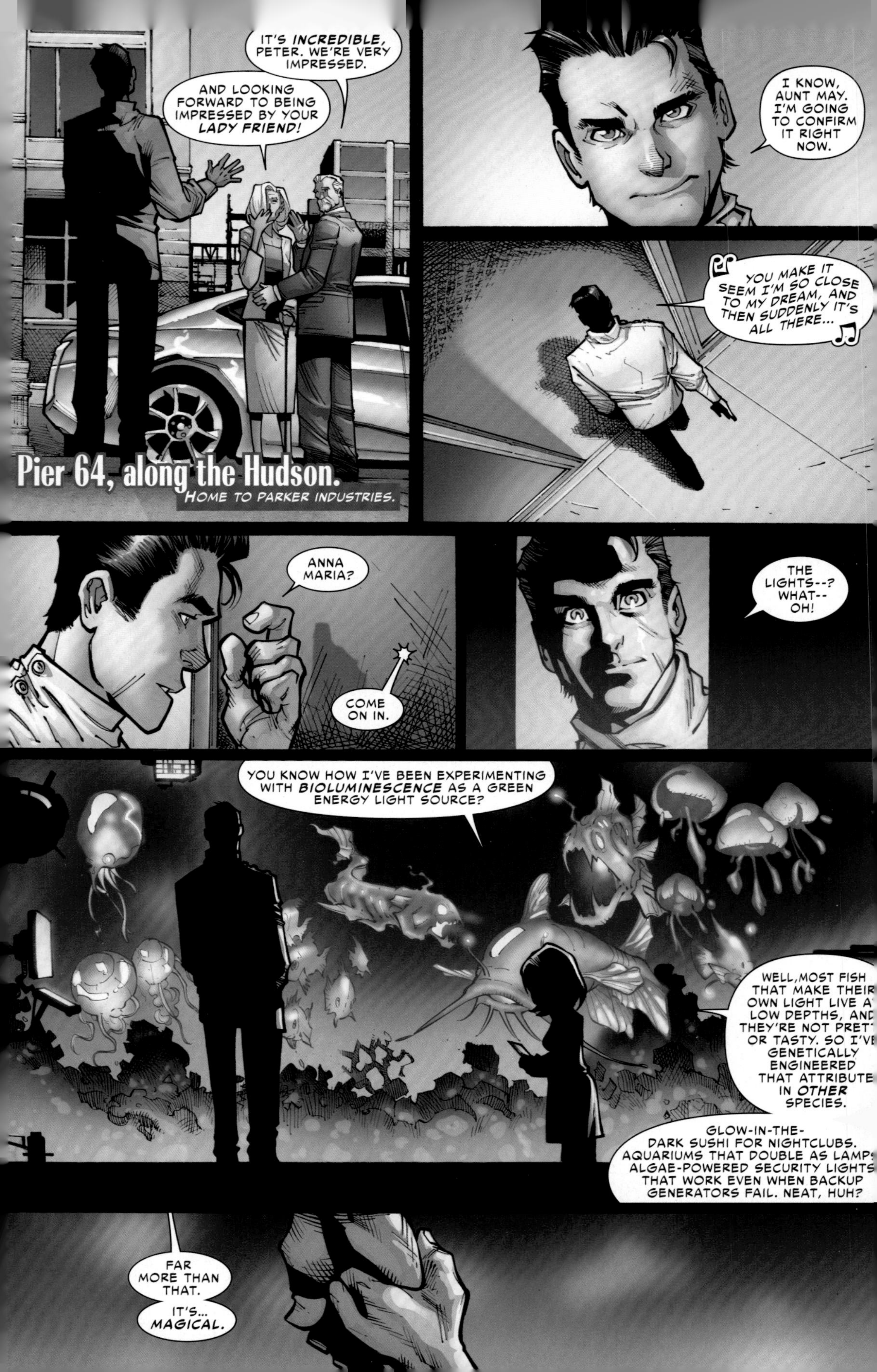
IT'S INCREDIBLE, PETER. WE'RE VERY IMPRESSED.
AND LOOKING FORWARD TO BEING IMPRESSED BY YOUR LADY FRIEND!
Pier 64, along the Hudson.
HOME TO PARKER INDUSTRIES.
I KNOW, AUNT MAY. I'M GOING TO CONFIRM IT RIGHT NOW.
YOU MAKE IT SEEM I'M SO CLOSE TO MY DREAM, AND THEN SUDDENLY IT'S ALL THERE...
ANNA MARIA?
COME ON IN.
THE LIGHTS--? WHAT-- OH!
YOU KNOW HOW I'VE BEEN EXPERIMENTING WITH BIOLUMINESCENCE AS A GREEN ENERGY LIGHT SOURCE?
WELL, MOST FISH THAT MAKE THEIR OWN LIGHT LIVE AT LOW DEPTHS, AND THEY'RE NOT PRETT OR TASTY. SO I'VE GENETICALLY ENGINEERED THAT ATTRIBUTE IN OTHER SPECIES.
GLOW-IN-THE-DARK SUSHI FOR NIGHTCLUBS. AQUARIUMS THAT DOUBLE AS LAMPS. ALGAE-POWERED SECURITY LIGHTS THAT WORK EVEN WHEN BACKUP GENERATORS FAIL. NEAT, HUH?
FAR MORE THAN THAT.
IT'S... MAGICAL.

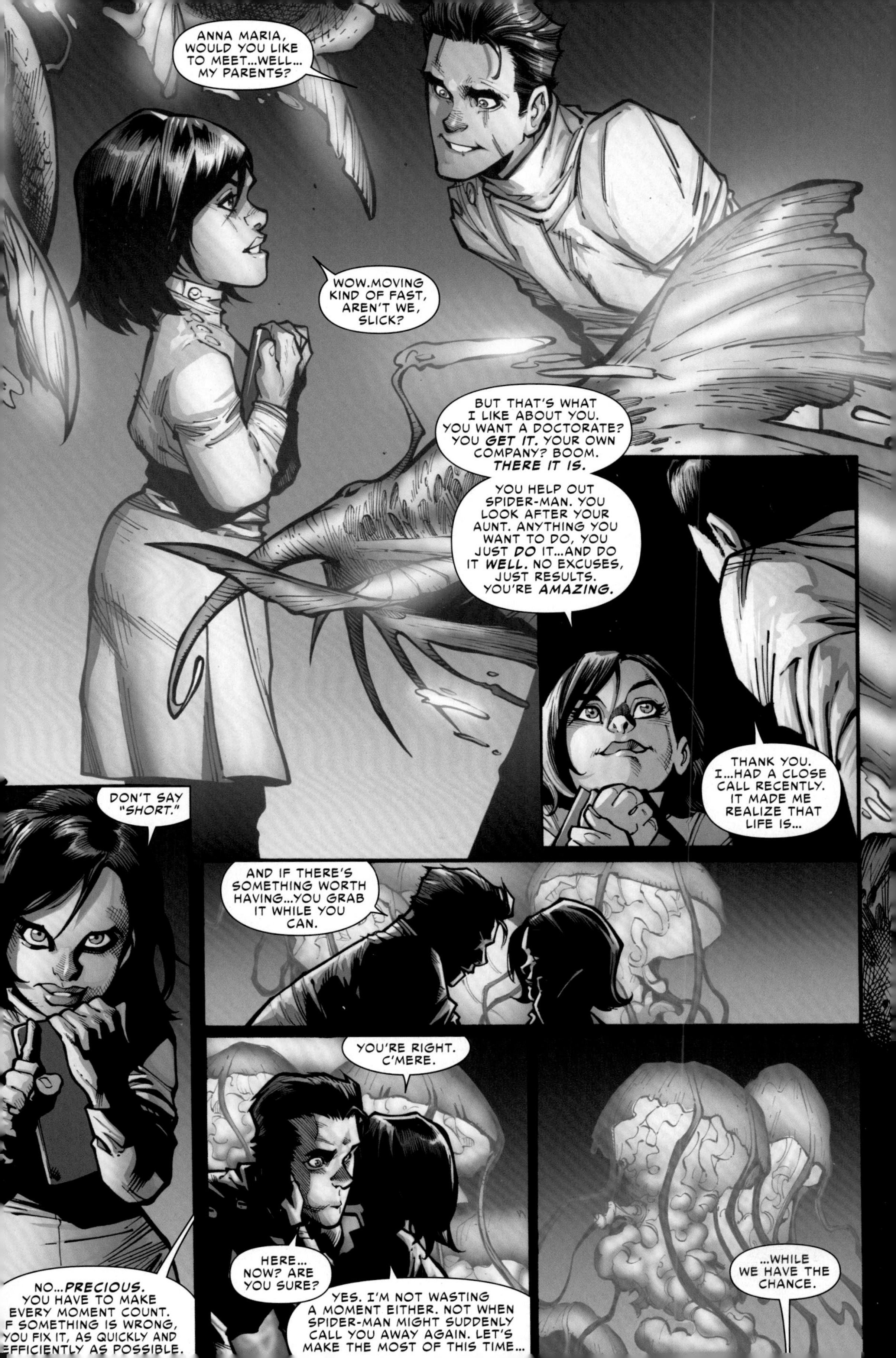
ANNA MARIA, WOULD YOU LIKE TO MEET...WELL... MY PARENTS?
WOW.MOVING KIND OF FAST, AREN'T WE, SLICK?
BUT THAT'S WHAT I LIKE ABOUT YOU. YOU WANT A DOCTORATE? YOU GET IT. YOUR OWN COMPANY? BOOM. THERE IT IS.
YOU HELP OUT SPIDER-MAN. YOU LOOK AFTER YOUR AUNT. ANYTHING YOU WANT TO DO, YOU JUST DO IT...AND DO IT WELL. NO EXCUSES, JUST RESULTS. YOU'RE AMAZING.
THANK YOU. I...HAD A CLOSE CALL RECENTLY. IT MADE ME REALIZE THAT LIFE IS...
DON'T SAY "SHORT."
NO...PRECIOUS. YOU HAVE TO MAKE EVERY MOMENT COUNT. F SOMETHING IS WRONG, YOU FIX IT, AS QUICKLY AND EFFICIENTLY AS POSSIBLE.
AND IF THERE'S SOMETHING WORTH HAVING...YOU GRAB IT WHILE YOU CAN.
YOU'RE RIGHT. C'MERE.
HERE... NOW? ARE YOU SURE?
YES. I'M NOT WASTING A MOMENT EITHER. NOT WHEN SPIDER-MAN MIGHT SUDDENLY CALL YOU AWAY AGAIN. LET'S MAKE THE MOST OF THIS TIME...
...WHILE WE HAVE THE CHANCE.

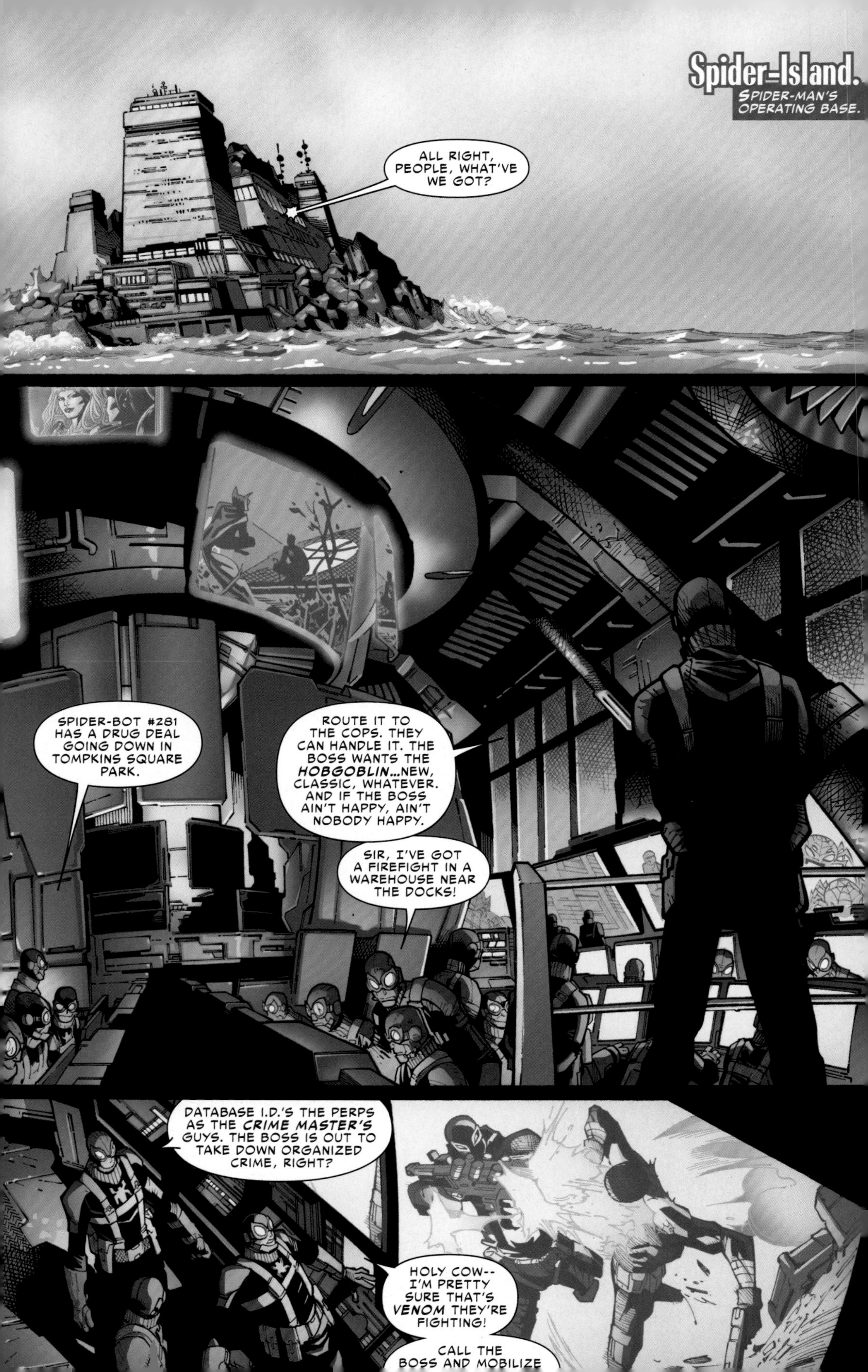
Spider-Island.
SPIDER-MAN'S OPERATING BASE.
ALL RIGHT, PEOPLE, WHAT'VE WE GOT?
SPIDER-BOT #281 HAS A DRUG DEAL GOING DOWN IN TOMPKINS SQUARE PARK.
ROUTE IT TO THE COPS. THEY CAN HANDLE IT. THE BOSS WANTS THE HOBGOBLIN...NEW, CLASSIC, WHATEVER. AND IF THE BOSS AIN'T HAPPY, AIN'T NOBODY HAPPY.
SIR, I'VE GOT A FIREFIGHT IN A WAREHOUSE NEAR THE DOCKS!
DATABASE I.D.'S THE PERPS AS THE CRIME MASTER'S GUYS. THE BOSS IS OUT TO TAKE DOWN ORGANIZED CRIME, RIGHT?
HOLY COW-- I'M PRETTY SURE THAT'S VENOM THEY'RE FIGHTING!
CALL THE BOSS AND MOBILIZE

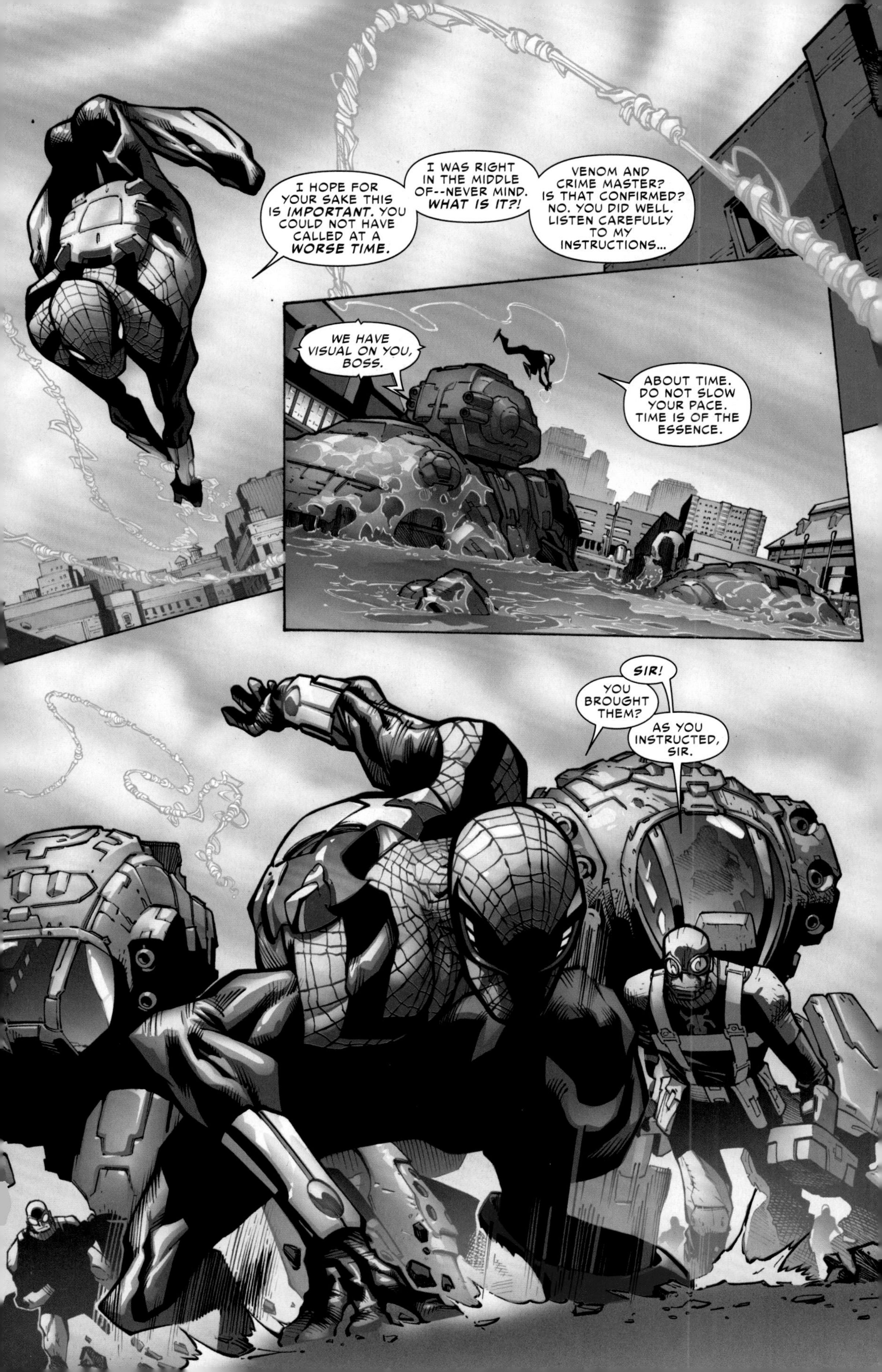
I HOPE FOR YOUR SAKE THIS IS IMPORTANT. YOU COULD NOT HAVE CALLED AT A WORSE TIME.
I WAS RIGHT IN THE MIDDLE OF--NEVER MIND. WHAT IS IT?!
VENOM AND CRIME MASTER? IS THAT CONFIRMED? NO. YOU DID WELL. LISTEN CAREFULLY TO MY INSTRUCTIONS...
WE HAVE VISUAL ON YOU, BOSS.
ABOUT TIME. DO NOT SLOW YOUR PACE. TIME IS OF THE ESSENCE.
SIR!
YOU BROUGHT THEM?
AS YOU INSTRUCTED, SIR.

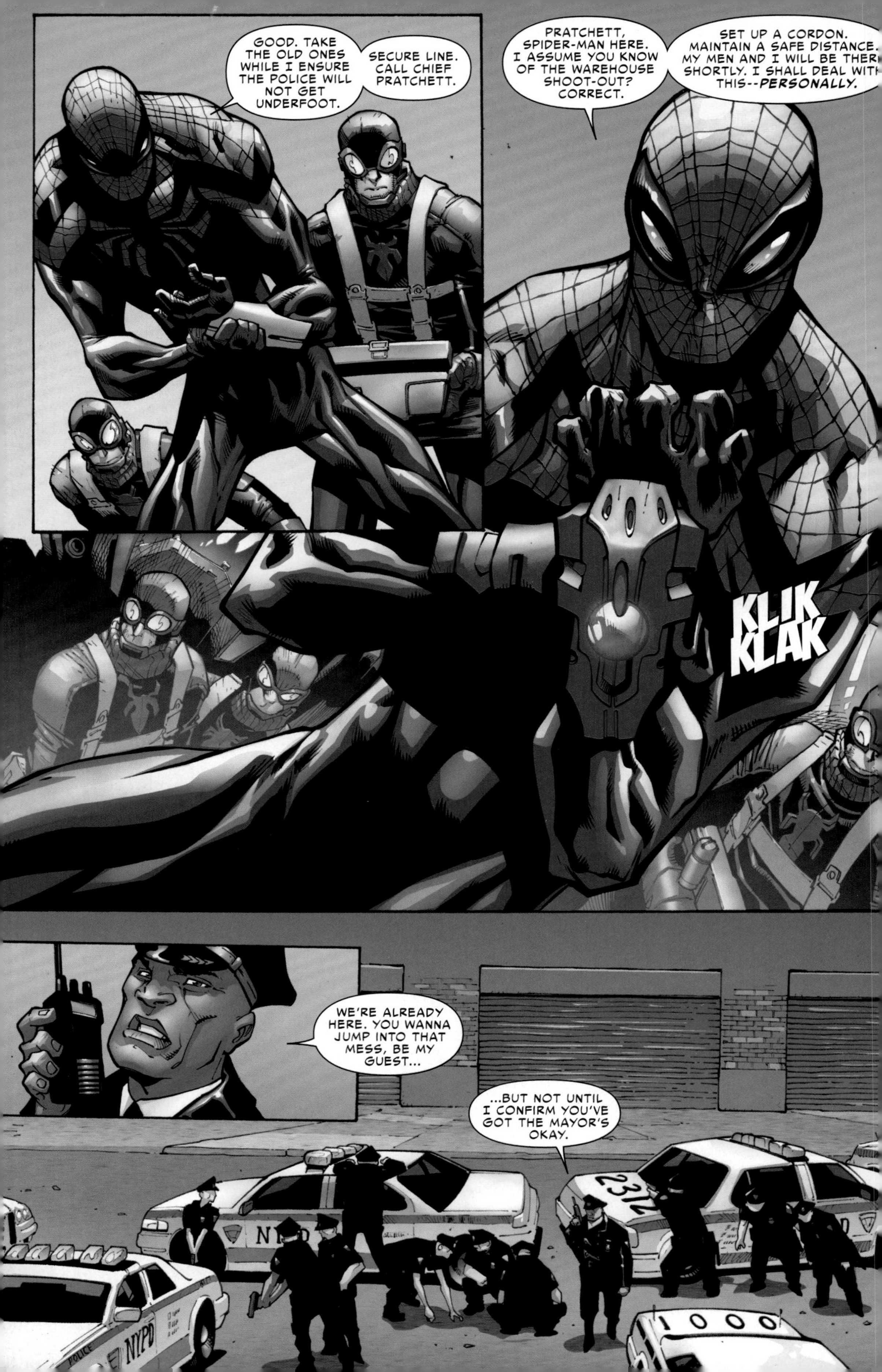
GOOD. TAKE THE OLD ONES WHILE I ENSURE THE POLICE WILL NOT GET UNDERFOOT.
SECURE LINE. CALL CHIEF PRATCHETT.
PRATCHETT, SPIDER-MAN HERE. I ASSUME YOU KNOW OF THE WAREHOUSE SHOOT-OUT? CORRECT.
SET UP A CORDON. MAINTAIN A SAFE DISTANCE. MY MEN AND I WILL BE THERE SHORTLY. I SHALL DEAL WITH THIS--PERSONALLY.
KLIK KLAK
WE'RE ALREADY HERE. YOU WANNA JUMP INTO THAT MESS, BE MY GUEST...
...BUT NOT UNTIL I CONFIRM YOU'VE GOT THE MAYOR'S OKAY.

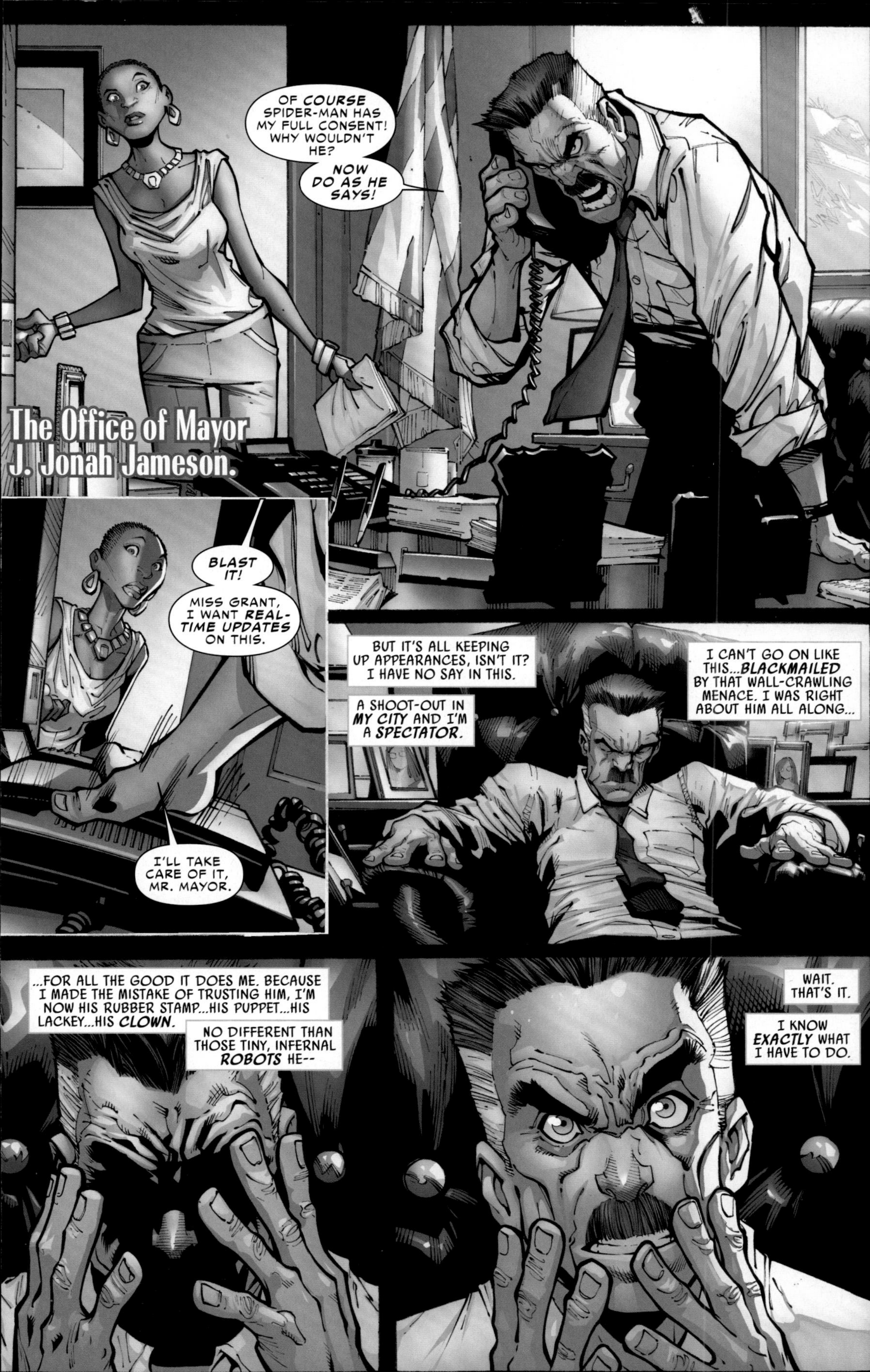
The Office of Mayor J. Jonah Jameson.
OF COURSE SPIDER-MAN HAS MY FULL CONSENT! WHY WOULDN'T HE?
NOW DO AS HE SAYS!
BLAST IT!
MISS GRANT, I WANT REAL-TIME UPDATES ON THIS.
I'LL TAKE CARE OF IT, MR. MAYOR.
BUT IT'S ALL KEEPING UP APPEARANCES, ISN'T IT? I HAVE NO SAY IN THIS.
A SHOOT-OUT IN MY CITY AND I'M A SPECTATOR.
I CAN'T GO ON LIKE THIS...BLACKMAILED BY THAT WALL-CRAWLING MENACE. I WAS RIGHT ABOUT HIM ALL ALONG...
...FOR ALL THE GOOD IT DOES ME. BECAUSE I MADE THE MISTAKE OF TRUSTING HIM, I'M NOW HIS RUBBER STAMP...HIS PUPPET...HIS LACKEY...HIS CLOWN.
NO DIFFERENT THAN THOSE TINY, INFERNAL ROBOTS HE--
WAIT. THAT'S IT.
I KNOW EXACTLY WHAT I HAVE TO DO.

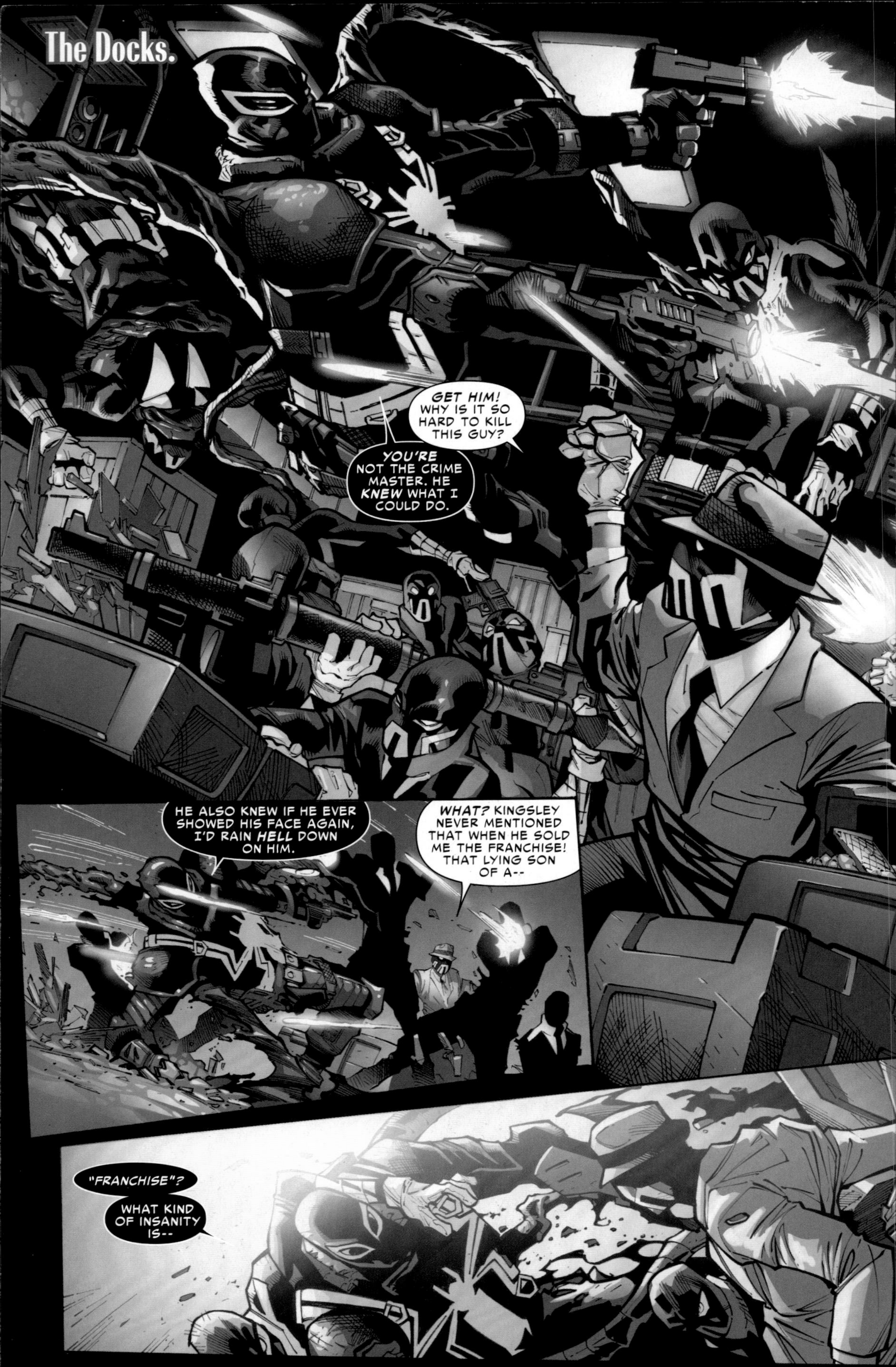
The Docks.
GET HIM! WHY IS IT SO HARD TO KILL THIS GUY?
YOU'RE NOT THE CRIME MASTER. HE KNEW WHAT I COULD DO.
HE ALSO KNEW IF HE EVER SHOWED HIS FACE AGAIN, I'D RAIN HELL DOWN ON HIM.
WHAT? KINGSLEY NEVER MENTIONED THAT WHEN HE SOLD ME THE FRANCHISE! THAT LYING SON OF A--
"FRANCHISE"?
WHAT KIND OF INSANITY IS--

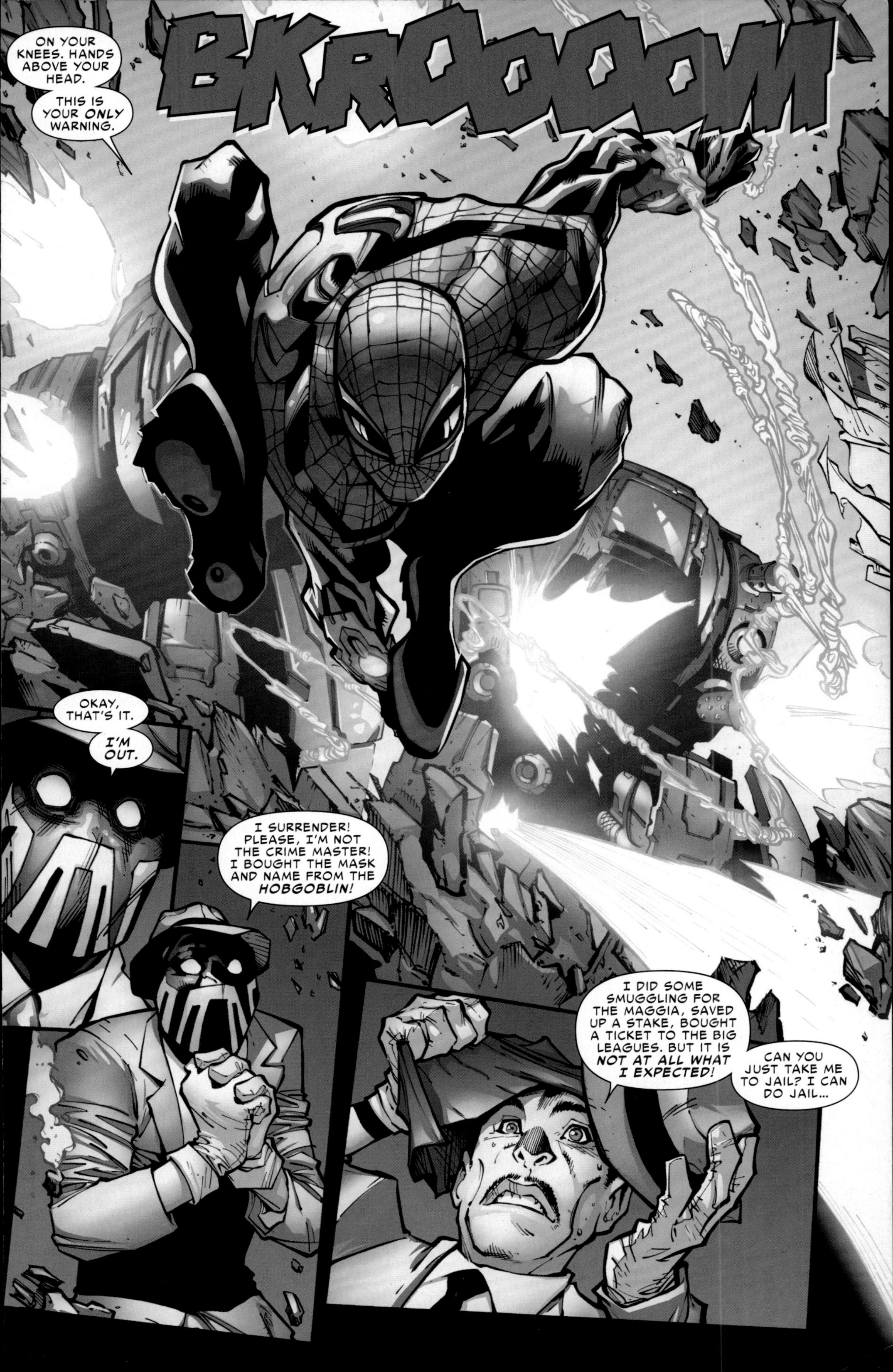
BKROOOOOM
ON YOUR KNEES. HANDS ABOVE YOUR HEAD.
THIS IS YOUR ONLY WARNING.
OKAY, THAT'S IT.
I'M OUT.
I SURRENDER! PLEASE, I'M NOT THE CRIME MASTER! I BOUGHT THE MASK AND NAME FROM THE HOBGOBLIN!
I DID SOME SMUGGLING FOR THE MAGGIA, SAVED UP A STAKE, BOUGHT A TICKET TO THE BIG LEAGUES. BUT IT IS NOT AT ALL WHAT I EXPECTED!
CAN YOU JUST TAKE ME TO JAIL? I CAN DO JAIL...

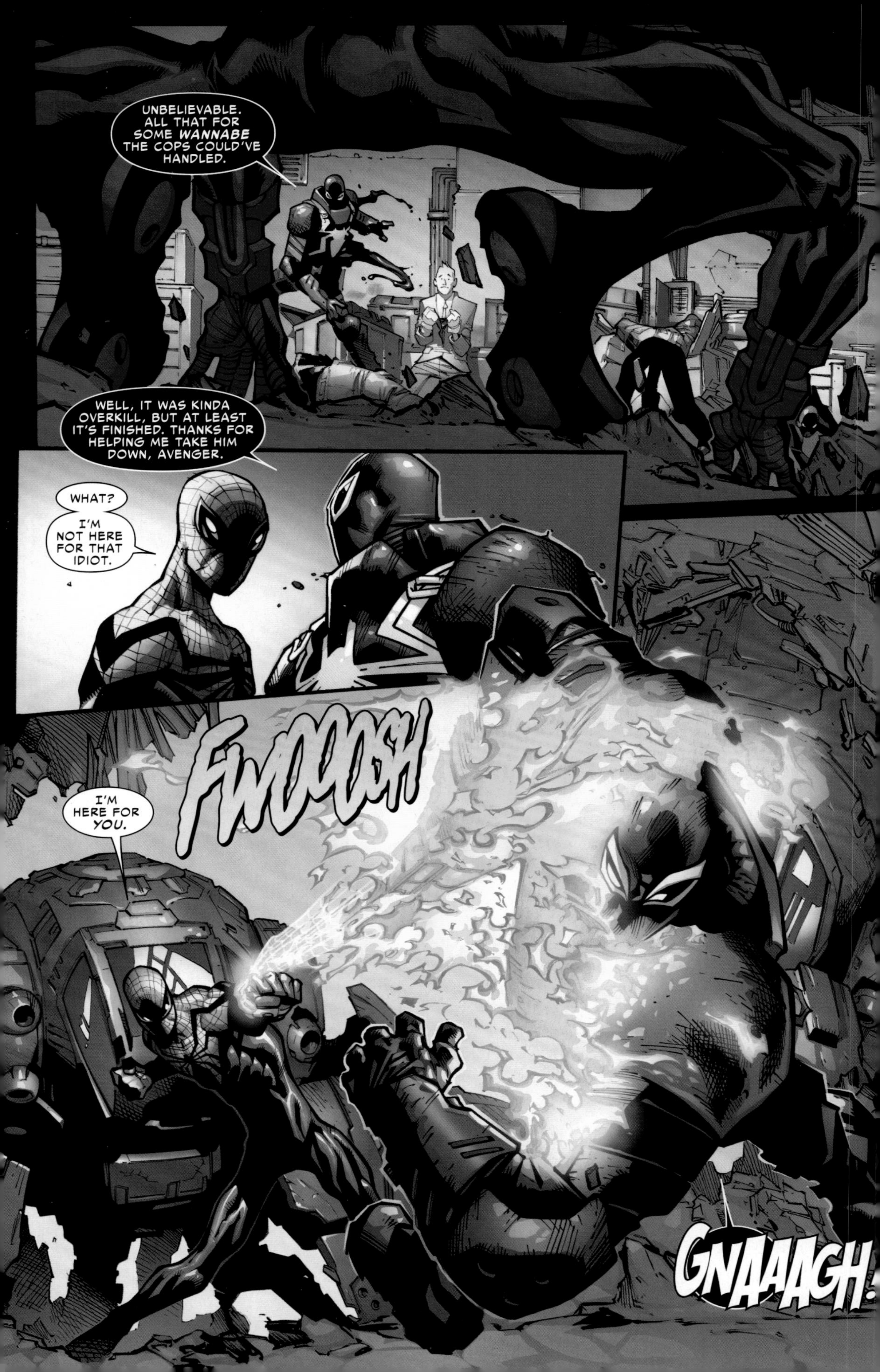

UNBELIEVABLE. ALL THAT FOR SOME WANNABE THE COPS COULD'VE HANDLED.
WELL, IT WAS KINDA OVERKILL, BUT AT LEAST IT'S FINISHED. THANKS FOR HELPING ME TAKE HIM DOWN, AVENGER.
WHAT?
I'M NOT HERE FOR THAT IDIOT.
FWOOOSH
I'M HERE FOR YOU.
GNAAAGH!

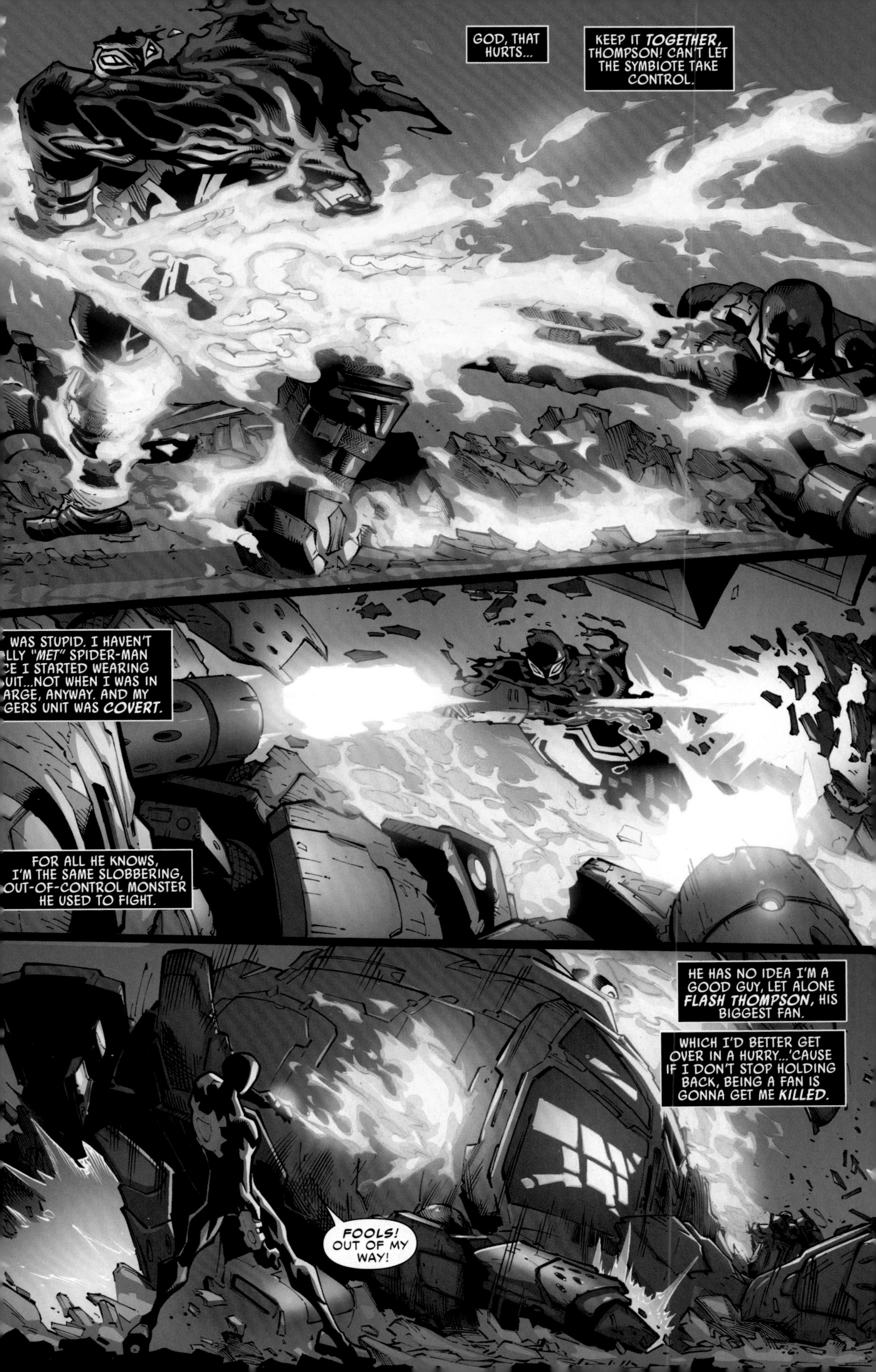
GOD, THAT HURTS...
KEEP IT TOGETHER, THOMPSON! CAN'T LET THE SYMBIOTE TAKE CONTROL.
' WAS STUPID. I HAVEN'T LLY "MET" SPIDER-MAN CE I STARTED WEARING UIT...NOT WHEN I WAS IN ARGE, ANYWAY. AND MY GERS UNIT WAS COVERT.
FOR ALL HE KNOWS, I'M THE SAME SLOBBERING, OUT-OF-CONTROL MONSTER HE USED TO FIGHT.
HE HAS NO IDEA I'M A GOOD GUY, LET ALONE FLASH THOMPSON, HIS BIGGEST FAN.
WHICH I'D BETTER GET OVER IN A HURRY...'CAUSE IF I DON'T STOP HOLDING BACK, BEING A FAN IS GONNA GET ME KILLED.
FOOLS! OUT OF MY WAY!

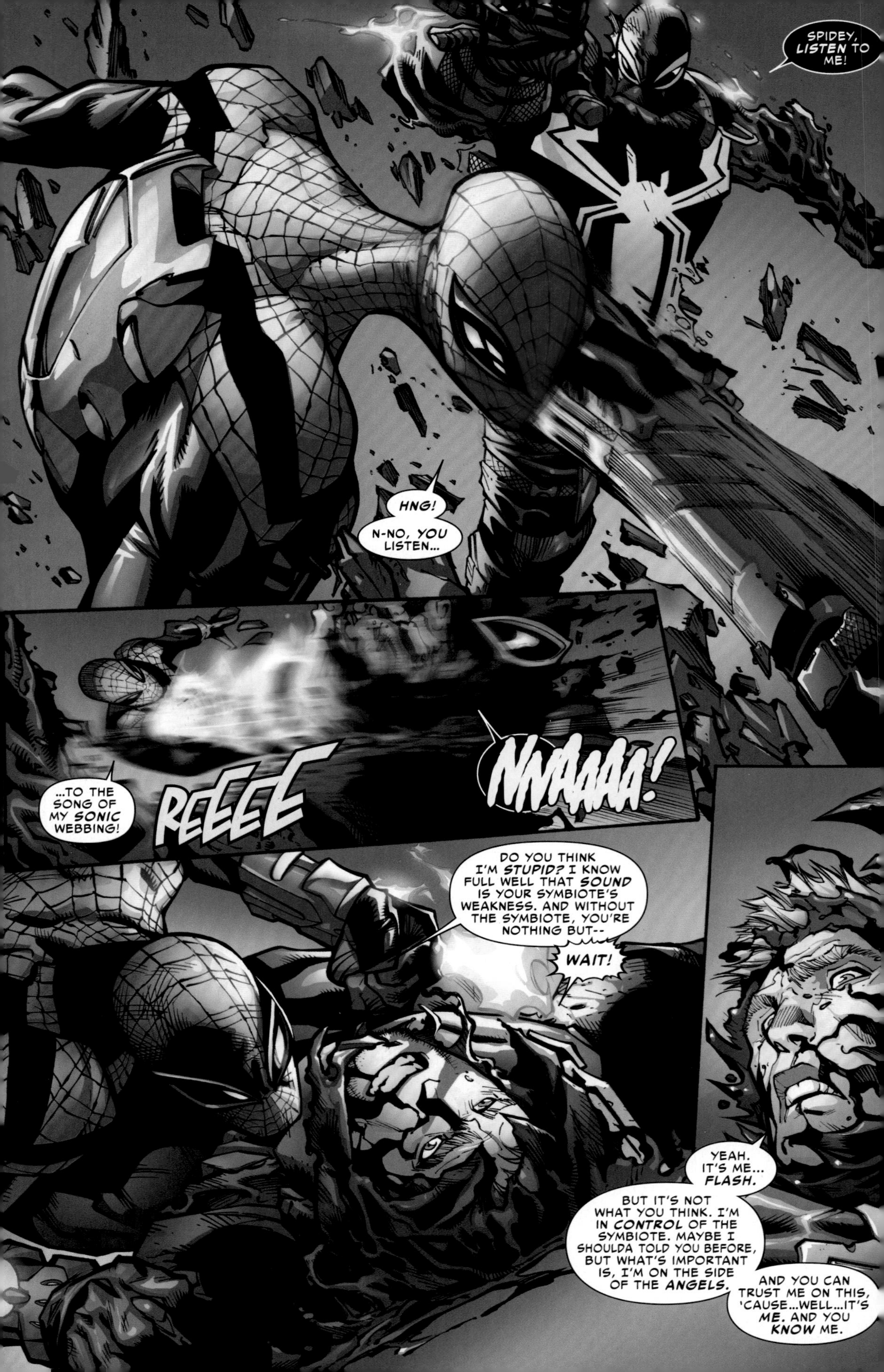
SPIDEY, LISTEN TO ME!
HNG!
N-NO, YOU LISTEN...
...TO THE SONG OF MY SONIC WEBBING!
REEEE
NNAAAAA!
DO YOU THINK I'M STUPID? I KNOW FULL WELL THAT SOUND IS YOUR SYMBIOTE'S WEAKNESS. AND WITHOUT THE SYMBIOTE, YOU'RE NOTHING BUT--
WAIT!
YEAH. IT'S ME... FLASH.
BUT IT'S NOT WHAT YOU THINK. I'M IN CONTROL OF THE SYMBIOTE. MAYBE I SHOULDA TOLD YOU BEFORE, BUT WHAT'S IMPORTANT IS, I'M ON THE SIDE OF THE ANGELS.
AND YOU CAN TRUST ME ON THIS, 'CAUSE...WELL...IT'S ME. AND YOU KNOW ME.

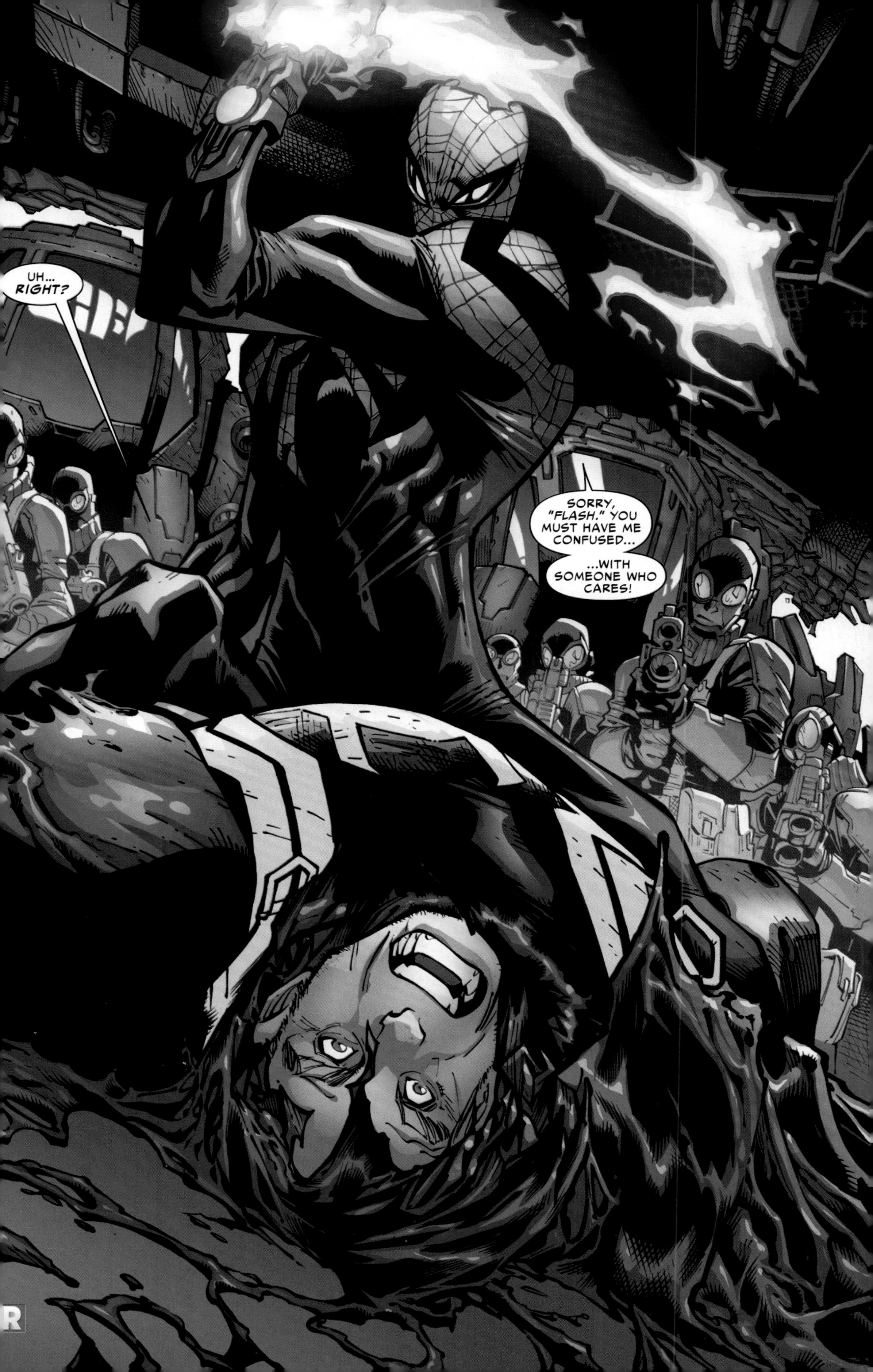
UH... RIGHT?
SORRY, "FLASH." YOU MUST HAVE ME CONFUSED...
...WITH SOMEONE WHO CARES!

23

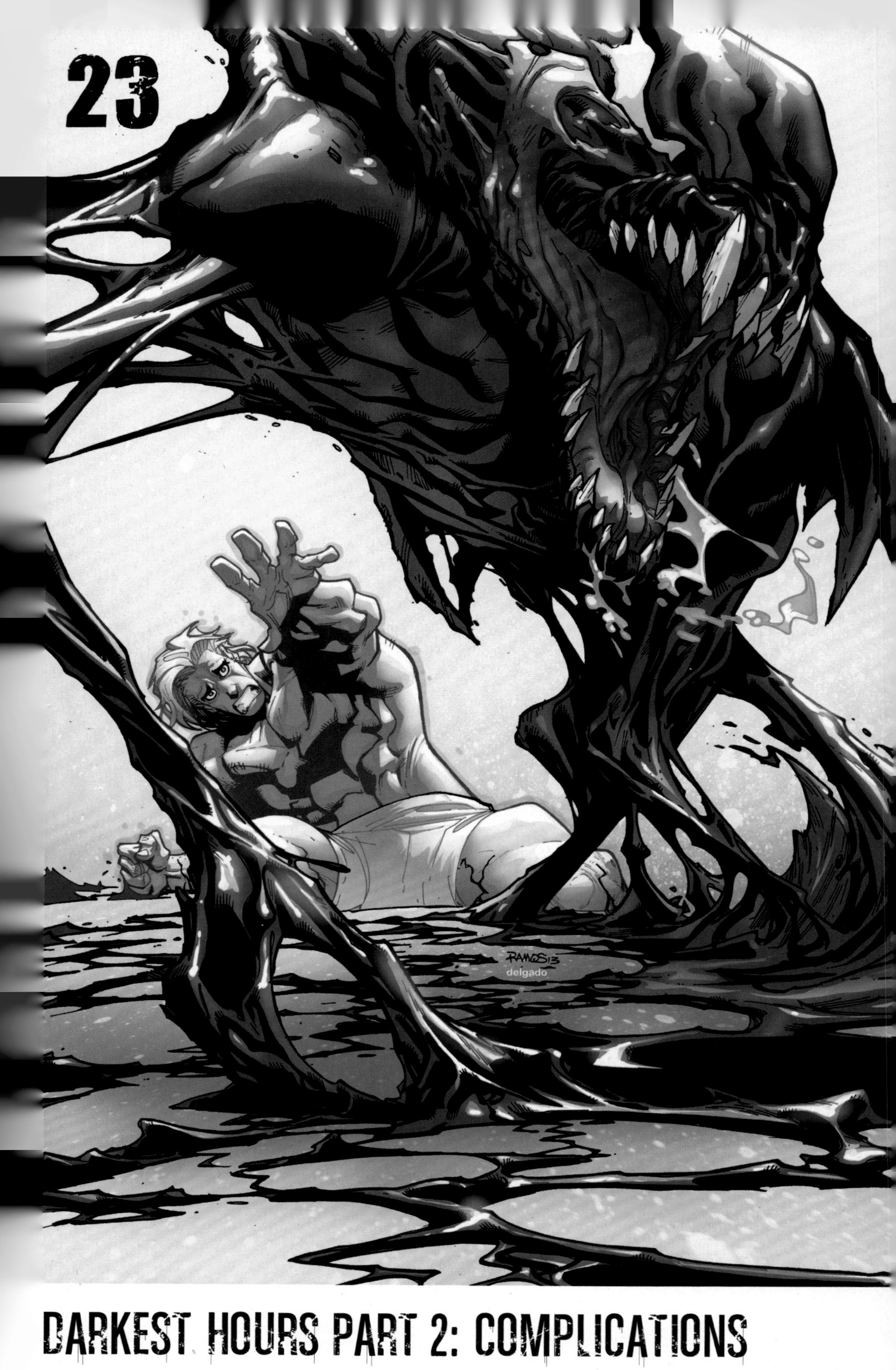
RAMOS'13
delgado

DARKEST HOURS PART 2: COMPLICATIONS

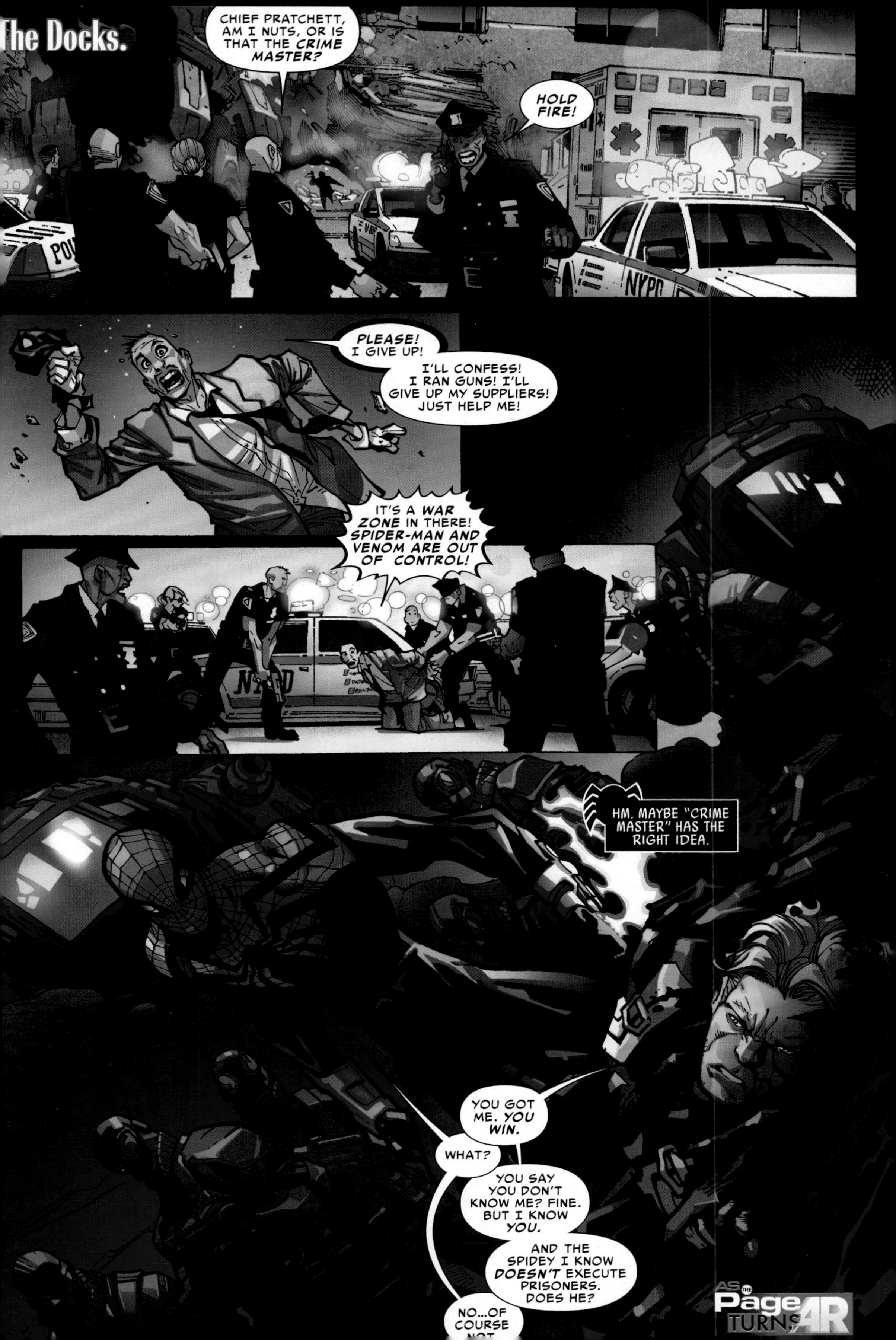

The Docks.
CHIEF PRATCHETT, AM I NUTS, OR IS THAT THE CRIME MASTER?
HOLD FIRE!
PLEASE! I GIVE UP!
I'LL CONFESS! I RAN GUNS! I'LL GIVE UP MY SUPPLIERS! JUST HELP ME!
IT'S A WAR ZONE IN THERE! SPIDER-MAN AND VENOM ARE OUT OF CONTROL!
NYPD
HM. MAYBE "CRIME MASTER" HAS THE RIGHT IDEA.
YOU GOT ME. YOU WIN.
WHAT?
YOU SAY YOU DON'T KNOW ME? FINE. BUT I KNOW YOU.
AND THE SPIDEY I KNOW DOESN'T EXECUTE PRISONERS. DOES HE?
NO...OF COURSE
AS THE Page TURNS AR

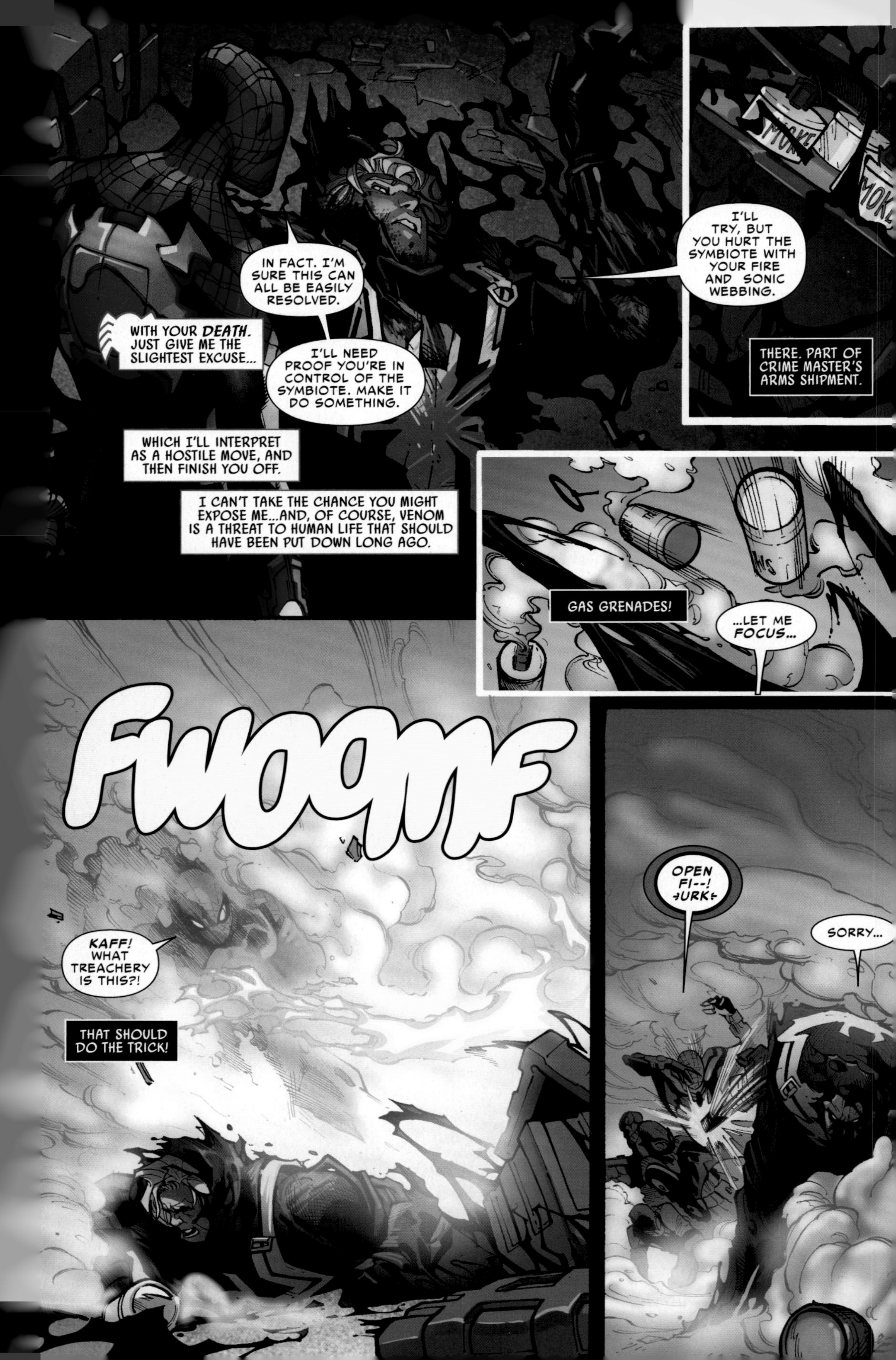
IN FACT. I'M SURE THIS CAN ALL BE EASILY RESOLVED.
WITH YOUR DEATH. JUST GIVE ME THE SLIGHTEST EXCUSE...
I'LL NEED PROOF YOU'RE IN CONTROL OF THE SYMBIOTE. MAKE IT DO SOMETHING.
WHICH I'LL INTERPRET AS A HOSTILE MOVE, AND THEN FINISH YOU OFF.
I CAN'T TAKE THE CHANCE YOU MIGHT EXPOSE ME...AND, OF COURSE, VENOM IS A THREAT TO HUMAN LIFE THAT SHOULD HAVE BEEN PUT DOWN LONG AGO.
I'LL TRY, BUT YOU HURT THE SYMBIOTE WITH YOUR FIRE AND SONIC WEBBING.
THERE. PART OF CRIME MASTER'S ARMS SHIPMENT.
GAS GRENADES!
...LET ME FOCUS...
FWOOMF
KAFF! WHAT TREACHERY IS THIS?!
THAT SHOULD DO THE TRICK!
OPEN FI--! ‹URK›
SORRY...

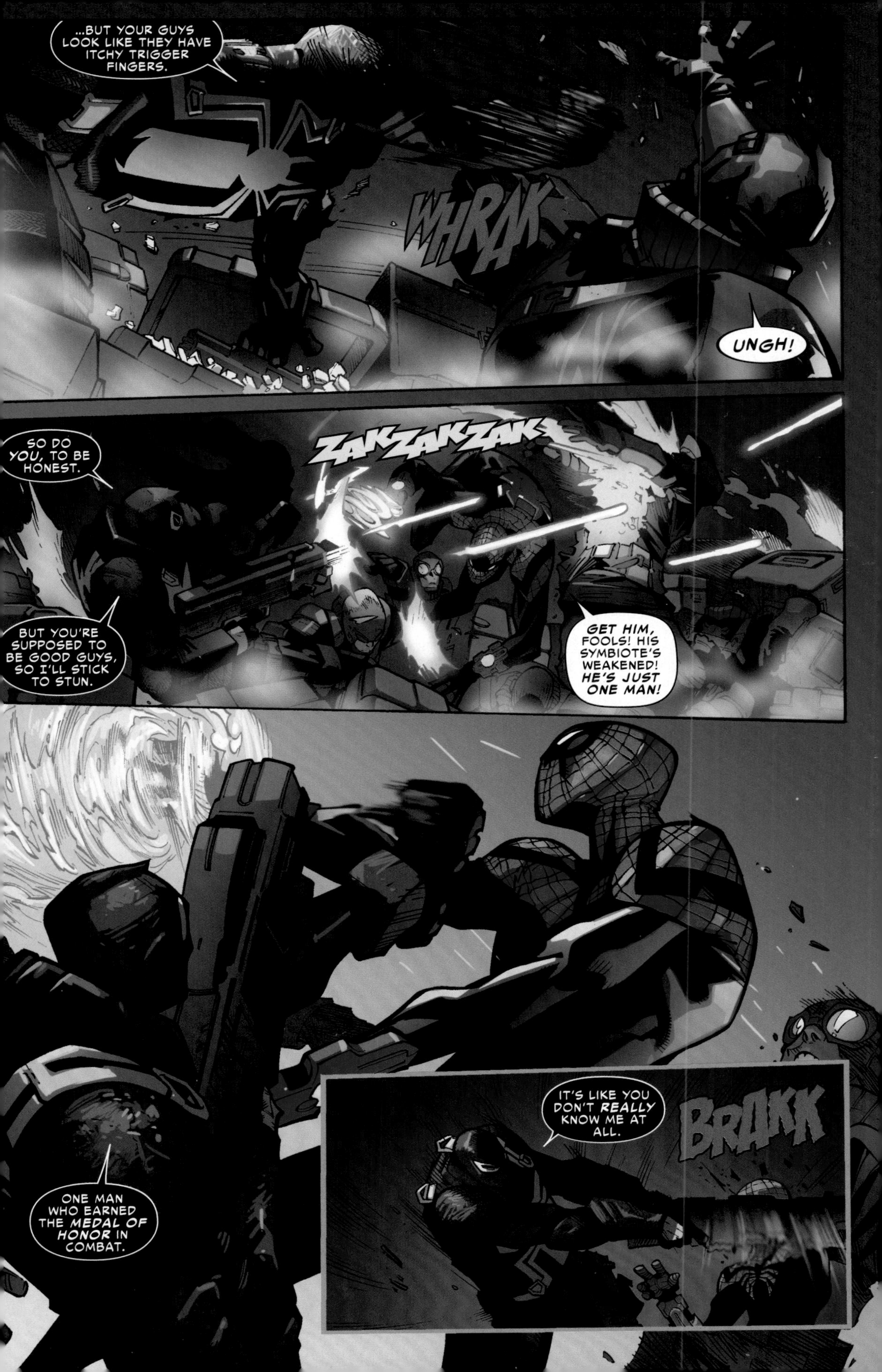
...BUT YOUR GUYS LOOK LIKE THEY HAVE ITCHY TRIGGER FINGERS.
WHRAK
UNGH!
SO DO *YOU*, TO BE HONEST.
ZAK ZAK ZAK
BUT YOU'RE SUPPOSED TO BE GOOD GUYS, SO I'LL STICK TO STUN.
GET HIM, FOOLS! HIS SYMBIOTE'S WEAKENED! *HE'S JUST ONE MAN!*
ONE MAN WHO EARNED THE *MEDAL OF HONOR* IN COMBAT.
IT'S LIKE YOU DON'T *REALLY* KNOW ME AT ALL.
BRAKK

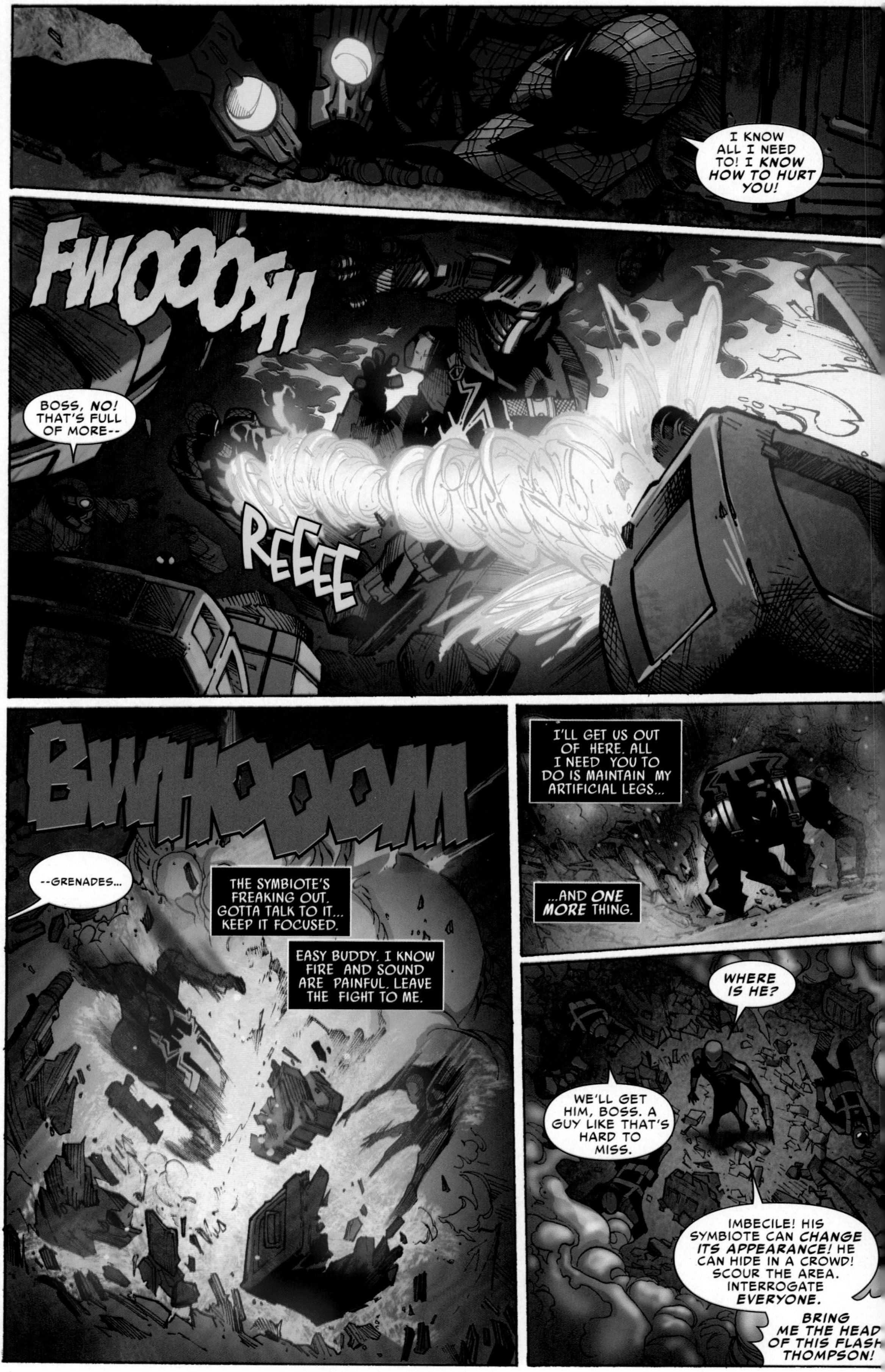
I KNOW ALL I NEED TO! I KNOW HOW TO HURT YOU!
FWOOOSH
BOSS, NO! THAT'S FULL OF MORE--
REEEEE
BWHOOOM
--GRENADES...
THE SYMBIOTE'S FREAKING OUT. GOTTA TALK TO IT... KEEP IT FOCUSED.
EASY BUDDY. I KNOW FIRE AND SOUND ARE PAINFUL. LEAVE THE FIGHT TO ME.
I'LL GET US OUT OF HERE. ALL I NEED YOU TO DO IS MAINTAIN MY ARTIFICIAL LEGS...
...AND ONE MORE THING.
WHERE IS HE?
WE'LL GET HIM, BOSS. A GUY LIKE THAT'S HARD TO MISS.
IMBECILE! HIS SYMBIOTE CAN CHANGE ITS APPEARANCE! HE CAN HIDE IN A CROWD! SCOUR THE AREA. INTERROGATE EVERYONE.
BRING ME THE HEAD OF THIS FLASH THOMPSON!

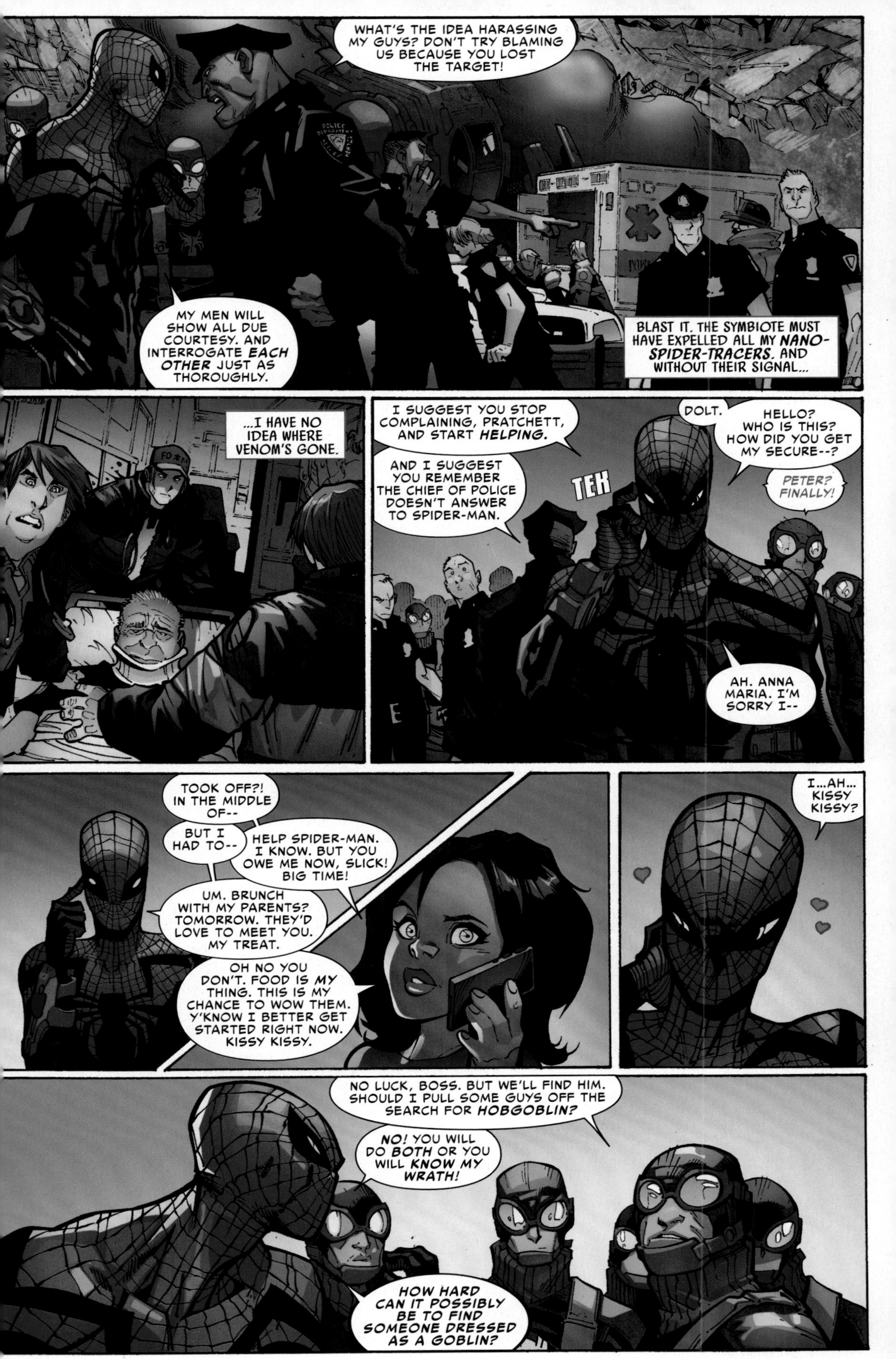
WHAT'S THE IDEA HARASSING MY GUYS? DON'T TRY BLAMING US BECAUSE YOU LOST THE TARGET!
MY MEN WILL SHOW ALL DUE COURTESY. AND INTERROGATE EACH OTHER JUST AS THOROUGHLY.
BLAST IT. THE SYMBIOTE MUST HAVE EXPELLED ALL MY NANO-SPIDER-TRACERS. AND WITHOUT THEIR SIGNAL...
...I HAVE NO IDEA WHERE VENOM'S GONE.
I SUGGEST YOU STOP COMPLAINING, PRATCHETT, AND START HELPING.
AND I SUGGEST YOU REMEMBER THE CHIEF OF POLICE DOESN'T ANSWER TO SPIDER-MAN.
TEK
DOLT.
HELLO? WHO IS THIS? HOW DID YOU GET MY SECURE--?
PETER? FINALLY!
AH. ANNA MARIA. I'M SORRY I--
TOOK OFF?! IN THE MIDDLE OF--
BUT I HAD TO--
HELP SPIDER-MAN. I KNOW. BUT YOU OWE ME NOW, SLICK! BIG TIME!
UM. BRUNCH WITH MY PARENTS? TOMORROW. THEY'D LOVE TO MEET YOU. MY TREAT.
OH NO YOU DON'T. FOOD IS MY THING. THIS IS MY CHANCE TO WOW THEM. Y'KNOW I BETTER GET STARTED RIGHT NOW. KISSY KISSY.
I...AH... KISSY KISSY?
NO LUCK, BOSS. BUT WE'LL FIND HIM. SHOULD I PULL SOME GUYS OFF THE SEARCH FOR HOBGOBLIN?
NO! YOU WILL DO BOTH OR YOU WILL KNOW MY WRATH!
HOW HARD CAN IT POSSIBLY BE TO FIND SOMEONE DRESSED AS A GOBLIN?

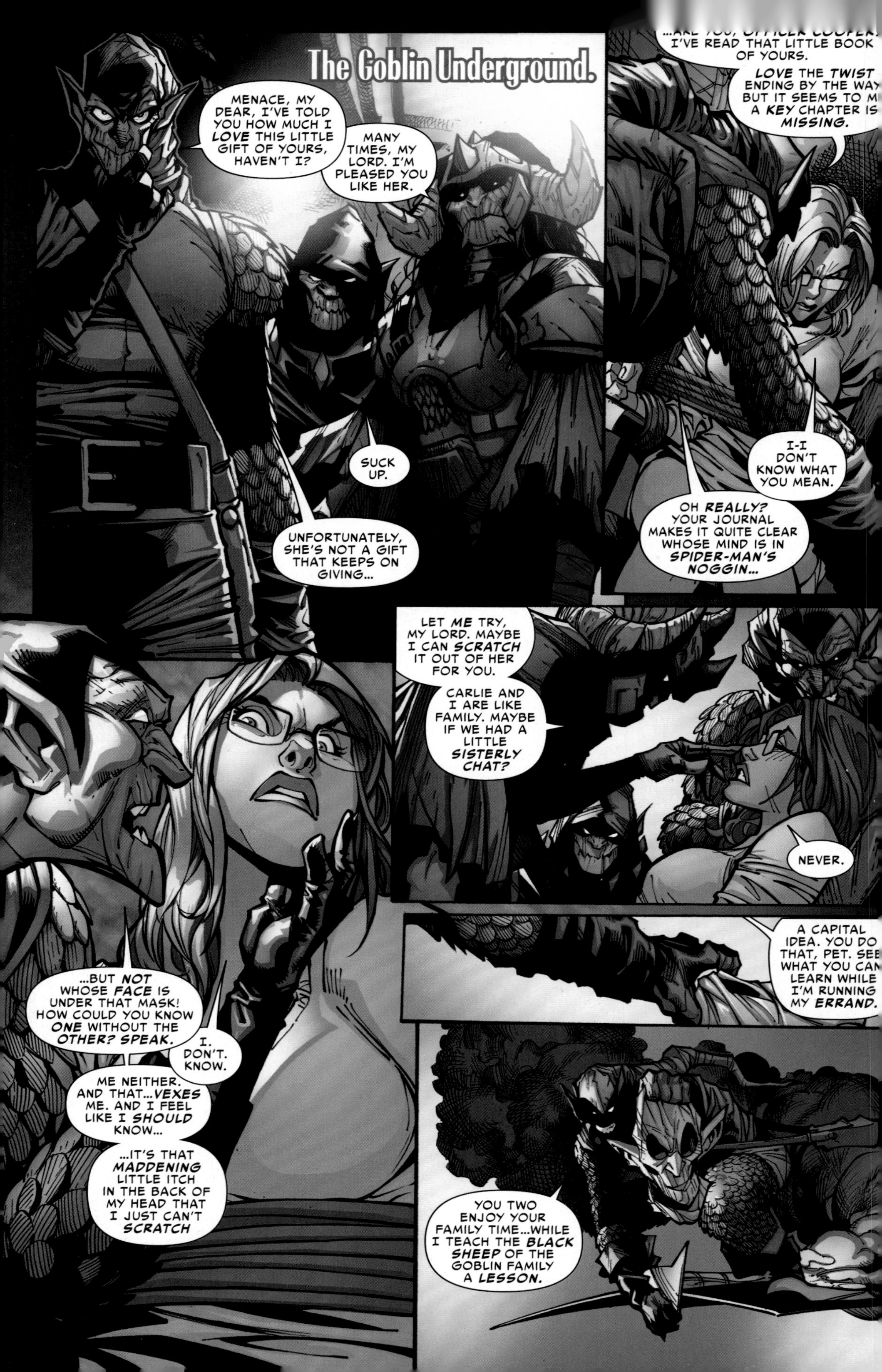
The Goblin Underground.
MENACE, MY DEAR, I'VE TOLD YOU HOW MUCH I LOVE THIS LITTLE GIFT OF YOURS, HAVEN'T I?
MANY TIMES, MY LORD. I'M PLEASED YOU LIKE HER.
SUCK UP.
UNFORTUNATELY, SHE'S NOT A GIFT THAT KEEPS ON GIVING...
I'VE READ THAT LITTLE BOOK OF YOURS.
LOVE THE TWIST ENDING BY THE WAY BUT IT SEEMS TO M A KEY CHAPTER IS MISSING.
I-I DON'T KNOW WHAT YOU MEAN.
OH REALLY? YOUR JOURNAL MAKES IT QUITE CLEAR WHOSE MIND IS IN SPIDER-MAN'S NOGGIN...
...BUT NOT WHOSE FACE IS UNDER THAT MASK! HOW COULD YOU KNOW ONE WITHOUT THE OTHER? SPEAK.
I. DON'T. KNOW.
ME NEITHER. AND THAT...VEXES ME. AND I FEEL LIKE I SHOULD KNOW...
...IT'S THAT MADDENING LITTLE ITCH IN THE BACK OF MY HEAD THAT I JUST CAN'T SCRATCH
LET ME TRY, MY LORD. MAYBE I CAN SCRATCH IT OUT OF HER FOR YOU.
CARLIE AND I ARE LIKE FAMILY. MAYBE IF WE HAD A LITTLE SISTERLY CHAT?
NEVER.
A CAPITAL IDEA. YOU DO THAT, PET. SEE WHAT YOU CAN LEARN WHILE I'M RUNNING MY ERRAND.
YOU TWO ENJOY YOUR FAMILY TIME...WHILE I TEACH THE BLACK SHEEP OF THE GOBLIN FAMILY A LESSON.

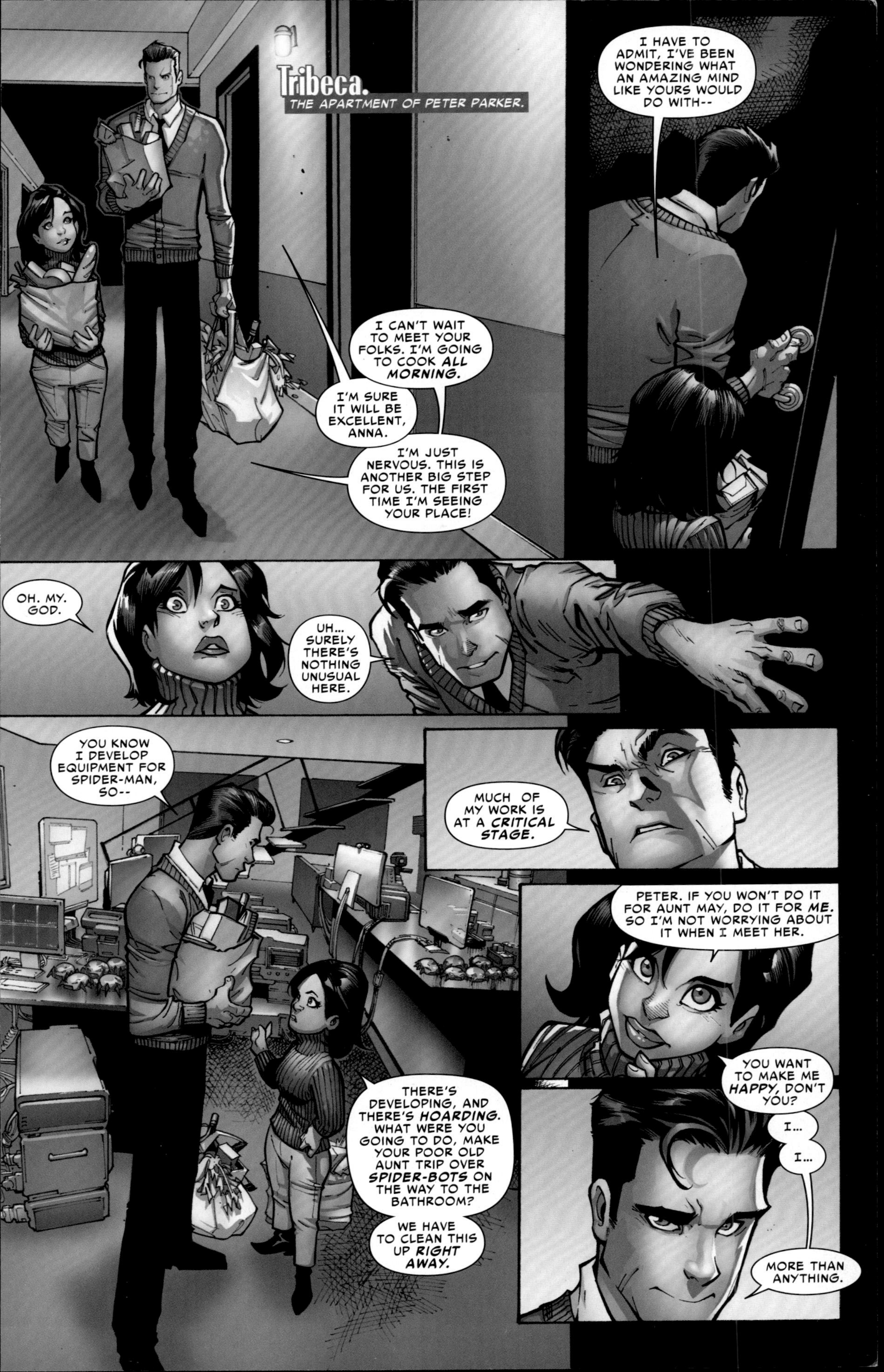
Tribeca.
THE APARTMENT OF PETER PARKER.
I CAN'T WAIT TO MEET YOUR FOLKS. I'M GOING TO COOK ALL MORNING.
I'M SURE IT WILL BE EXCELLENT, ANNA.
I'M JUST NERVOUS. THIS IS ANOTHER BIG STEP FOR US. THE FIRST TIME I'M SEEING YOUR PLACE!
I HAVE TO ADMIT, I'VE BEEN WONDERING WHAT AN AMAZING MIND LIKE YOURS WOULD DO WITH--
OH. MY. GOD.
UH... SURELY THERE'S NOTHING UNUSUAL HERE.
YOU KNOW I DEVELOP EQUIPMENT FOR SPIDER-MAN, SO--
THERE'S DEVELOPING, AND THERE'S HOARDING. WHAT WERE YOU GOING TO DO, MAKE YOUR POOR OLD AUNT TRIP OVER SPIDER-BOTS ON THE WAY TO THE BATHROOM?
WE HAVE TO CLEAN THIS UP RIGHT AWAY.
MUCH OF MY WORK IS AT A CRITICAL STAGE.
PETER. IF YOU WON'T DO IT FOR AUNT MAY, DO IT FOR ME. SO I'M NOT WORRYING ABOUT IT WHEN I MEET HER.
YOU WANT TO MAKE ME HAPPY, DON'T YOU?
I...
I...
MORE THAN ANYTHING.

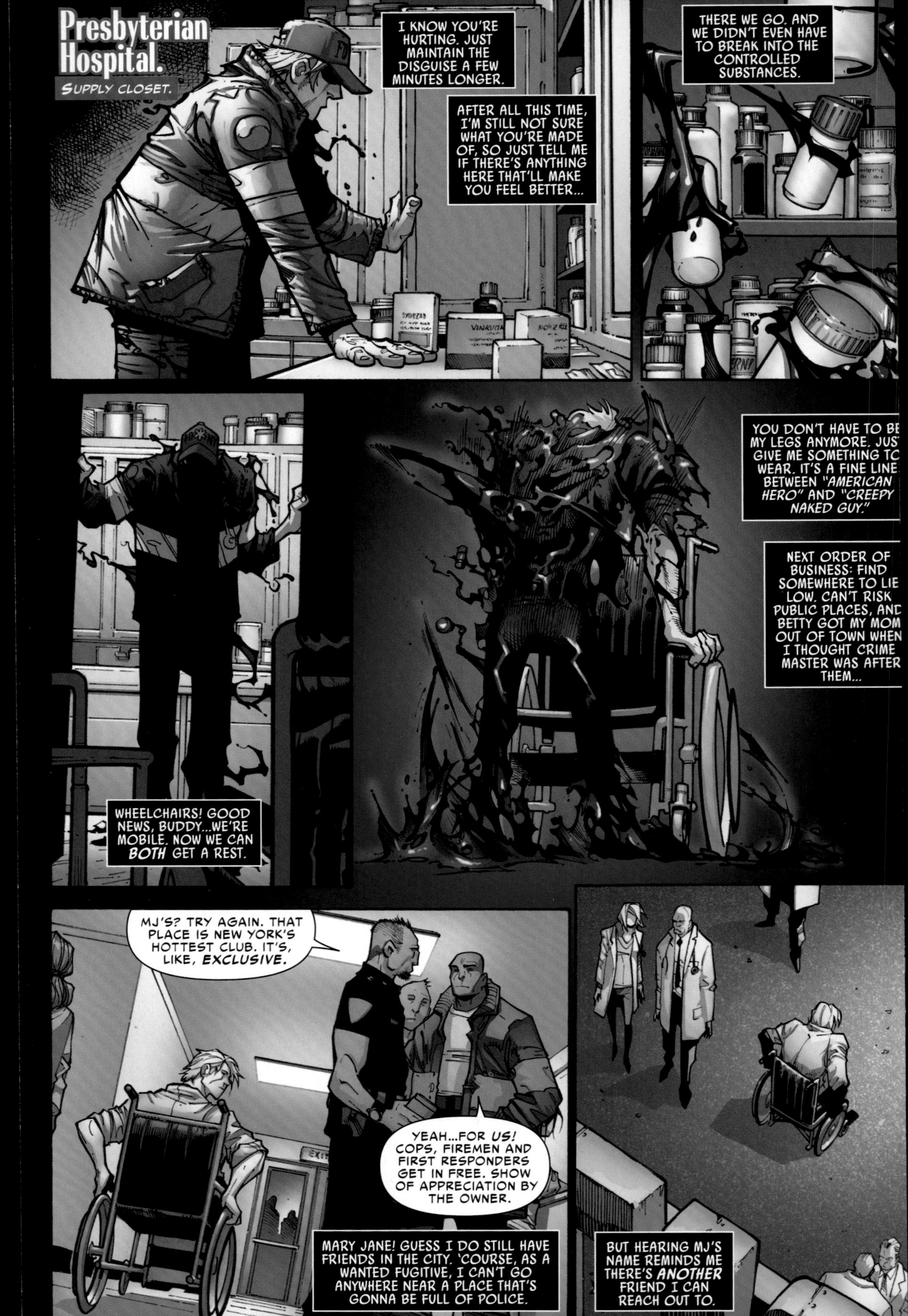
Presbyterian Hospital.
SUPPLY CLOSET.
I KNOW YOU'RE HURTING. JUST MAINTAIN THE DISGUISE A FEW MINUTES LONGER.
AFTER ALL THIS TIME, I'M STILL NOT SURE WHAT YOU'RE MADE OF, SO JUST TELL ME IF THERE'S ANYTHING HERE THAT'LL MAKE YOU FEEL BETTER...
THERE WE GO. AND WE DIDN'T EVEN HAVE TO BREAK INTO THE CONTROLLED SUBSTANCES.
WHEELCHAIRS! GOOD NEWS, BUDDY...WE'RE MOBILE. NOW WE CAN BOTH GET A REST.
YOU DON'T HAVE TO BE MY LEGS ANYMORE. JUST GIVE ME SOMETHING TO WEAR. IT'S A FINE LINE BETWEEN "AMERICAN HERO" AND "CREEPY NAKED GUY."
NEXT ORDER OF BUSINESS: FIND SOMEWHERE TO LIE LOW. CAN'T RISK PUBLIC PLACES, AND BETTY GOT MY MOM OUT OF TOWN WHEN I THOUGHT CRIME MASTER WAS AFTER THEM...
MJ'S? TRY AGAIN. THAT PLACE IS NEW YORK'S HOTTEST CLUB. IT'S, LIKE, EXCLUSIVE.
YEAH...FOR US! COPS, FIREMEN AND FIRST RESPONDERS GET IN FREE. SHOW OF APPRECIATION BY THE OWNER.
MARY JANE! GUESS I DO STILL HAVE FRIENDS IN THE CITY. 'COURSE, AS A WANTED FUGITIVE, I CAN'T GO ANYWHERE NEAR A PLACE THAT'S GONNA BE FULL OF POLICE.
BUT HEARING MJ'S NAME REMINDS ME THERE'S ANOTHER FRIEND I CAN REACH OUT TO.

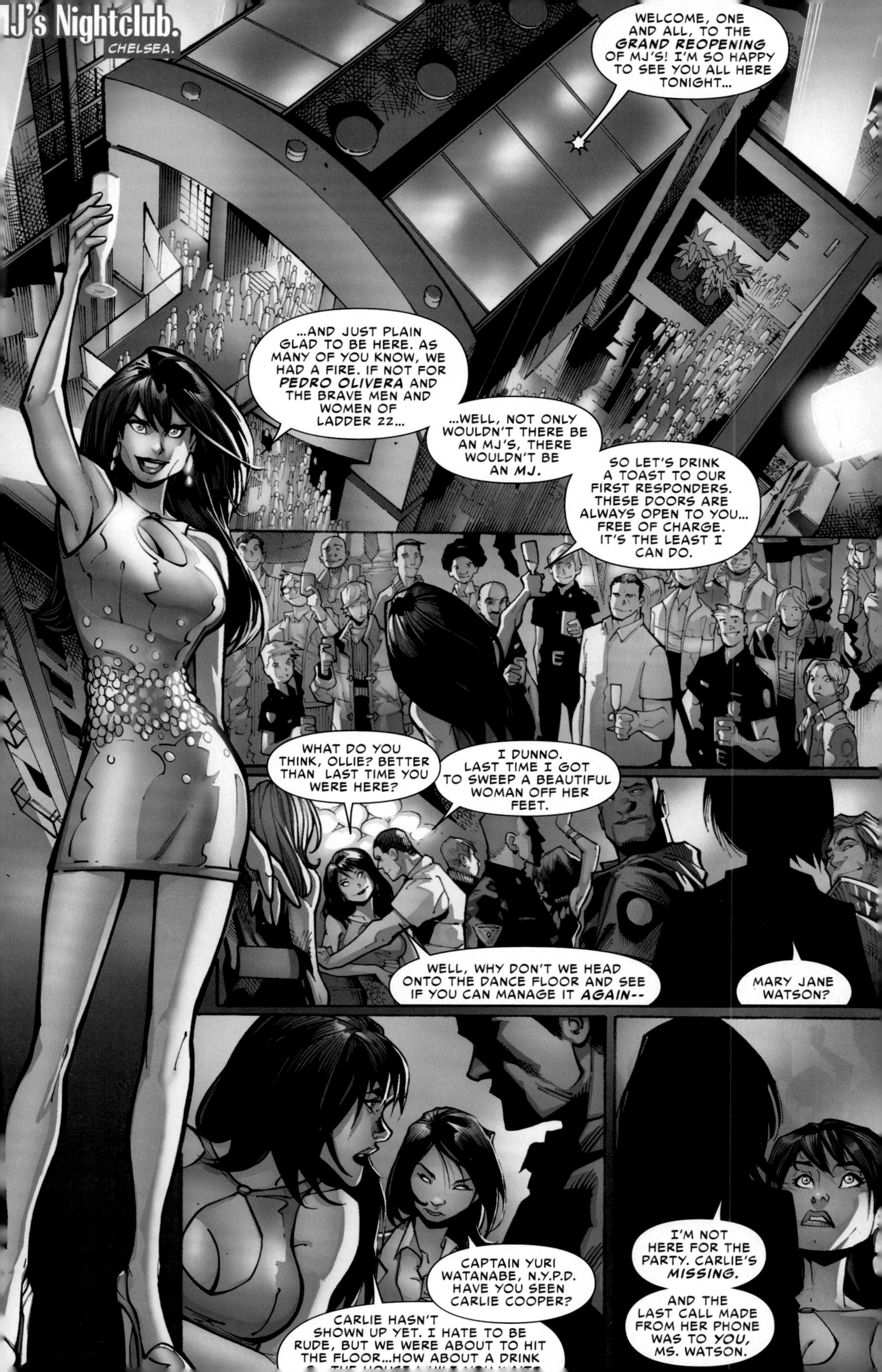
MJ's Nightclub.
CHELSEA.
WELCOME, ONE AND ALL, TO THE GRAND REOPENING OF MJ'S! I'M SO HAPPY TO SEE YOU ALL HERE TONIGHT...
...AND JUST PLAIN GLAD TO BE HERE. AS MANY OF YOU KNOW, WE HAD A FIRE. IF NOT FOR PEDRO OLIVERA AND THE BRAVE MEN AND WOMEN OF LADDER 22...
...WELL, NOT ONLY WOULDN'T THERE BE AN MJ'S, THERE WOULDN'T BE AN MJ.
SO LET'S DRINK A TOAST TO OUR FIRST RESPONDERS. THESE DOORS ARE ALWAYS OPEN TO YOU... FREE OF CHARGE. IT'S THE LEAST I CAN DO.
WHAT DO YOU THINK, OLLIE? BETTER THAN LAST TIME YOU WERE HERE?
I DUNNO. LAST TIME I GOT TO SWEEP A BEAUTIFUL WOMAN OFF HER FEET.
WELL, WHY DON'T WE HEAD ONTO THE DANCE FLOOR AND SEE IF YOU CAN MANAGE IT AGAIN--
MARY JANE WATSON?
CAPTAIN YURI WATANABE, N.Y.P.D. HAVE YOU SEEN CARLIE COOPER?
CARLIE HASN'T SHOWN UP YET. I HATE TO BE RUDE, BUT WE WERE ABOUT TO HIT THE FLOOR...HOW ABOUT A DRINK
I'M NOT HERE FOR THE PARTY. CARLIE'S MISSING.
AND THE LAST CALL MADE FROM HER PHONE WAS TO YOU, MS. WATSON.

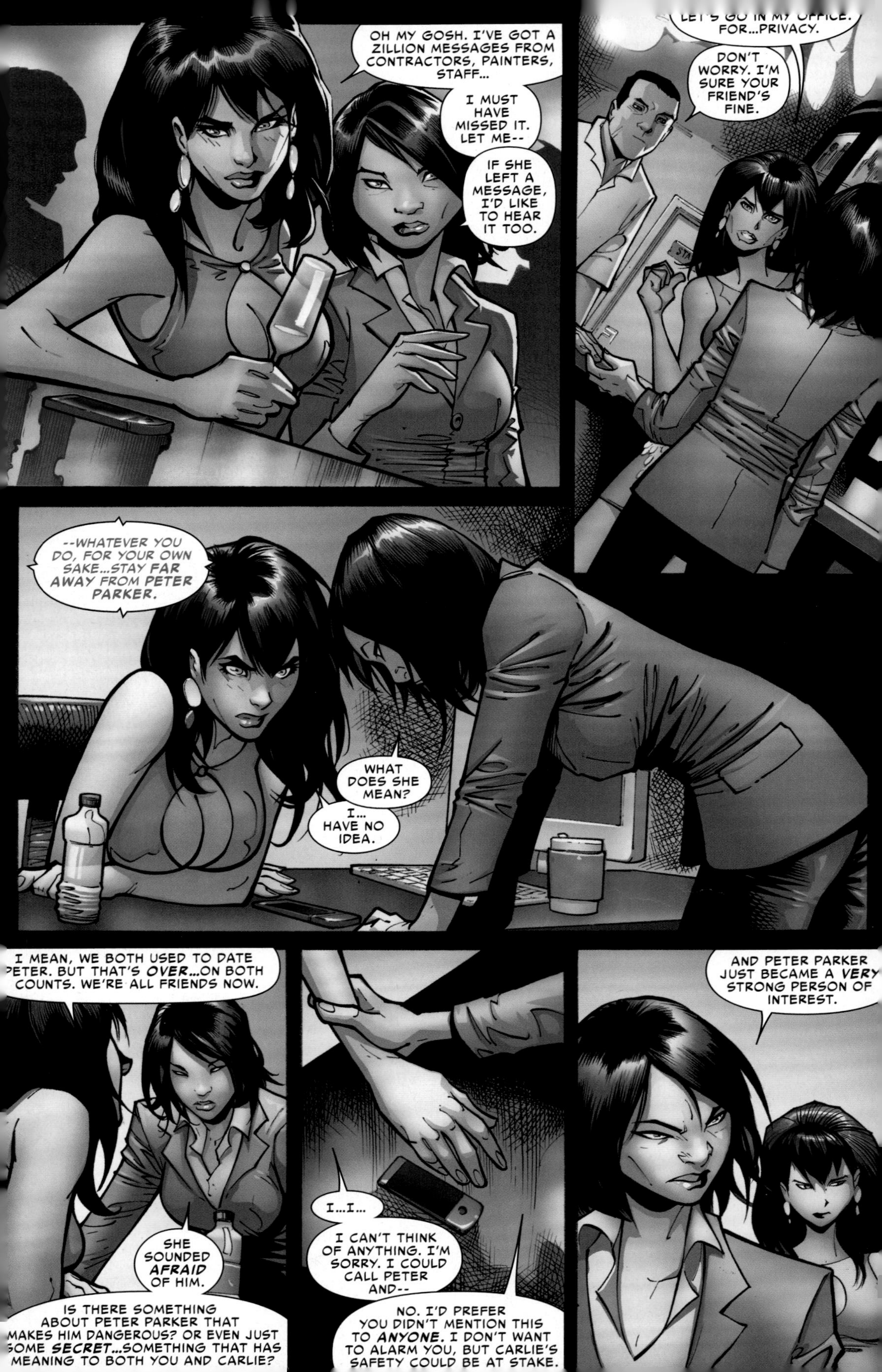
OH MY GOSH. I'VE GOT A ZILLION MESSAGES FROM CONTRACTORS, PAINTERS, STAFF...
I MUST HAVE MISSED IT. LET ME--
IF SHE LEFT A MESSAGE, I'D LIKE TO HEAR IT TOO.
LET'S GO IN MY OFFICE. FOR...PRIVACY.
DON'T WORRY. I'M SURE YOUR FRIEND'S FINE.
--WHATEVER YOU DO, FOR YOUR OWN SAKE...STAY FAR AWAY FROM PETER PARKER.
WHAT DOES SHE MEAN?
I... HAVE NO IDEA.
I MEAN, WE BOTH USED TO DATE PETER. BUT THAT'S OVER...ON BOTH COUNTS. WE'RE ALL FRIENDS NOW.
SHE SOUNDED AFRAID OF HIM.
IS THERE SOMETHING ABOUT PETER PARKER THAT MAKES HIM DANGEROUS? OR EVEN JUST SOME SECRET...SOMETHING THAT HAS MEANING TO BOTH YOU AND CARLIE?
I...I...
I CAN'T THINK OF ANYTHING. I'M SORRY. I COULD CALL PETER AND--
NO. I'D PREFER YOU DIDN'T MENTION THIS TO ANYONE. I DON'T WANT TO ALARM YOU, BUT CARLIE'S SAFETY COULD BE AT STAKE.
AND PETER PARKER JUST BECAME A VERY STRONG PERSON OF INTEREST.

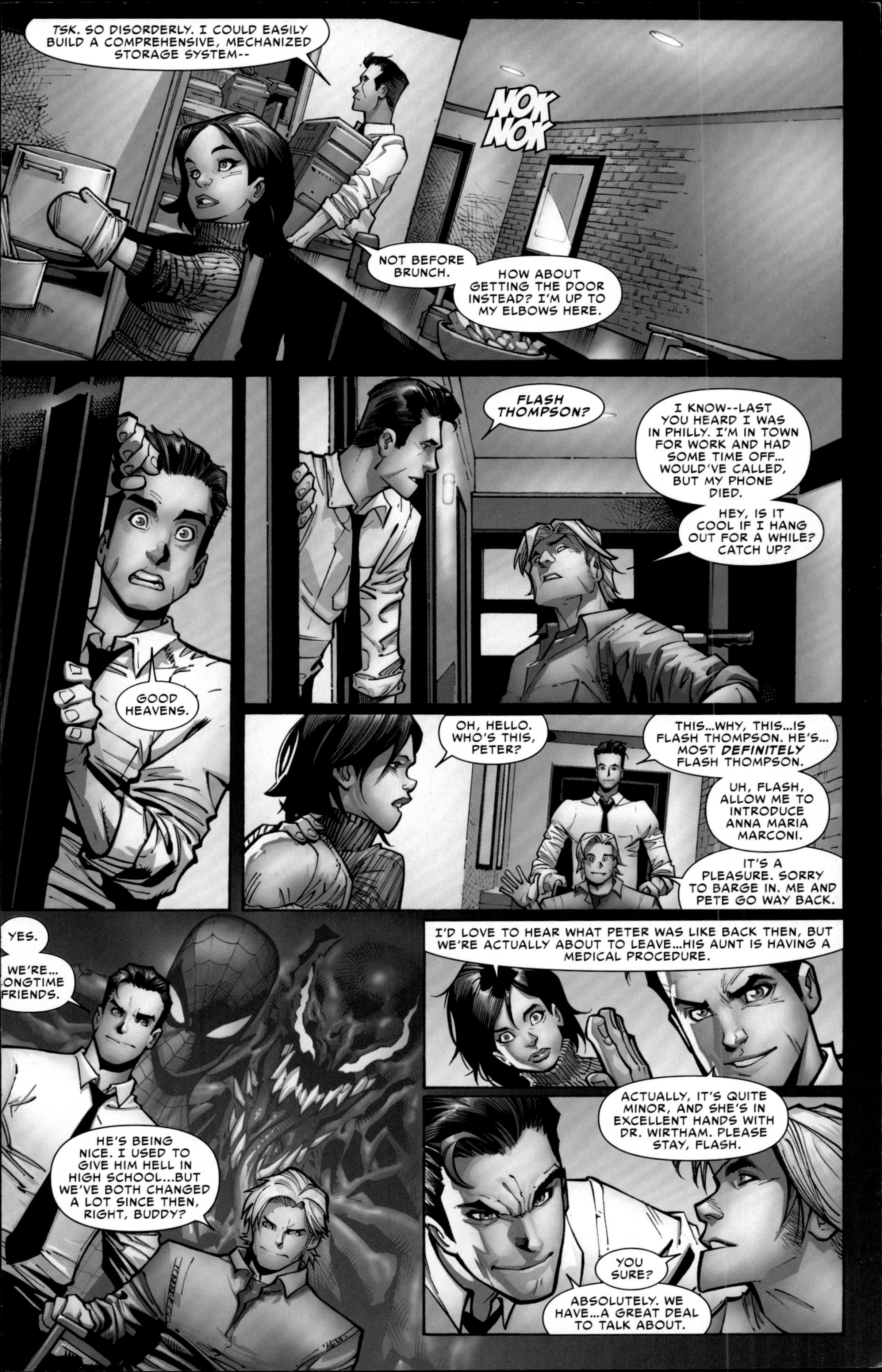
TSK. SO DISORDERLY. I COULD EASILY BUILD A COMPREHENSIVE, MECHANIZED STORAGE SYSTEM--
NOK NOK
NOT BEFORE BRUNCH.
HOW ABOUT GETTING THE DOOR INSTEAD? I'M UP TO MY ELBOWS HERE.
GOOD HEAVENS.
FLASH THOMPSON?
I KNOW--LAST YOU HEARD I WAS IN PHILLY. I'M IN TOWN FOR WORK AND HAD SOME TIME OFF... WOULD'VE CALLED, BUT MY PHONE DIED.
HEY, IS IT COOL IF I HANG OUT FOR A WHILE? CATCH UP?
OH, HELLO. WHO'S THIS, PETER?
THIS...WHY, THIS...IS FLASH THOMPSON. HE'S... MOST DEFINITELY FLASH THOMPSON.
UH, FLASH, ALLOW ME TO INTRODUCE ANNA MARIA MARCONI.
IT'S A PLEASURE. SORRY TO BARGE IN. ME AND PETE GO WAY BACK.
YES.
WE'RE... LONGTIME FRIENDS.
HE'S BEING NICE. I USED TO GIVE HIM HELL IN HIGH SCHOOL...BUT WE'VE BOTH CHANGED A LOT SINCE THEN, RIGHT, BUDDY?
I'D LOVE TO HEAR WHAT PETER WAS LIKE BACK THEN, BUT WE'RE ACTUALLY ABOUT TO LEAVE...HIS AUNT IS HAVING A MEDICAL PROCEDURE.
ACTUALLY, IT'S QUITE MINOR, AND SHE'S IN EXCELLENT HANDS WITH DR. WIRTHAM. PLEASE STAY, FLASH.
YOU SURE?
ABSOLUTELY. WE HAVE...A GREAT DEAL TO TALK ABOUT.

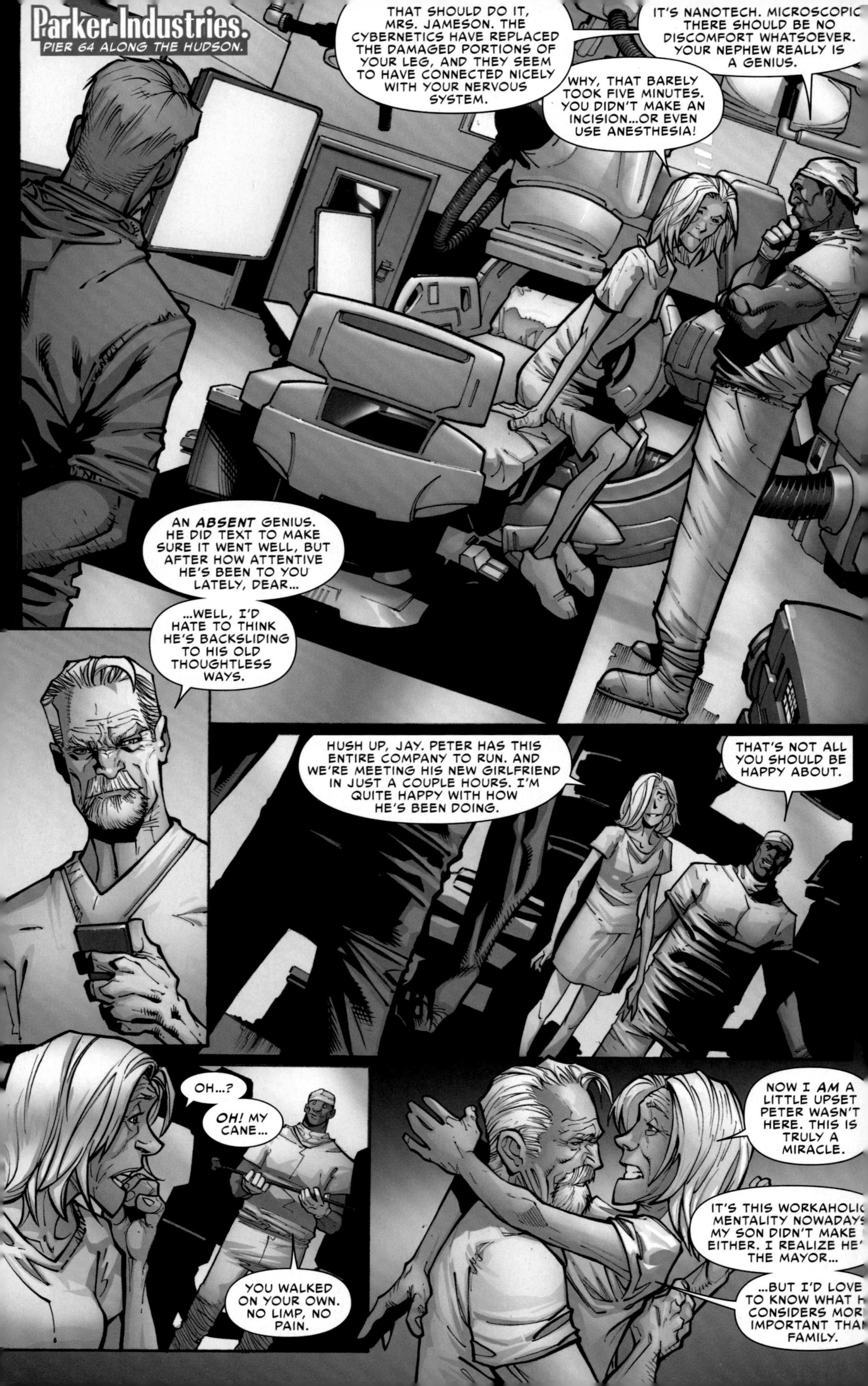
Parker Industries.
PIER 64 ALONG THE HUDSON.
THAT SHOULD DO IT, MRS. JAMESON. THE CYBERNETICS HAVE REPLACED THE DAMAGED PORTIONS OF YOUR LEG, AND THEY SEEM TO HAVE CONNECTED NICELY WITH YOUR NERVOUS SYSTEM.
WHY, THAT BARELY TOOK FIVE MINUTES. YOU DIDN'T MAKE AN INCISION...OR EVEN USE ANESTHESIA!
IT'S NANOTECH. MICROSCOPIC THERE SHOULD BE NO DISCOMFORT WHATSOEVER. YOUR NEPHEW REALLY IS A GENIUS.
AN ABSENT GENIUS. HE DID TEXT TO MAKE SURE IT WENT WELL, BUT AFTER HOW ATTENTIVE HE'S BEEN TO YOU LATELY, DEAR...
...WELL, I'D HATE TO THINK HE'S BACKSLIDING TO HIS OLD THOUGHTLESS WAYS.
HUSH UP, JAY. PETER HAS THIS ENTIRE COMPANY TO RUN. AND WE'RE MEETING HIS NEW GIRLFRIEND IN JUST A COUPLE HOURS. I'M QUITE HAPPY WITH HOW HE'S BEEN DOING.
THAT'S NOT ALL YOU SHOULD BE HAPPY ABOUT.
OH...?
OH! MY CANE...
YOU WALKED ON YOUR OWN. NO LIMP, NO PAIN.
NOW I AM A LITTLE UPSET PETER WASN'T HERE. THIS IS TRULY A MIRACLE.
IT'S THIS WORKAHOLIC MENTALITY NOWADAYS MY SON DIDN'T MAKE EITHER. I REALIZE HE THE MAYOR...
...BUT I'D LOVE TO KNOW WHAT H CONSIDERS MOR IMPORTANT THA FAMILY.

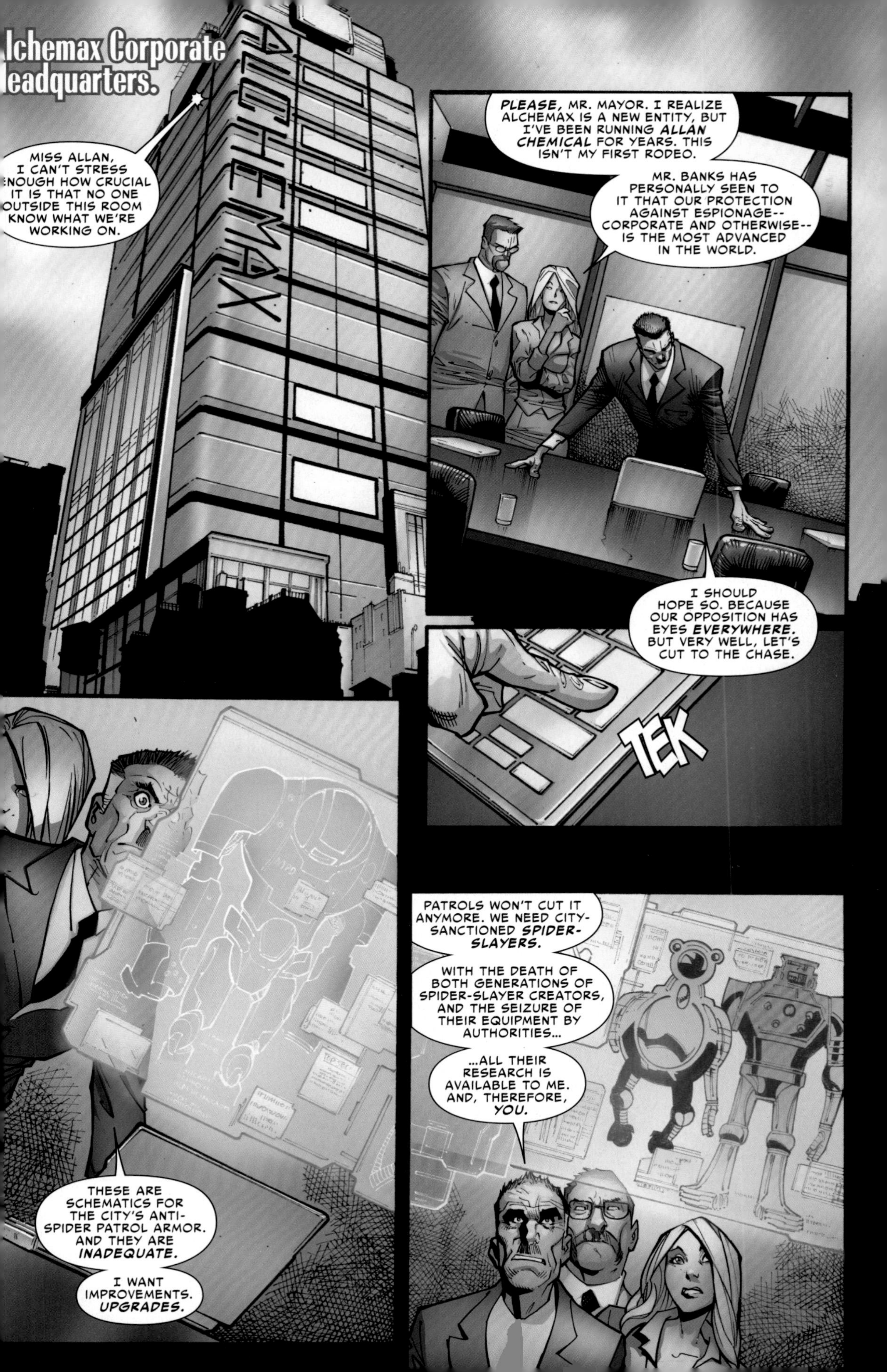
lchemax Corporate leadquarters.
MISS ALLAN, I CAN'T STRESS ENOUGH HOW CRUCIAL IT IS THAT NO ONE OUTSIDE THIS ROOM KNOW WHAT WE'RE WORKING ON.
PLEASE, MR. MAYOR. I REALIZE ALCHEMAX IS A NEW ENTITY, BUT I'VE BEEN RUNNING ALLAN CHEMICAL FOR YEARS. THIS ISN'T MY FIRST RODEO.
MR. BANKS HAS PERSONALLY SEEN TO IT THAT OUR PROTECTION AGAINST ESPIONAGE-- CORPORATE AND OTHERWISE-- IS THE MOST ADVANCED IN THE WORLD.
I SHOULD HOPE SO. BECAUSE OUR OPPOSITION HAS EYES EVERYWHERE. BUT VERY WELL, LET'S CUT TO THE CHASE.
TEK
THESE ARE SCHEMATICS FOR THE CITY'S ANTI-SPIDER PATROL ARMOR. AND THEY ARE INADEQUATE.
I WANT IMPROVEMENTS. UPGRADES.
PATROLS WON'T CUT IT ANYMORE. WE NEED CITY-SANCTIONED SPIDER-SLAYERS.
WITH THE DEATH OF BOTH GENERATIONS OF SPIDER-SLAYER CREATORS, AND THE SEIZURE OF THEIR EQUIPMENT BY AUTHORITIES...
...ALL THEIR RESEARCH IS AVAILABLE TO ME. AND, THEREFORE, YOU.

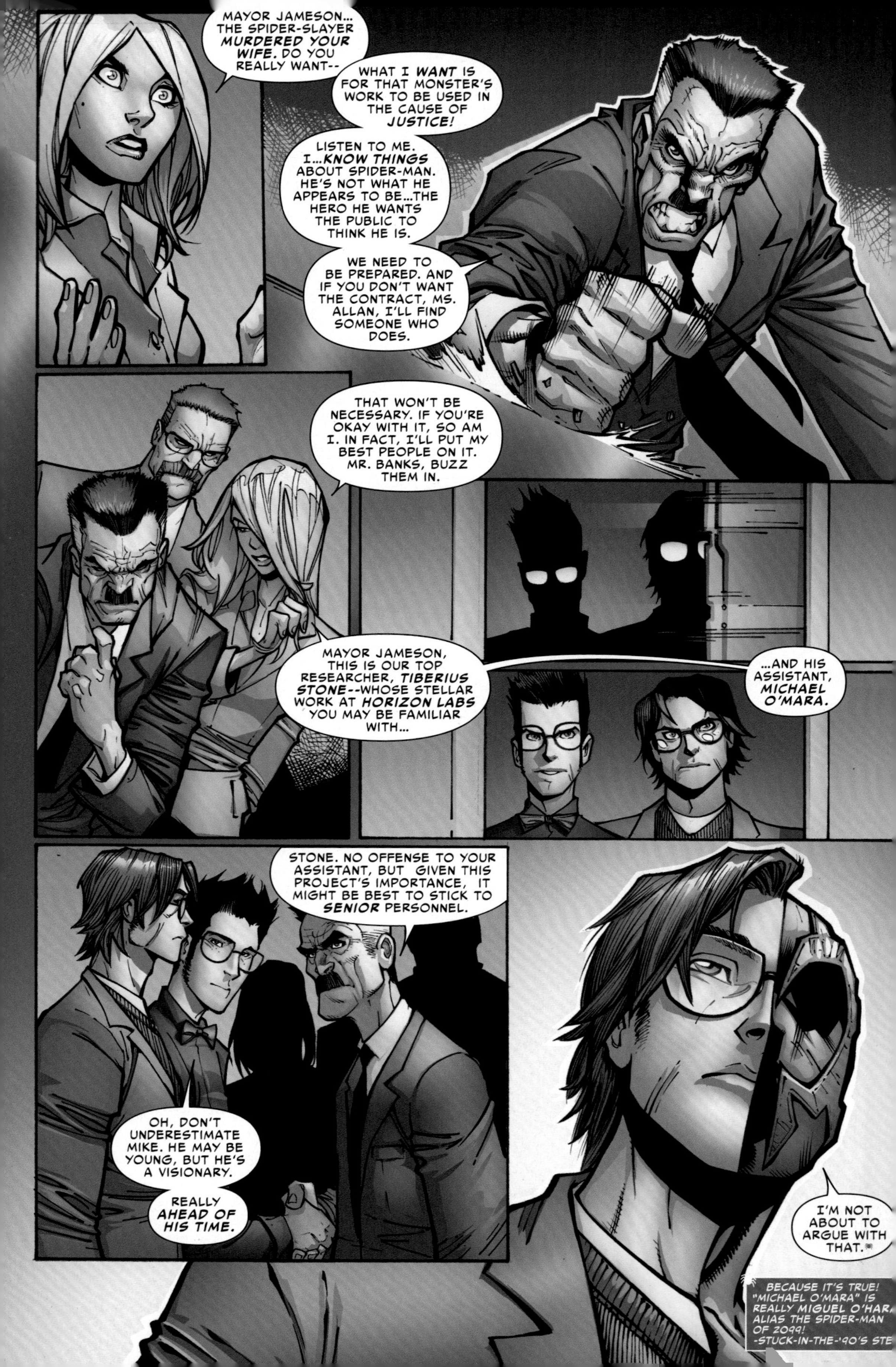
MAYOR JAMESON... THE SPIDER-SLAYER MURDERED YOUR WIFE. DO YOU REALLY WANT--
WHAT I WANT IS FOR THAT MONSTER'S WORK TO BE USED IN THE CAUSE OF JUSTICE!
LISTEN TO ME. I...KNOW THINGS ABOUT SPIDER-MAN. HE'S NOT WHAT HE APPEARS TO BE...THE HERO HE WANTS THE PUBLIC TO THINK HE IS.
WE NEED TO BE PREPARED. AND IF YOU DON'T WANT THE CONTRACT, MS. ALLAN, I'LL FIND SOMEONE WHO DOES.
THAT WON'T BE NECESSARY. IF YOU'RE OKAY WITH IT, SO AM I. IN FACT, I'LL PUT MY BEST PEOPLE ON IT. MR. BANKS, BUZZ THEM IN.
MAYOR JAMESON, THIS IS OUR TOP RESEARCHER, TIBERIUS STONE--WHOSE STELLAR WORK AT HORIZON LABS YOU MAY BE FAMILIAR WITH...
...AND HIS ASSISTANT, MICHAEL O'MARA.
STONE. NO OFFENSE TO YOUR ASSISTANT, BUT GIVEN THIS PROJECT'S IMPORTANCE, IT MIGHT BE BEST TO STICK TO SENIOR PERSONNEL.
OH, DON'T UNDERESTIMATE MIKE. HE MAY BE YOUNG, BUT HE'S A VISIONARY.
REALLY AHEAD OF HIS TIME.
I'M NOT ABOUT TO ARGUE WITH THAT.
BECAUSE IT'S TRUE! "MICHAEL O'MARA" IS REALLY MIGUEL O'HAR ALIAS THE SPIDER-MAN OF 2099! -STUCK-IN-THE-'90'S STE

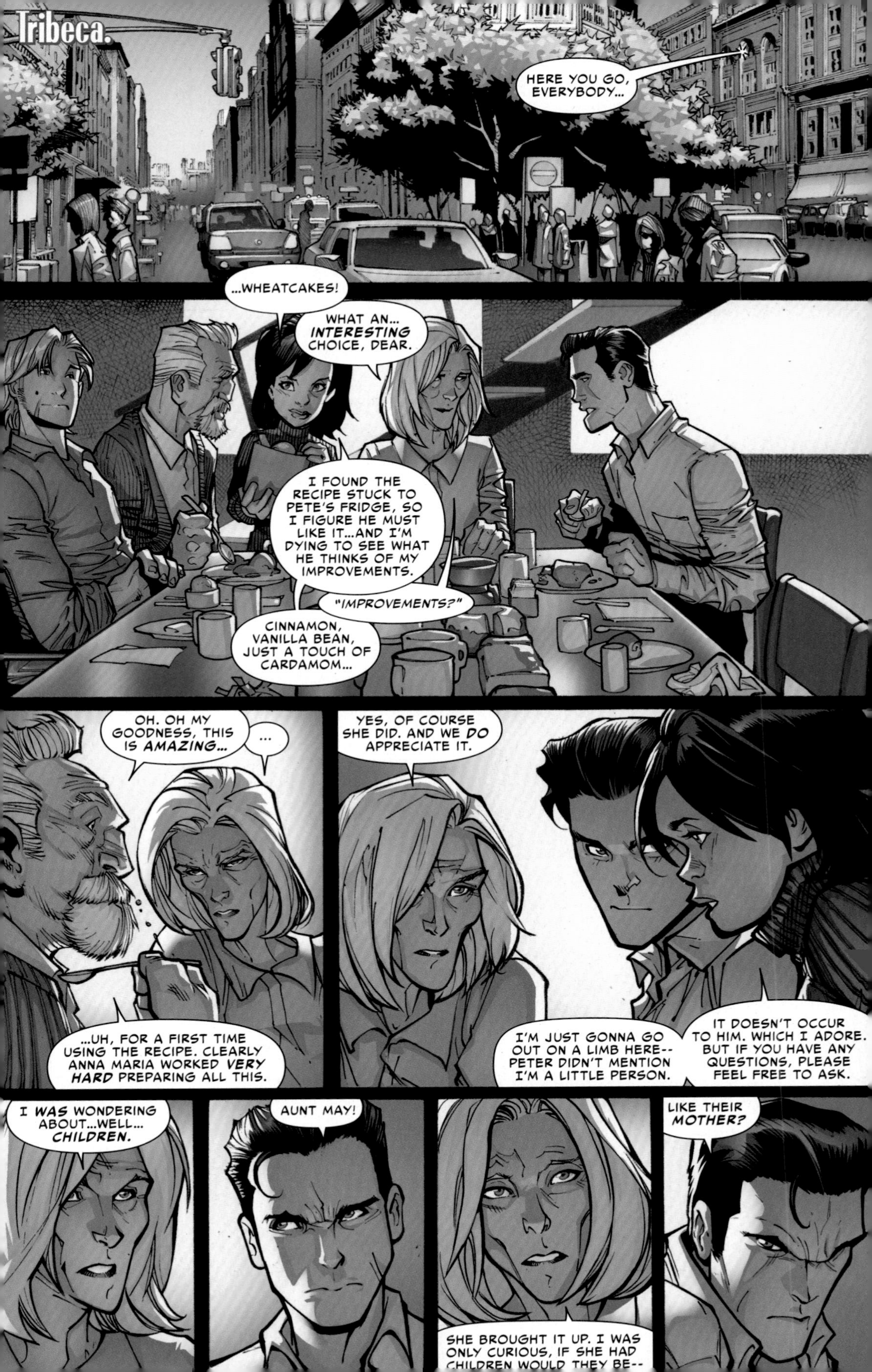
Tribeca.
HERE YOU GO, EVERYBODY...
...WHEATCAKES!
WHAT AN... INTERESTING CHOICE, DEAR.
I FOUND THE RECIPE STUCK TO PETE'S FRIDGE, SO I FIGURE HE MUST LIKE IT...AND I'M DYING TO SEE WHAT HE THINKS OF MY IMPROVEMENTS.
"IMPROVEMENTS?"
CINNAMON, VANILLA BEAN, JUST A TOUCH OF CARDAMOM...
OH. OH MY GOODNESS, THIS IS AMAZING...
...
...UH, FOR A FIRST TIME USING THE RECIPE. CLEARLY ANNA MARIA WORKED VERY HARD PREPARING ALL THIS.
YES, OF COURSE SHE DID. AND WE DO APPRECIATE IT.
I'M JUST GONNA GO OUT ON A LIMB HERE-- PETER DIDN'T MENTION I'M A LITTLE PERSON.
IT DOESN'T OCCUR TO HIM. WHICH I ADORE. BUT IF YOU HAVE ANY QUESTIONS, PLEASE FEEL FREE TO ASK.
I WAS WONDERING ABOUT...WELL... CHILDREN.
AUNT MAY!
SHE BROUGHT IT UP. I WAS ONLY CURIOUS, IF SHE HAD CHILDREN WOULD THEY BE--
LIKE THEIR MOTHER?

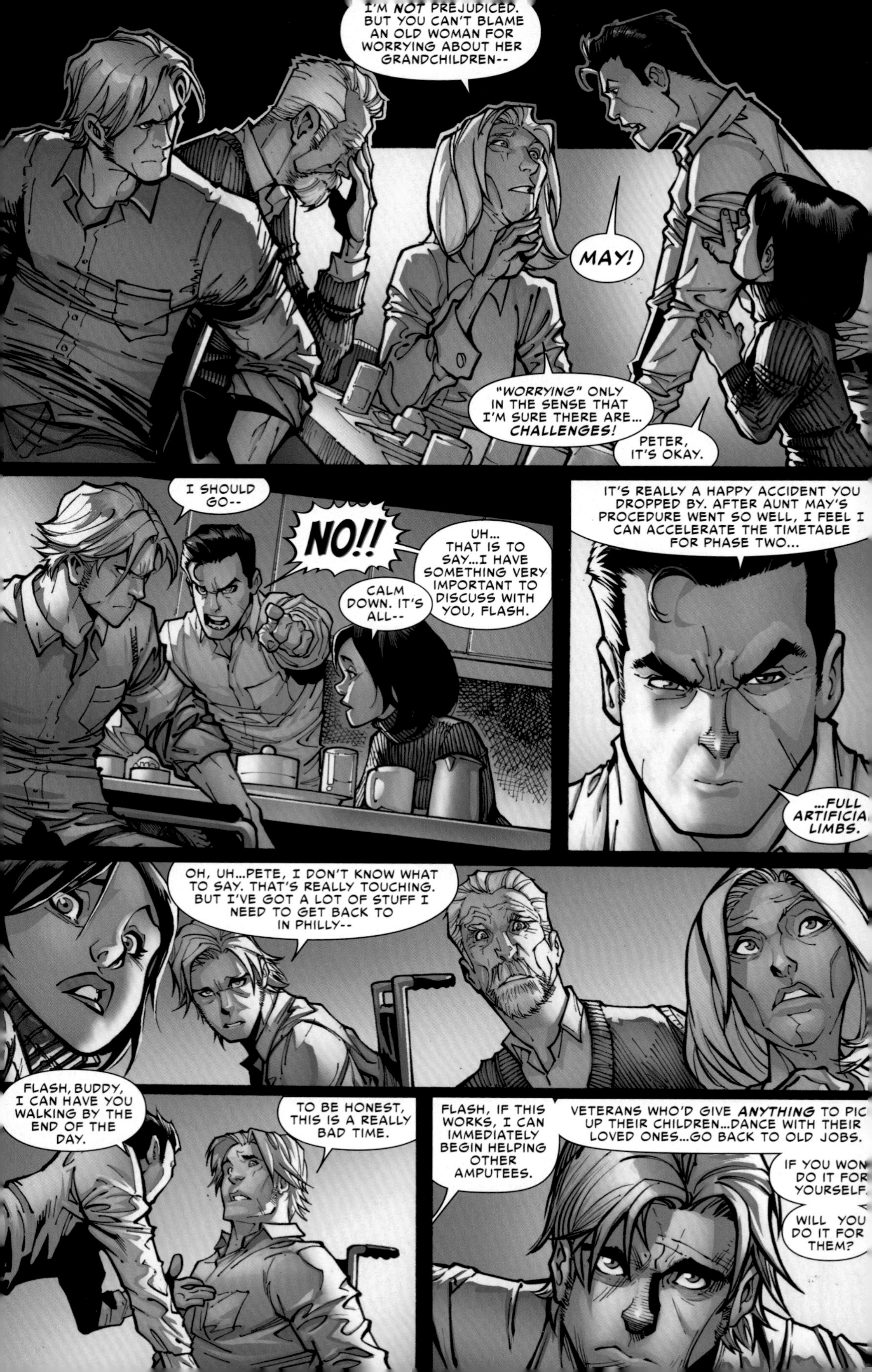
I'M NOT PREJUDICED. BUT YOU CAN'T BLAME AN OLD WOMAN FOR WORRYING ABOUT HER GRANDCHILDREN--
MAY!
"WORRYING" ONLY IN THE SENSE THAT I'M SURE THERE ARE... CHALLENGES!
PETER, IT'S OKAY.
I SHOULD GO--
NO!!
UH... THAT IS TO SAY...I HAVE SOMETHING VERY IMPORTANT TO DISCUSS WITH YOU, FLASH.
CALM DOWN. IT'S ALL--
IT'S REALLY A HAPPY ACCIDENT YOU DROPPED BY. AFTER AUNT MAY'S PROCEDURE WENT SO WELL, I FEEL I CAN ACCELERATE THE TIMETABLE FOR PHASE TWO...
...FULL ARTIFICIA LIMBS.
OH, UH...PETE, I DON'T KNOW WHAT TO SAY. THAT'S REALLY TOUCHING. BUT I'VE GOT A LOT OF STUFF I NEED TO GET BACK TO IN PHILLY--
FLASH, BUDDY, I CAN HAVE YOU WALKING BY THE END OF THE DAY.
TO BE HONEST, THIS IS A REALLY BAD TIME.
FLASH, IF THIS WORKS, I CAN IMMEDIATELY BEGIN HELPING OTHER AMPUTEES.
VETERANS WHO'D GIVE ANYTHING TO PIC UP THEIR CHILDREN...DANCE WITH THEIR LOVED ONES...GO BACK TO OLD JOBS.
IF YOU WON DO IT FOR YOURSELF
WILL YOU DO IT FOR THEM?

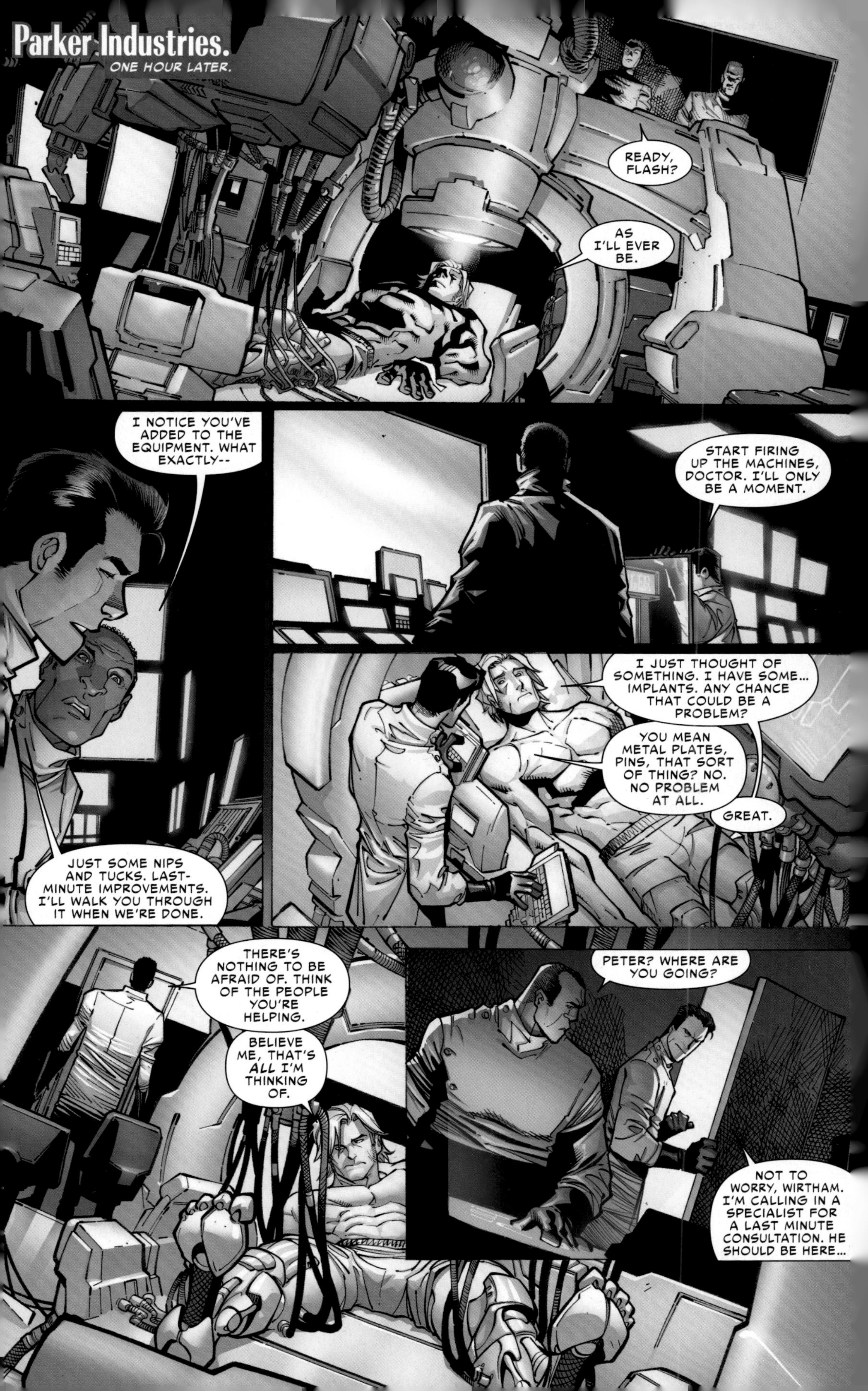
Parker Industries.
ONE HOUR LATER.
READY, FLASH?
AS I'LL EVER BE.
I NOTICE YOU'VE ADDED TO THE EQUIPMENT. WHAT EXACTLY--
JUST SOME NIPS AND TUCKS. LAST-MINUTE IMPROVEMENTS. I'LL WALK YOU THROUGH IT WHEN WE'RE DONE.
START FIRING UP THE MACHINES, DOCTOR. I'LL ONLY BE A MOMENT.
I JUST THOUGHT OF SOMETHING. I HAVE SOME... IMPLANTS. ANY CHANCE THAT COULD BE A PROBLEM?
YOU MEAN METAL PLATES, PINS, THAT SORT OF THING? NO. NO PROBLEM AT ALL.
GREAT.
THERE'S NOTHING TO BE AFRAID OF. THINK OF THE PEOPLE YOU'RE HELPING.
BELIEVE ME, THAT'S *ALL* I'M THINKING OF.
PETER? WHERE ARE YOU GOING?
NOT TO WORRY, WIRTHAM. I'M CALLING IN A SPECIALIST FOR A LAST MINUTE CONSULTATION. HE SHOULD BE HERE...

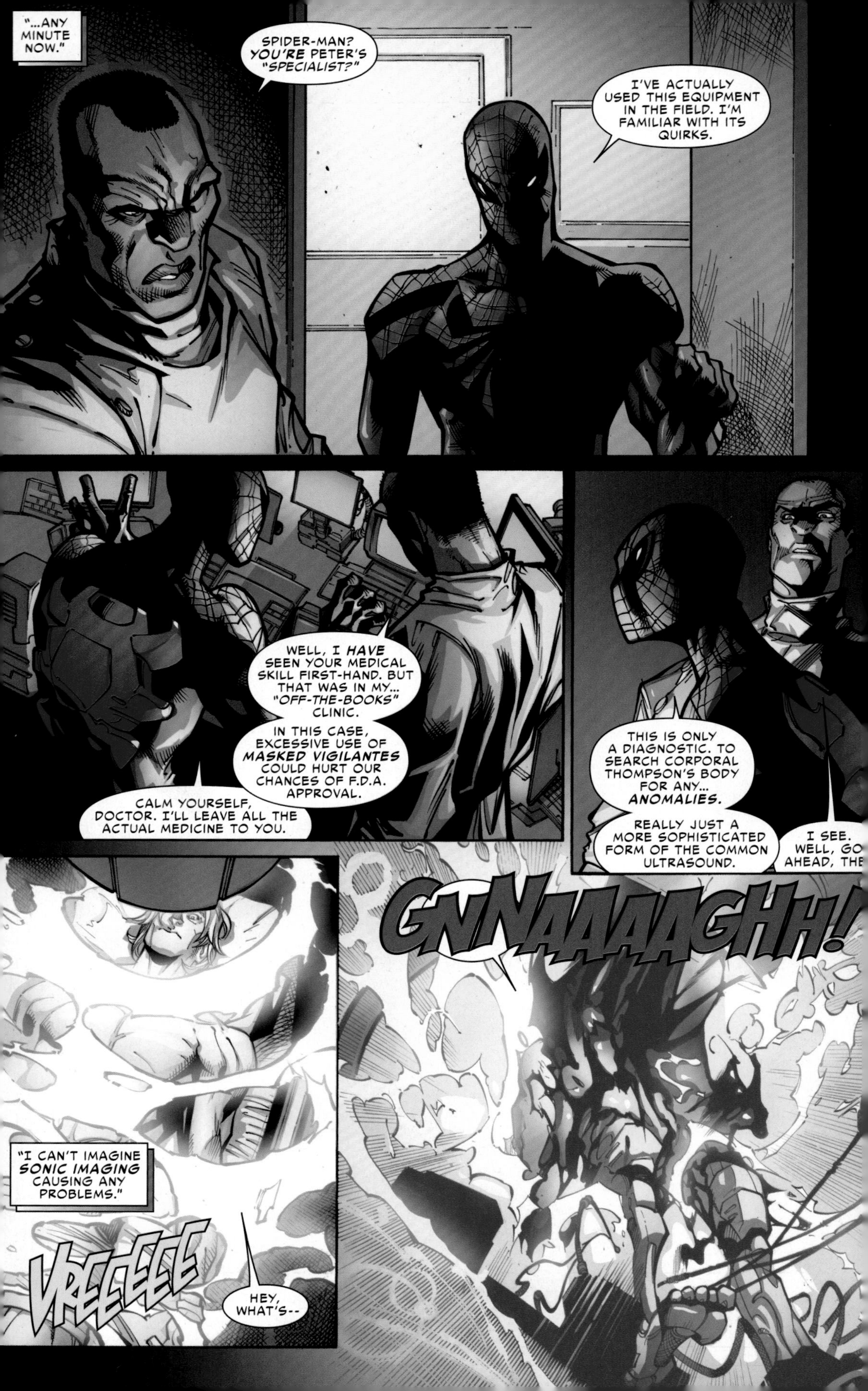
"...ANY MINUTE NOW."
SPIDER-MAN? YOU'RE PETER'S "SPECIALIST?"
I'VE ACTUALLY USED THIS EQUIPMENT IN THE FIELD. I'M FAMILIAR WITH ITS QUIRKS.
WELL, I HAVE SEEN YOUR MEDICAL SKILL FIRST-HAND. BUT THAT WAS IN MY... "OFF-THE-BOOKS" CLINIC.
IN THIS CASE, EXCESSIVE USE OF MASKED VIGILANTES COULD HURT OUR CHANCES OF F.D.A. APPROVAL.
CALM YOURSELF, DOCTOR. I'LL LEAVE ALL THE ACTUAL MEDICINE TO YOU.
THIS IS ONLY A DIAGNOSTIC. TO SEARCH CORPORAL THOMPSON'S BODY FOR ANY... ANOMALIES.
REALLY JUST A MORE SOPHISTICATED FORM OF THE COMMON ULTRASOUND.
I SEE. WELL, GO AHEAD, THE
"I CAN'T IMAGINE SONIC IMAGING CAUSING ANY PROBLEMS."
VREEEEE
HEY, WHAT'S--
GNNAAAAAGHH!

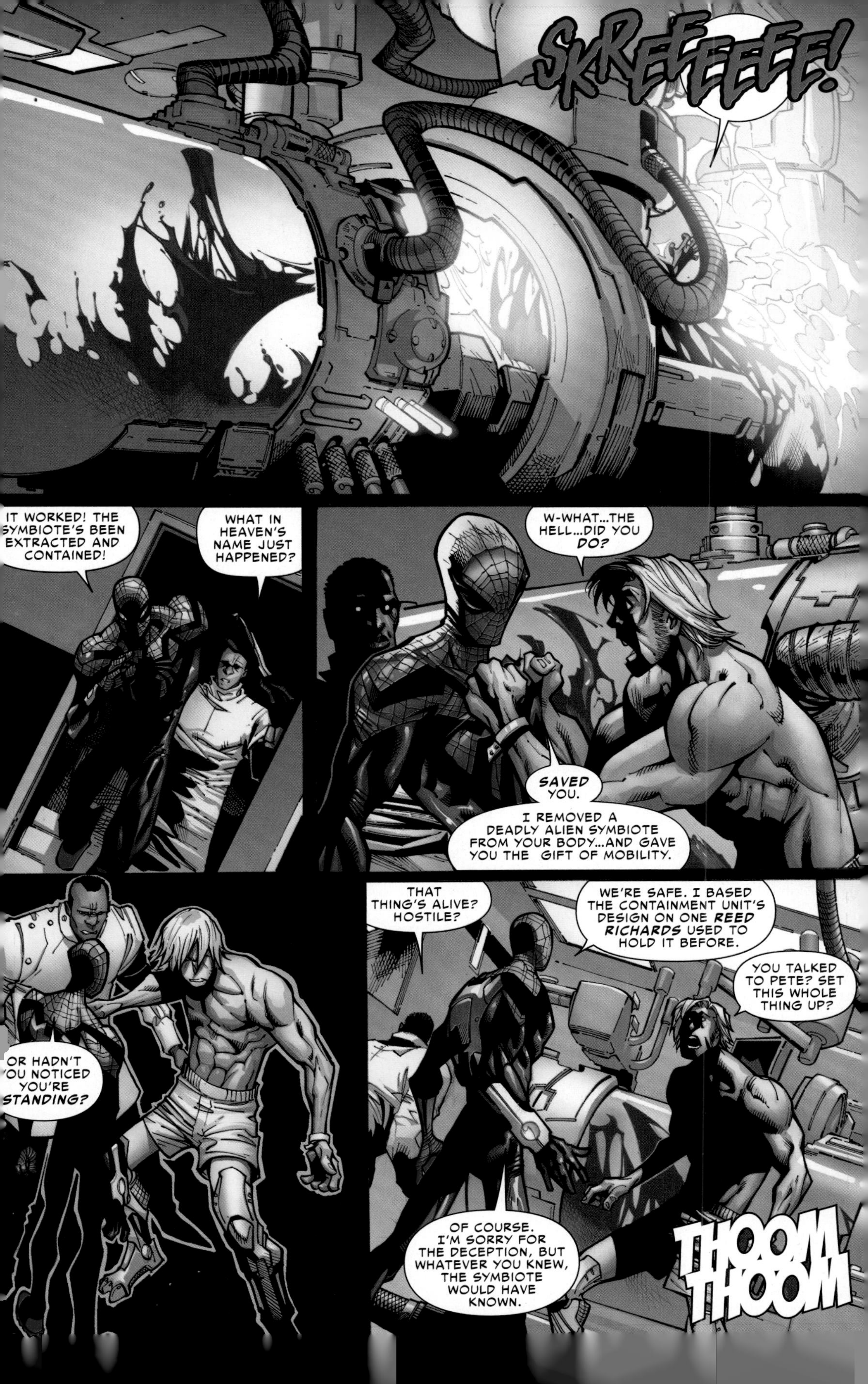
SKREEEEEE!
IT WORKED! THE SYMBIOTE'S BEEN EXTRACTED AND CONTAINED!
WHAT IN HEAVEN'S NAME JUST HAPPENED?
W-WHAT...THE HELL...DID YOU DO?
SAVED YOU.
I REMOVED A DEADLY ALIEN SYMBIOTE FROM YOUR BODY...AND GAVE YOU THE GIFT OF MOBILITY.
OR HADN'T YOU NOTICED YOU'RE STANDING?
THAT THING'S ALIVE? HOSTILE?
WE'RE SAFE. I BASED THE CONTAINMENT UNIT'S DESIGN ON ONE REED RICHARDS USED TO HOLD IT BEFORE.
YOU TALKED TO PETE? SET THIS WHOLE THING UP?
OF COURSE. I'M SORRY FOR THE DECEPTION, BUT WHATEVER YOU KNEW, THE SYMBIOTE WOULD HAVE KNOWN.
THOOM THOOM

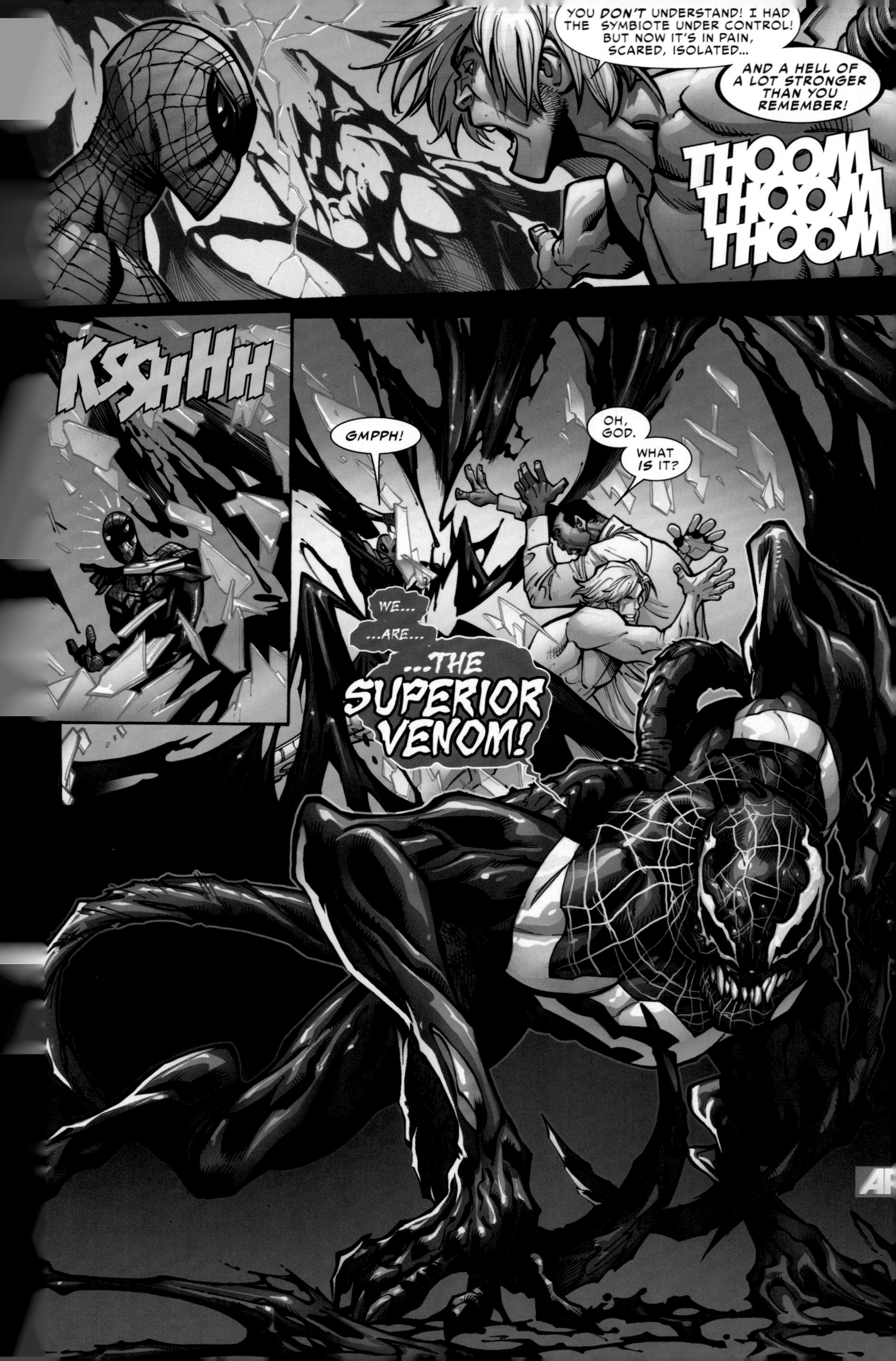
YOU DON'T UNDERSTAND! I HAD THE SYMBIOTE UNDER CONTROL! BUT NOW IT'S IN PAIN, SCARED, ISOLATED...
AND A HELL OF A LOT STRONGER THAN YOU REMEMBER!
THOOM THOOM THOOM
KSSHHH
GMPPH!
OH, GOD.
WHAT IS IT?
WE...
...ARE...
...THE SUPERIOR VENOM!

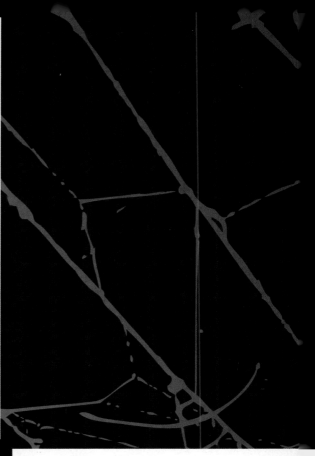

22 VARIANT
J. SCOTT CAMPBELL & EDGAR DELGADO

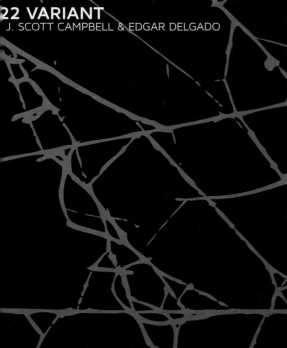

#24 VARIANT
BY STEFANO CASELLI & FRANK MARTIN

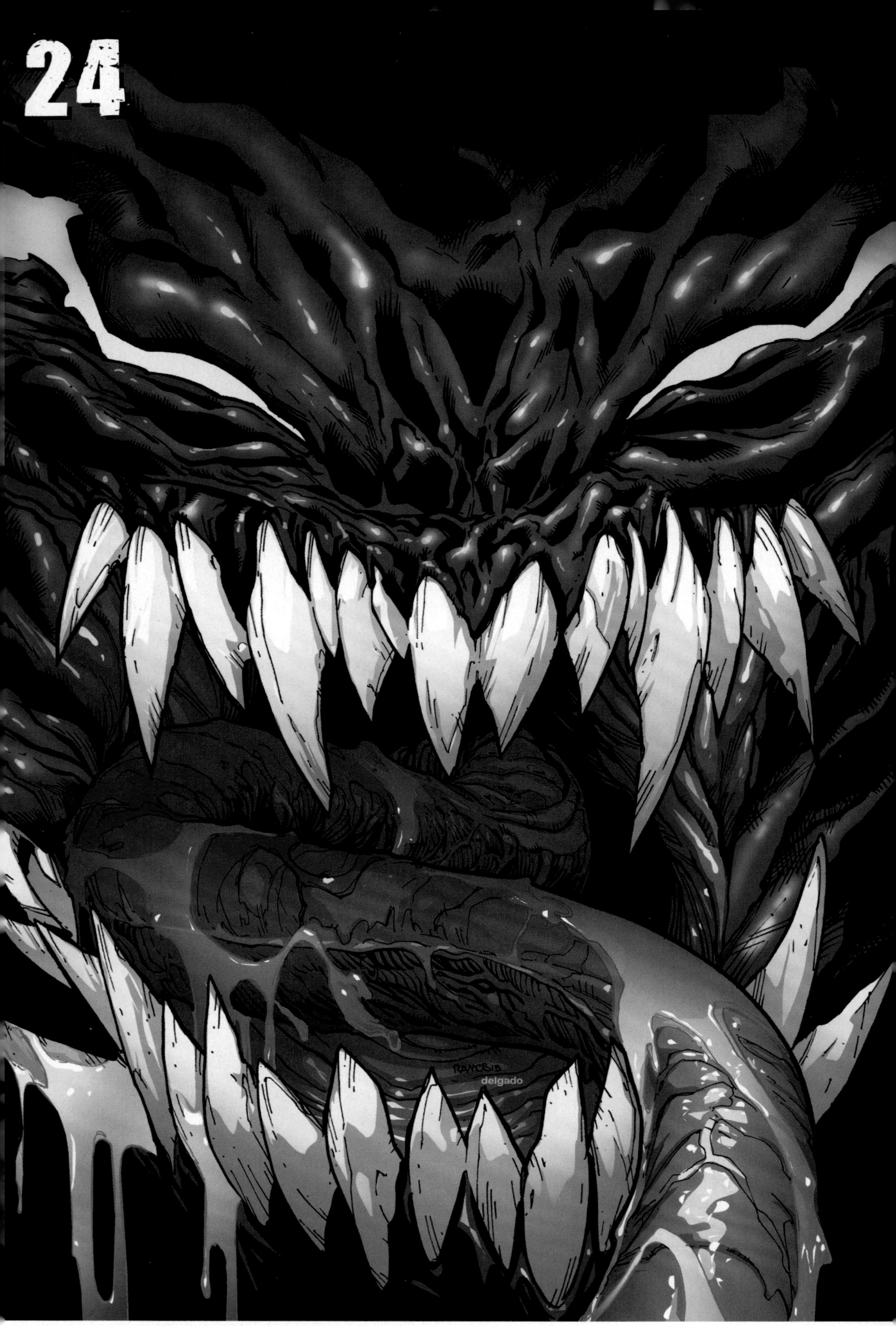
24

DARKEST HOURS PART 3: DARK EMBRACE

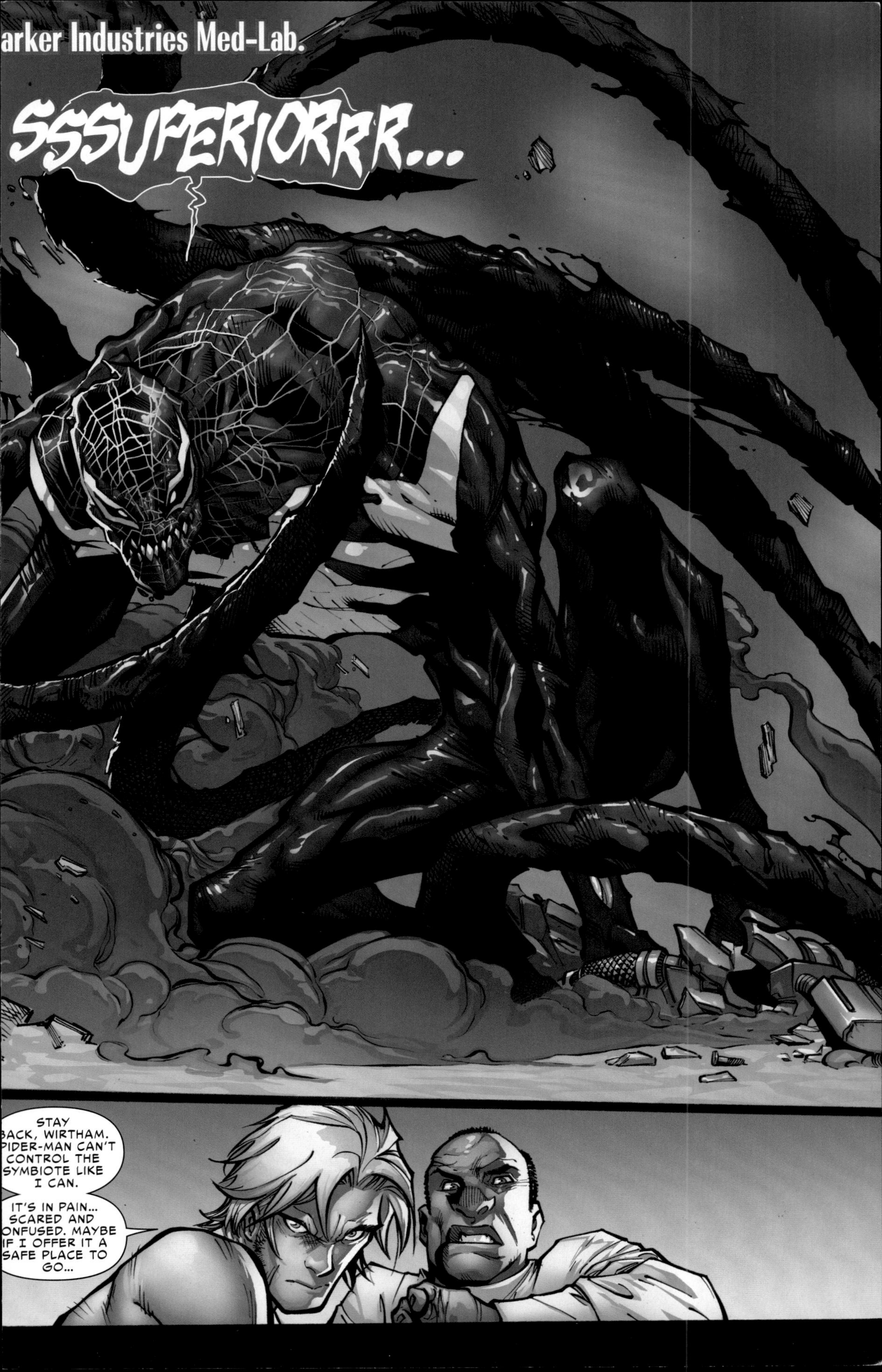

arker Industries Med-Lab.
SSSUPERIORRR...
STAY BACK, WIRTHAM. PIDER-MAN CAN'T CONTROL THE SYMBIOTE LIKE I CAN.
IT'S IN PAIN... SCARED AND ONFUSED. MAYBE IF I OFFER IT A SAFE PLACE TO GO...

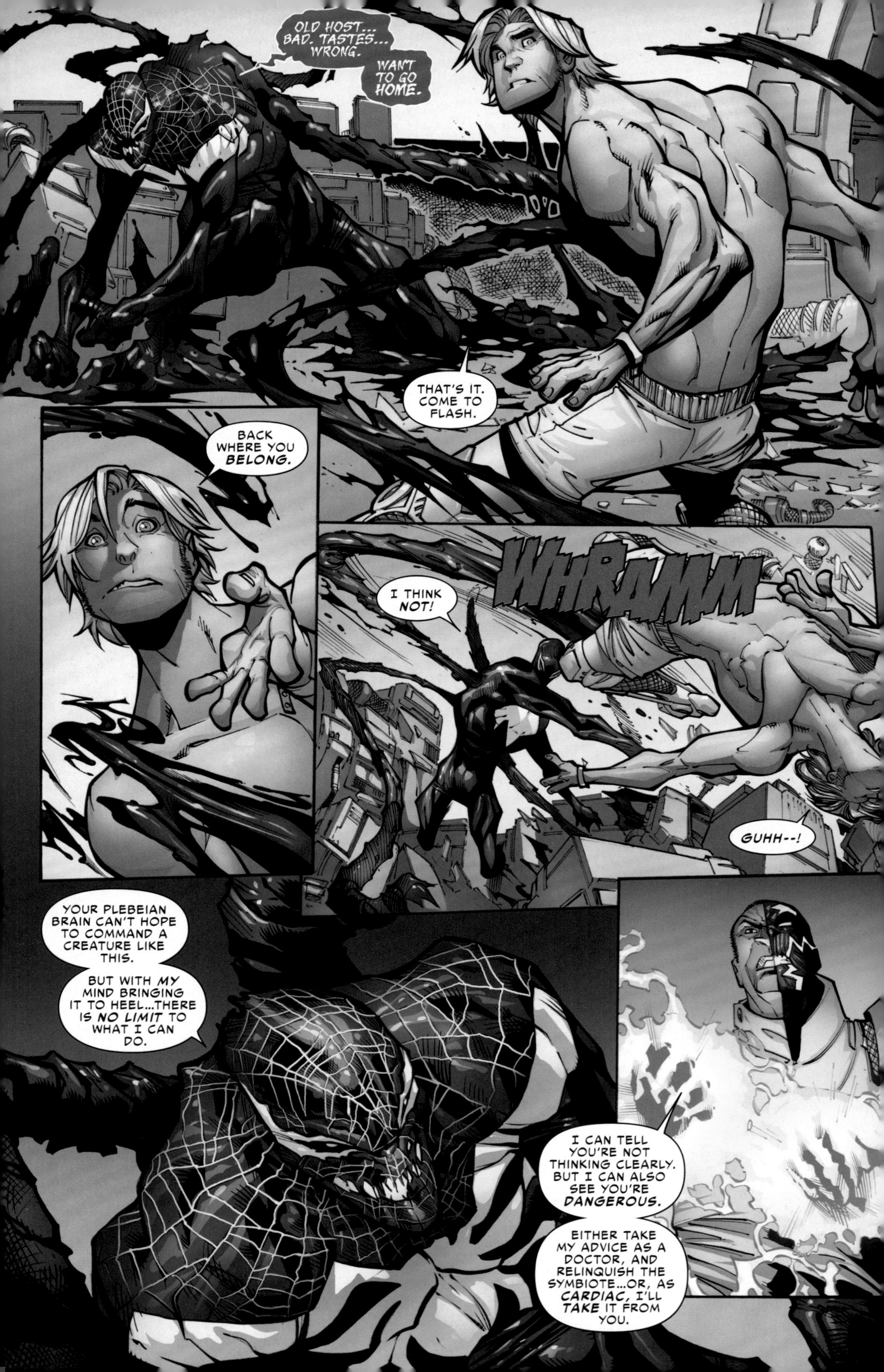
OLD HOST... BAD. TASTES... WRONG.
WANT TO GO HOME.
THAT'S IT. COME TO FLASH.
BACK WHERE YOU BELONG.
I THINK NOT!
WHRAMM
GUHH--!
YOUR PLEBEIAN BRAIN CAN'T HOPE TO COMMAND A CREATURE LIKE THIS.
BUT WITH MY MIND BRINGING IT TO HEEL...THERE IS NO LIMIT TO WHAT I CAN DO.
I CAN TELL YOU'RE NOT THINKING CLEARLY. BUT I CAN ALSO SEE YOU'RE DANGEROUS.
EITHER TAKE MY ADVICE AS A DOCTOR, AND RELINQUISH THE SYMBIOTE...OR, AS CARDIAC, I'LL TAKE IT FROM YOU.

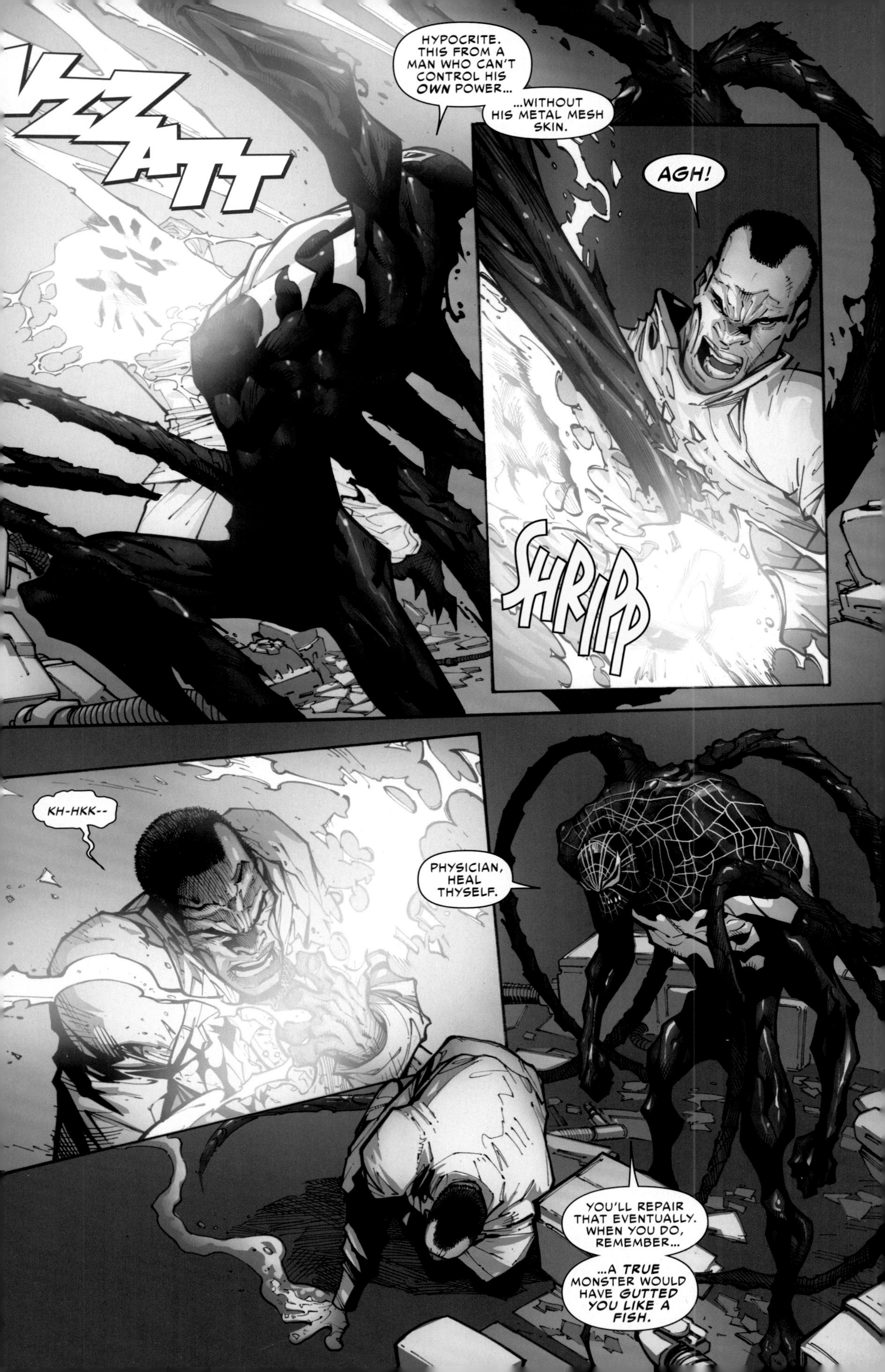

ZZAAT
HYPOCRITE. THIS FROM A MAN WHO CAN'T CONTROL HIS OWN POWER...
...WITHOUT HIS METAL MESH SKIN.
AGH!
SHRIPP
KH-HKK--
PHYSICIAN, HEAL THYSELF.
YOU'LL REPAIR THAT EVENTUALLY. WHEN YOU DO, REMEMBER...
...A TRUE MONSTER WOULD HAVE GUTTED YOU LIKE A FISH.

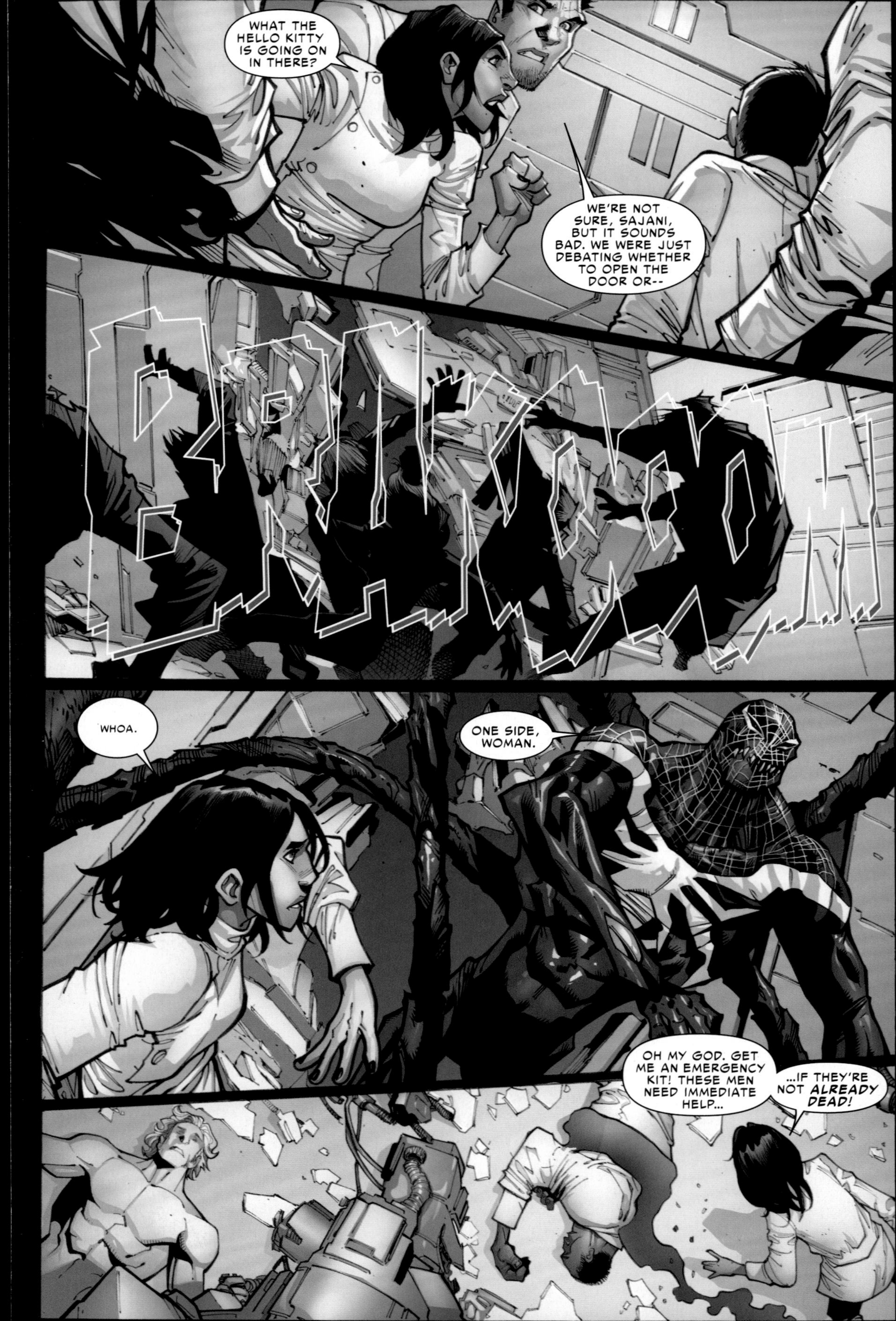
WHAT THE HELLO KITTY IS GOING ON IN THERE?
WE'RE NOT SURE, SAJANI, BUT IT SOUNDS BAD. WE WERE JUST DEBATING WHETHER TO OPEN THE DOOR OR--
WHOA.
ONE SIDE, WOMAN.
OH MY GOD. GET ME AN EMERGENCY KIT! THESE MEN NEED IMMEDIATE HELP...
...IF THEY'RE NOT *ALREADY DEAD!*

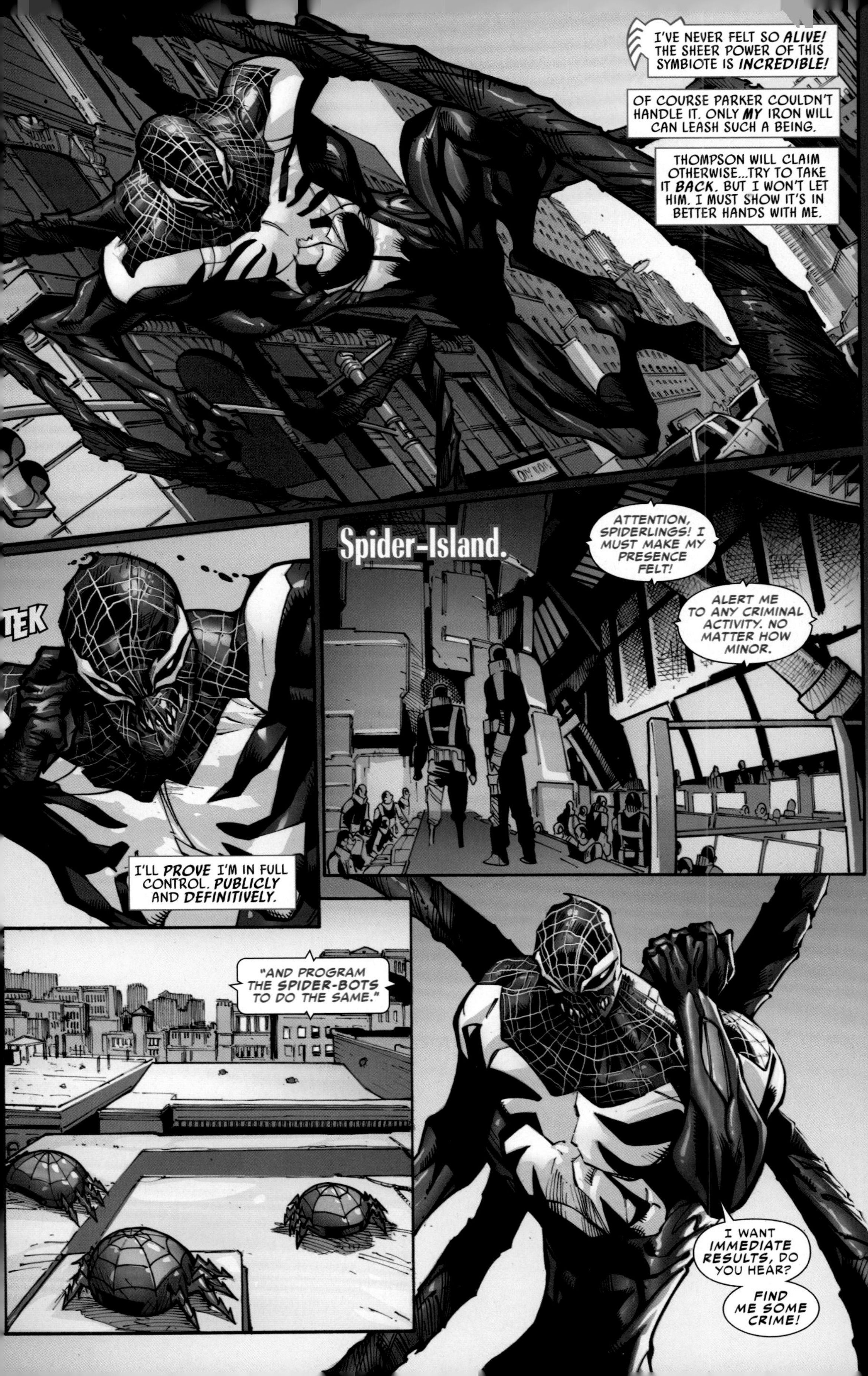

I'VE NEVER FELT SO ALIVE! THE SHEER POWER OF THIS SYMBIOTE IS INCREDIBLE!
OF COURSE PARKER COULDN'T HANDLE IT. ONLY MY IRON WILL CAN LEASH SUCH A BEING.
THOMPSON WILL CLAIM OTHERWISE...TRY TO TAKE IT BACK. BUT I WON'T LET HIM. I MUST SHOW IT'S IN BETTER HANDS WITH ME.
TEK
I'LL PROVE I'M IN FULL CONTROL. PUBLICLY AND DEFINITIVELY.
Spider-Island.
ATTENTION, SPIDERLINGS! I MUST MAKE MY PRESENCE FELT!
ALERT ME TO ANY CRIMINAL ACTIVITY. NO MATTER HOW MINOR.
"AND PROGRAM THE SPIDER-BOTS TO DO THE SAME."
I WANT IMMEDIATE RESULTS, DO YOU HEAR?
FIND ME SOME CRIME!

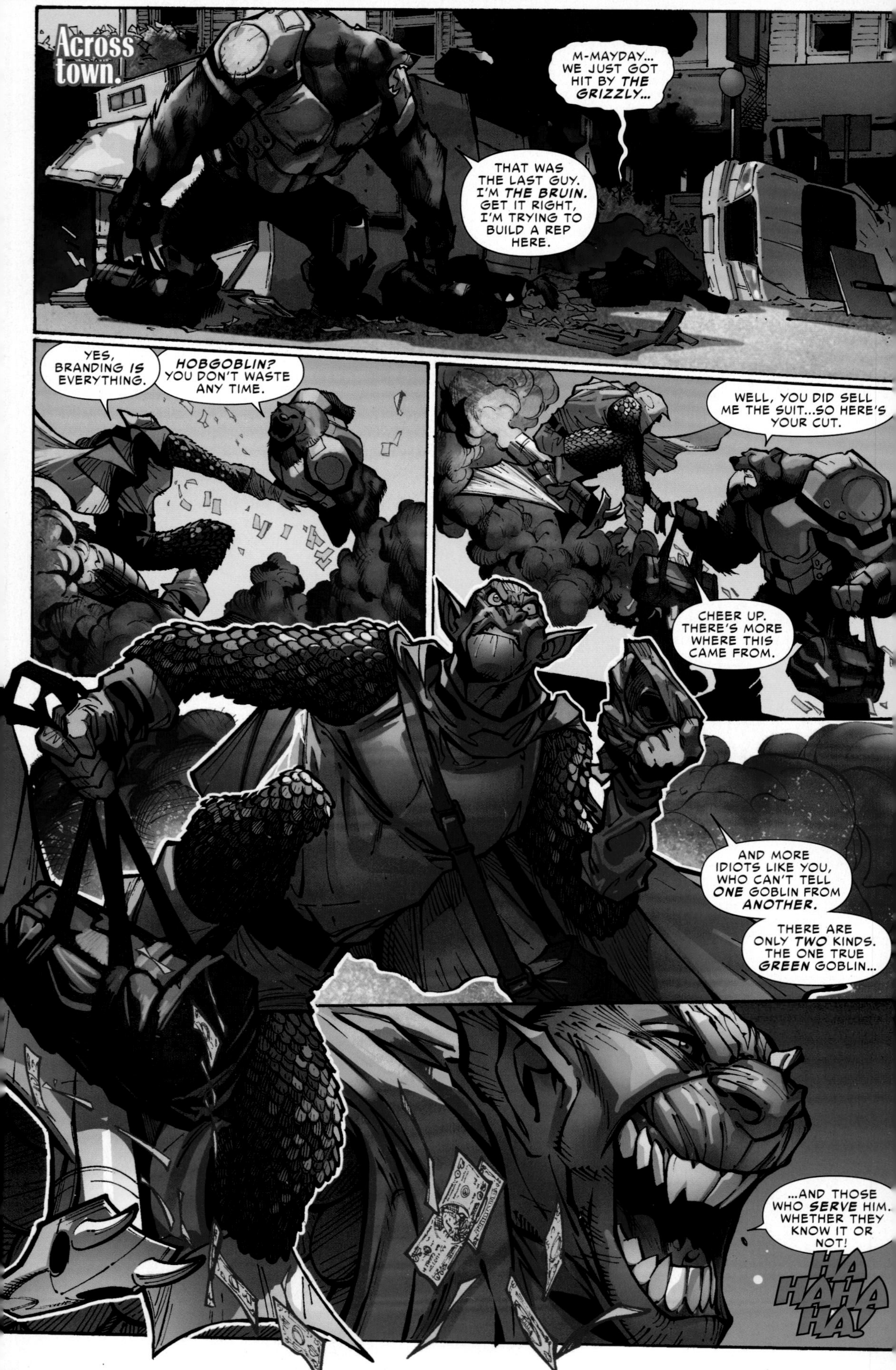

Across town.
M-MAYDAY... WE JUST GOT HIT BY THE GRIZZLY...
THAT WAS THE LAST GUY. I'M THE BRUIN. GET IT RIGHT, I'M TRYING TO BUILD A REP HERE.
YES, BRANDING IS EVERYTHING.
HOBGOBLIN? YOU DON'T WASTE ANY TIME.
WELL, YOU DID SELL ME THE SUIT...SO HERE'S YOUR CUT.
CHEER UP. THERE'S MORE WHERE THIS CAME FROM.
AND MORE IDIOTS LIKE YOU, WHO CAN'T TELL ONE GOBLIN FROM ANOTHER.
THERE ARE ONLY TWO KINDS. THE ONE TRUE GREEN GOBLIN...
...AND THOSE WHO SERVE HIM. WHETHER THEY KNOW IT OR NOT!
HA HAHAHA HA!

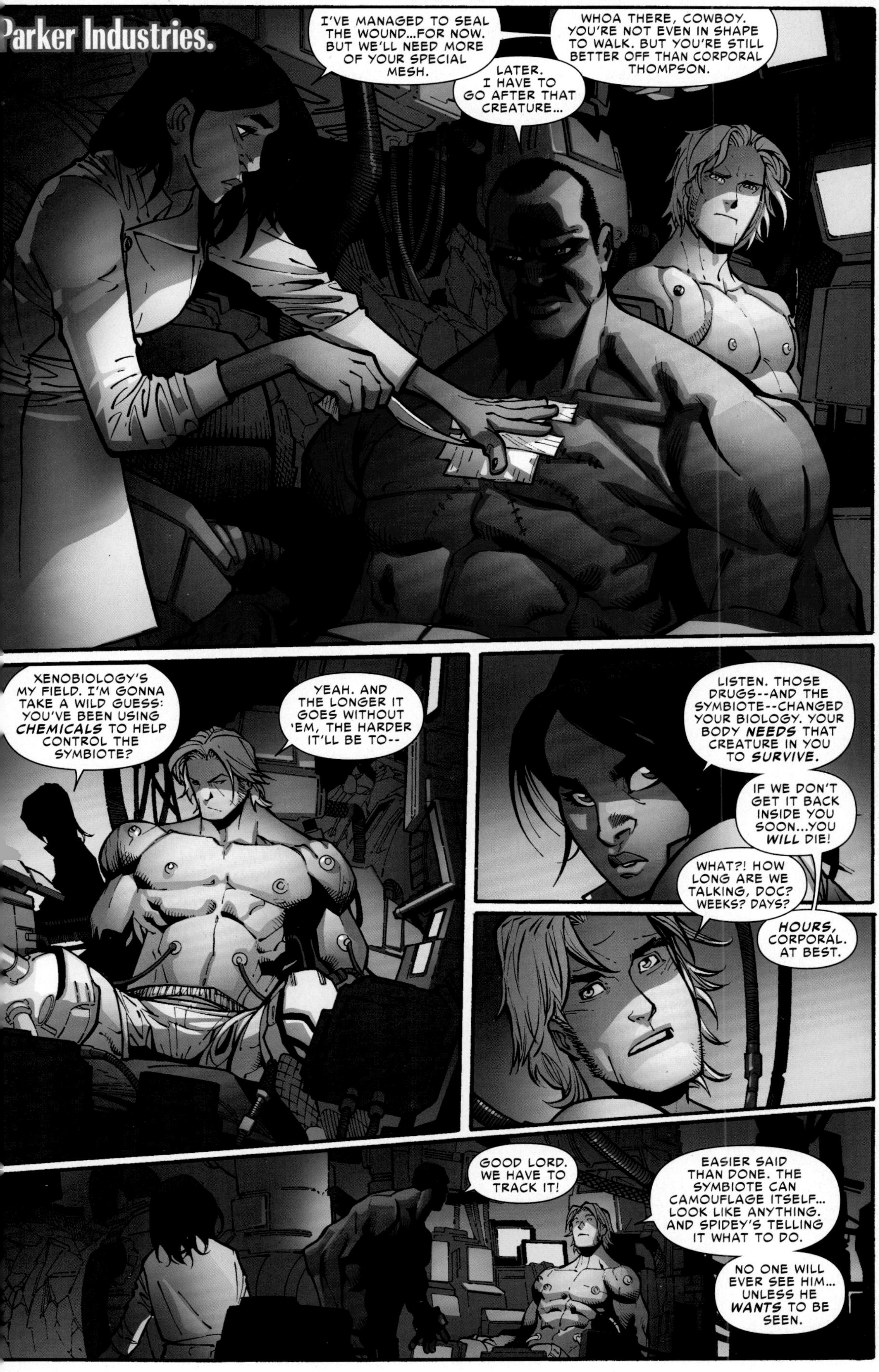
Parker Industries.
I'VE MANAGED TO SEAL THE WOUND...FOR NOW. BUT WE'LL NEED MORE OF YOUR SPECIAL MESH.
LATER. I HAVE TO GO AFTER THAT CREATURE...
WHOA THERE, COWBOY. YOU'RE NOT EVEN IN SHAPE TO WALK. BUT YOU'RE STILL BETTER OFF THAN CORPORAL THOMPSON.
XENOBIOLOGY'S MY FIELD. I'M GONNA TAKE A WILD GUESS: YOU'VE BEEN USING *CHEMICALS* TO HELP CONTROL THE SYMBIOTE?
YEAH. AND THE LONGER IT GOES WITHOUT 'EM, THE HARDER IT'LL BE TO--
LISTEN. THOSE DRUGS--AND THE SYMBIOTE--CHANGED YOUR BIOLOGY. YOUR BODY *NEEDS* THAT CREATURE IN YOU TO *SURVIVE.*
IF WE DON'T GET IT BACK INSIDE YOU SOON...YOU *WILL* DIE!
WHAT?! HOW LONG ARE WE TALKING, DOC? WEEKS? DAYS?
HOURS, CORPORAL. AT BEST.
GOOD LORD. WE HAVE TO TRACK IT!
EASIER SAID THAN DONE. THE SYMBIOTE CAN CAMOUFLAGE ITSELF... LOOK LIKE ANYTHING. AND SPIDEY'S TELLING IT WHAT TO DO.
NO ONE WILL EVER SEE HIM... UNLESS HE *WANTS* TO BE SEEN.

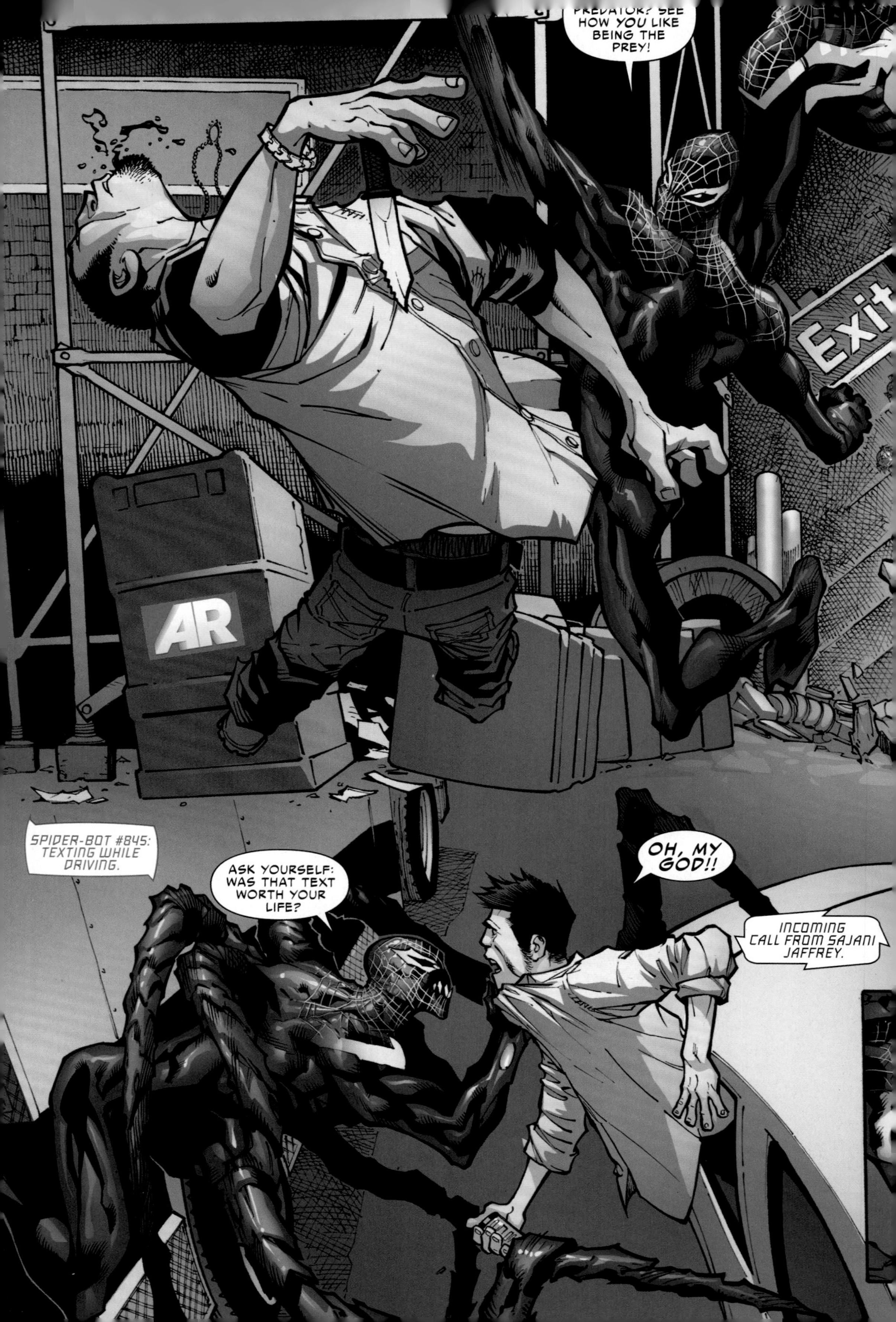
PREDATOR? SEE HOW YOU LIKE BEING THE PREY!
SPIDER-BOT #845: TEXTING WHILE DRIVING.
ASK YOURSELF: WAS THAT TEXT WORTH YOUR LIFE?
OH, MY GOD!!
INCOMING CALL FROM SAJANI JAFFREY.
EXIT
AR

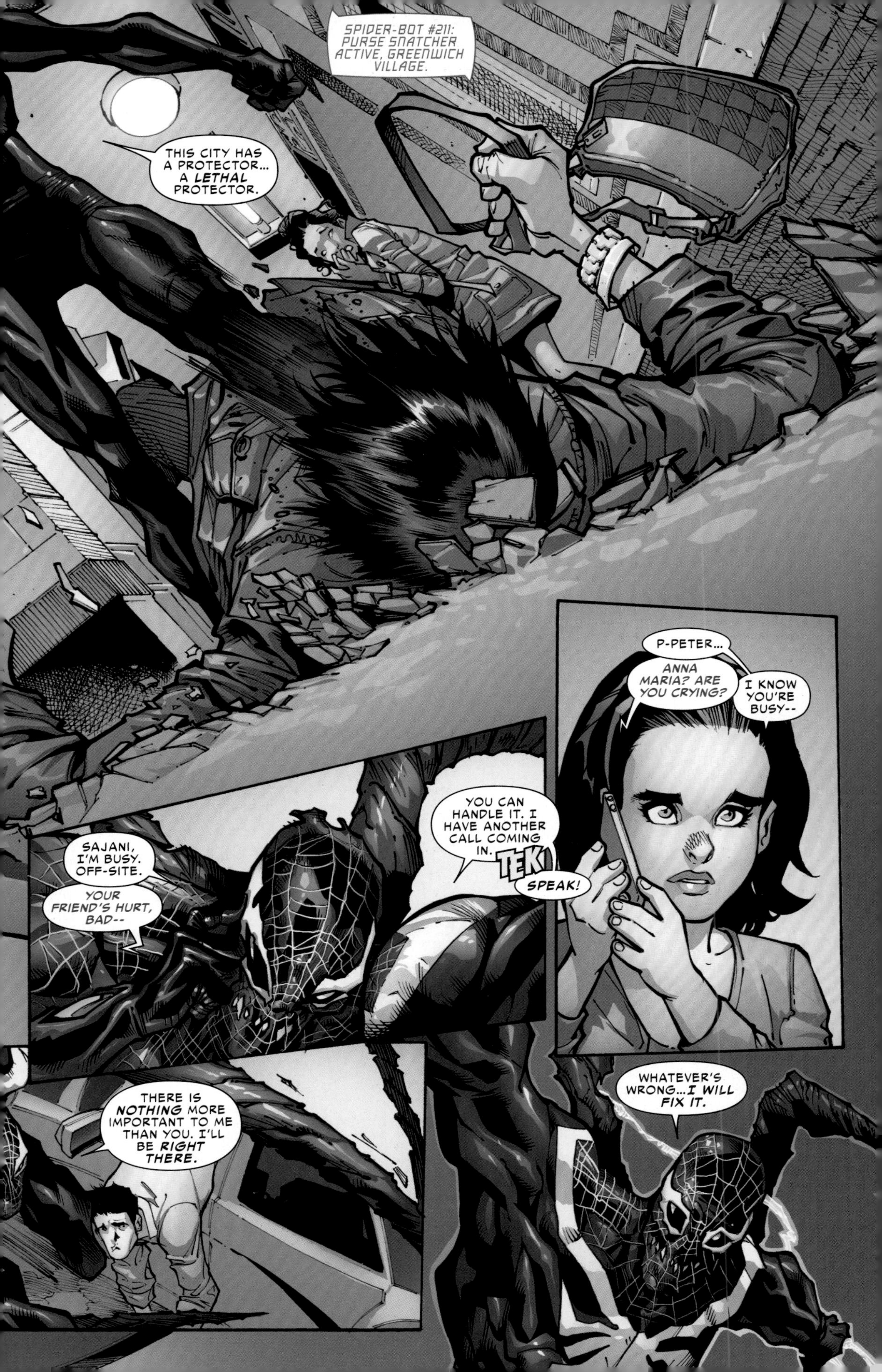
SPIDER-BOT #211: PURSE SNATCHER ACTIVE, GREENWICH VILLAGE.
THIS CITY HAS A PROTECTOR... A LETHAL PROTECTOR.
P-PETER...
ANNA MARIA? ARE YOU CRYING?
I KNOW YOU'RE BUSY--
SAJANI, I'M BUSY. OFF-SITE.
YOUR FRIEND'S HURT, BAD--
YOU CAN HANDLE IT. I HAVE ANOTHER CALL COMING IN.
TEK
SPEAK!
THERE IS NOTHING MORE IMPORTANT TO ME THAN YOU. I'LL BE RIGHT THERE.
WHATEVER'S WRONG... I WILL FIX IT.

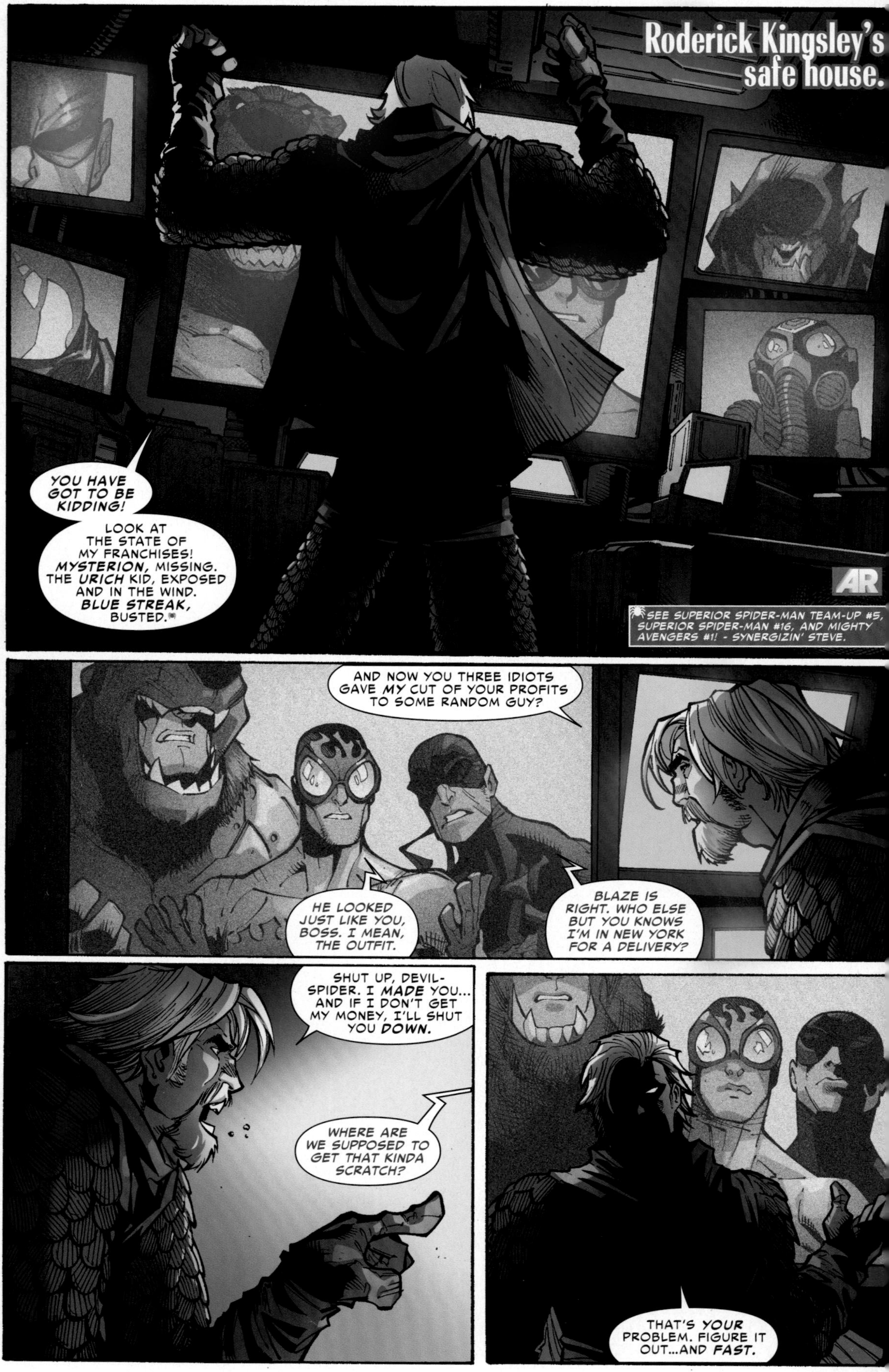
Roderick Kingsley's safe house.
YOU HAVE GOT TO BE KIDDING!
LOOK AT THE STATE OF MY FRANCHISES! MYSTERION, MISSING. THE URICH KID, EXPOSED AND IN THE WIND. BLUE STREAK, BUSTED.*
*SEE SUPERIOR SPIDER-MAN TEAM-UP #5, SUPERIOR SPIDER-MAN #16, AND MIGHTY AVENGERS #1! - SYNERGIZIN' STEVE.
AND NOW YOU THREE IDIOTS GAVE MY CUT OF YOUR PROFITS TO SOME RANDOM GUY?
HE LOOKED JUST LIKE YOU, BOSS. I MEAN, THE OUTFIT.
BLAZE IS RIGHT. WHO ELSE BUT YOU KNOWS I'M IN NEW YORK FOR A DELIVERY?
SHUT UP, DEVIL-SPIDER. I MADE YOU... AND IF I DON'T GET MY MONEY, I'LL SHUT YOU DOWN.
WHERE ARE WE SUPPOSED TO GET THAT KINDA SCRATCH?
THAT'S YOUR PROBLEM. FIGURE IT OUT...AND FAST.

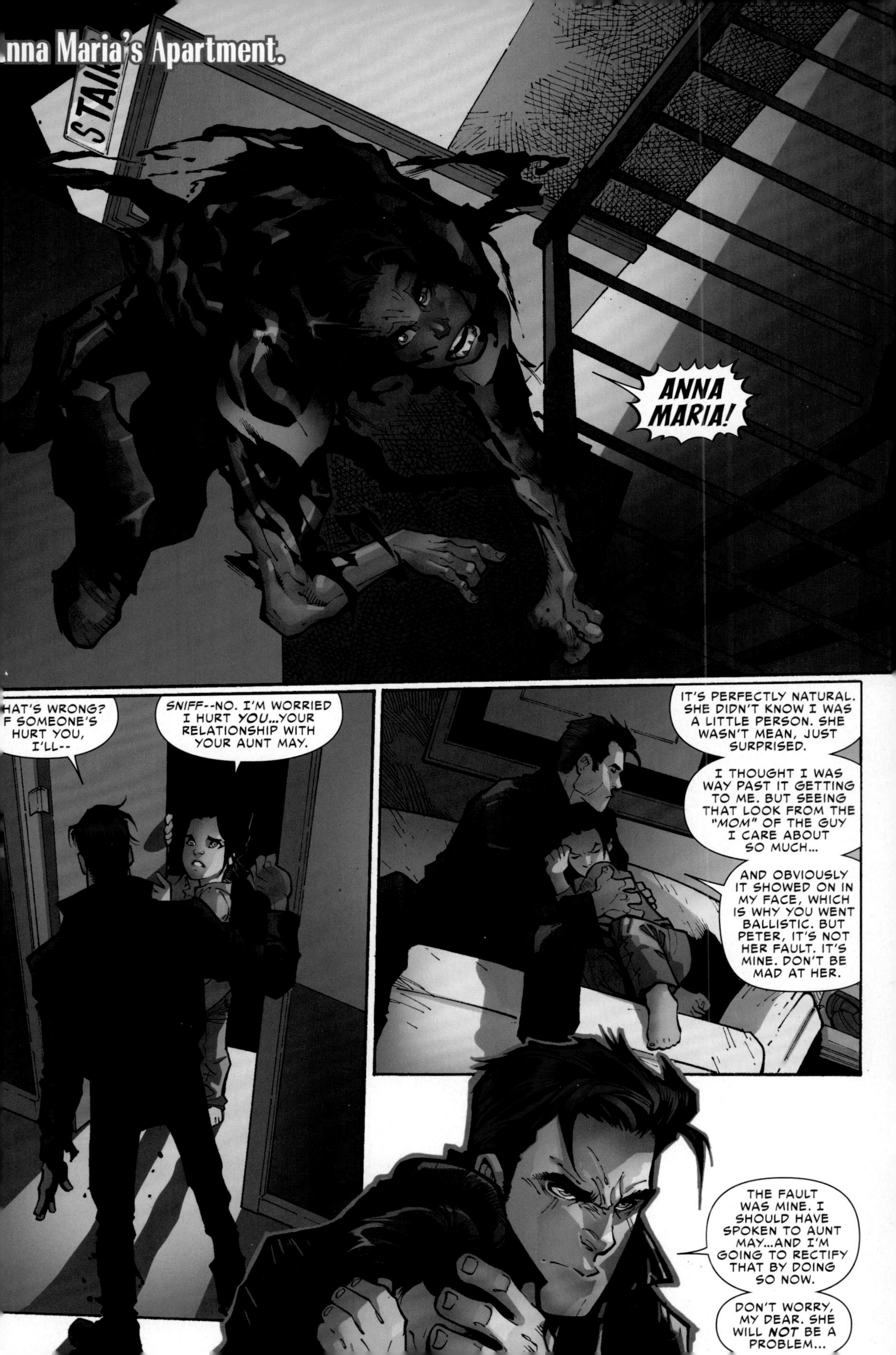
nna Maria's Apartment.
STAIR
ANNA MARIA!
HAT'S WRONG? F SOMEONE'S HURT YOU, I'LL--
SNIFF--NO. I'M WORRIED I HURT YOU...YOUR RELATIONSHIP WITH YOUR AUNT MAY.
IT'S PERFECTLY NATURAL. SHE DIDN'T KNOW I WAS A LITTLE PERSON. SHE WASN'T MEAN, JUST SURPRISED.
I THOUGHT I WAS WAY PAST IT GETTING TO ME. BUT SEEING THAT LOOK FROM THE "MOM" OF THE GUY I CARE ABOUT SO MUCH...
AND OBVIOUSLY IT SHOWED ON IN MY FACE, WHICH IS WHY YOU WENT BALLISTIC. BUT PETER, IT'S NOT HER FAULT. IT'S MINE. DON'T BE MAD AT HER.
THE FAULT WAS MINE. I SHOULD HAVE SPOKEN TO AUNT MAY...AND I'M GOING TO RECTIFY THAT BY DOING SO NOW.
DON'T WORRY, MY DEAR. SHE WILL NOT BE A PROBLEM...

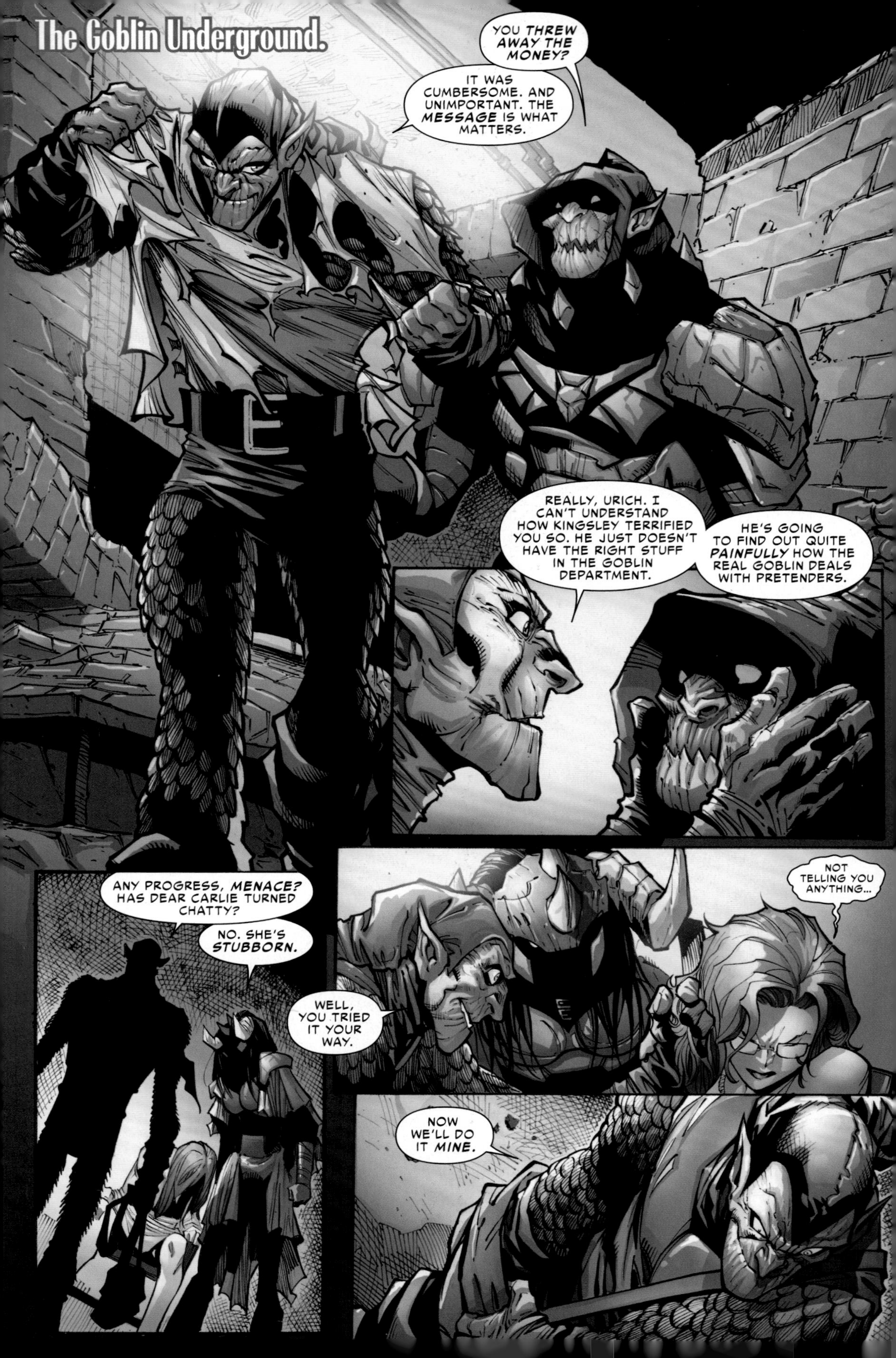
The Goblin Underground.
YOU THREW AWAY THE MONEY?
IT WAS CUMBERSOME. AND UNIMPORTANT. THE MESSAGE IS WHAT MATTERS.
REALLY, URICH. I CAN'T UNDERSTAND HOW KINGSLEY TERRIFIED YOU SO. HE JUST DOESN'T HAVE THE RIGHT STUFF IN THE GOBLIN DEPARTMENT.
HE'S GOING TO FIND OUT QUITE PAINFULLY HOW THE REAL GOBLIN DEALS WITH PRETENDERS.
ANY PROGRESS, MENACE? HAS DEAR CARLIE TURNED CHATTY?
NO. SHE'S STUBBORN.
NOT TELLING YOU ANYTHING...
WELL, YOU TRIED IT YOUR WAY.
NOW WE'LL DO IT MINE.

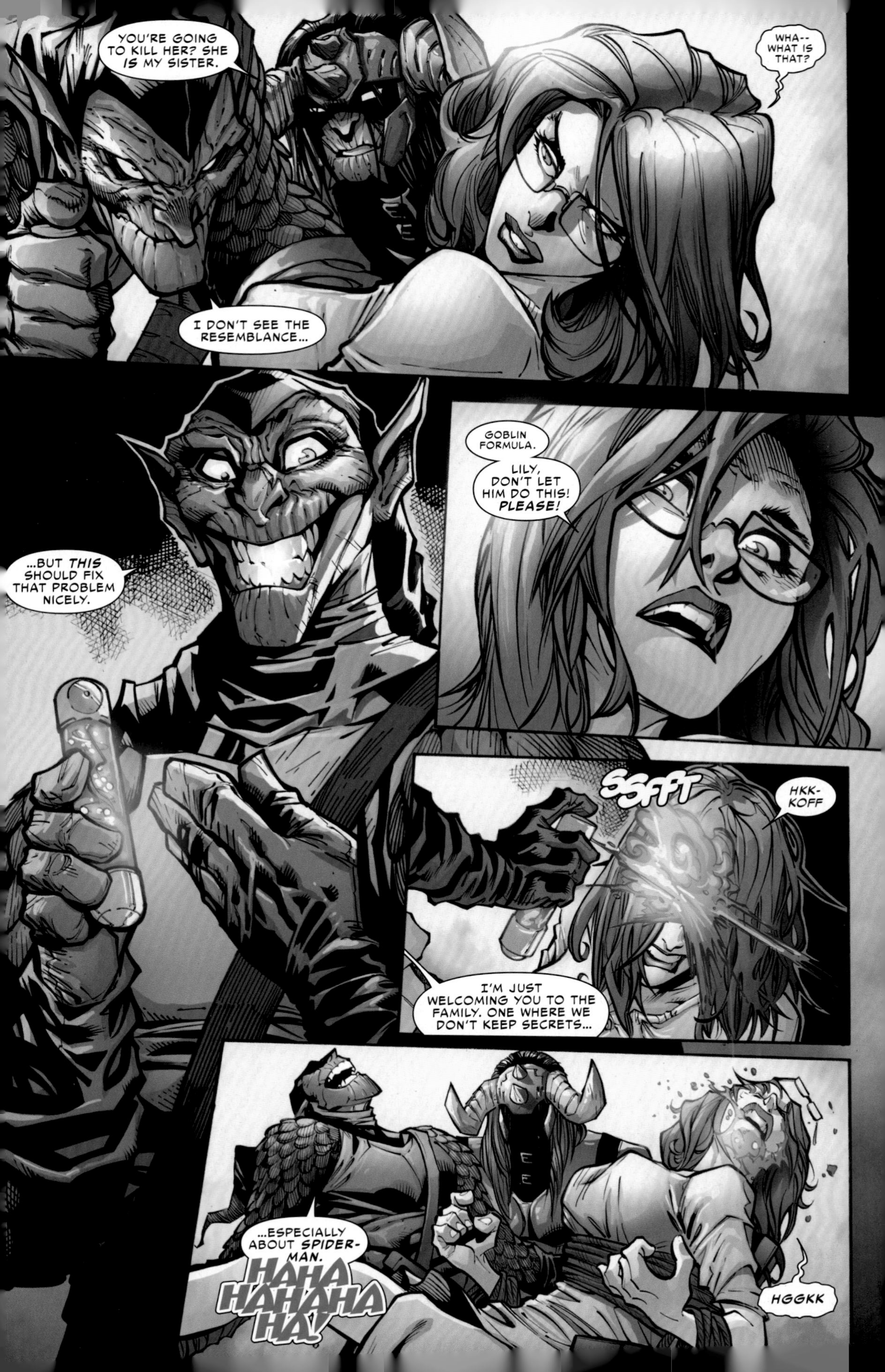
YOU'RE GOING TO KILL HER? SHE *IS* MY SISTER.
WHA-- WHAT IS THAT?
I DON'T SEE THE RESEMBLANCE...
...BUT *THIS* SHOULD FIX THAT PROBLEM NICELY.
GOBLIN FORMULA.
LILY, DON'T LET HIM DO THIS! *PLEASE!*
SSFFT
HKK-KOFF
I'M JUST WELCOMING YOU TO THE FAMILY. ONE WHERE WE DON'T KEEP SECRETS...
...ESPECIALLY ABOUT *SPIDER-MAN.*
HAHA HAHAHA HA!
HGGKK

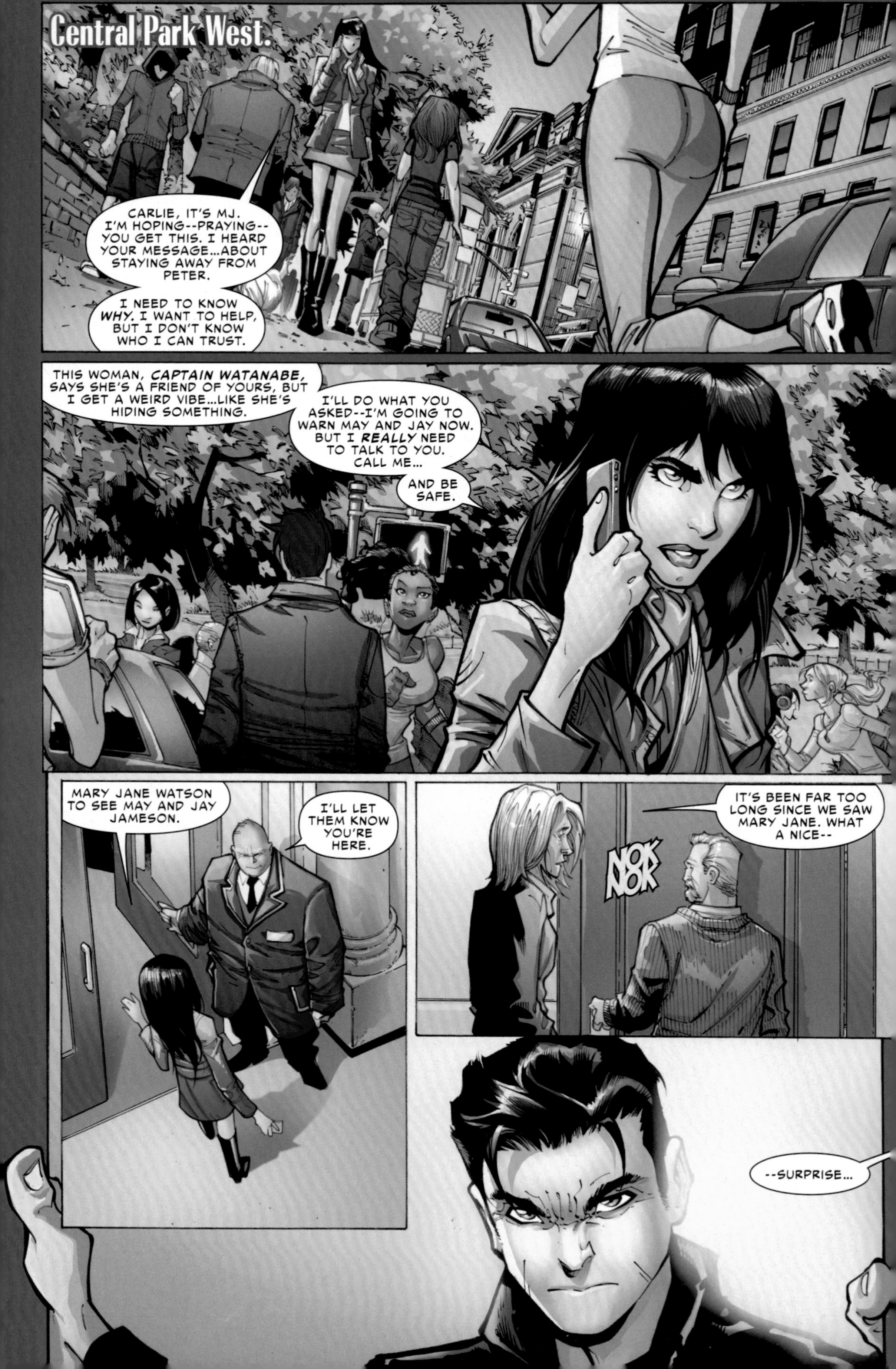
Central Park West.
CARLIE, IT'S MJ. I'M HOPING--PRAYING--YOU GET THIS. I HEARD YOUR MESSAGE...ABOUT STAYING AWAY FROM PETER.
I NEED TO KNOW WHY. I WANT TO HELP, BUT I DON'T KNOW WHO I CAN TRUST.
THIS WOMAN, CAPTAIN WATANABE, SAYS SHE'S A FRIEND OF YOURS, BUT I GET A WEIRD VIBE...LIKE SHE'S HIDING SOMETHING.
I'LL DO WHAT YOU ASKED--I'M GOING TO WARN MAY AND JAY NOW. BUT I REALLY NEED TO TALK TO YOU. CALL ME...
AND BE SAFE.
MARY JANE WATSON TO SEE MAY AND JAY JAMESON.
I'LL LET THEM KNOW YOU'RE HERE.
IT'S BEEN FAR TOO LONG SINCE WE SAW MARY JANE. WHAT A NICE--
NOK NOK
--SURPRISE...

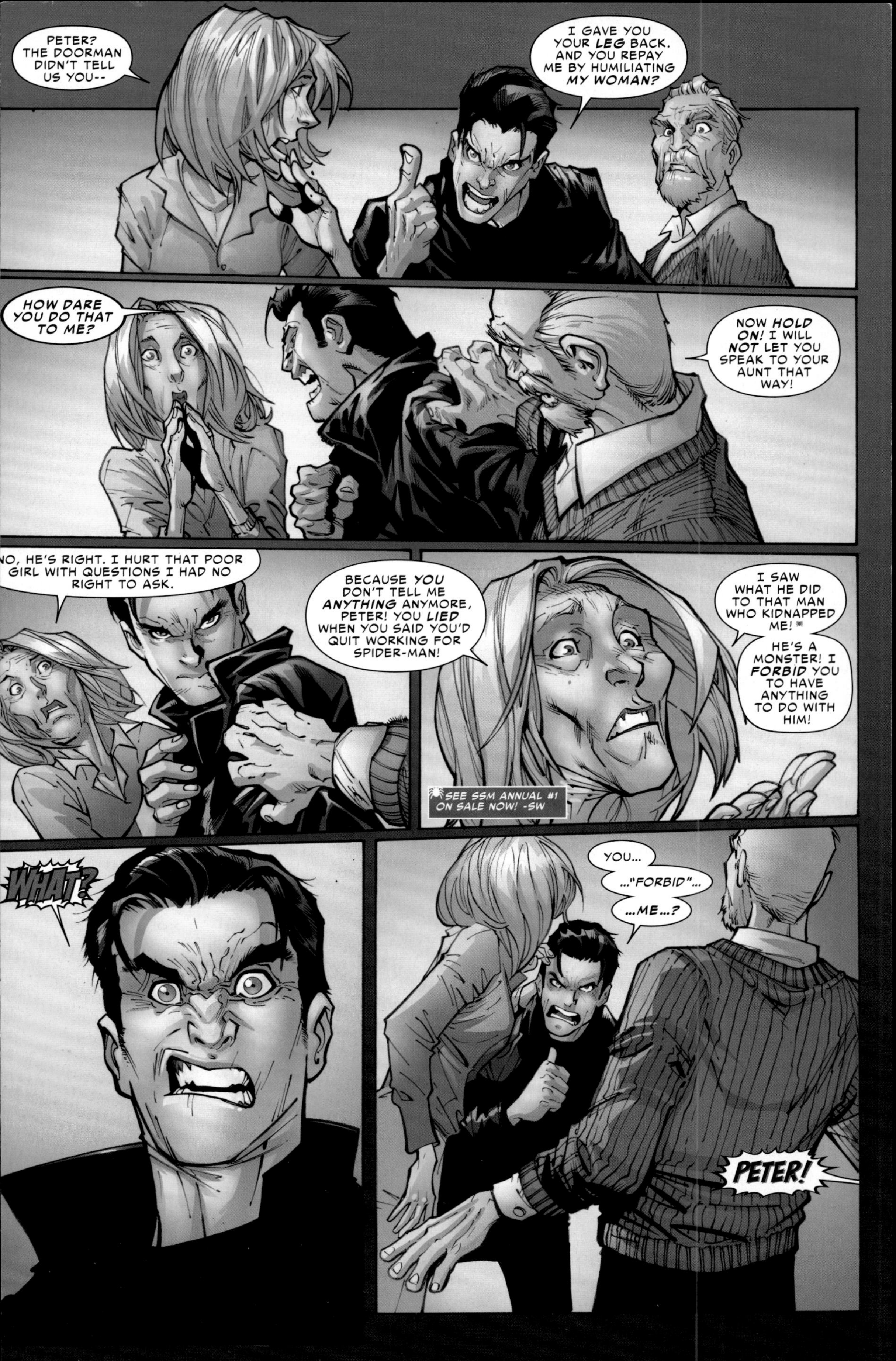
PETER? THE DOORMAN DIDN'T TELL US YOU--
I GAVE YOU YOUR LEG BACK. AND YOU REPAY ME BY HUMILIATING MY WOMAN?
HOW DARE YOU DO THAT TO ME?
NOW HOLD ON! I WILL NOT LET YOU SPEAK TO YOUR AUNT THAT WAY!
NO, HE'S RIGHT. I HURT THAT POOR GIRL WITH QUESTIONS I HAD NO RIGHT TO ASK.
BECAUSE YOU DON'T TELL ME ANYTHING ANYMORE, PETER! YOU LIED WHEN YOU SAID YOU'D QUIT WORKING FOR SPIDER-MAN!
I SAW WHAT HE DID TO THAT MAN WHO KIDNAPPED ME!
HE'S A MONSTER! I FORBID YOU TO HAVE ANYTHING TO DO WITH HIM!
SEE SSM ANNUAL #1 ON SALE NOW! -SW
WHAT?
YOU...
..."FORBID"...
...ME...?
PETER!

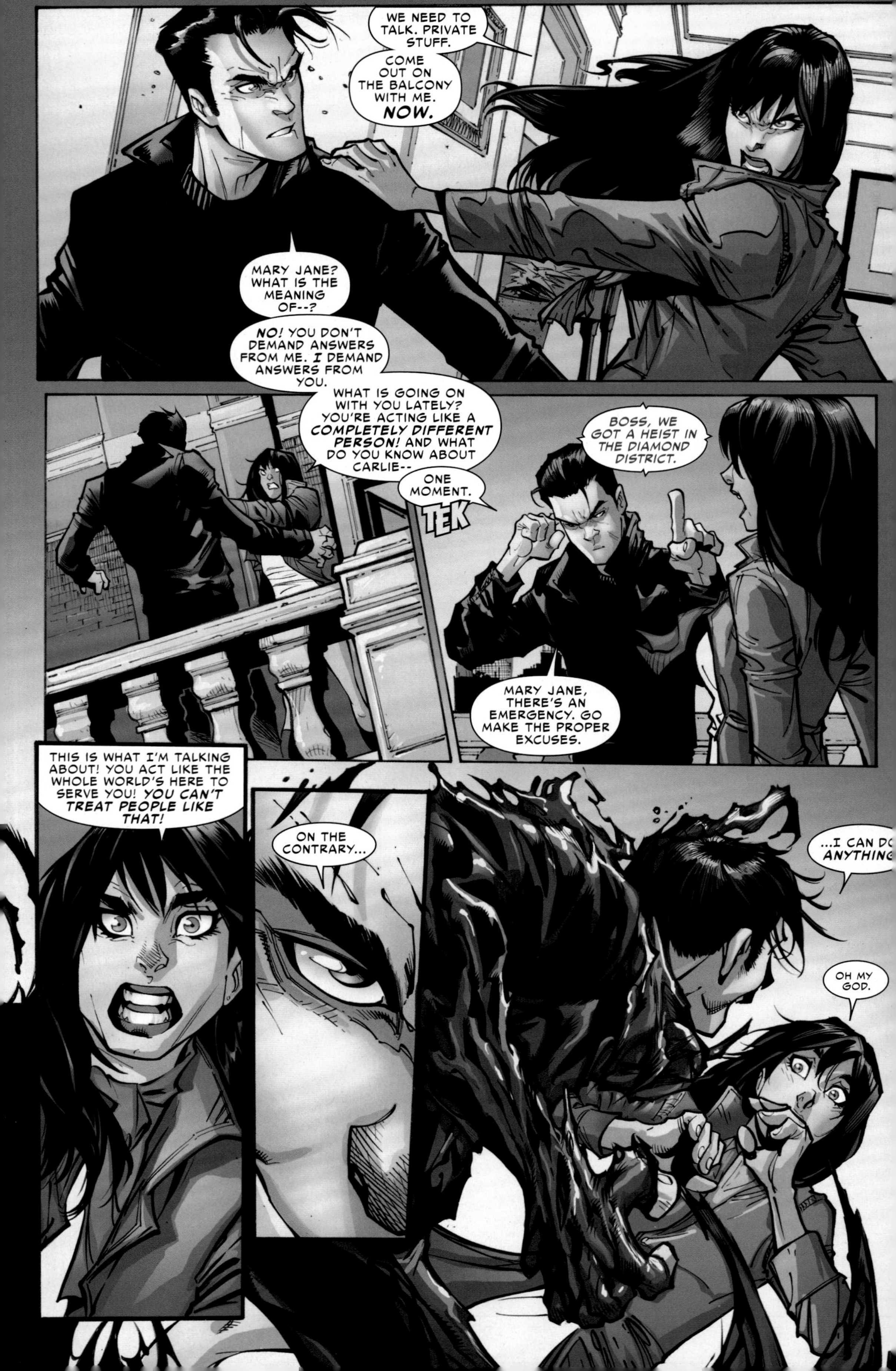
WE NEED TO TALK. PRIVATE STUFF.
COME OUT ON THE BALCONY WITH ME. NOW.
MARY JANE? WHAT IS THE MEANING OF--?
NO! YOU DON'T DEMAND ANSWERS FROM ME. I DEMAND ANSWERS FROM YOU.
WHAT IS GOING ON WITH YOU LATELY? YOU'RE ACTING LIKE A COMPLETELY DIFFERENT PERSON! AND WHAT DO YOU KNOW ABOUT CARLIE--
ONE MOMENT.
TEK
BOSS, WE GOT A HEIST IN THE DIAMOND DISTRICT.
MARY JANE, THERE'S AN EMERGENCY. GO MAKE THE PROPER EXCUSES.
THIS IS WHAT I'M TALKING ABOUT! YOU ACT LIKE THE WHOLE WORLD'S HERE TO SERVE YOU! YOU CAN'T TREAT PEOPLE LIKE THAT!
ON THE CONTRARY...
...I CAN DO ANYTHING
OH MY GOD.

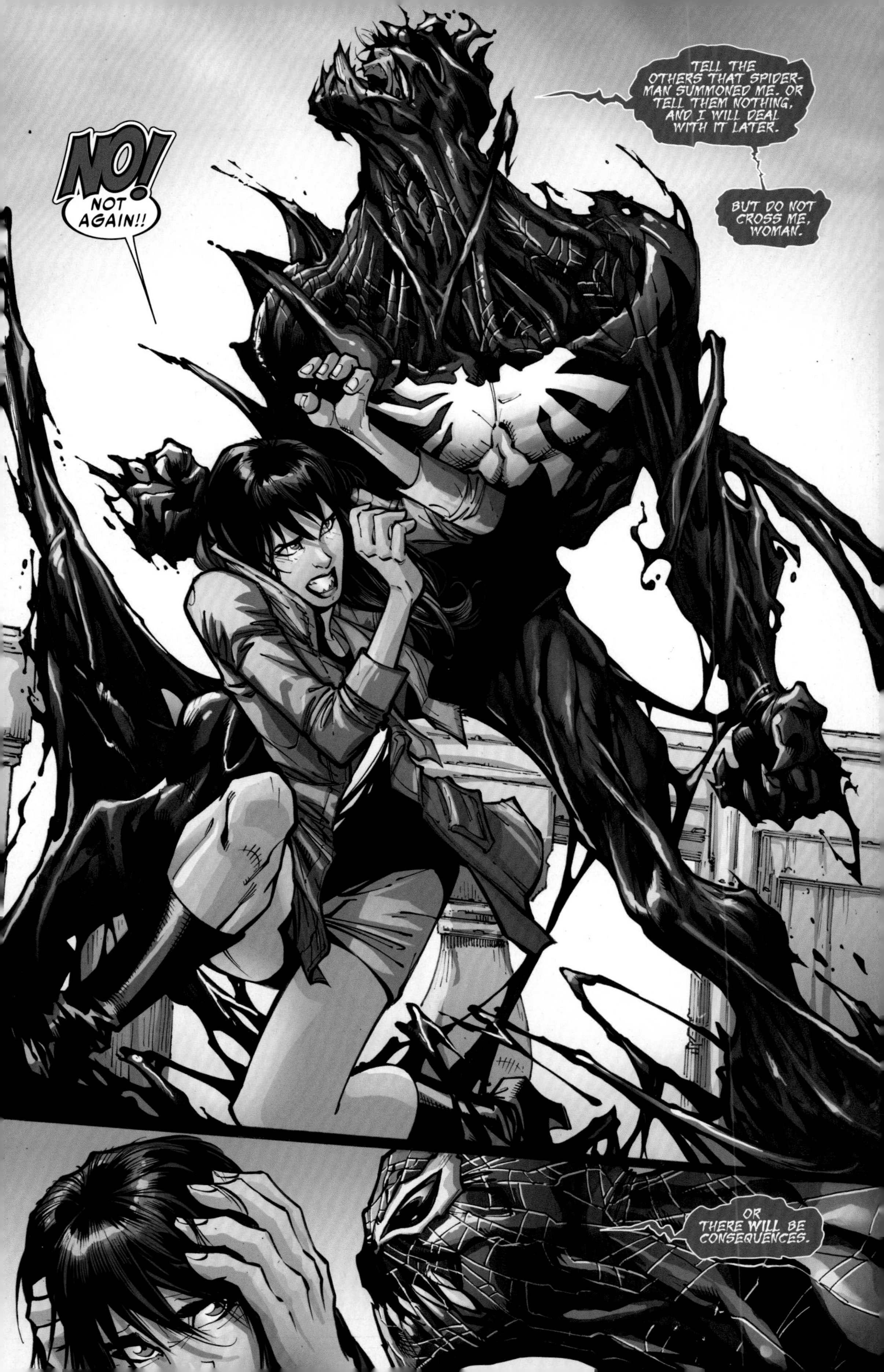
NO!
NOT AGAIN!!
TELL THE OTHERS THAT SPIDER-MAN SUMMONED ME. OR TELL THEM NOTHING, AND I WILL DEAL WITH IT LATER.
BUT DO NOT CROSS ME, WOMAN.
OR THERE WILL BE CONSEQUENCES.

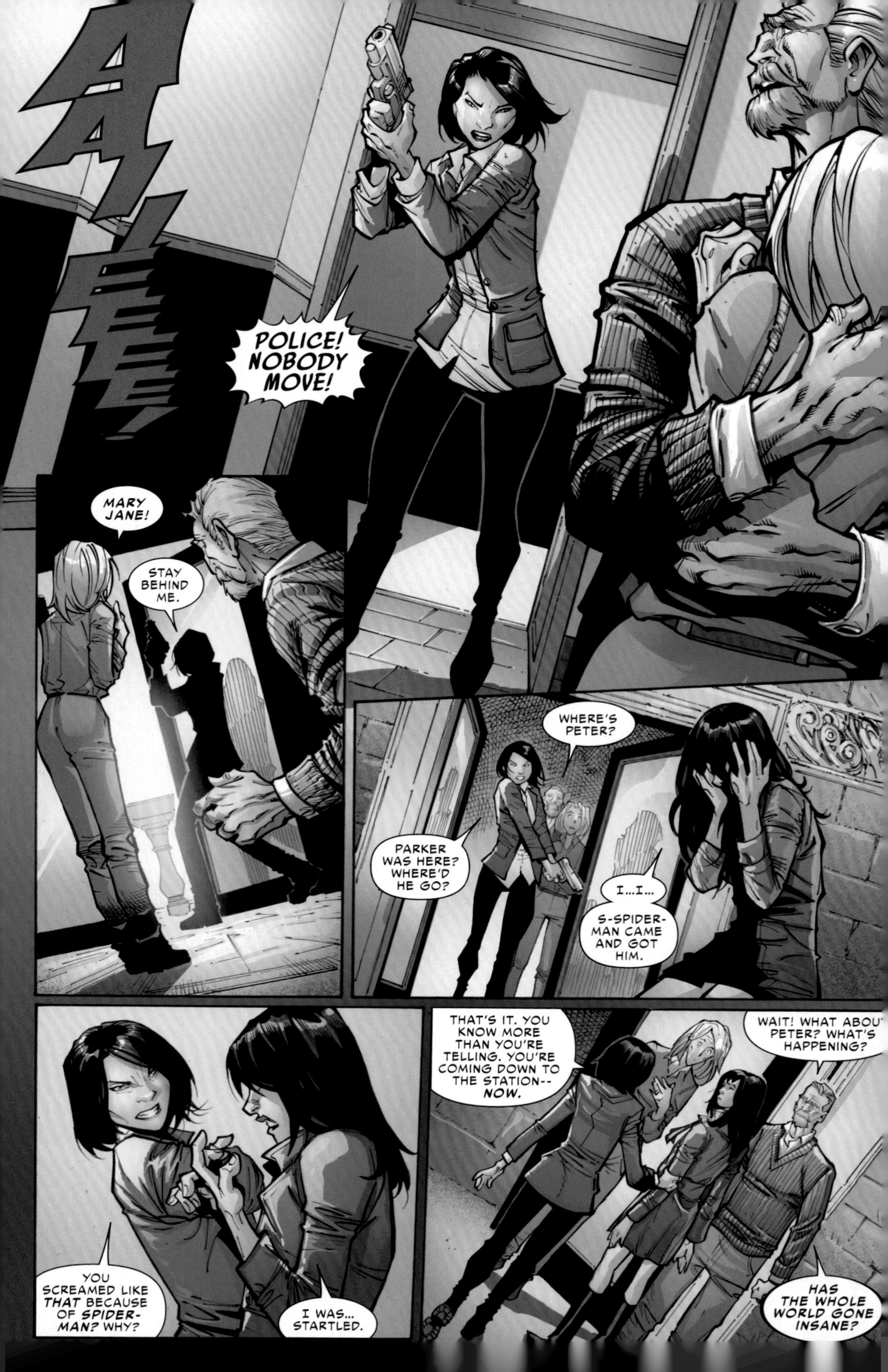
AAIEEEE!
POLICE! NOBODY MOVE!
MARY JANE!
STAY BEHIND ME.
WHERE'S PETER?
PARKER WAS HERE? WHERE'D HE GO?
I...I...
S-SPIDER-MAN CAME AND GOT HIM.
YOU SCREAMED LIKE THAT BECAUSE OF SPIDER-MAN? WHY?
I WAS... STARTLED.
THAT'S IT. YOU KNOW MORE THAN YOU'RE TELLING. YOU'RE COMING DOWN TO THE STATION-- NOW.
WAIT! WHAT ABOU PETER? WHAT'S HAPPENING?
HAS THE WHOLE WORLD GONE INSANE?

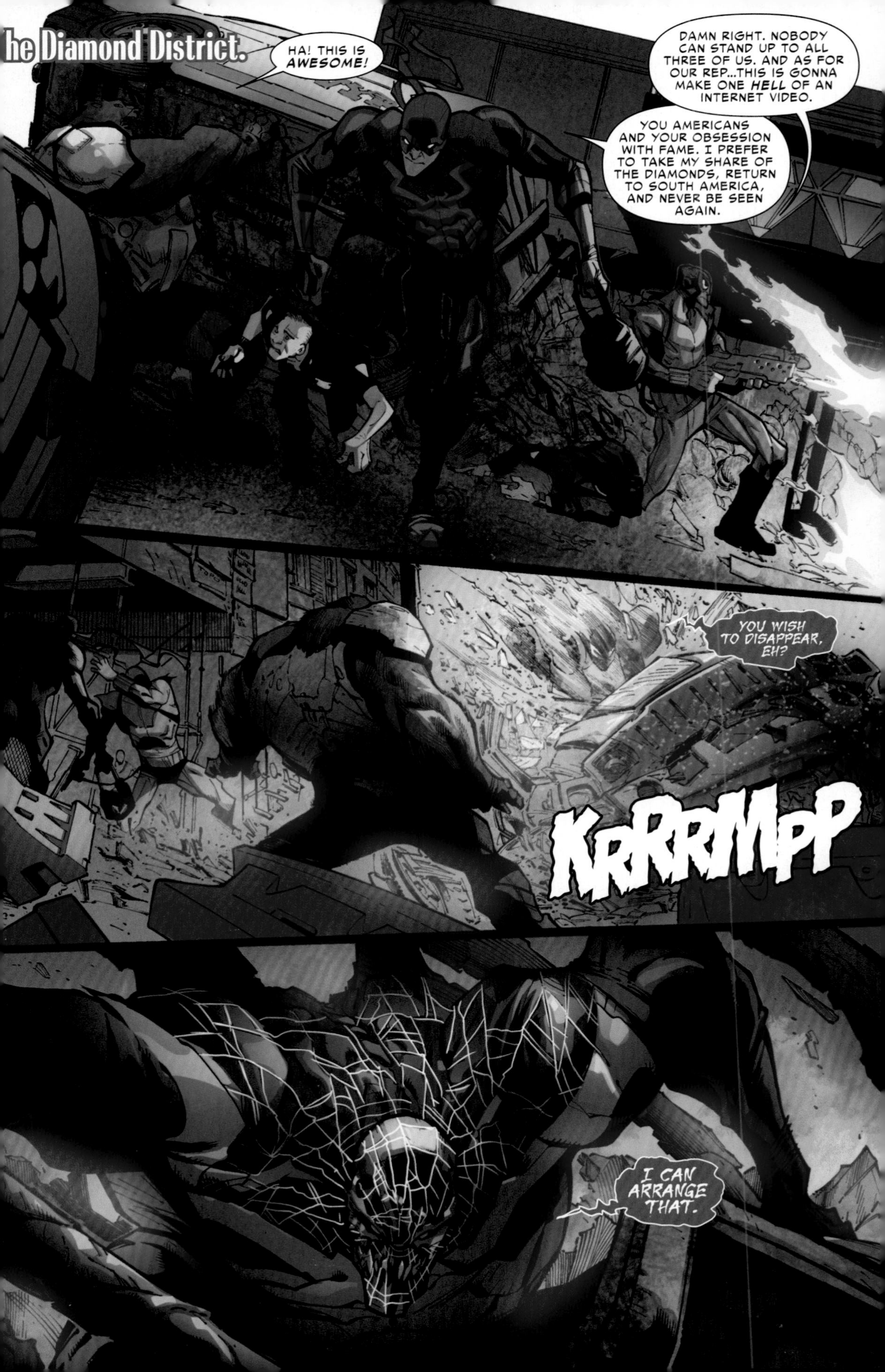
he Diamond District.
HA! THIS IS AWESOME!
DAMN RIGHT. NOBODY CAN STAND UP TO ALL THREE OF US. AND AS FOR OUR REP...THIS IS GONNA MAKE ONE HELL OF AN INTERNET VIDEO.
YOU AMERICANS AND YOUR OBSESSION WITH FAME. I PREFER TO TAKE MY SHARE OF THE DIAMONDS, RETURN TO SOUTH AMERICA, AND NEVER BE SEEN AGAIN.
YOU WISH TO DISAPPEAR, EH?
KRRRMPP
I CAN ARRANGE THAT.

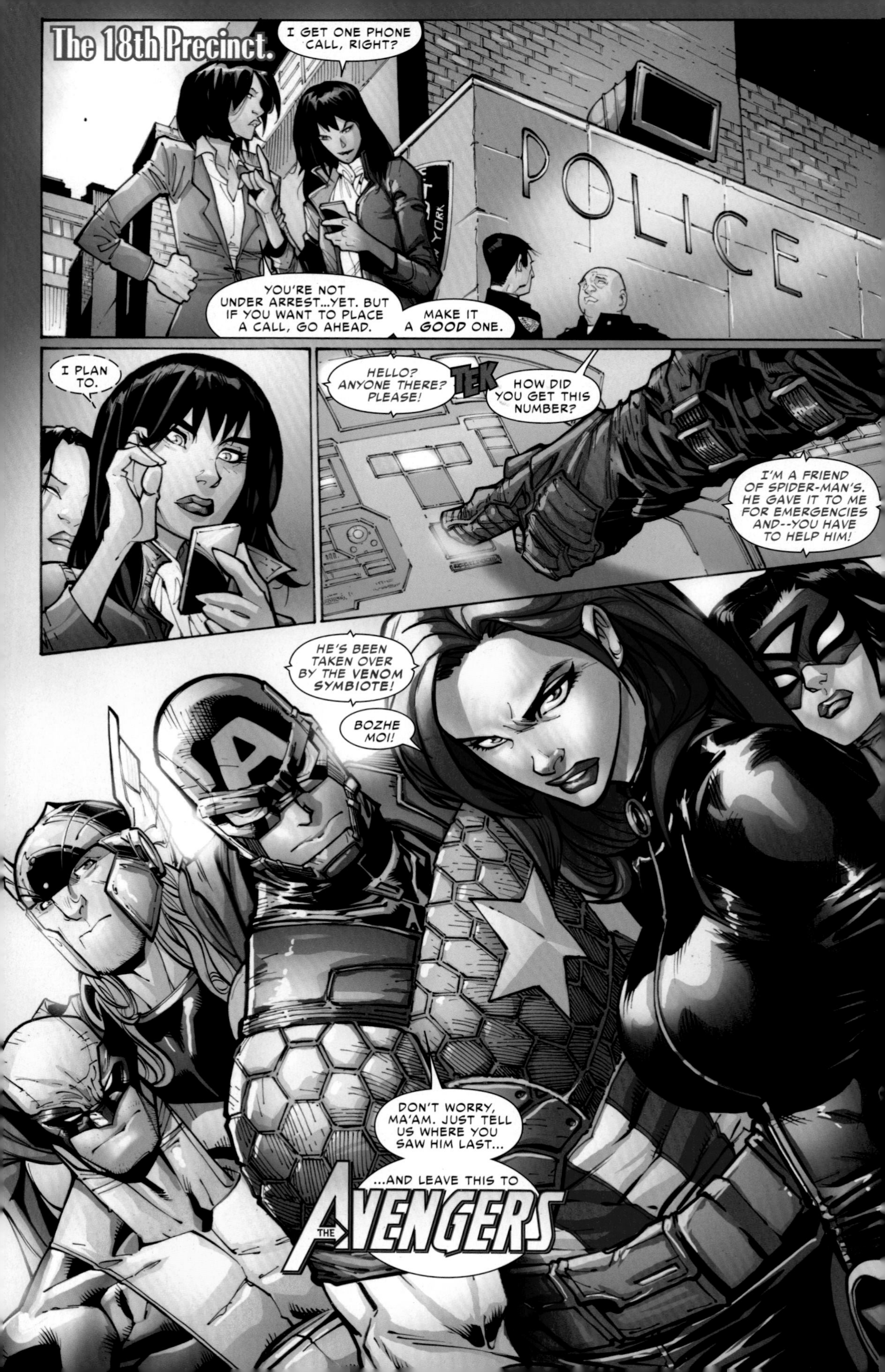
The 18th Precinct.
I GET ONE PHONE CALL, RIGHT?
POLICE
YOU'RE NOT UNDER ARREST...YET. BUT IF YOU WANT TO PLACE A CALL, GO AHEAD.
MAKE IT A GOOD ONE.
I PLAN TO.
HELLO? ANYONE THERE? PLEASE!
TEK
HOW DID YOU GET THIS NUMBER?
I'M A FRIEND OF SPIDER-MAN'S. HE GAVE IT TO ME FOR EMERGENCIES AND--YOU HAVE TO HELP HIM!
HE'S BEEN TAKEN OVER BY THE VENOM SYMBIOTE!
BOZHE MOI!
DON'T WORRY, MA'AM. JUST TELL US WHERE YOU SAW HIM LAST...
...AND LEAVE THIS TO
THE AVENGERS

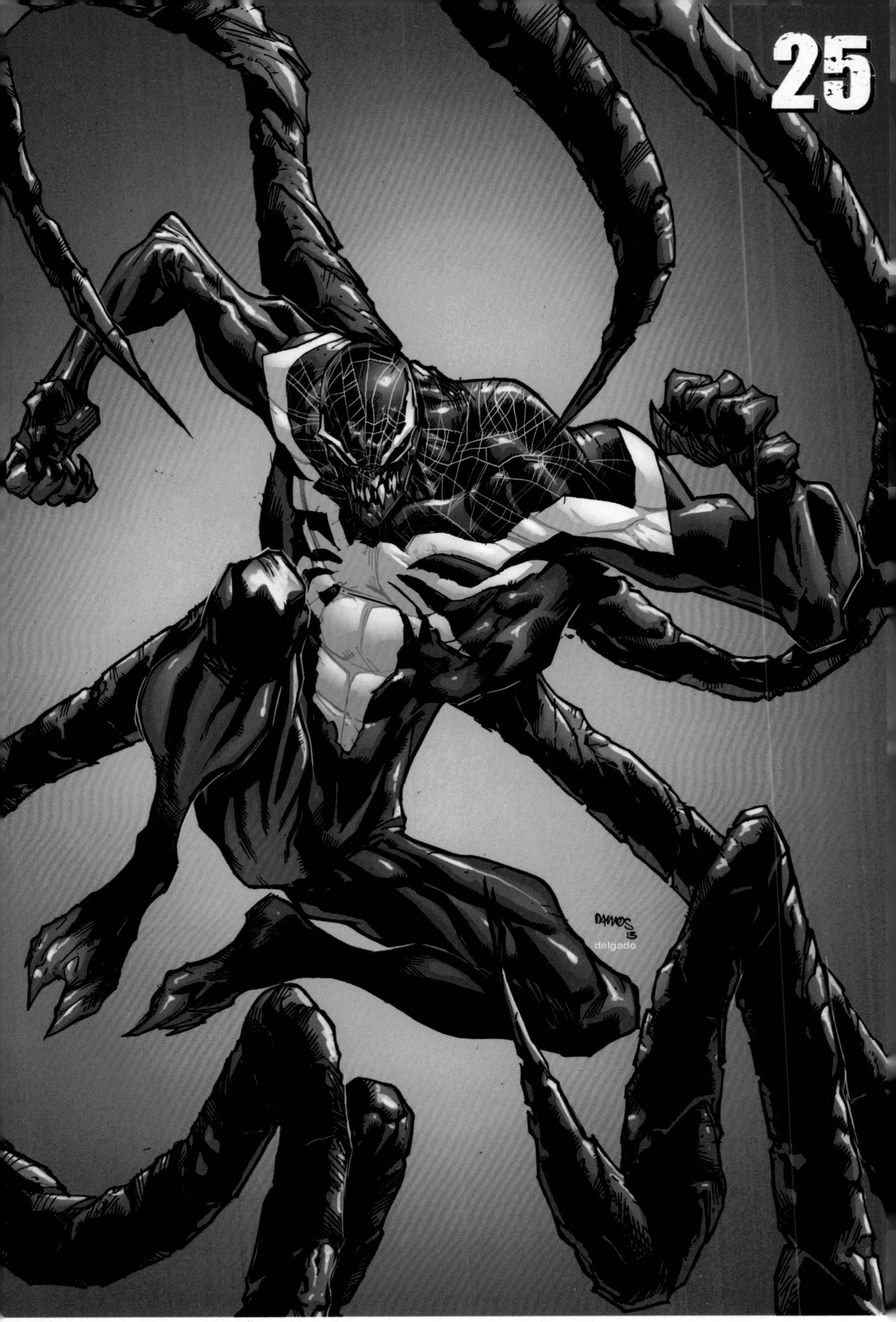
25
RAMOS 13
delgado

DARKEST HOURS PART 5: BEFORE THE DAWN

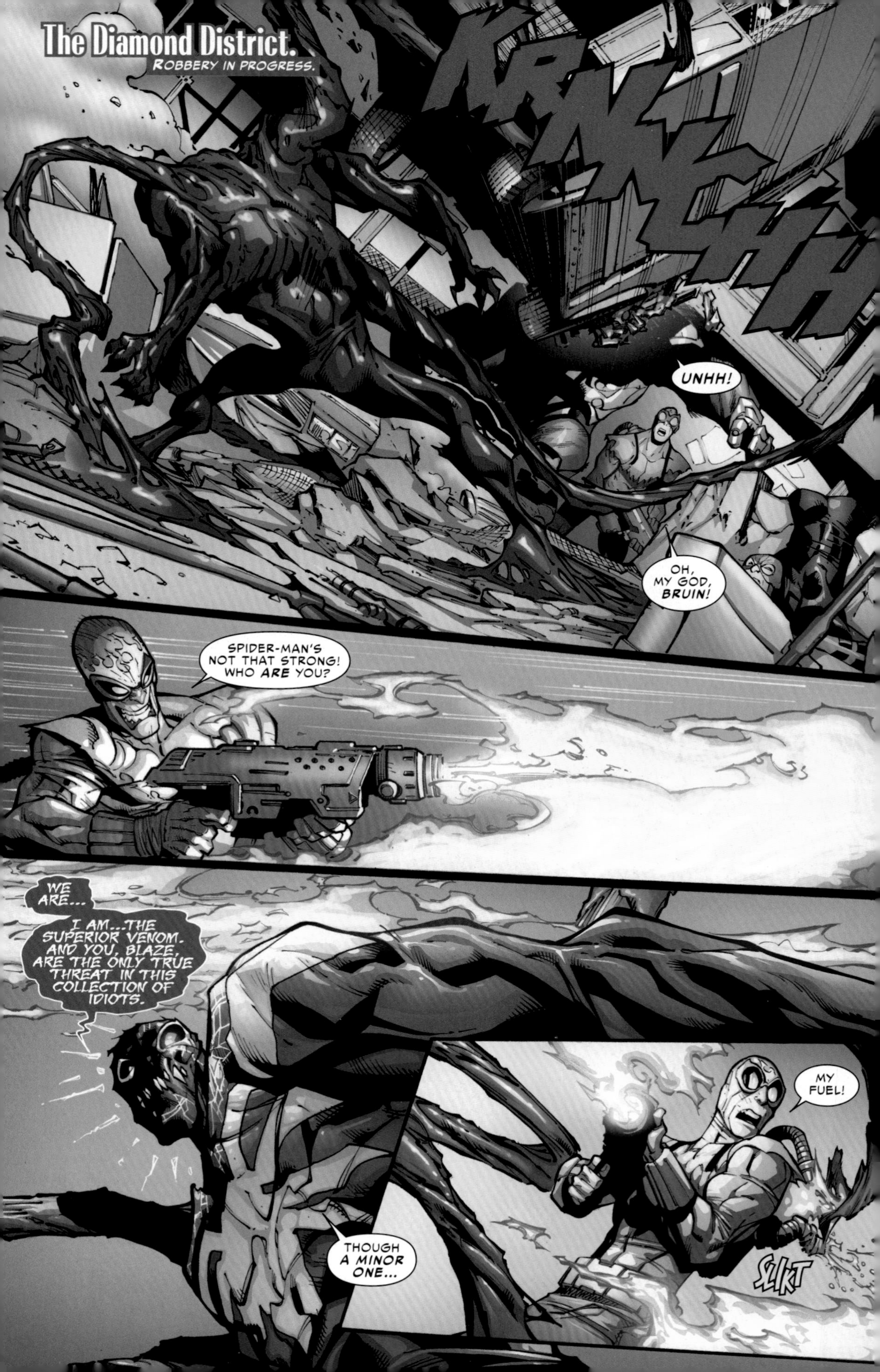
The Diamond District.
ROBBERY IN PROGRESS.
KRAKASHH
UNHH!
OH, MY GOD, BRUIN!
SPIDER-MAN'S NOT THAT STRONG! WHO ARE YOU?
WE ARE...
I AM...THE SUPERIOR VENOM. AND YOU, BLAZE, ARE THE ONLY TRUE THREAT IN THIS COLLECTION OF IDIOTS.
THOUGH A MINOR ONE...
MY FUEL!
SLIKT

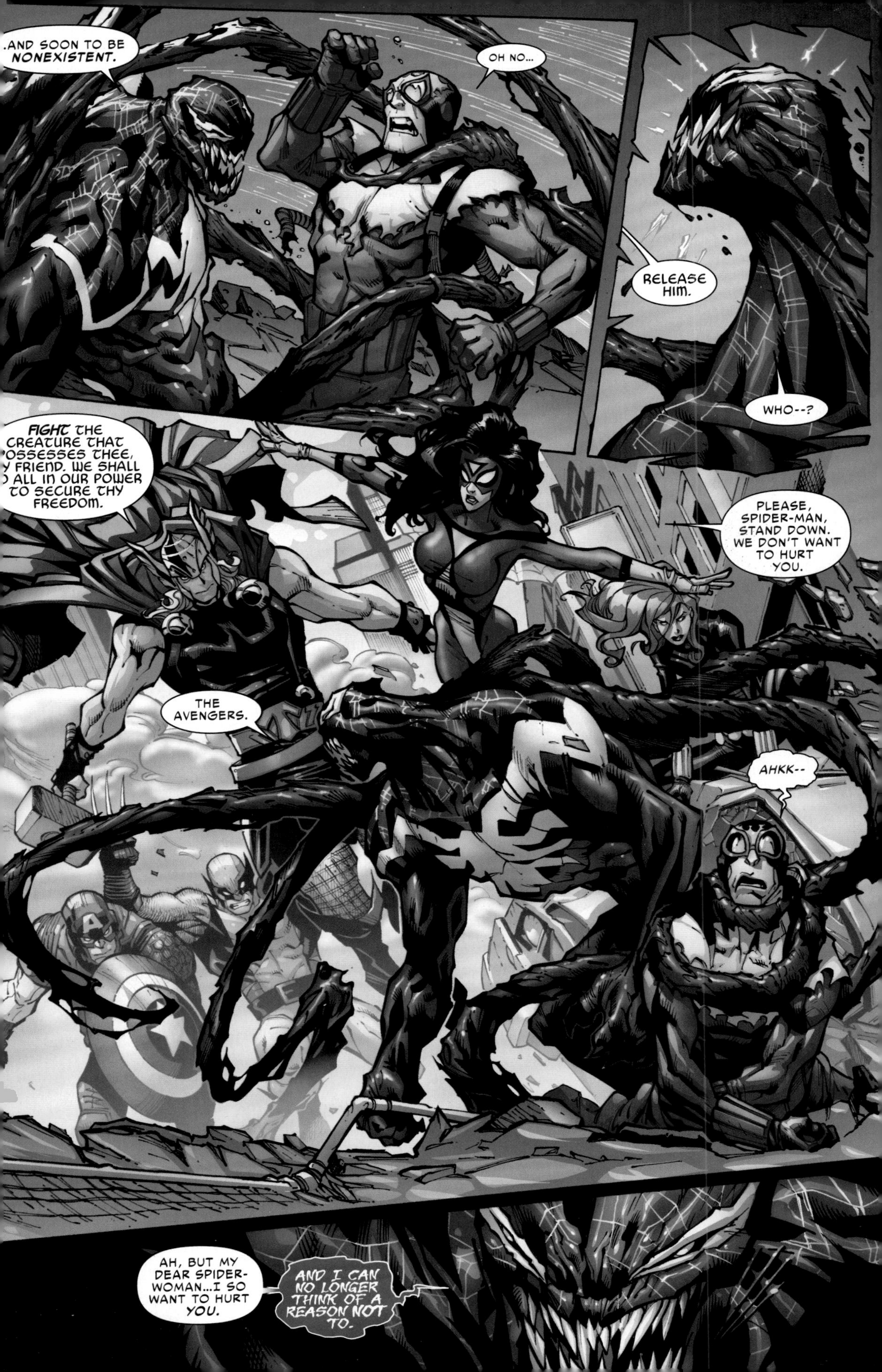
..AND SOON TO BE NONEXISTENT.
OH NO...
RELEASE HIM.
WHO--?
FIGHT THE CREATURE THAT POSSESSES THEE, MY FRIEND. WE SHALL DO ALL IN OUR POWER TO SECURE THY FREEDOM.
PLEASE, SPIDER-MAN, STAND DOWN. WE DON'T WANT TO HURT YOU.
THE AVENGERS.
AHKK--
AH, BUT MY DEAR SPIDER-WOMAN...I SO WANT TO HURT YOU.
AND I CAN NO LONGER THINK OF A REASON NOT TO.

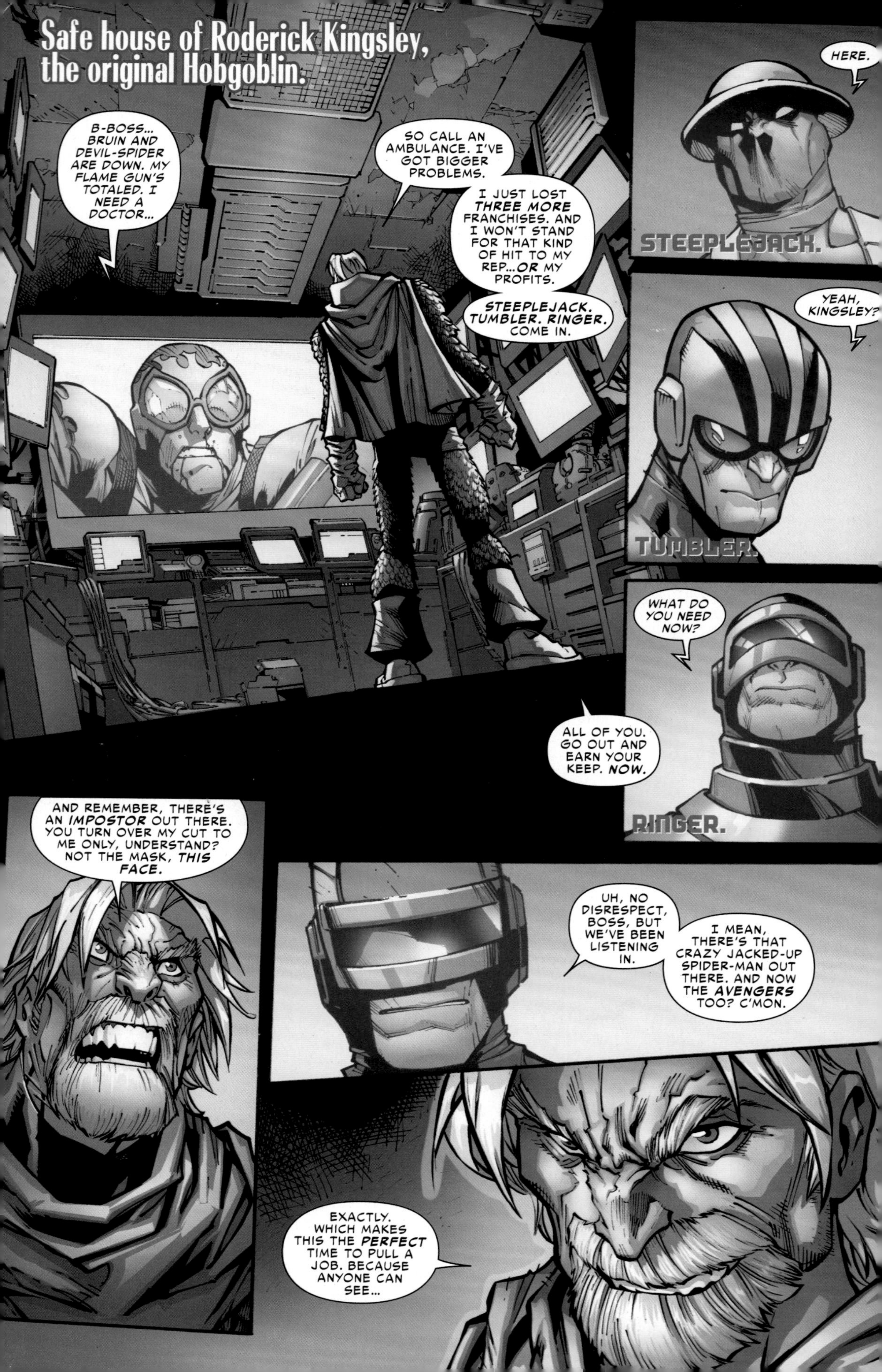

Safe house of Roderick Kingsley, the original Hobgoblin.
B-BOSS... BRUIN AND DEVIL-SPIDER ARE DOWN. MY FLAME GUN'S TOTALED. I NEED A DOCTOR...
SO CALL AN AMBULANCE. I'VE GOT BIGGER PROBLEMS.
I JUST LOST THREE MORE FRANCHISES. AND I WON'T STAND FOR THAT KIND OF HIT TO MY REP...OR MY PROFITS.
STEEPLEJACK. TUMBLER. RINGER. COME IN.
HERE.
STEEPLEJACK.
YEAH, KINGSLEY?
TUMBLER.
WHAT DO YOU NEED NOW?
ALL OF YOU. GO OUT AND EARN YOUR KEEP. NOW.
RINGER.
AND REMEMBER, THERE'S AN IMPOSTOR OUT THERE. YOU TURN OVER MY CUT TO ME ONLY, UNDERSTAND? NOT THE MASK, THIS FACE.
UH, NO DISRESPECT, BOSS, BUT WE'VE BEEN LISTENING IN.
I MEAN, THERE'S THAT CRAZY JACKED-UP SPIDER-MAN OUT THERE. AND NOW THE AVENGERS TOO? C'MON.
EXACTLY. WHICH MAKES THIS THE PERFECT TIME TO PULL A JOB. BECAUSE ANYONE CAN SEE...

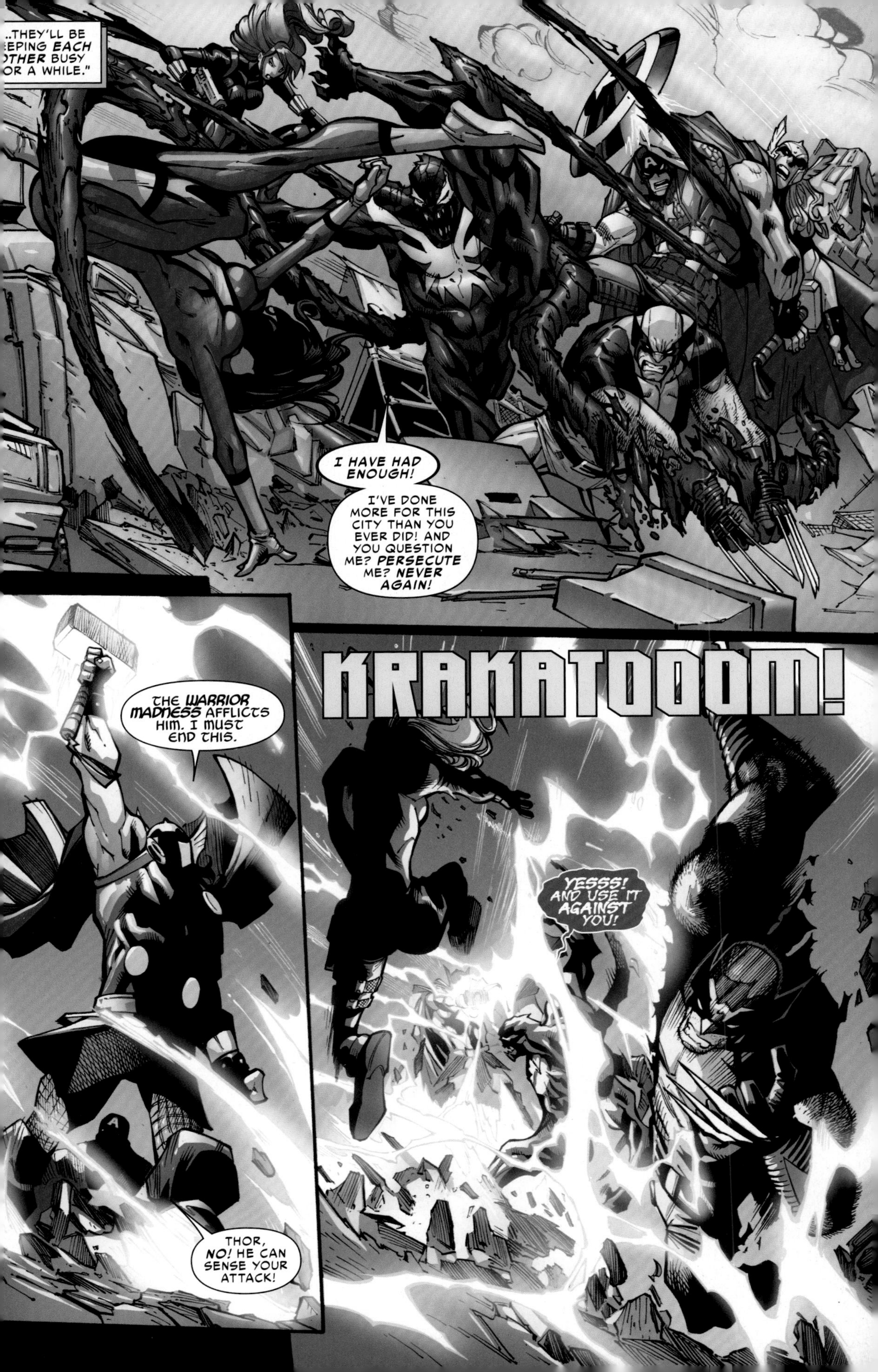

...THEY'LL BE KEEPING EACH OTHER BUSY FOR A WHILE."
I HAVE HAD ENOUGH!
I'VE DONE MORE FOR THIS CITY THAN YOU EVER DID! AND YOU QUESTION ME? PERSECUTE ME? NEVER AGAIN!
THE WARRIOR MADNESS AFFLICTS HIM. I MUST END THIS.
THOR, NO! HE CAN SENSE YOUR ATTACK!
KRAKATOOOM!
YESSS! AND USE IT AGAINST YOU!

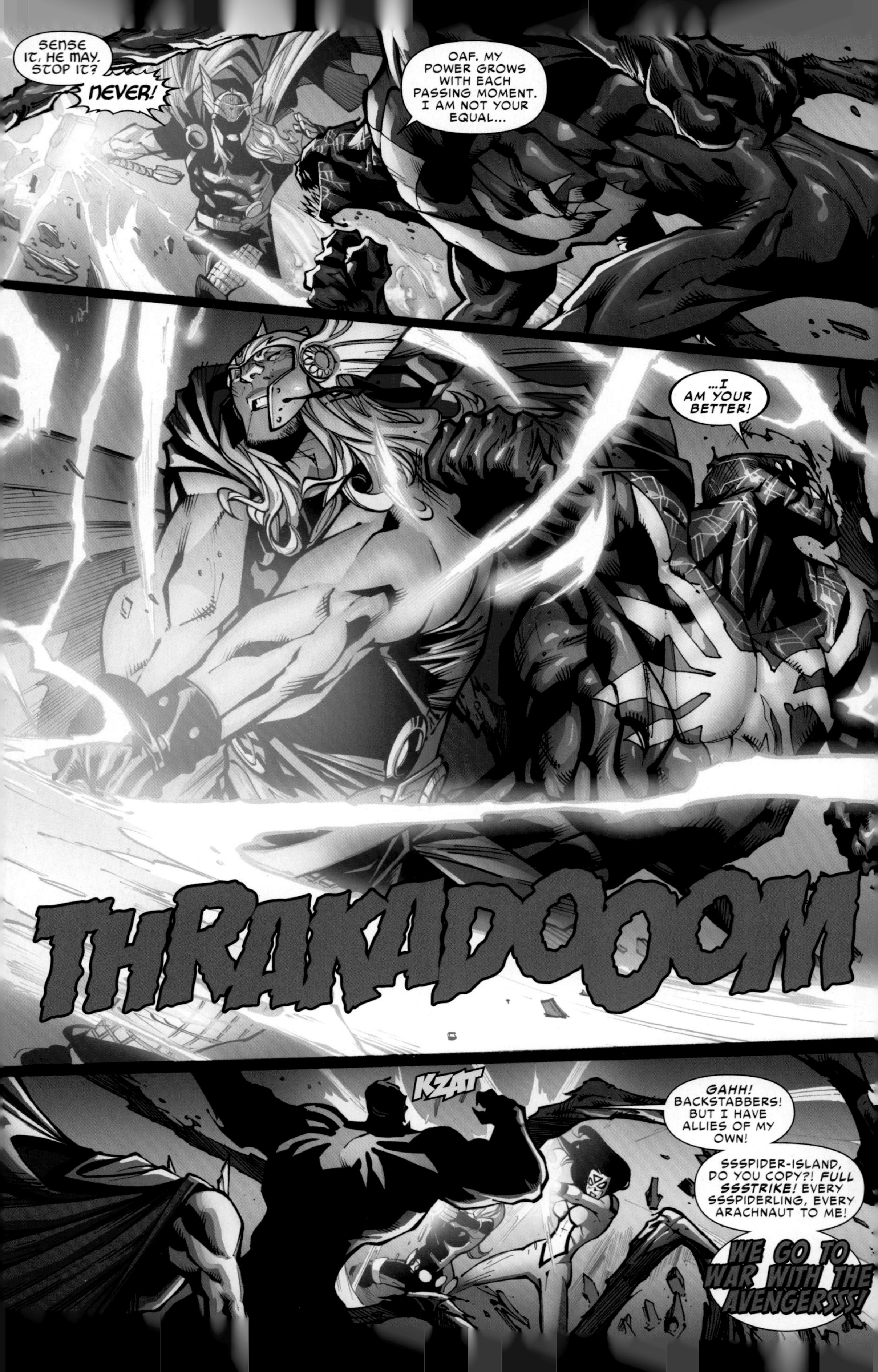
SENSE IT, HE MAY. STOP IT? NEVER!
OAF. MY POWER GROWS WITH EACH PASSING MOMENT. I AM NOT YOUR EQUAL...
...I AM YOUR BETTER!
THRAKADOOOM
KZAT
GAHH! BACKSTABBERS! BUT I HAVE ALLIES OF MY OWN!
SSSPIDER-ISLAND, DO YOU COPY?! FULL SSSTRIKE! EVERY SSSPIDERLING, EVERY ARACHNAUT TO ME!
WE GO TO WAR WITH THE AVENGERSSS!

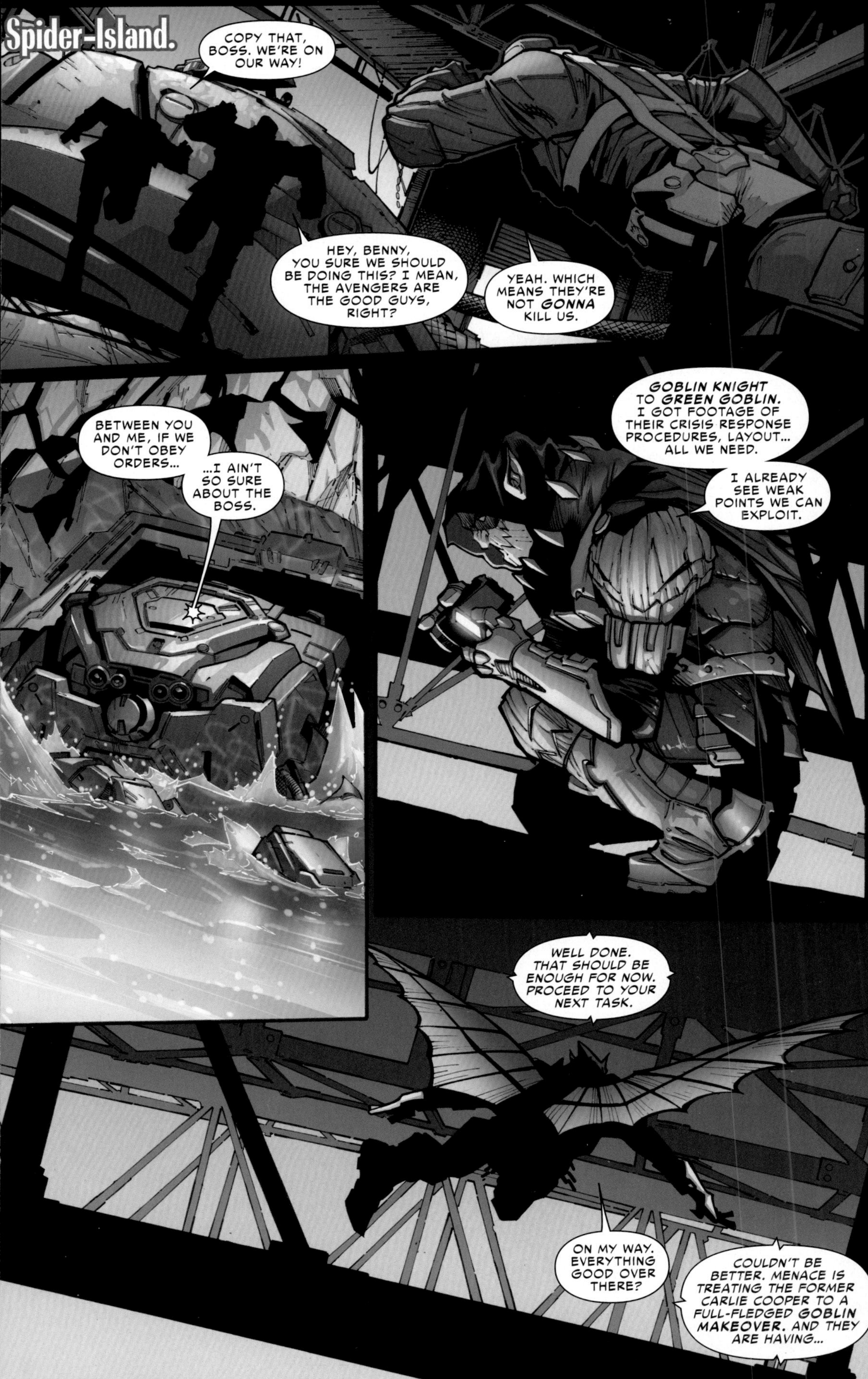
Spider-Island.
COPY THAT, BOSS. WE'RE ON OUR WAY!
HEY, BENNY, YOU SURE WE SHOULD BE DOING THIS? I MEAN, THE AVENGERS ARE THE GOOD GUYS, RIGHT?
YEAH. WHICH MEANS THEY'RE NOT GONNA KILL US.
BETWEEN YOU AND ME, IF WE DON'T OBEY ORDERS...
...I AIN'T SO SURE ABOUT THE BOSS.
GOBLIN KNIGHT TO GREEN GOBLIN. I GOT FOOTAGE OF THEIR CRISIS RESPONSE PROCEDURES, LAYOUT... ALL WE NEED.
I ALREADY SEE WEAK POINTS WE CAN EXPLOIT.
WELL DONE. THAT SHOULD BE ENOUGH FOR NOW. PROCEED TO YOUR NEXT TASK.
ON MY WAY. EVERYTHING GOOD OVER THERE?
COULDN'T BE BETTER. MENACE IS TREATING THE FORMER CARLIE COOPER TO A FULL-FLEDGED GOBLIN MAKEOVER. AND THEY ARE HAVING...

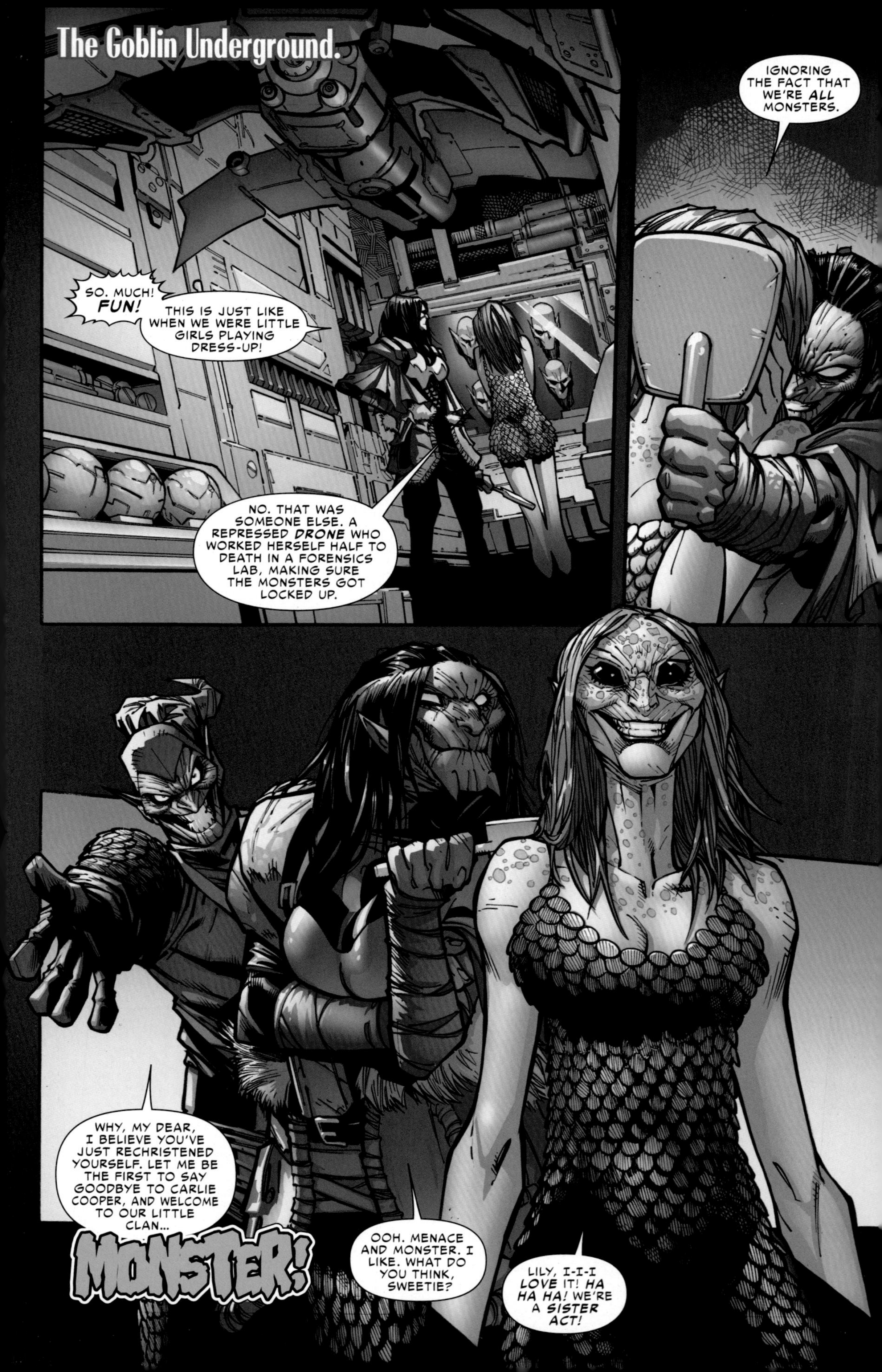
The Goblin Underground.
SO. MUCH! FUN!
THIS IS JUST LIKE WHEN WE WERE LITTLE GIRLS PLAYING DRESS-UP!
NO. THAT WAS SOMEONE ELSE. A REPRESSED DRONE WHO WORKED HERSELF HALF TO DEATH IN A FORENSICS LAB, MAKING SURE THE MONSTERS GOT LOCKED UP.
IGNORING THE FACT THAT WE'RE ALL MONSTERS.
WHY, MY DEAR, I BELIEVE YOU'VE JUST RECHRISTENED YOURSELF. LET ME BE THE FIRST TO SAY GOODBYE TO CARLIE COOPER, AND WELCOME TO OUR LITTLE CLAN...
MONSTER!
OOH. MENACE AND MONSTER. I LIKE. WHAT DO YOU THINK, SWEETIE?
LILY, I-I-I LOVE IT! HA HA HA! WE'RE A SISTER ACT!

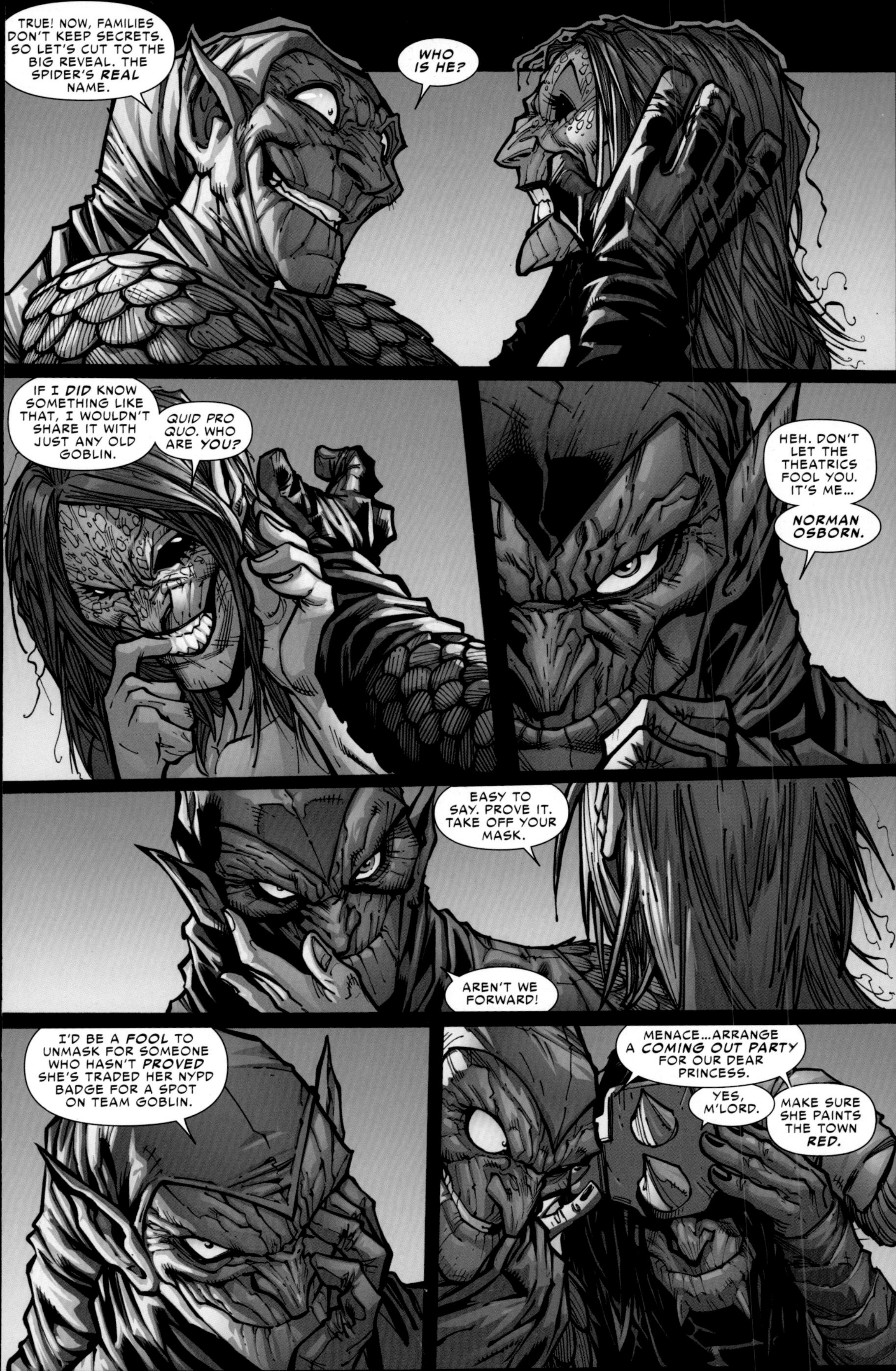
TRUE! NOW, FAMILIES DON'T KEEP SECRETS. SO LET'S CUT TO THE BIG REVEAL. THE SPIDER'S REAL NAME.
WHO IS HE?
IF I DID KNOW SOMETHING LIKE THAT, I WOULDN'T SHARE IT WITH JUST ANY OLD GOBLIN.
QUID PRO QUO. WHO ARE YOU?
HEH. DON'T LET THE THEATRICS FOOL YOU. IT'S ME...
NORMAN OSBORN.
EASY TO SAY. PROVE IT. TAKE OFF YOUR MASK.
AREN'T WE FORWARD!
I'D BE A FOOL TO UNMASK FOR SOMEONE WHO HASN'T PROVED SHE'S TRADED HER NYPD BADGE FOR A SPOT ON TEAM GOBLIN.
MENACE...ARRANGE A COMING OUT PARTY FOR OUR DEAR PRINCESS.
YES, M'LORD.
MAKE SURE SHE PAINTS THE TOWN RED.

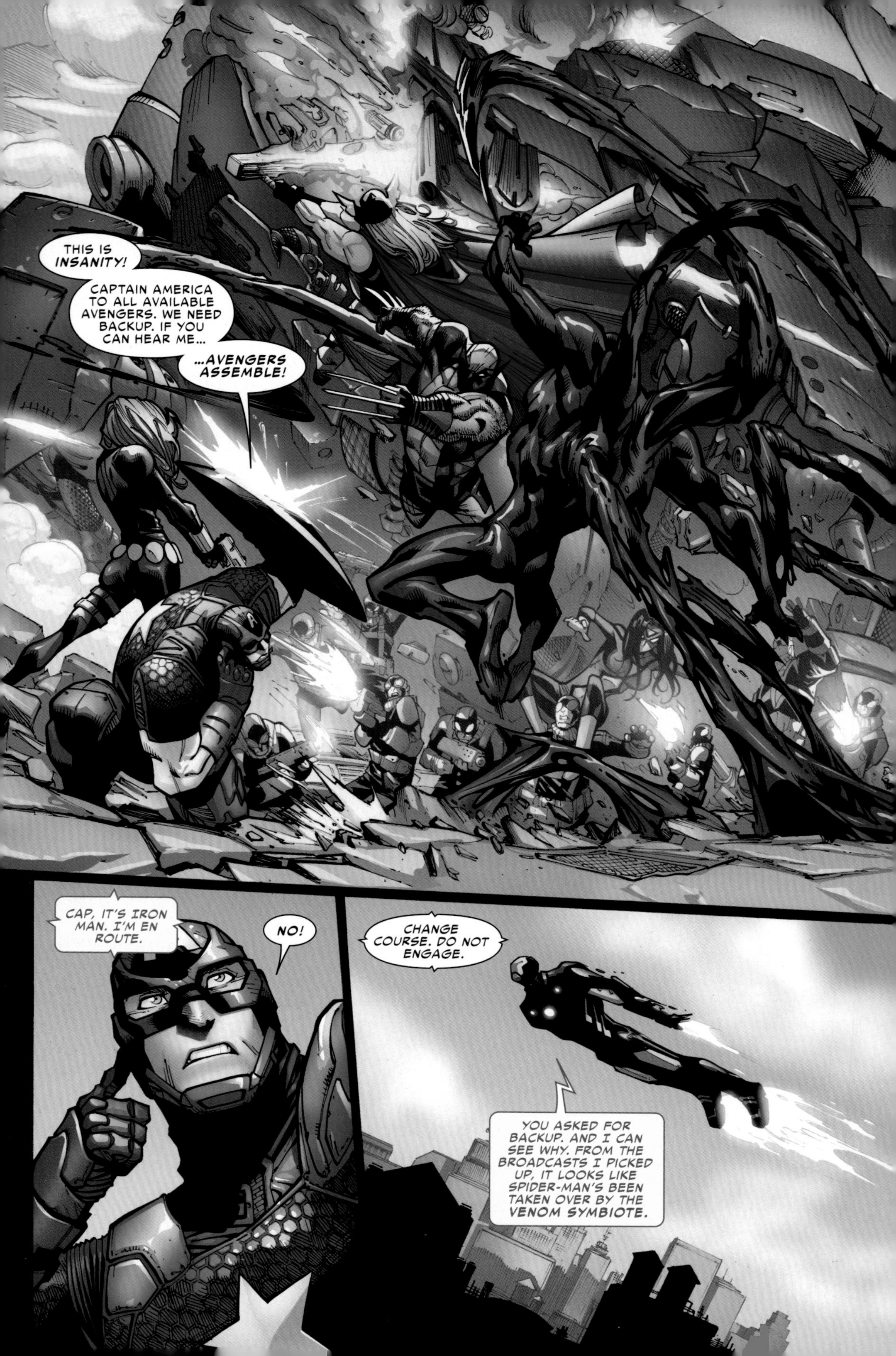
THIS IS INSANITY!
CAPTAIN AMERICA TO ALL AVAILABLE AVENGERS. WE NEED BACKUP. IF YOU CAN HEAR ME...
...AVENGERS ASSEMBLE!
CAP, IT'S IRON MAN. I'M EN ROUTE.
NO!
CHANGE COURSE. DO NOT ENGAGE.
YOU ASKED FOR BACKUP. AND I CAN SEE WHY. FROM THE BROADCASTS I PICKED UP, IT LOOKS LIKE SPIDER-MAN'S BEEN TAKEN OVER BY THE VENOM SYMBIOTE.

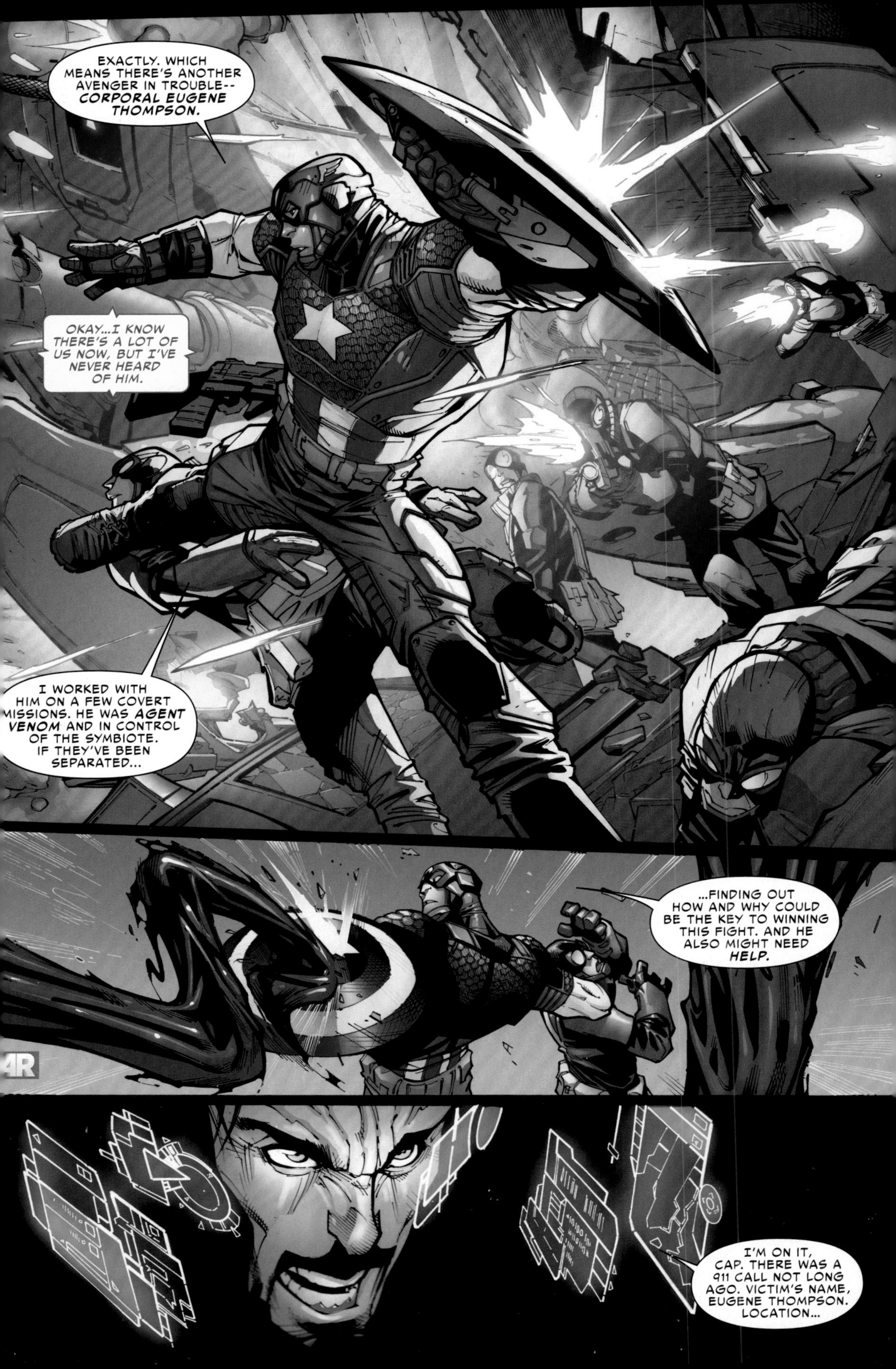
EXACTLY. WHICH MEANS THERE'S ANOTHER AVENGER IN TROUBLE-- CORPORAL EUGENE THOMPSON.
OKAY...I KNOW THERE'S A LOT OF US NOW, BUT I'VE NEVER HEARD OF HIM.
I WORKED WITH HIM ON A FEW COVERT MISSIONS. HE WAS AGENT VENOM AND IN CONTROL OF THE SYMBIOTE. IF THEY'VE BEEN SEPARATED...
...FINDING OUT HOW AND WHY COULD BE THE KEY TO WINNING THIS FIGHT. AND HE ALSO MIGHT NEED HELP.
I'M ON IT, CAP. THERE WAS A 911 CALL NOT LONG AGO. VICTIM'S NAME, EUGENE THOMPSON. LOCATION...

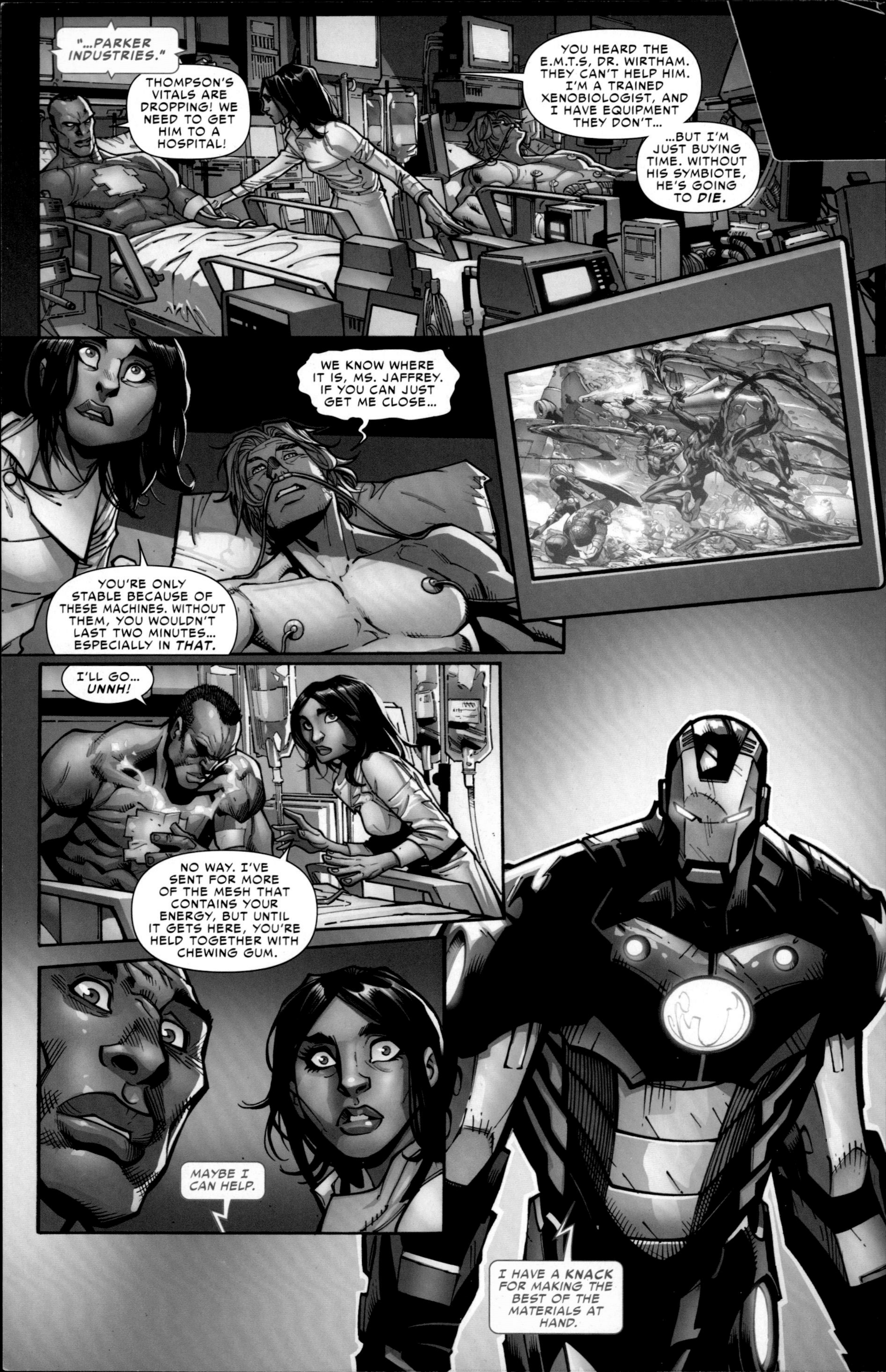
"...PARKER INDUSTRIES."
THOMPSON'S VITALS ARE DROPPING! WE NEED TO GET HIM TO A HOSPITAL!
YOU HEARD THE E.M.T.S, DR. WIRTHAM. THEY CAN'T HELP HIM. I'M A TRAINED XENOBIOLOGIST, AND I HAVE EQUIPMENT THEY DON'T...
...BUT I'M JUST BUYING TIME. WITHOUT HIS SYMBIOTE, HE'S GOING TO DIE.
WE KNOW WHERE IT IS, MS. JAFFREY. IF YOU CAN JUST GET ME CLOSE...
YOU'RE ONLY STABLE BECAUSE OF THESE MACHINES. WITHOUT THEM, YOU WOULDN'T LAST TWO MINUTES... ESPECIALLY IN THAT.
I'LL GO... UNNH!
NO WAY. I'VE SENT FOR MORE OF THE MESH THAT CONTAINS YOUR ENERGY, BUT UNTIL IT GETS HERE, YOU'RE HELD TOGETHER WITH CHEWING GUM.
MAYBE I CAN HELP.
I HAVE A KNACK FOR MAKING THE BEST OF THE MATERIALS AT HAND.

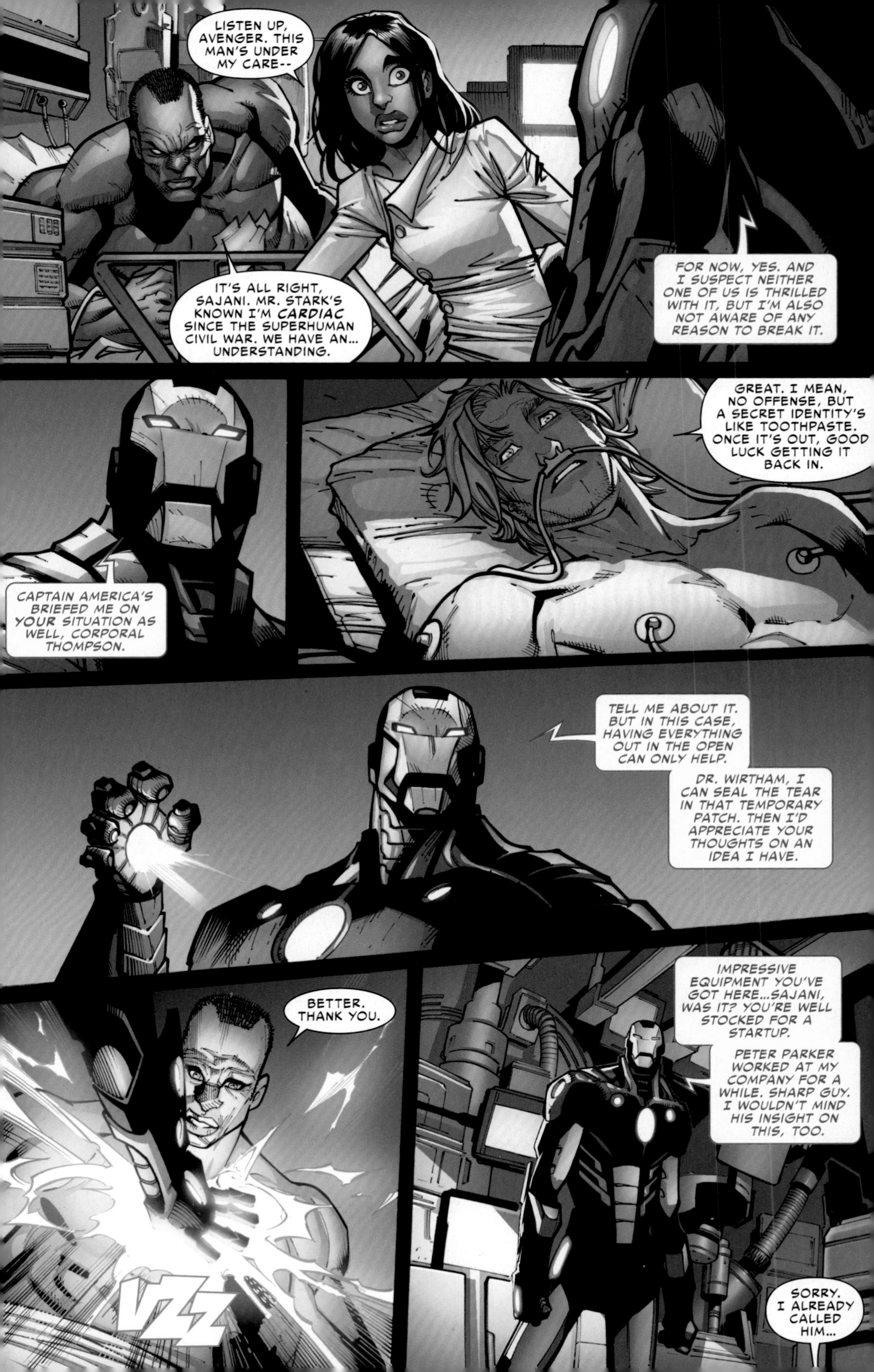
LISTEN UP, AVENGER. THIS MAN'S UNDER MY CARE--
IT'S ALL RIGHT, SAJANI. MR. STARK'S KNOWN I'M CARDIAC SINCE THE SUPERHUMAN CIVIL WAR. WE HAVE AN... UNDERSTANDING.
FOR NOW, YES. AND I SUSPECT NEITHER ONE OF US IS THRILLED WITH IT, BUT I'M ALSO NOT AWARE OF ANY REASON TO BREAK IT.
CAPTAIN AMERICA'S BRIEFED ME ON YOUR SITUATION AS WELL, CORPORAL THOMPSON.
GREAT. I MEAN, NO OFFENSE, BUT A SECRET IDENTITY'S LIKE TOOTHPASTE. ONCE IT'S OUT, GOOD LUCK GETTING IT BACK IN.
TELL ME ABOUT IT. BUT IN THIS CASE, HAVING EVERYTHING OUT IN THE OPEN CAN ONLY HELP.
DR. WIRTHAM, I CAN SEAL THE TEAR IN THAT TEMPORARY PATCH. THEN I'D APPRECIATE YOUR THOUGHTS ON AN IDEA I HAVE.
VZZ
BETTER. THANK YOU.
IMPRESSIVE EQUIPMENT YOU'VE GOT HERE...SAJANI, WAS IT? YOU'RE WELL STOCKED FOR A STARTUP.
PETER PARKER WORKED AT MY COMPANY FOR A WHILE. SHARP GUY. I WOULDN'T MIND HIS INSIGHT ON THIS, TOO.
SORRY. I ALREADY CALLED HIM...

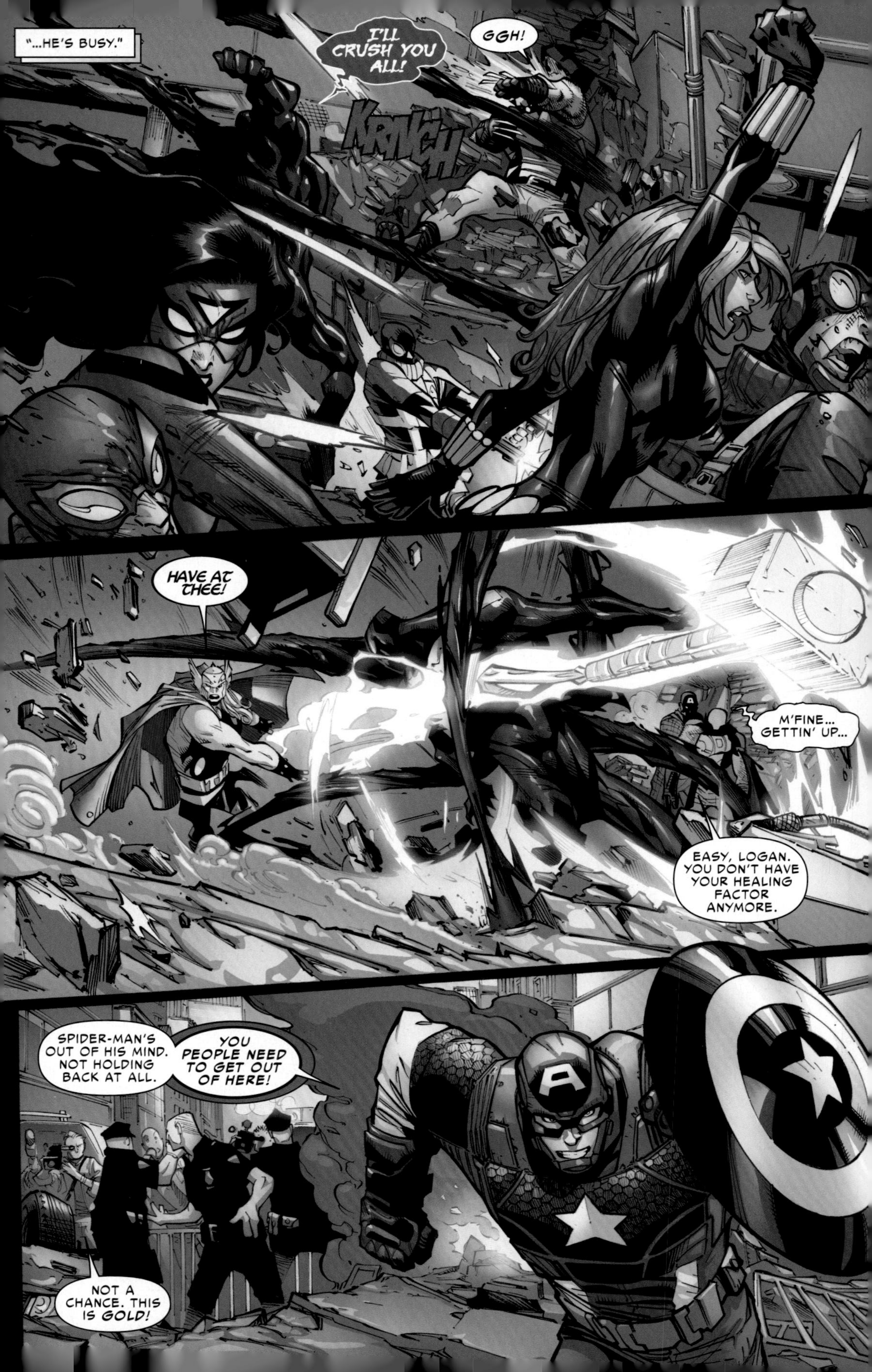
"...HE'S BUSY."
I'LL CRUSH YOU ALL!
GGH!
KRNCH
HAVE AT THEE!
M'FINE... GETTIN' UP...
EASY, LOGAN. YOU DON'T HAVE YOUR HEALING FACTOR ANYMORE.
SPIDER-MAN'S OUT OF HIS MIND. NOT HOLDING BACK AT ALL.
YOU PEOPLE NEED TO GET OUT OF HERE!
NOT A CHANCE. THIS IS GOLD!

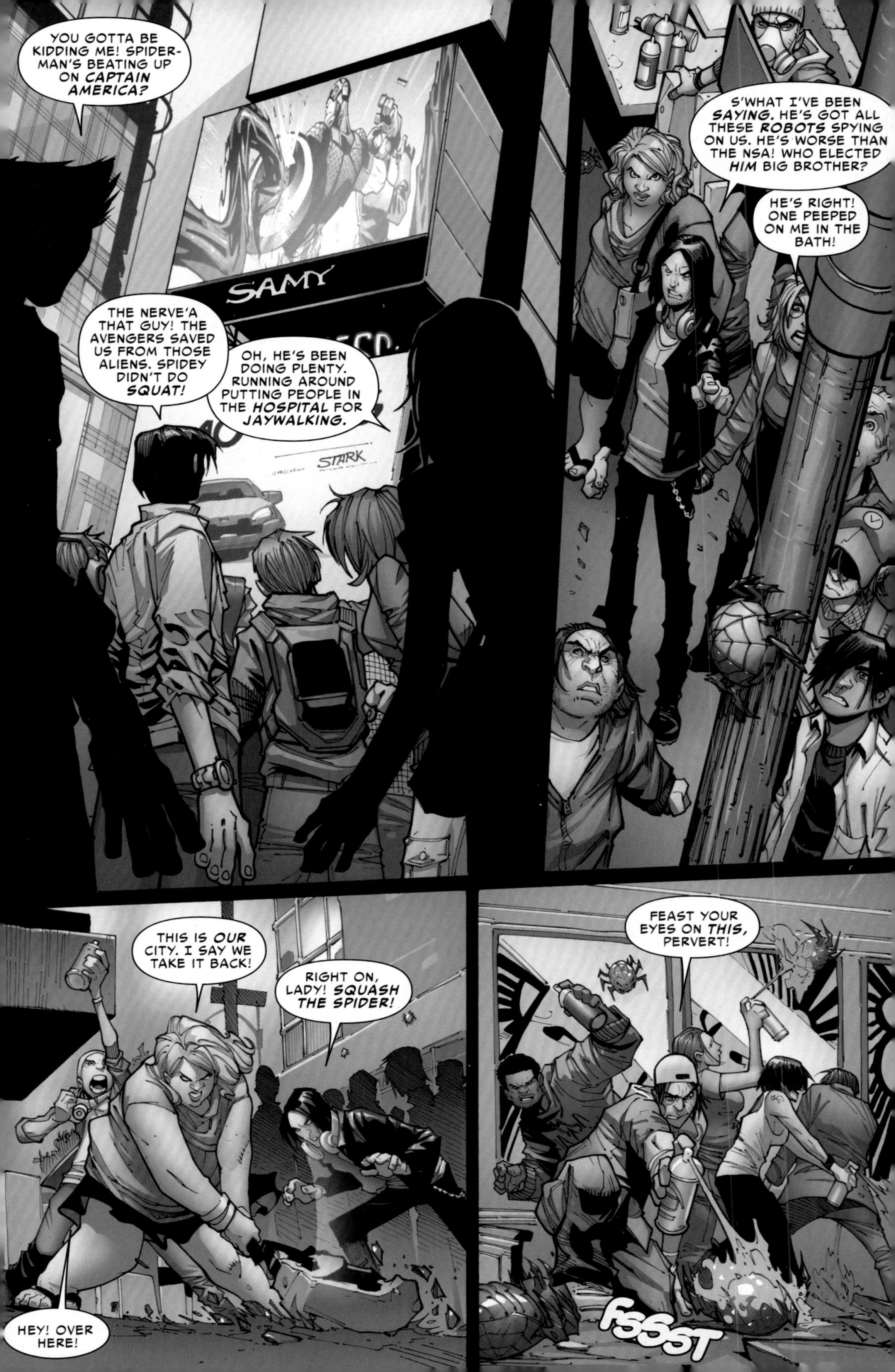
YOU GOTTA BE KIDDING ME! SPIDER-MAN'S BEATING UP ON CAPTAIN AMERICA?
SAMY
THE NERVE'A THAT GUY! THE AVENGERS SAVED US FROM THOSE ALIENS. SPIDEY DIDN'T DO SQUAT!
OH, HE'S BEEN DOING PLENTY. RUNNING AROUND PUTTING PEOPLE IN THE HOSPITAL FOR JAYWALKING.
STARK
S'WHAT I'VE BEEN SAYING. HE'S GOT ALL THESE ROBOTS SPYING ON US. HE'S WORSE THAN THE NSA! WHO ELECTED HIM BIG BROTHER?
HE'S RIGHT! ONE PEEPED ON ME IN THE BATH!
THIS IS OUR CITY. I SAY WE TAKE IT BACK!
RIGHT ON, LADY! SQUASH THE SPIDER!
HEY! OVER HERE!
FEAST YOUR EYES ON THIS, PERVERT!
FSSST

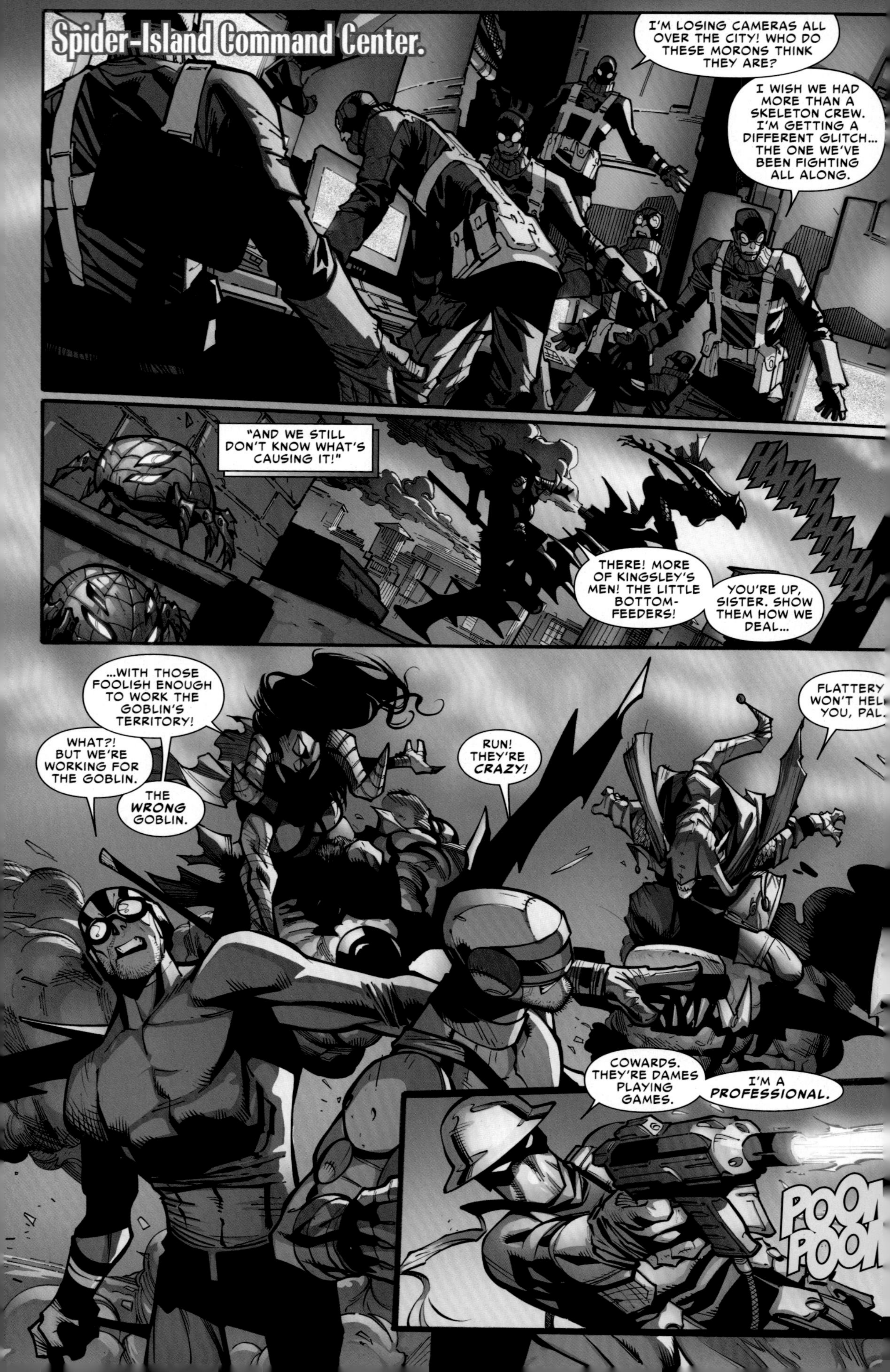
Spider-Island Command Center.
I'M LOSING CAMERAS ALL OVER THE CITY! WHO DO THESE MORONS THINK THEY ARE?
I WISH WE HAD MORE THAN A SKELETON CREW. I'M GETTING A DIFFERENT GLITCH... THE ONE WE'VE BEEN FIGHTING ALL ALONG.
"AND WE STILL DON'T KNOW WHAT'S CAUSING IT!"
HAHAHAHAHAHA
THERE! MORE OF KINGSLEY'S MEN! THE LITTLE BOTTOM-FEEDERS!
YOU'RE UP, SISTER. SHOW THEM HOW WE DEAL...
...WITH THOSE FOOLISH ENOUGH TO WORK THE GOBLIN'S TERRITORY!
WHAT?! BUT WE'RE WORKING FOR THE GOBLIN.
THE *WRONG* GOBLIN.
RUN! THEY'RE *CRAZY*!
FLATTERY WON'T HEL YOU, PAL.
COWARDS. THEY'RE DAMES PLAYING GAMES.
I'M A *PROFESSIONAL.*
POOM POOM

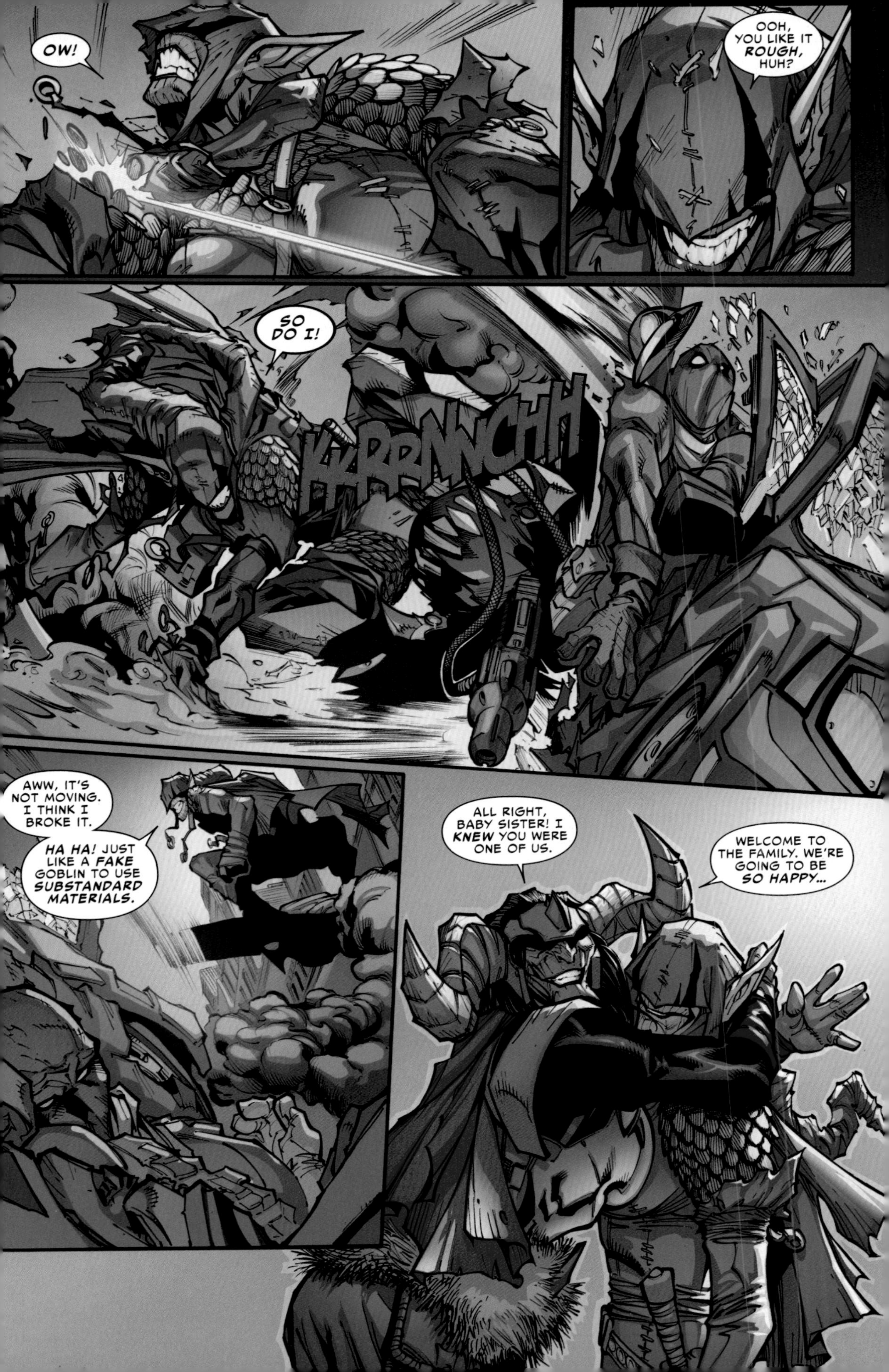
OW!
OOH, YOU LIKE IT ROUGH, HUH?
SO DO I!
KKRRNNCHH
AWW, IT'S NOT MOVING. I THINK I BROKE IT.
HA HA! JUST LIKE A FAKE GOBLIN TO USE SUBSTANDARD MATERIALS.
ALL RIGHT, BABY SISTER! I KNEW YOU WERE ONE OF US.
WELCOME TO THE FAMILY. WE'RE GOING TO BE SO HAPPY...

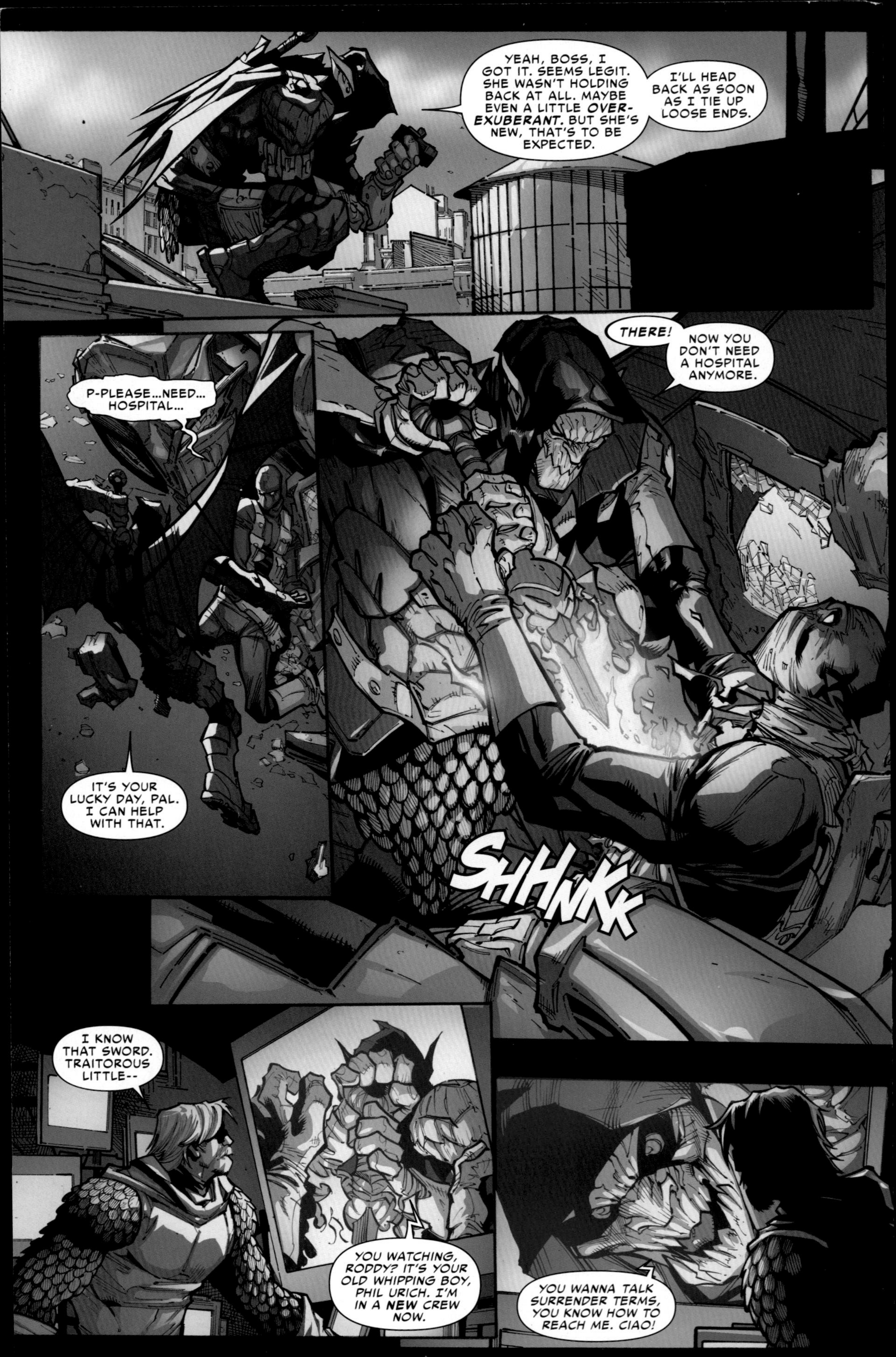
YEAH, BOSS, I GOT IT. SEEMS LEGIT. SHE WASN'T HOLDING BACK AT ALL. MAYBE EVEN A LITTLE OVER-EXUBERANT. BUT SHE'S NEW, THAT'S TO BE EXPECTED.
I'LL HEAD BACK AS SOON AS I TIE UP LOOSE ENDS.
P-PLEASE...NEED... HOSPITAL...
IT'S YOUR LUCKY DAY, PAL. I CAN HELP WITH THAT.
SHHNKK
THERE!
NOW YOU DON'T NEED A HOSPITAL ANYMORE.
I KNOW THAT SWORD. TRAITOROUS LITTLE--
YOU WATCHING, RODDY? IT'S YOUR OLD WHIPPING BOY, PHIL URICH. I'M IN A NEW CREW NOW.
YOU WANNA TALK SURRENDER TERMS, YOU KNOW HOW TO REACH ME. CIAO!

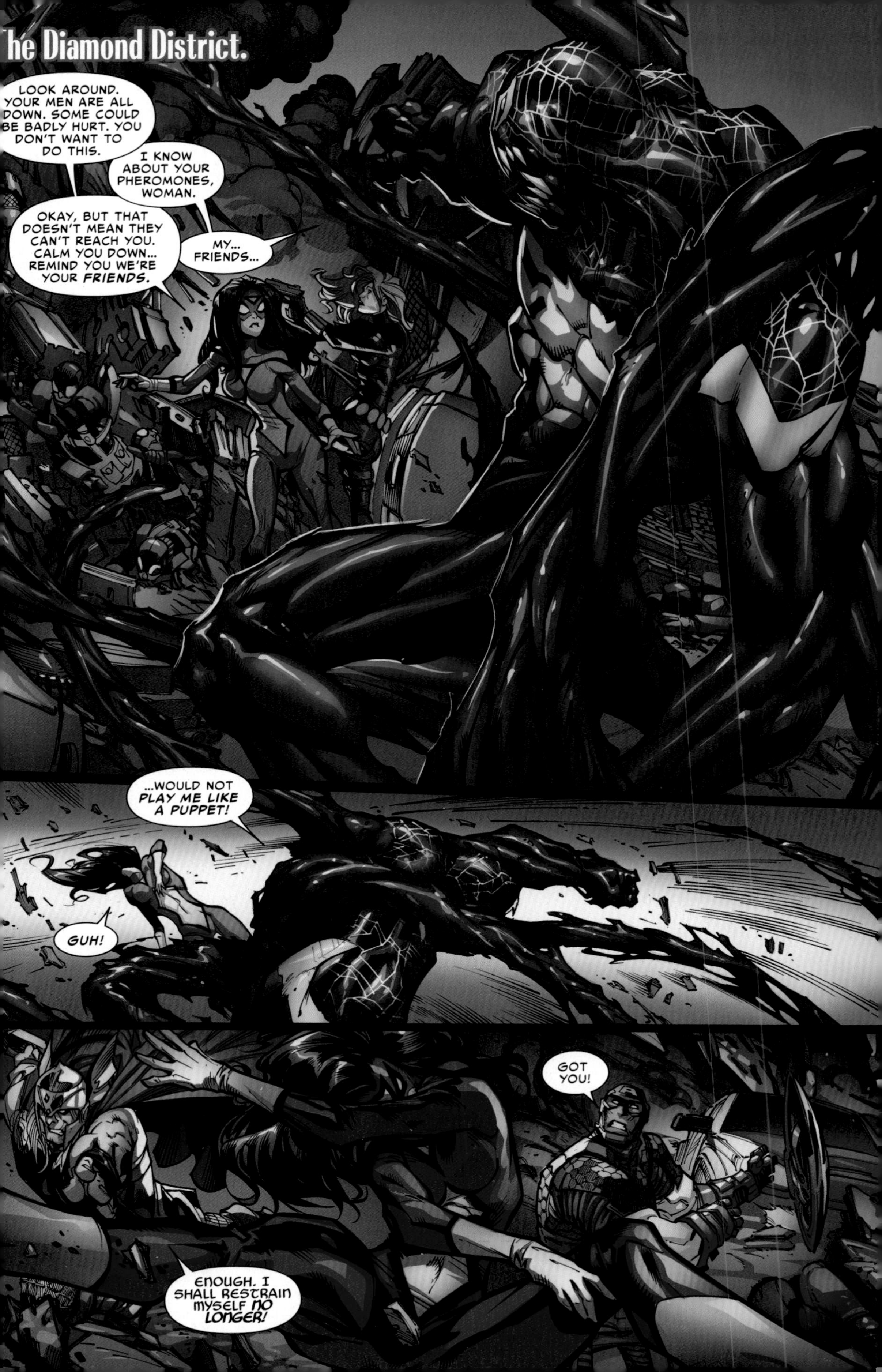
The Diamond District.
LOOK AROUND. YOUR MEN ARE ALL DOWN. SOME COULD BE BADLY HURT. YOU DON'T WANT TO DO THIS.
I KNOW ABOUT YOUR PHEROMONES, WOMAN.
OKAY, BUT THAT DOESN'T MEAN THEY CAN'T REACH YOU. CALM YOU DOWN... REMIND YOU WE'RE YOUR FRIENDS.
MY... FRIENDS...
...WOULD NOT PLAY ME LIKE A PUPPET!
GUH!
GOT YOU!
ENOUGH. I SHALL RESTRAIN MYSELF NO LONGER!

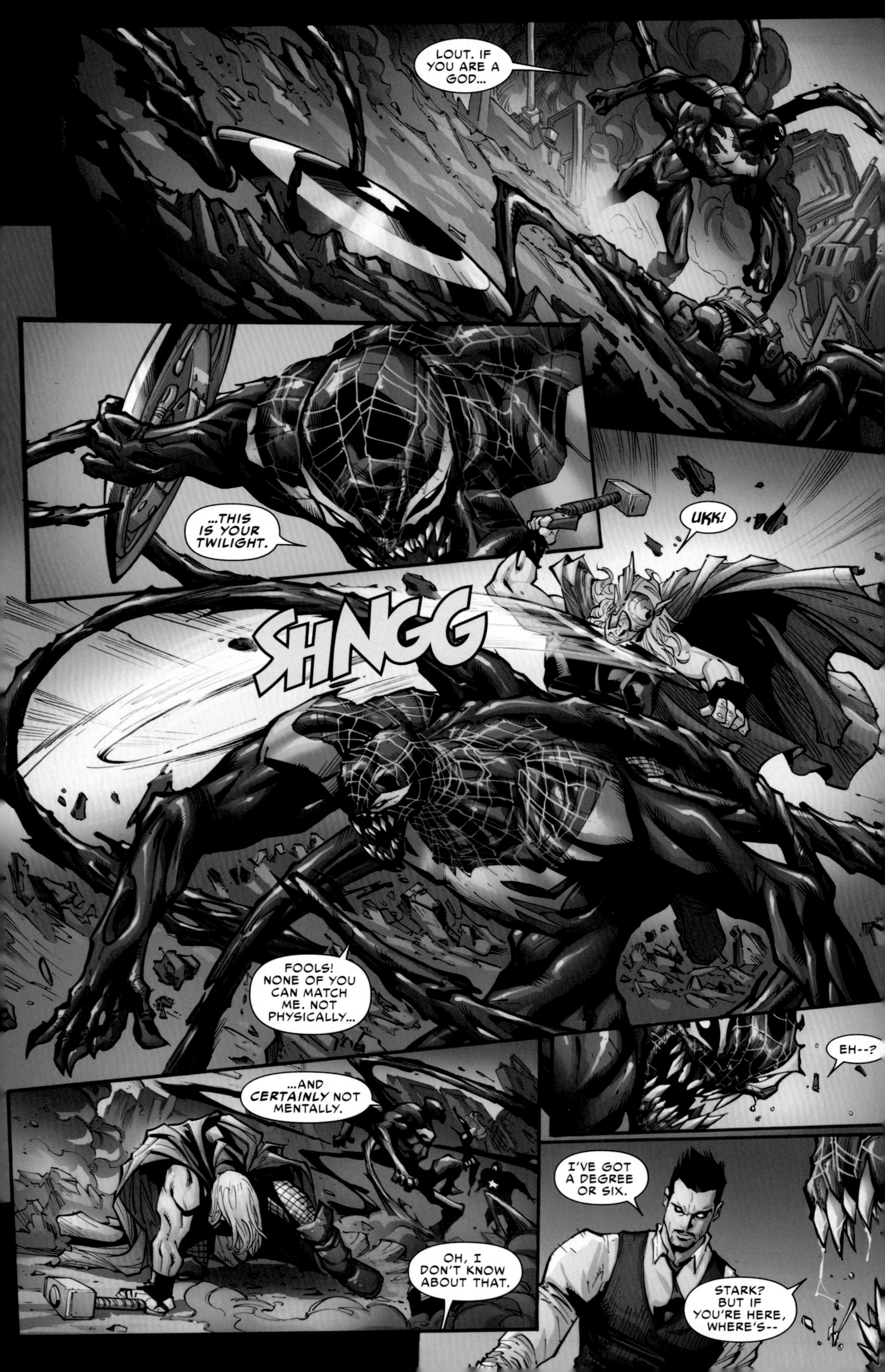
LOUT. IF YOU ARE A GOD...
...THIS IS YOUR TWILIGHT.
UKK!
SHNGG
FOOLS! NONE OF YOU CAN MATCH ME. NOT PHYSICALLY...
EH--?
...AND CERTAINLY NOT MENTALLY.
OH, I DON'T KNOW ABOUT THAT.
I'VE GOT A DEGREE OR SIX.
STARK? BUT IF YOU'RE HERE, WHERE'S--

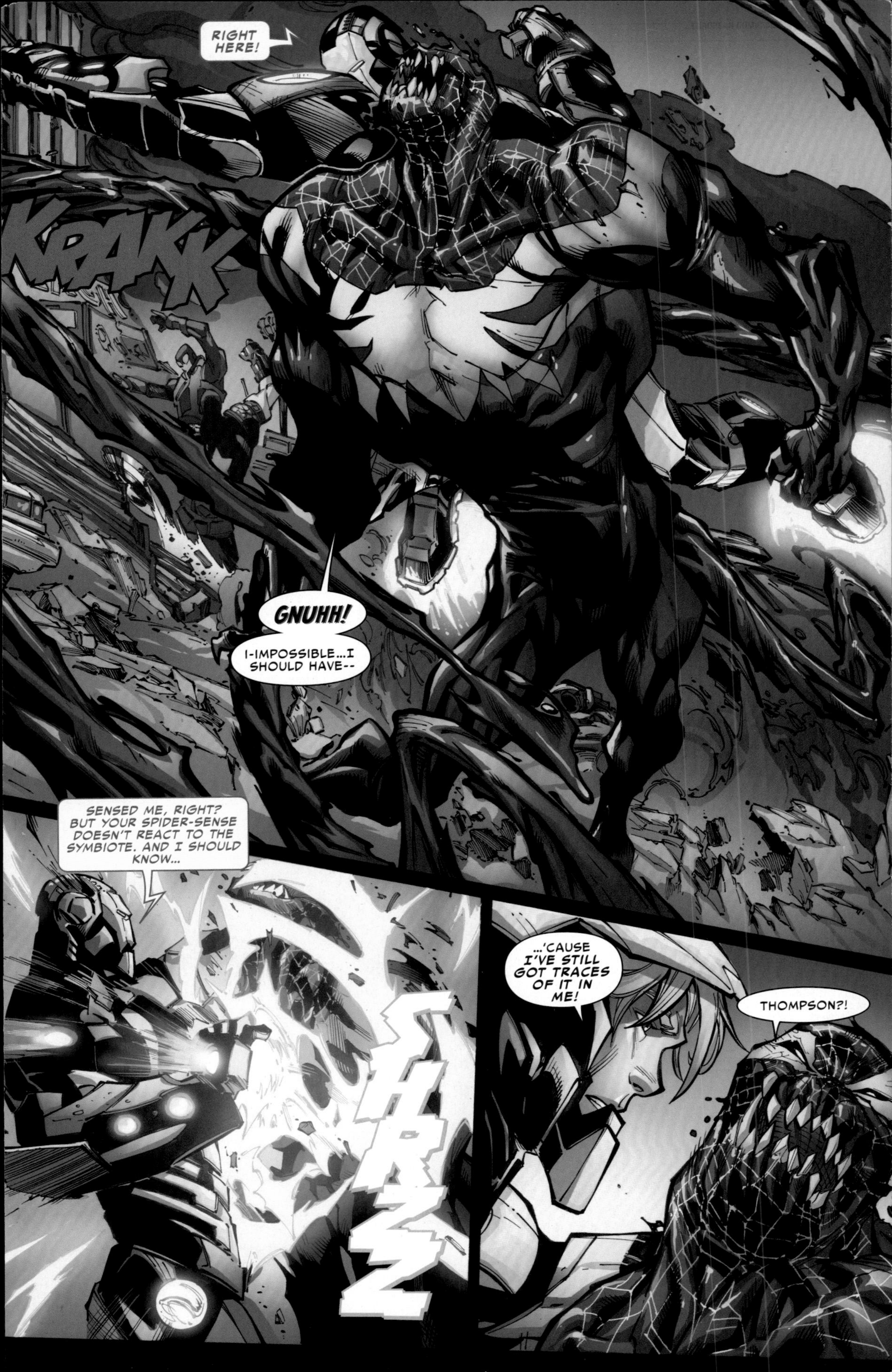
RIGHT HERE!
KRAKK
GNUHH!
I-IMPOSSIBLE...I SHOULD HAVE--
SENSED ME, RIGHT? BUT YOUR SPIDER-SENSE DOESN'T REACT TO THE SYMBIOTE. AND I SHOULD KNOW...
SHRZZ
...'CAUSE I'VE STILL GOT TRACES OF IT IN ME!
THOMPSON?!

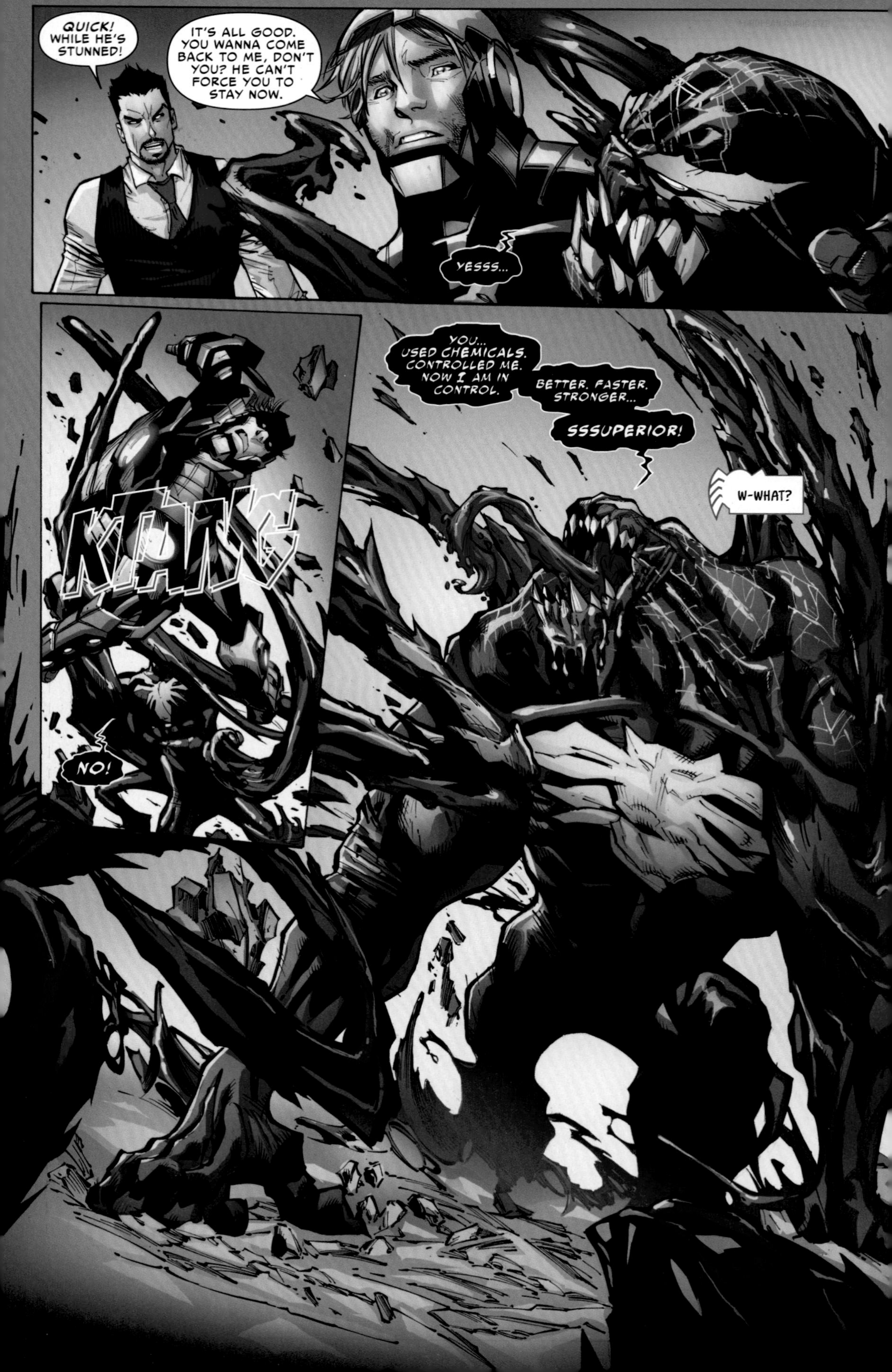
QUICK! WHILE HE'S STUNNED!
IT'S ALL GOOD. YOU WANNA COME BACK TO ME, DON'T YOU? HE CAN'T FORCE YOU TO STAY NOW.
YESSS...
KTANG
NO!
YOU... USED CHEMICALS. CONTROLLED ME. NOW I AM IN CONTROL.
BETTER. FASTER. STRONGER...
SSSUPERIOR!
W-WHAT?

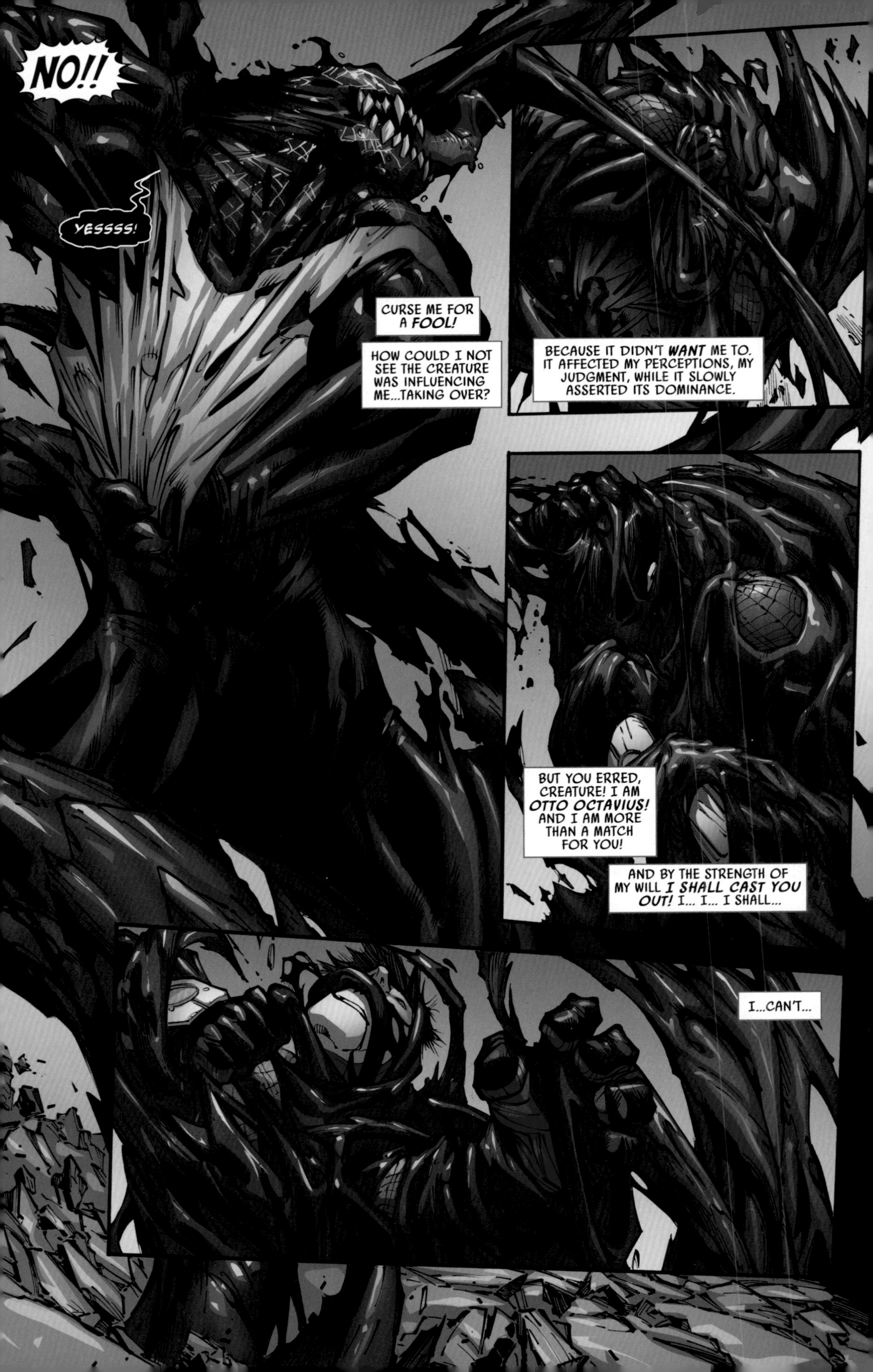
NO!!
YESSSS!
CURSE ME FOR A *FOOL!*
HOW COULD I NOT SEE THE CREATURE WAS INFLUENCING ME...TAKING OVER?
BECAUSE IT DIDN'T *WANT* ME TO. IT AFFECTED MY PERCEPTIONS, MY JUDGMENT, WHILE IT SLOWLY ASSERTED ITS DOMINANCE.
BUT YOU ERRED, CREATURE! I AM *OTTO OCTAVIUS!* AND I AM MORE THAN A MATCH FOR YOU!
AND BY THE STRENGTH OF MY WILL *I SHALL CAST YOU OUT!* I... I... I SHALL...
I...CAN'T...

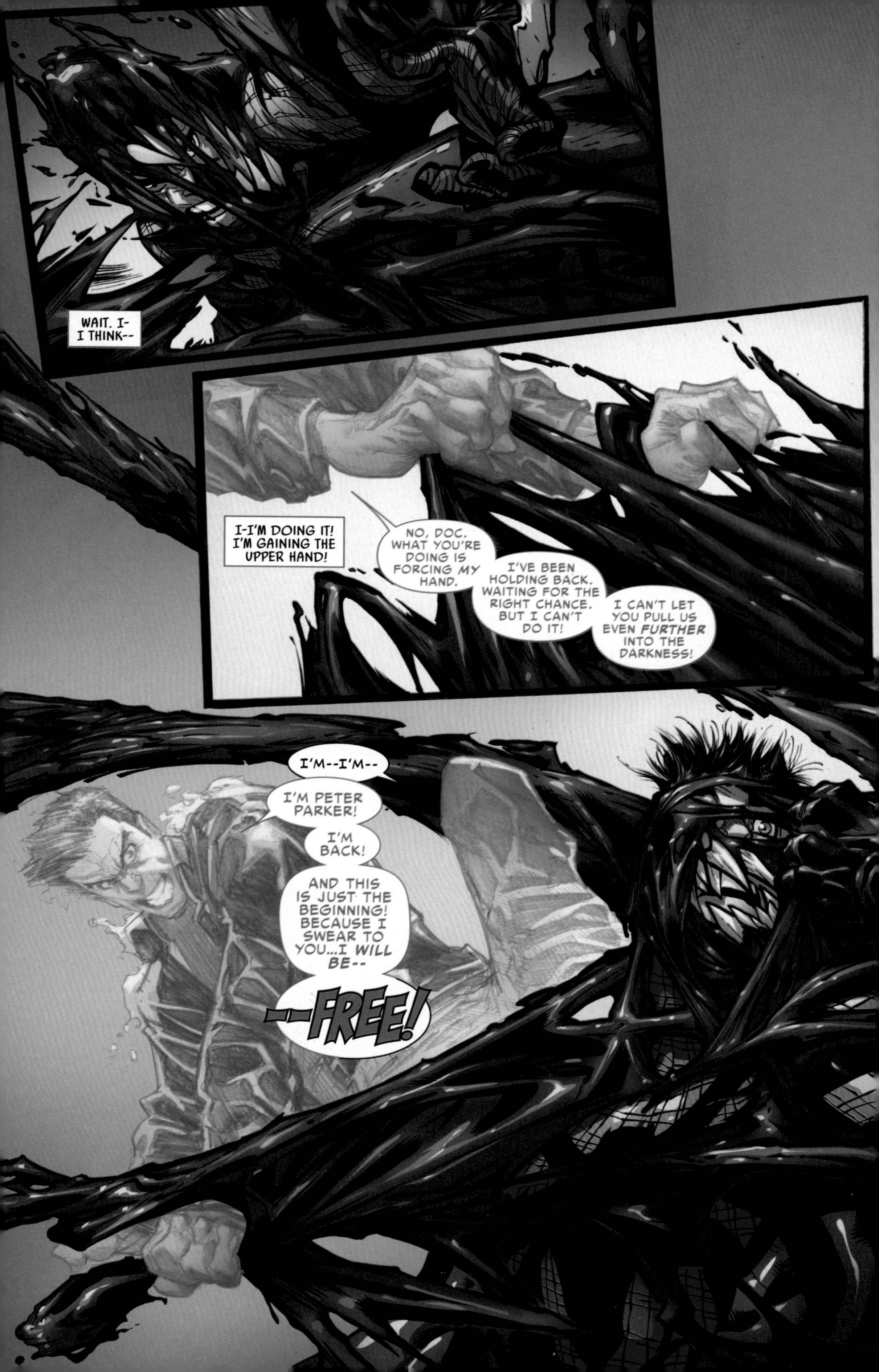
WAIT. I-
I THINK--
I-I'M DOING IT! I'M GAINING THE UPPER HAND!
NO, DOC. WHAT YOU'RE DOING IS FORCING MY HAND.
I'VE BEEN HOLDING BACK. WAITING FOR THE RIGHT CHANCE. BUT I CAN'T DO IT!
I CAN'T LET YOU PULL US EVEN FURTHER INTO THE DARKNESS!
I'M--I'M--
I'M PETER PARKER!
I'M BACK!
AND THIS IS JUST THE BEGINNING! BECAUSE I SWEAR TO YOU...I WILL BE--
--FREE!

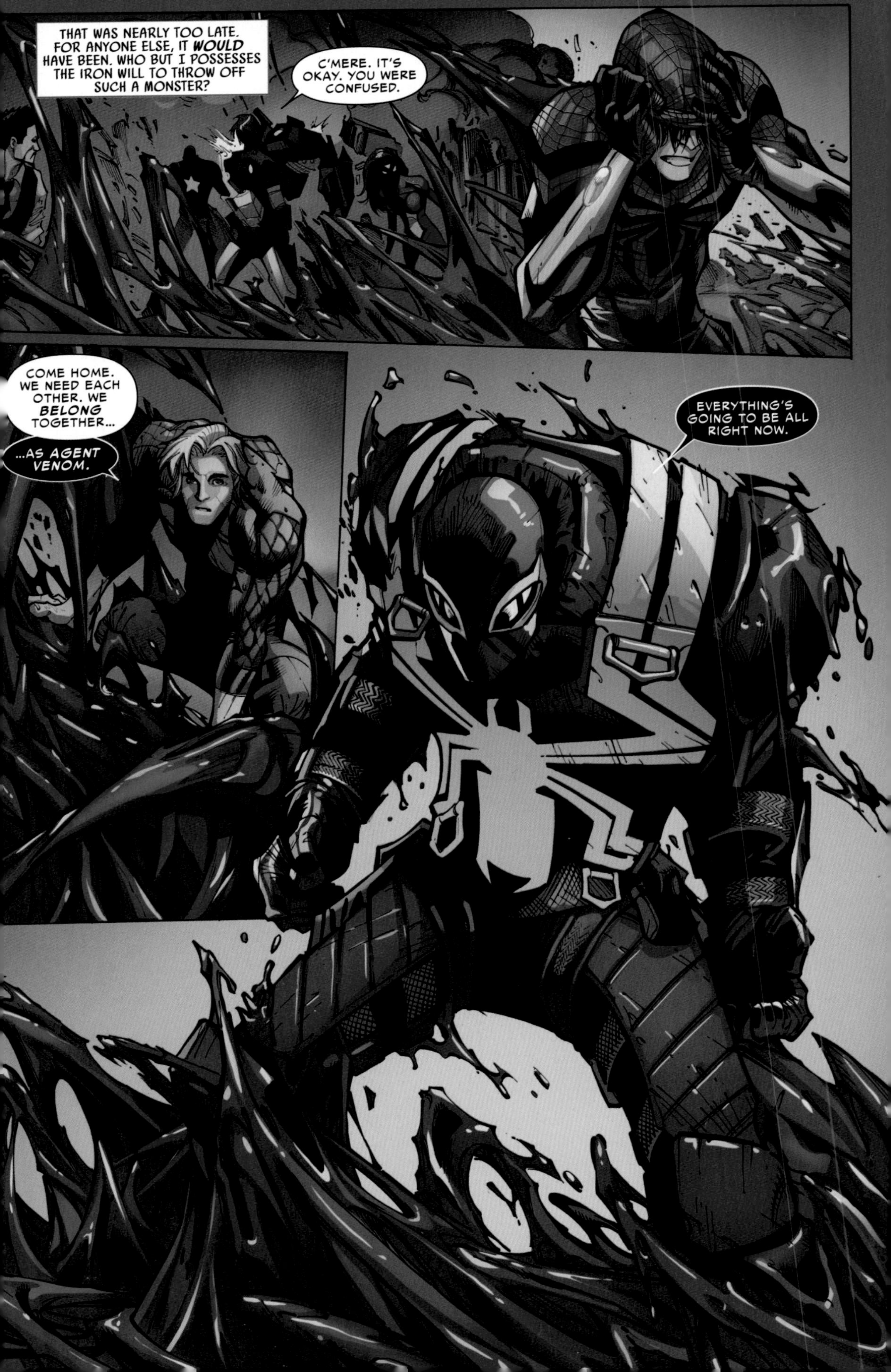

THAT WAS NEARLY TOO LATE. FOR ANYONE ELSE, IT *WOULD* HAVE BEEN. WHO BUT I POSSESSES THE IRON WILL TO THROW OFF SUCH A MONSTER?
C'MERE. IT'S OKAY. YOU WERE CONFUSED.
COME HOME. WE NEED EACH OTHER. WE *BELONG* TOGETHER...
...AS *AGENT VENOM.*
EVERYTHING'S GOING TO BE ALL RIGHT NOW.

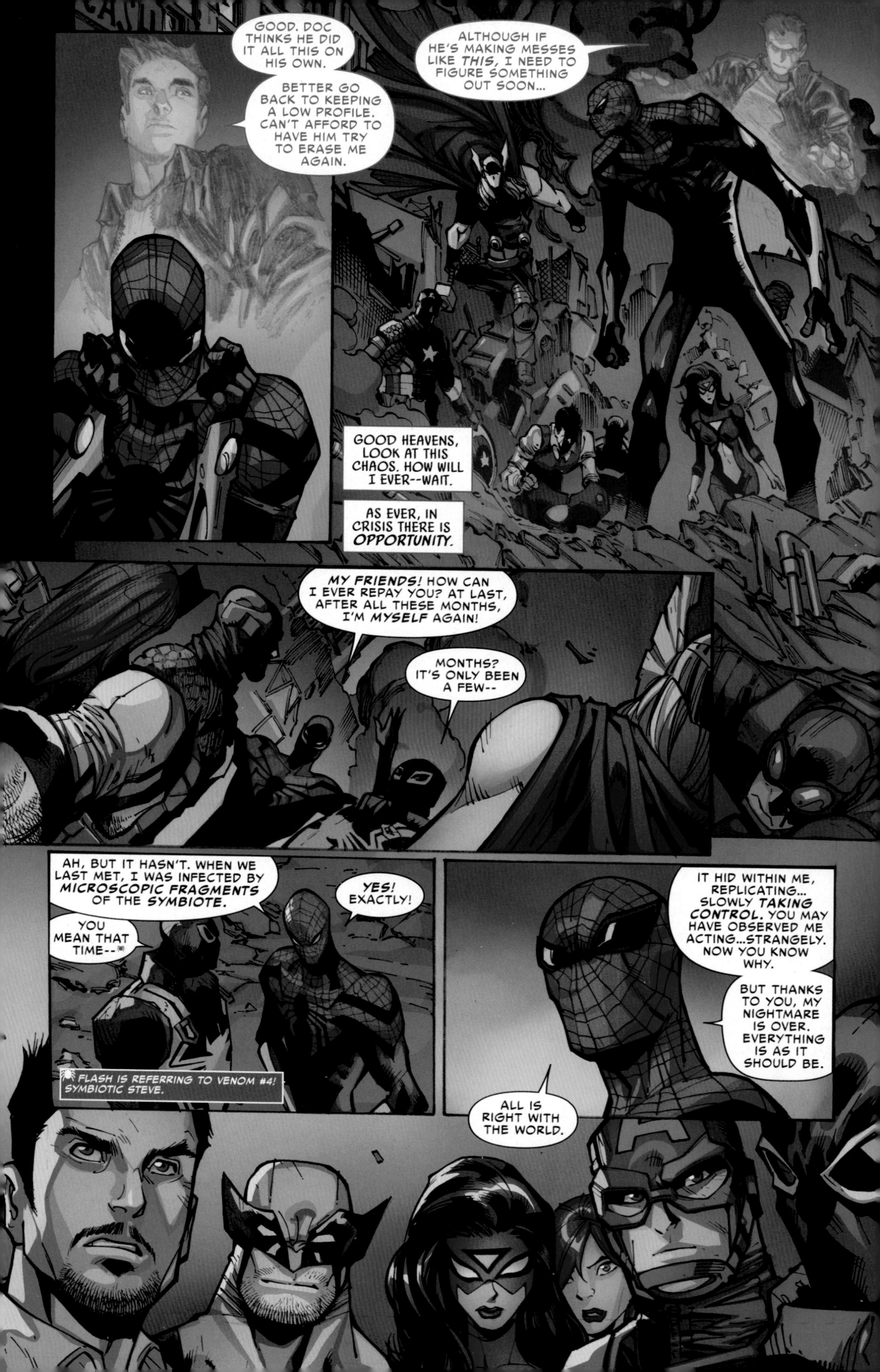
GOOD. DOC THINKS HE DID IT ALL THIS ON HIS OWN.
BETTER GO BACK TO KEEPING A LOW PROFILE. CAN'T AFFORD TO HAVE HIM TRY TO ERASE ME AGAIN.
ALTHOUGH IF HE'S MAKING MESSES LIKE THIS, I NEED TO FIGURE SOMETHING OUT SOON...
GOOD HEAVENS, LOOK AT THIS CHAOS. HOW WILL I EVER--WAIT.
AS EVER, IN CRISIS THERE IS OPPORTUNITY.
MY FRIENDS! HOW CAN I EVER REPAY YOU? AT LAST, AFTER ALL THESE MONTHS, I'M MYSELF AGAIN!
MONTHS? IT'S ONLY BEEN A FEW--
AH, BUT IT HASN'T. WHEN WE LAST MET, I WAS INFECTED BY MICROSCOPIC FRAGMENTS OF THE SYMBIOTE.
YES! EXACTLY!
YOU MEAN THAT TIME--
FLASH IS REFERRING TO VENOM #4! SYMBIOTIC STEVE.
IT HID WITHIN ME, REPLICATING... SLOWLY TAKING CONTROL. YOU MAY HAVE OBSERVED ME ACTING...STRANGELY. NOW YOU KNOW WHY.
BUT THANKS TO YOU, MY NIGHTMARE IS OVER. EVERYTHING IS AS IT SHOULD BE.
ALL IS RIGHT WITH THE WORLD.

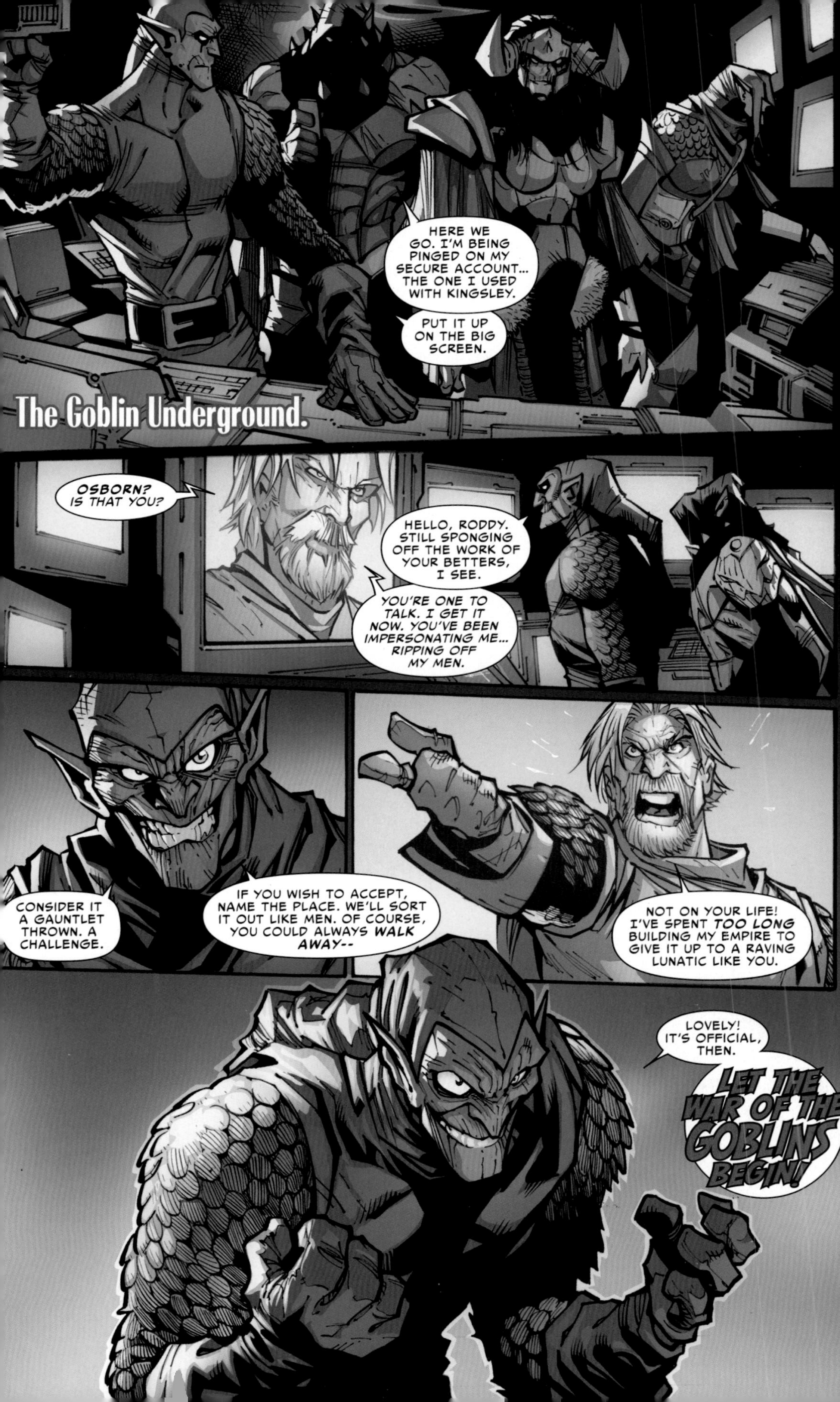
HERE WE GO. I'M BEING PINGED ON MY SECURE ACCOUNT... THE ONE I USED WITH KINGSLEY.
PUT IT UP ON THE BIG SCREEN.
The Goblin Underground.
OSBORN? IS THAT YOU?
HELLO, RODDY. STILL SPONGING OFF THE WORK OF YOUR BETTERS, I SEE.
YOU'RE ONE TO TALK. I GET IT NOW. YOU'VE BEEN IMPERSONATING ME... RIPPING OFF MY MEN.
CONSIDER IT A GAUNTLET THROWN. A CHALLENGE.
IF YOU WISH TO ACCEPT, NAME THE PLACE. WE'LL SORT IT OUT LIKE MEN. OF COURSE, YOU COULD ALWAYS WALK AWAY--
NOT ON YOUR LIFE! I'VE SPENT TOO LONG BUILDING MY EMPIRE TO GIVE IT UP TO A RAVING LUNATIC LIKE YOU.
LOVELY! IT'S OFFICIAL, THEN.
LET THE WAR OF THE GOBLINS BEGIN!

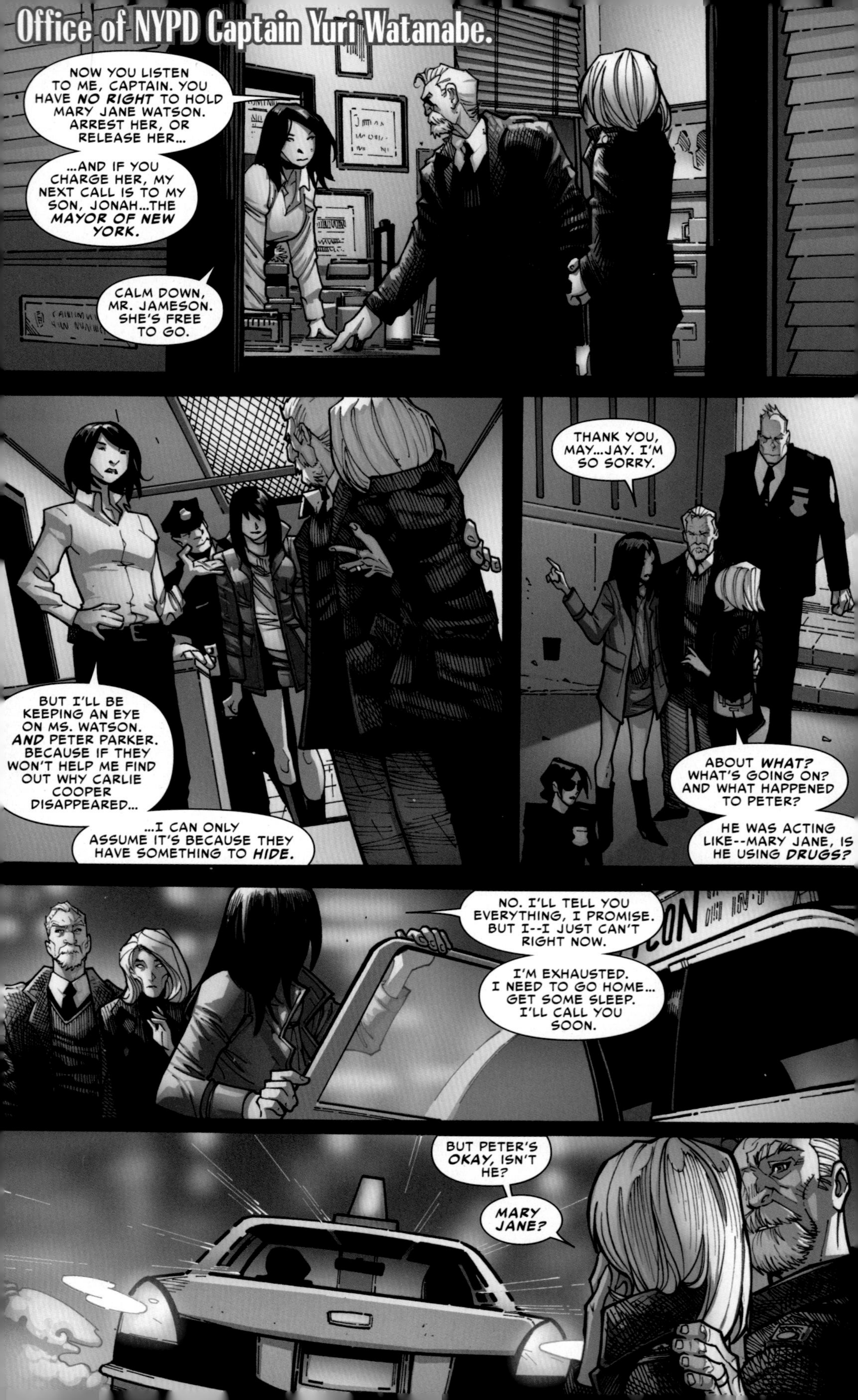
Office of NYPD Captain Yuri Watanabe.
NOW YOU LISTEN TO ME, CAPTAIN. YOU HAVE *NO RIGHT* TO HOLD MARY JANE WATSON. ARREST HER, OR RELEASE HER...
...AND IF YOU CHARGE HER, MY NEXT CALL IS TO MY SON, JONAH...THE *MAYOR OF NEW YORK.*
CALM DOWN, MR. JAMESON. SHE'S FREE TO GO.
BUT I'LL BE KEEPING AN EYE ON MS. WATSON. *AND* PETER PARKER. BECAUSE IF THEY WON'T HELP ME FIND OUT WHY CARLIE COOPER DISAPPEARED...
...I CAN ONLY ASSUME IT'S BECAUSE THEY HAVE SOMETHING TO *HIDE.*
THANK YOU, MAY...JAY. I'M SO SORRY.
ABOUT *WHAT?* WHAT'S GOING ON? AND WHAT HAPPENED TO PETER?
HE WAS ACTING LIKE--MARY JANE, IS HE USING *DRUGS?*
NO. I'LL TELL YOU EVERYTHING, I PROMISE. BUT I--I JUST CAN'T RIGHT NOW.
I'M EXHAUSTED. I NEED TO GO HOME... GET SOME SLEEP. I'LL CALL YOU SOON.
BUT PETER'S *OKAY,* ISN'T HE?
MARY JANE?

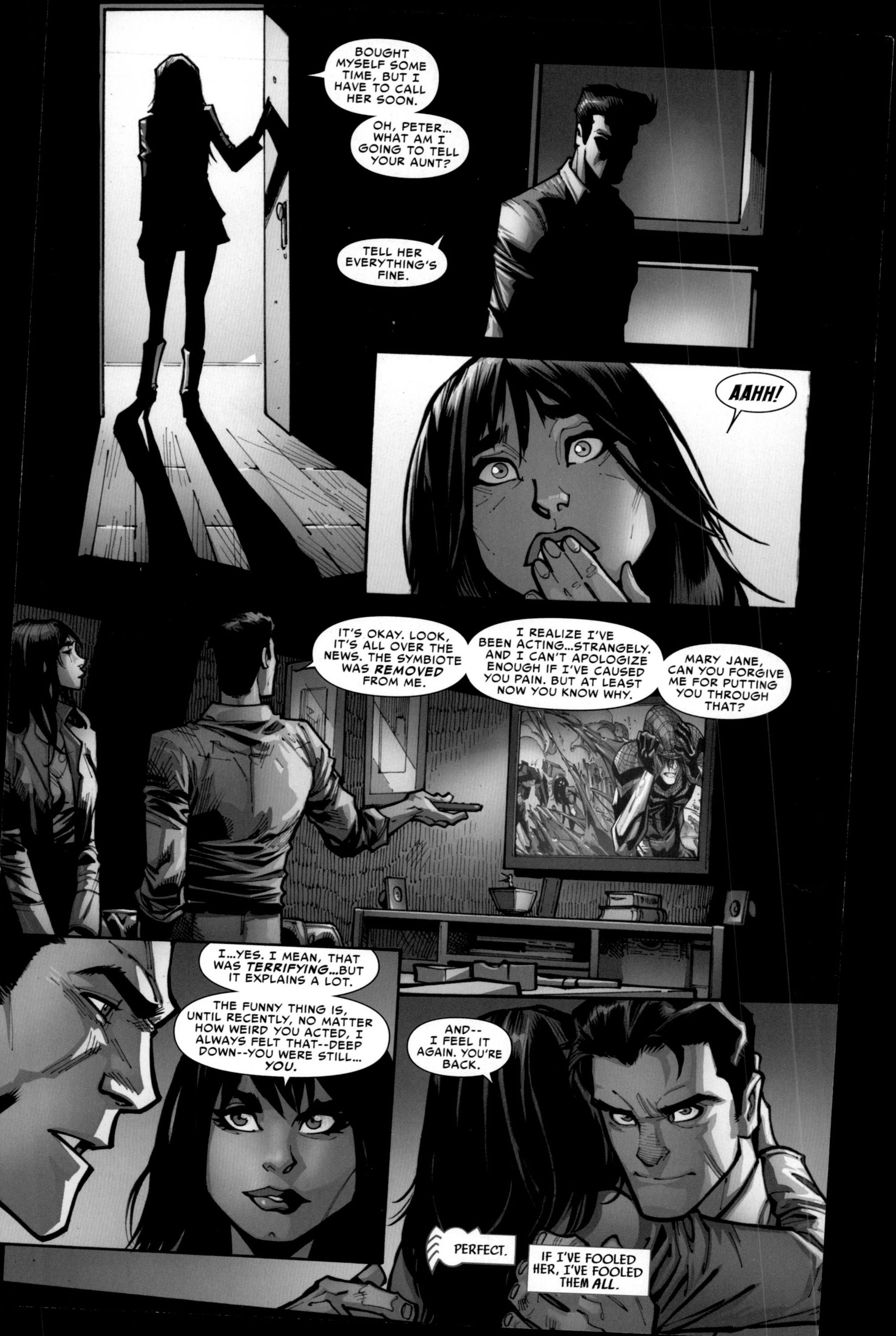

BOUGHT MYSELF SOME TIME, BUT I HAVE TO CALL HER SOON.
OH, PETER... WHAT AM I GOING TO TELL YOUR AUNT?
TELL HER EVERYTHING'S FINE.
AAHH!
IT'S OKAY. LOOK, IT'S ALL OVER THE NEWS. THE SYMBIOTE WAS *REMOVED* FROM ME.
I REALIZE I'VE BEEN ACTING...STRANGELY. AND I CAN'T APOLOGIZE ENOUGH IF I'VE CAUSED YOU PAIN. BUT AT LEAST NOW YOU KNOW WHY.
MARY JANE, CAN YOU FORGIVE ME FOR PUTTING YOU THROUGH THAT?
I...YES. I MEAN, THAT WAS *TERRIFYING*...BUT IT EXPLAINS A LOT.
THE FUNNY THING IS, UNTIL RECENTLY, NO MATTER HOW WEIRD YOU ACTED, I ALWAYS FELT THAT--DEEP DOWN--YOU WERE STILL... *YOU*.
AND-- I FEEL IT AGAIN. YOU'RE BACK.
PERFECT.
IF I'VE FOOLED HER, I'VE FOOLED THEM *ALL*.

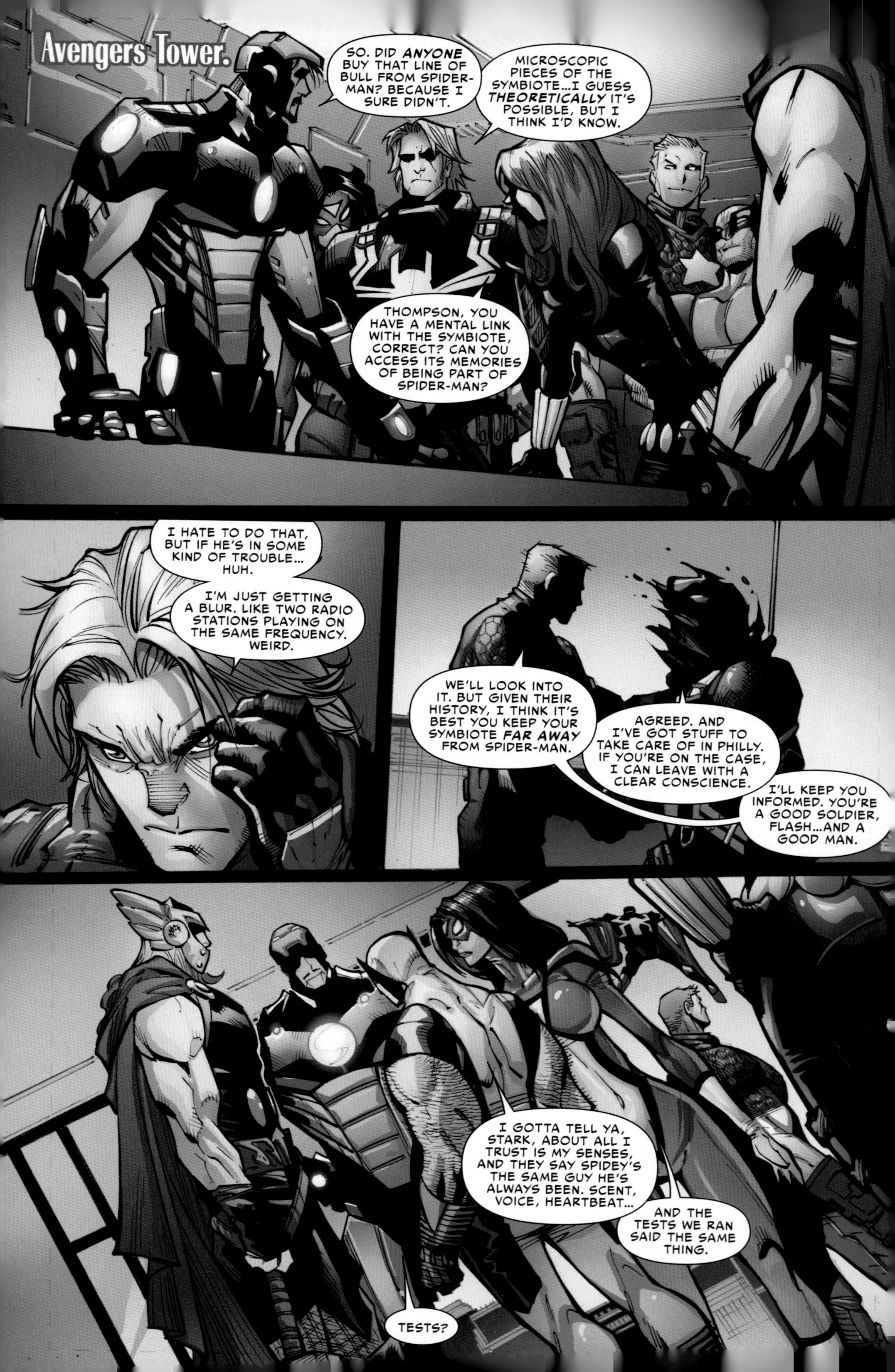
Avengers Tower.
SO. DID ANYONE BUY THAT LINE OF BULL FROM SPIDER-MAN? BECAUSE I SURE DIDN'T.
MICROSCOPIC PIECES OF THE SYMBIOTE...I GUESS THEORETICALLY IT'S POSSIBLE, BUT I THINK I'D KNOW.
THOMPSON, YOU HAVE A MENTAL LINK WITH THE SYMBIOTE, CORRECT? CAN YOU ACCESS ITS MEMORIES OF BEING PART OF SPIDER-MAN?
I HATE TO DO THAT, BUT IF HE'S IN SOME KIND OF TROUBLE... HUH.
I'M JUST GETTING A BLUR. LIKE TWO RADIO STATIONS PLAYING ON THE SAME FREQUENCY. WEIRD.
WE'LL LOOK INTO IT. BUT GIVEN THEIR HISTORY, I THINK IT'S BEST YOU KEEP YOUR SYMBIOTE FAR AWAY FROM SPIDER-MAN.
AGREED. AND I'VE GOT STUFF TO TAKE CARE OF IN PHILLY. IF YOU'RE ON THE CASE, I CAN LEAVE WITH A CLEAR CONSCIENCE.
I'LL KEEP YOU INFORMED. YOU'RE A GOOD SOLDIER, FLASH...AND A GOOD MAN.
I GOTTA TELL YA, STARK, ABOUT ALL I TRUST IS MY SENSES, AND THEY SAY SPIDEY'S THE SAME GUY HE'S ALWAYS BEEN. SCENT, VOICE, HEARTBEAT...
AND THE TESTS WE RAN SAID THE SAME THING.
TESTS?

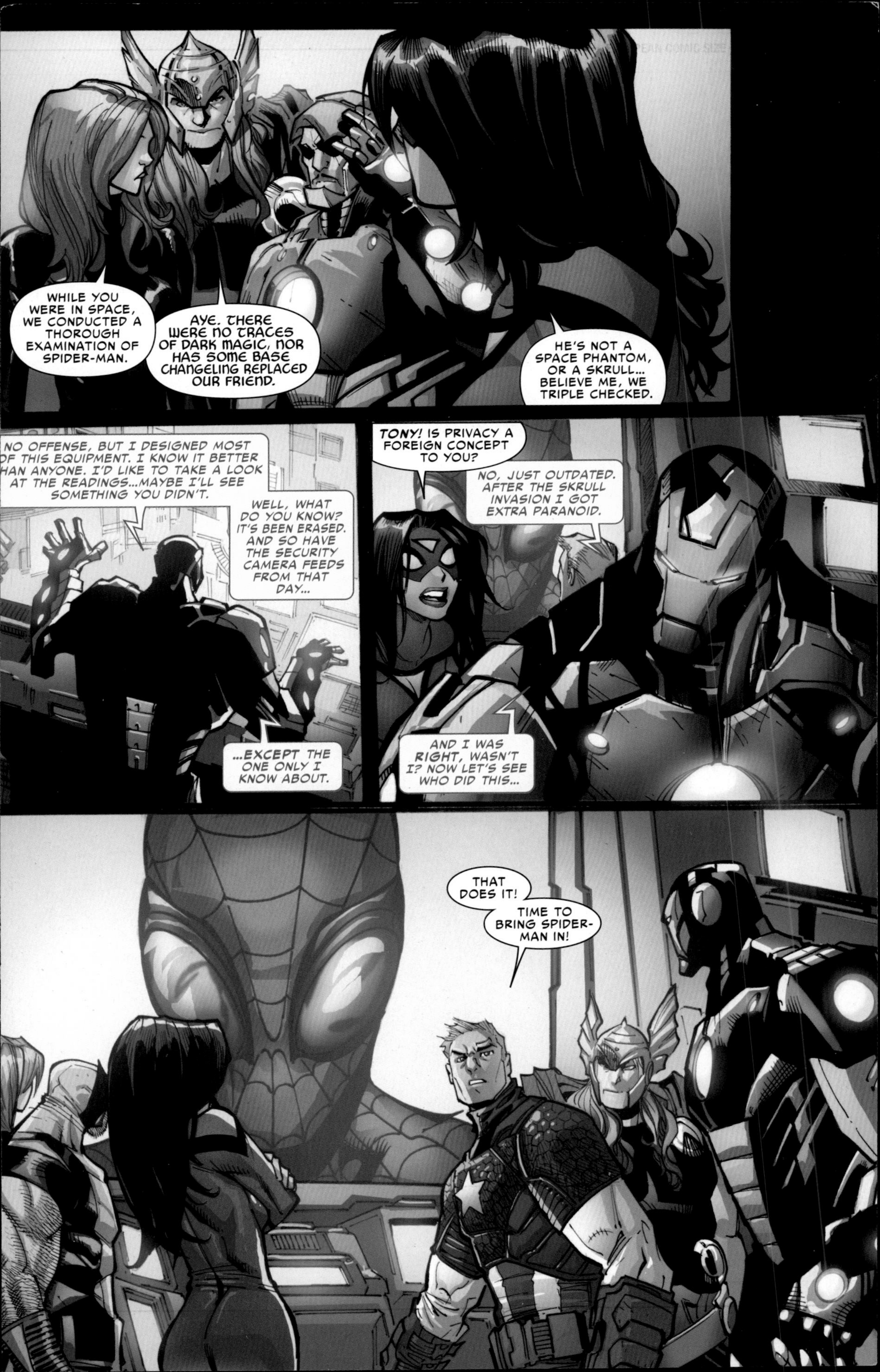
WHILE YOU WERE IN SPACE, WE CONDUCTED A THOROUGH EXAMINATION OF SPIDER-MAN.
AYE. THERE WERE NO TRACES OF DARK MAGIC, NOR HAS SOME BASE CHANGELING REPLACED OUR FRIEND.
HE'S NOT A SPACE PHANTOM, OR A SKRULL... BELIEVE ME, WE TRIPLE CHECKED.
NO OFFENSE, BUT I DESIGNED MOST OF THIS EQUIPMENT. I KNOW IT BETTER THAN ANYONE. I'D LIKE TO TAKE A LOOK AT THE READINGS...MAYBE I'LL SEE SOMETHING YOU DIDN'T.
WELL, WHAT DO YOU KNOW? IT'S BEEN ERASED. AND SO HAVE THE SECURITY CAMERA FEEDS FROM THAT DAY...
...EXCEPT THE ONE ONLY I KNOW ABOUT.
TONY! IS PRIVACY A FOREIGN CONCEPT TO YOU?
NO, JUST OUTDATED. AFTER THE SKRULL INVASION I GOT EXTRA PARANOID.
AND I WAS RIGHT, WASN'T I? NOW LET'S SEE WHO DID THIS...
THAT DOES IT!
TIME TO BRING SPIDER-MAN IN!

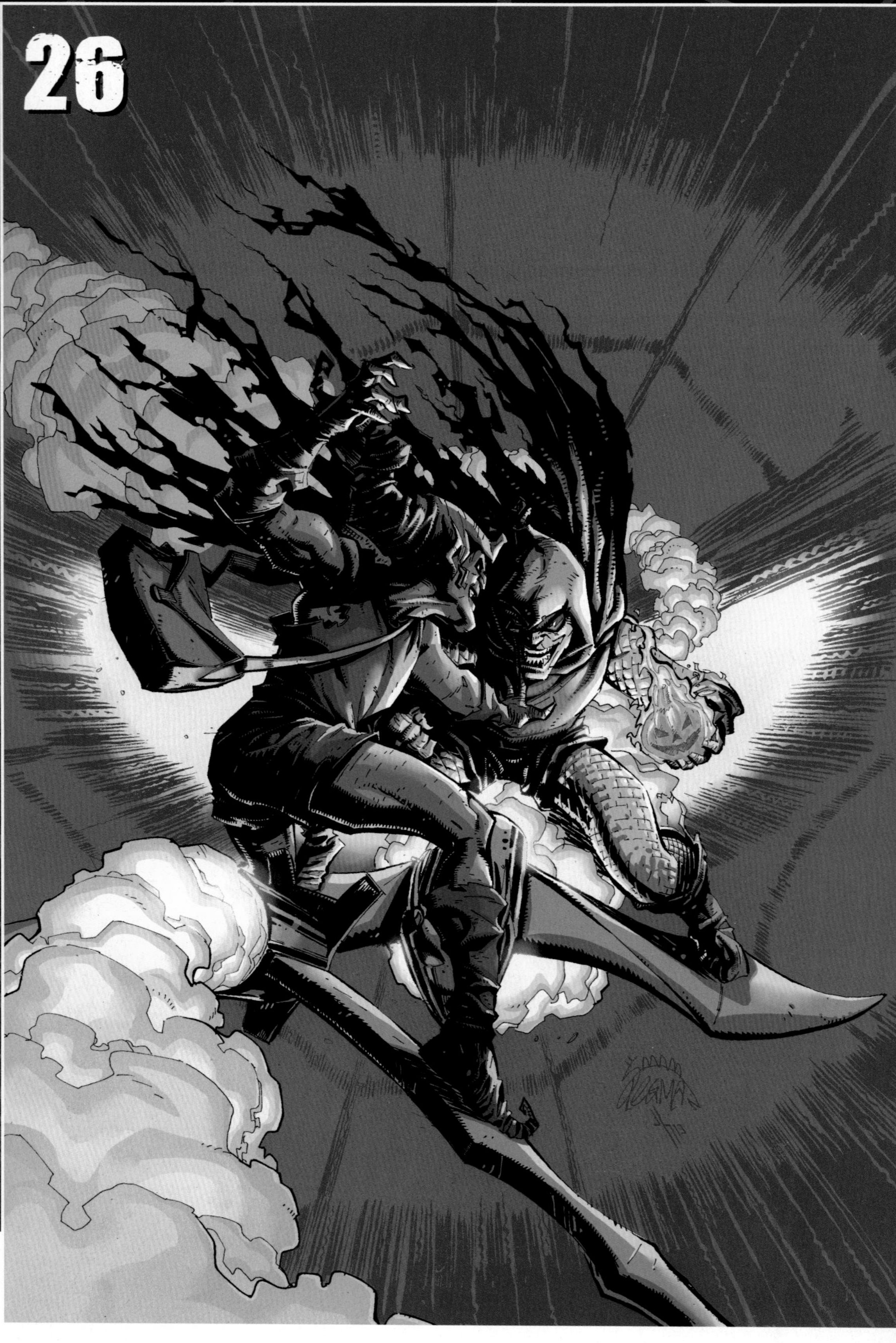
26

GOBLIN NATION PRELUDE: THE ARENA

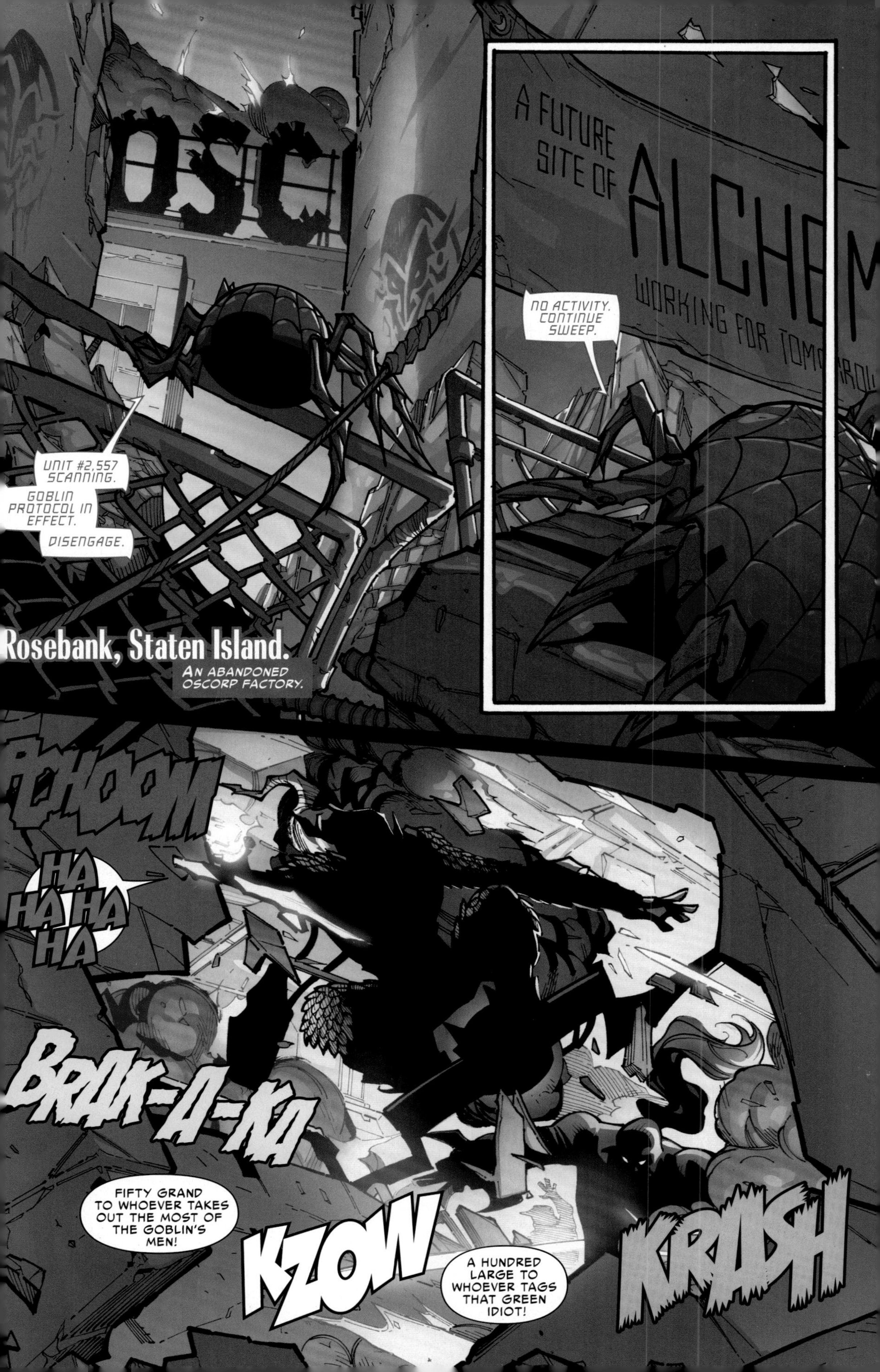

OSC
A FUTURE SITE OF ALCHEM
WORKING FOR TOMORROW
Rosebank, Staten Island.
AN ABANDONED OSCORP FACTORY.
UNIT #2,557 SCANNING.
GOBLIN PROTOCOL IN EFFECT.
DISENGAGE.
NO ACTIVITY. CONTINUE SWEEP.
FCHOOM
HA HA HA HA HA
BRAK-A-KA
FIFTY GRAND TO WHOEVER TAKES OUT THE MOST OF THE GOBLIN'S MEN!
KZOW
A HUNDRED LARGE TO WHOEVER TAGS THAT GREEN IDIOT!
KRASH

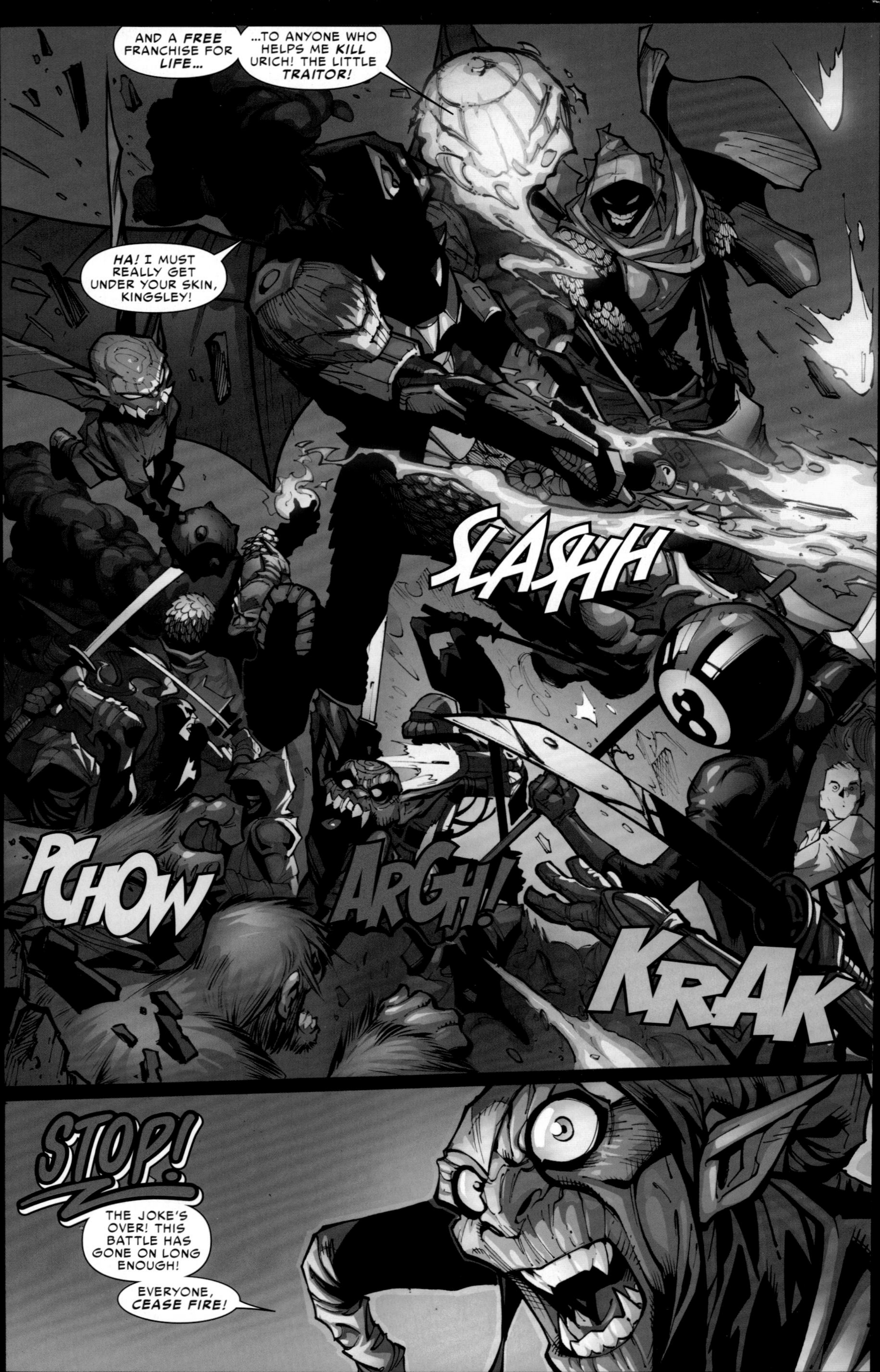

AND A FREE FRANCHISE FOR LIFE...
...TO ANYONE WHO HELPS ME KILL URICH! THE LITTLE TRAITOR!
HA! I MUST REALLY GET UNDER YOUR SKIN, KINGSLEY!
SLASHH
PCHOW
ARGH!
KRAK
STOP!
THE JOKE'S OVER! THIS BATTLE HAS GONE ON LONG ENOUGH!
EVERYONE, CEASE FIRE!

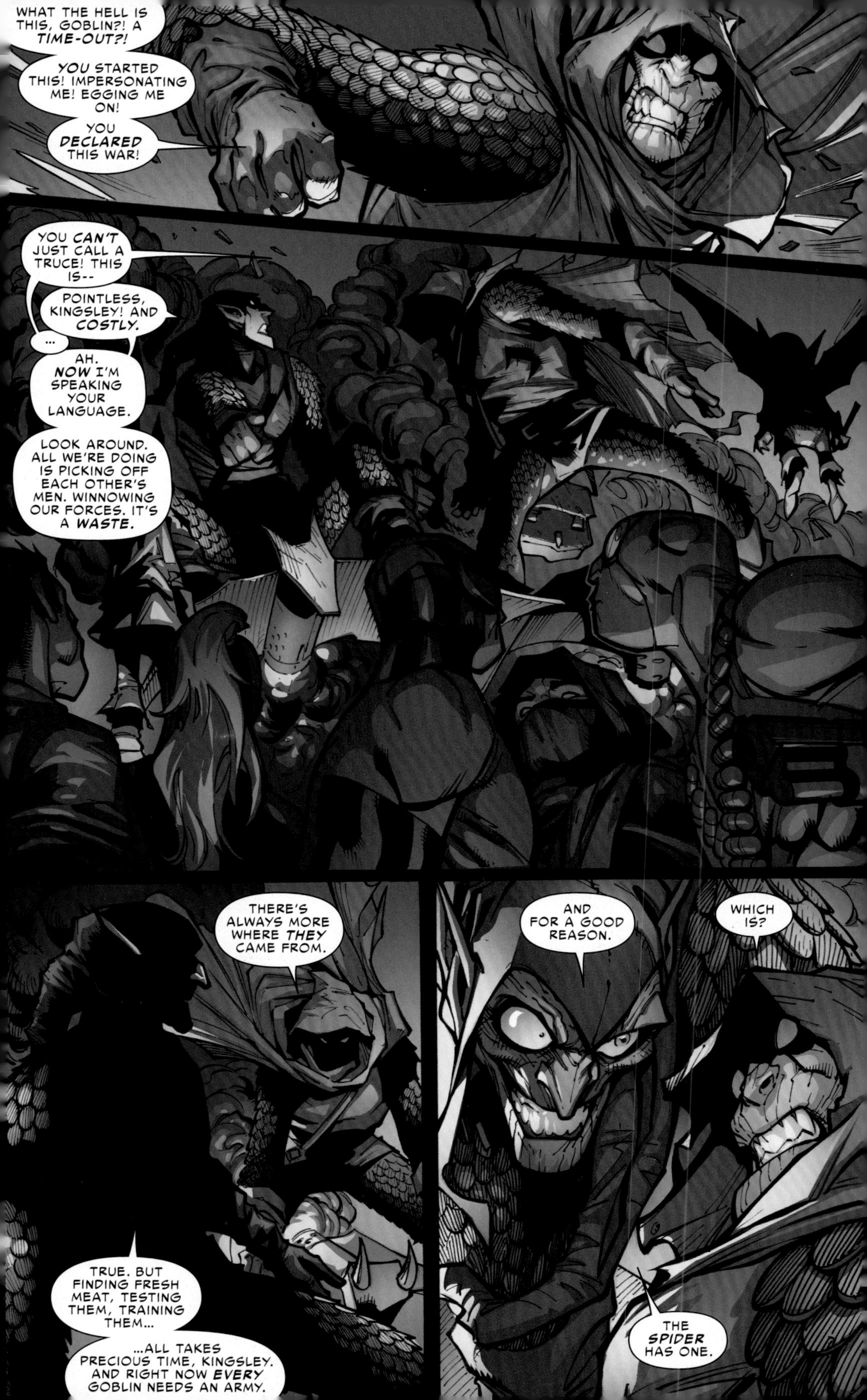
WHAT THE HELL IS THIS, GOBLIN?! A *TIME-OUT?!*
YOU STARTED THIS! IMPERSONATING ME! EGGING ME ON!
YOU *DECLARED* THIS WAR!
YOU *CAN'T* JUST CALL A TRUCE! THIS IS--
POINTLESS, KINGSLEY! AND *COSTLY.*
...
AH. *NOW* I'M SPEAKING YOUR LANGUAGE.
LOOK AROUND. ALL WE'RE DOING IS PICKING OFF EACH OTHER'S MEN. WINNOWING OUR FORCES. IT'S A *WASTE.*
THERE'S ALWAYS MORE WHERE *THEY* CAME FROM.
TRUE. BUT FINDING FRESH MEAT, TESTING THEM, TRAINING THEM...
...ALL TAKES PRECIOUS TIME, KINGSLEY. AND RIGHT NOW *EVERY* GOBLIN NEEDS AN ARMY.
AND FOR A GOOD REASON.
WHICH IS?
THE *SPIDER* HAS ONE.

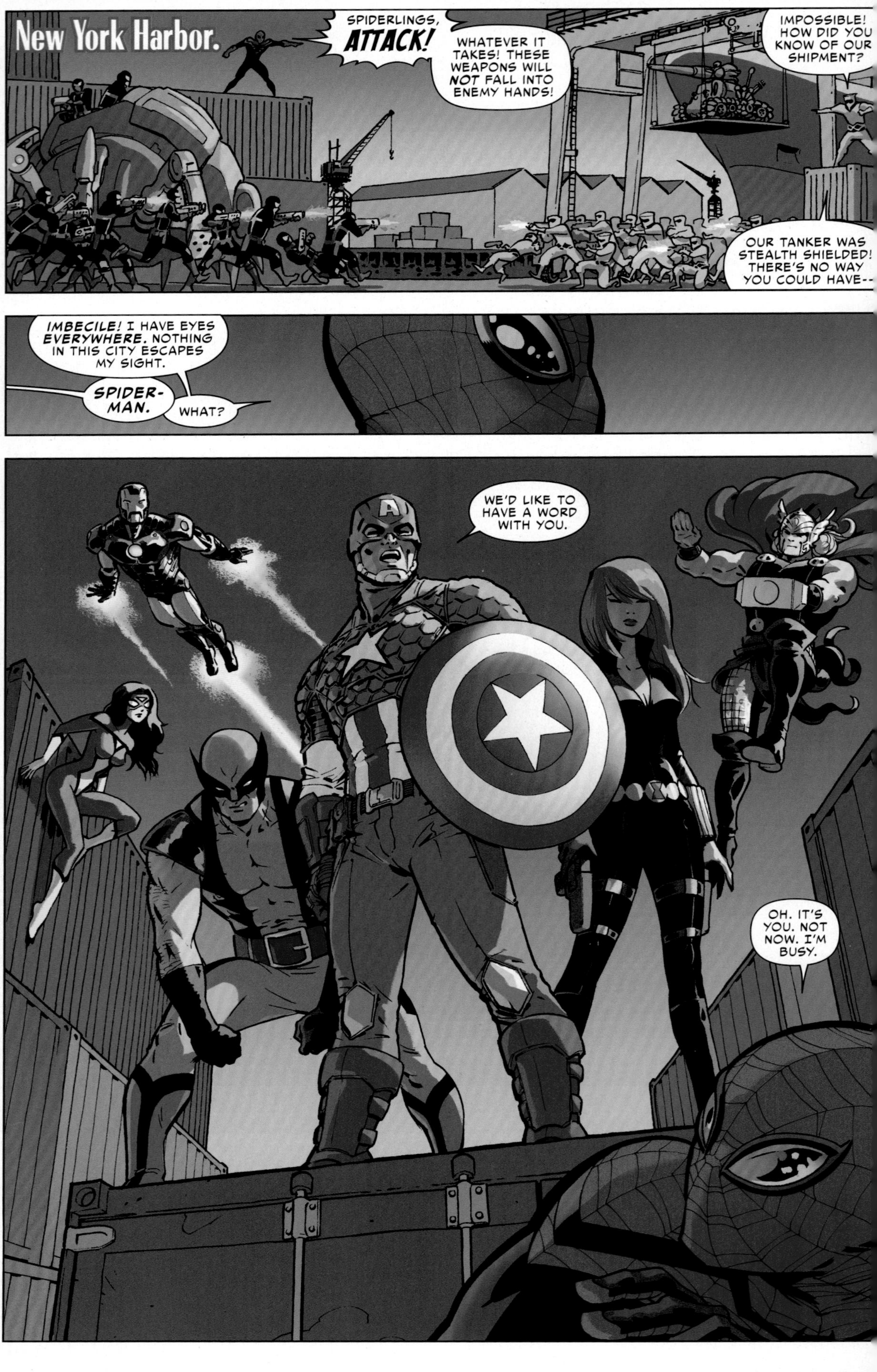
New York Harbor.
SPIDERLINGS, ATTACK!
WHATEVER IT TAKES! THESE WEAPONS WILL NOT FALL INTO ENEMY HANDS!
IMPOSSIBLE! HOW DID YOU KNOW OF OUR SHIPMENT?
OUR TANKER WAS STEALTH SHIELDED! THERE'S NO WAY YOU COULD HAVE--
IMBECILE! I HAVE EYES EVERYWHERE. NOTHING IN THIS CITY ESCAPES MY SIGHT.
SPIDER-MAN.
WHAT?
WE'D LIKE TO HAVE A WORD WITH YOU.
OH. IT'S YOU. NOT NOW. I'M BUSY.

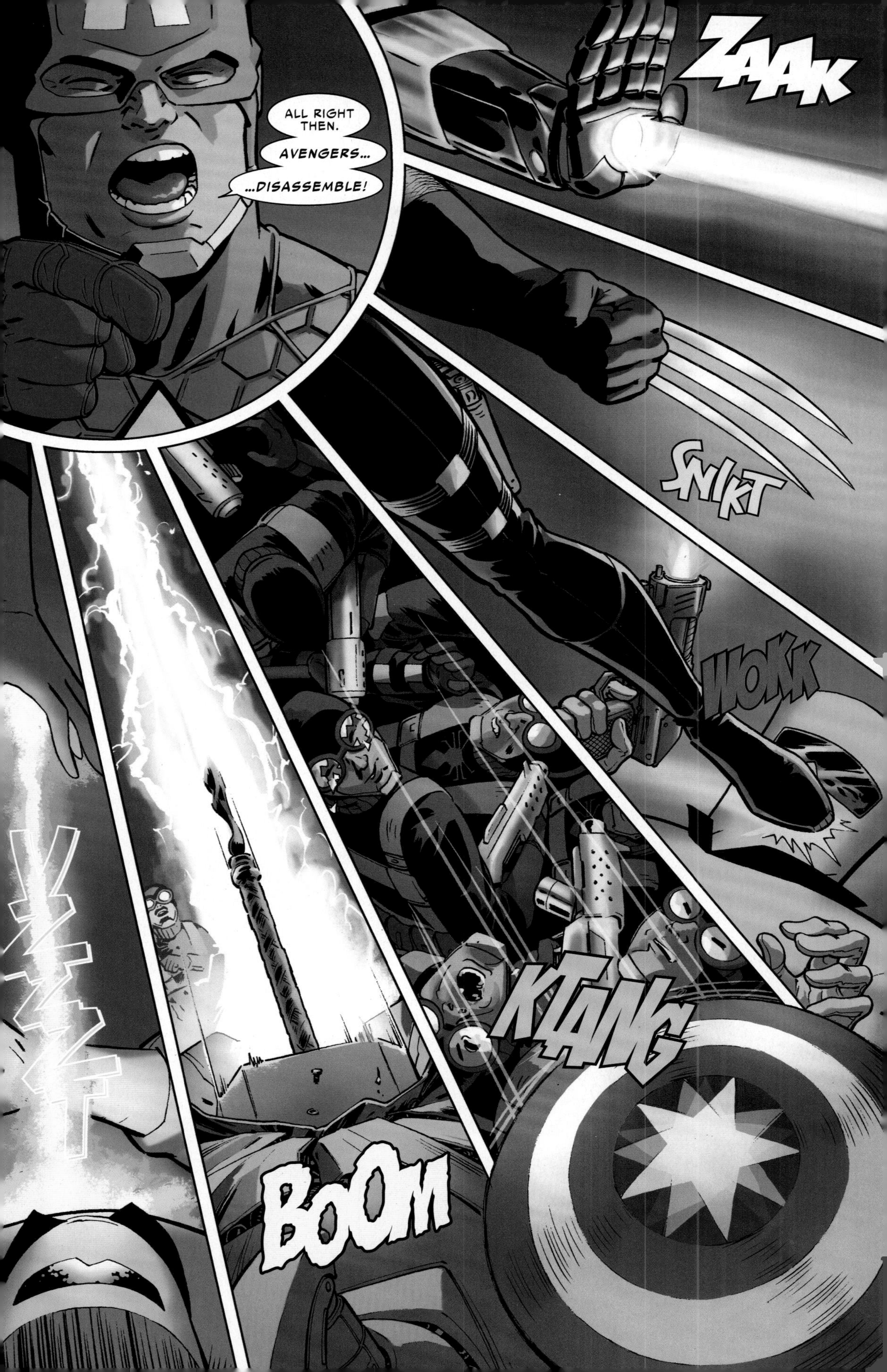
ALL RIGHT THEN.
AVENGERS...
...DISASSEMBLE!
ZAAAK
SNIKT
WOKK
KLANG
VZZZT
BOOM

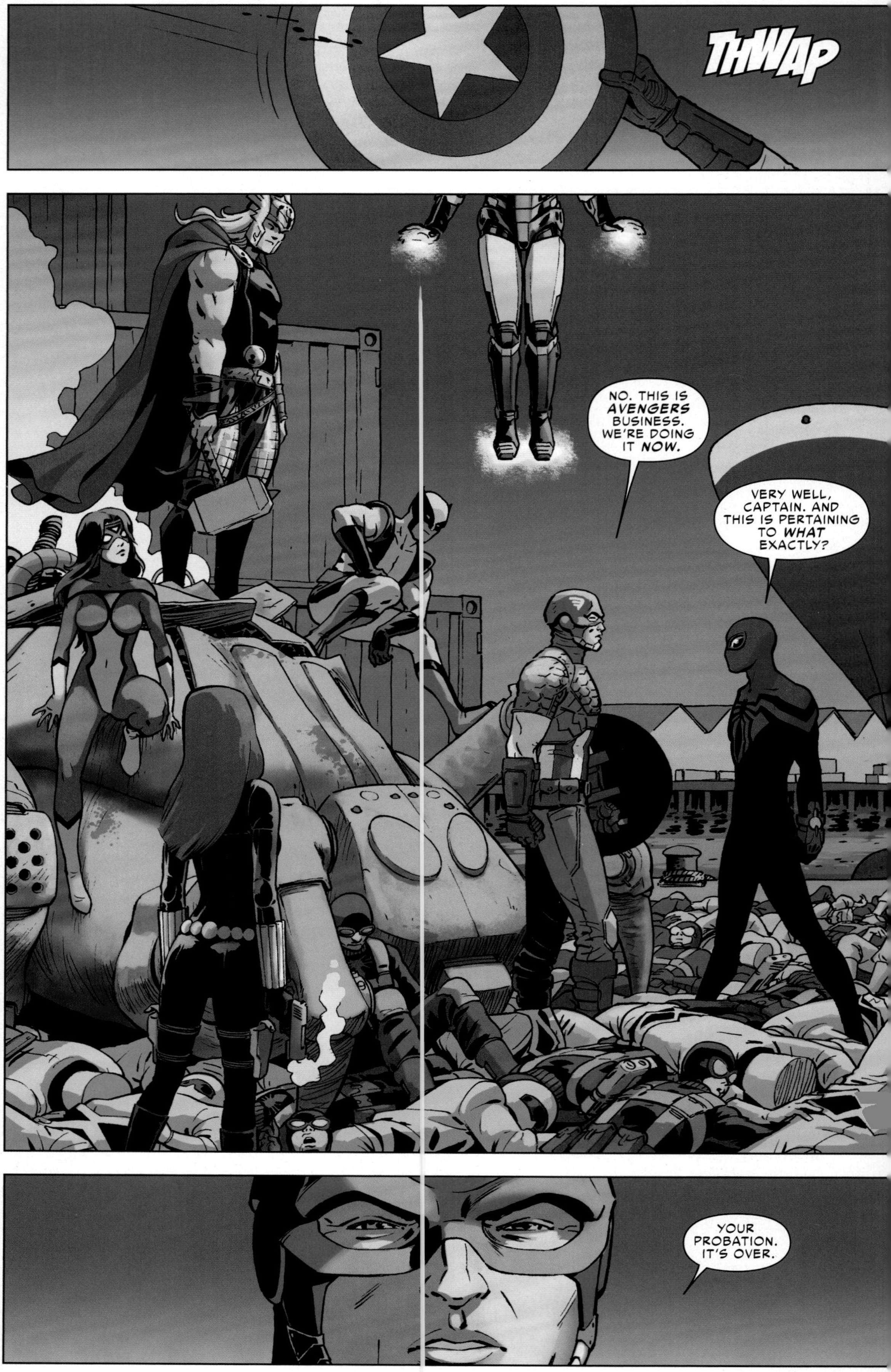
THWAP
NO. THIS IS AVENGERS BUSINESS. WE'RE DOING IT NOW.
VERY WELL, CAPTAIN. AND THIS IS PERTAINING TO WHAT EXACTLY?
YOUR PROBATION. IT'S OVER.

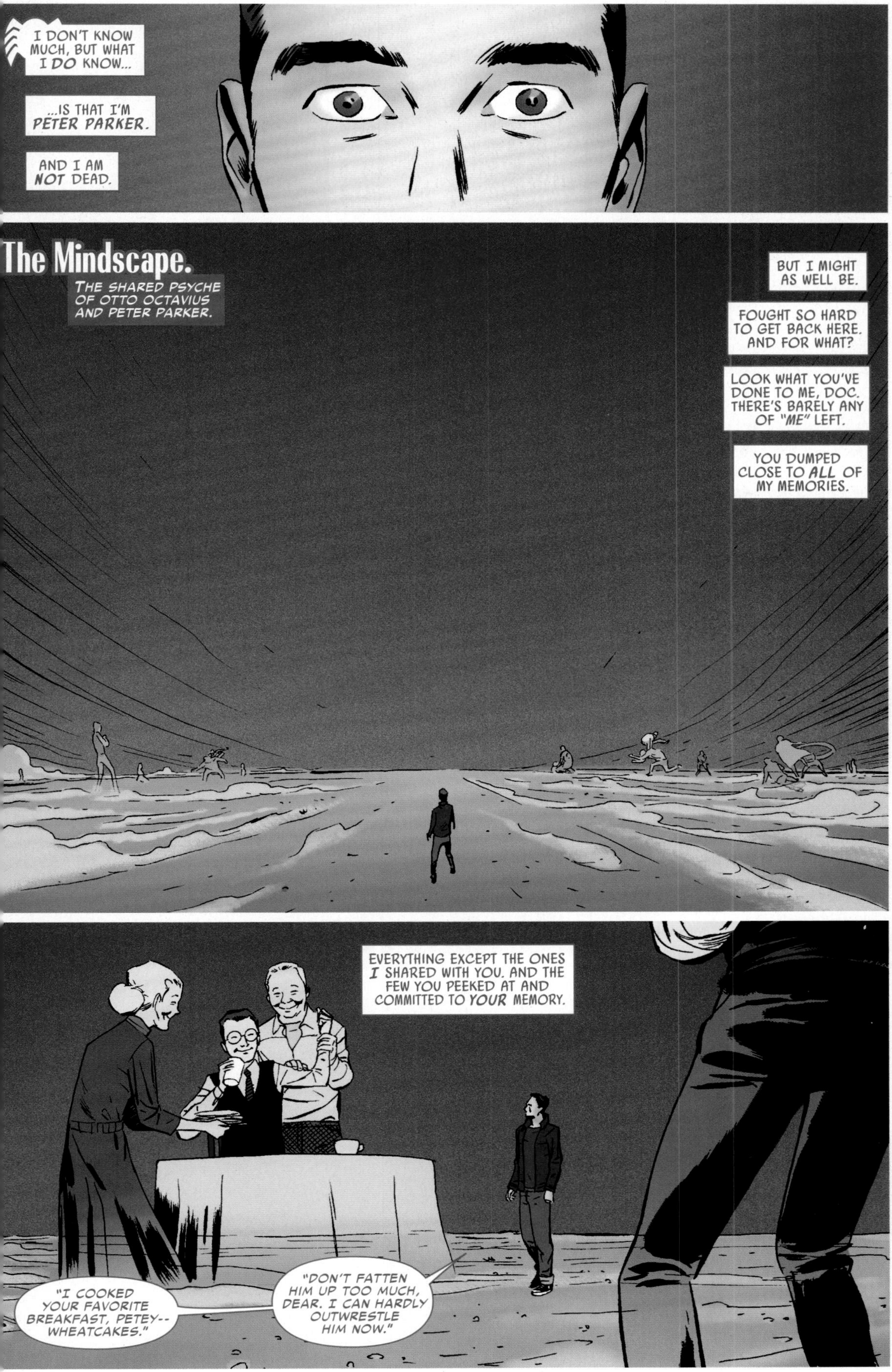
I DON'T KNOW MUCH, BUT WHAT I DO KNOW...
...IS THAT I'M PETER PARKER.
AND I AM NOT DEAD.
The Mindscape.
THE SHARED PSYCHE OF OTTO OCTAVIUS AND PETER PARKER.
BUT I MIGHT AS WELL BE.
FOUGHT SO HARD TO GET BACK HERE. AND FOR WHAT?
LOOK WHAT YOU'VE DONE TO ME, DOC. THERE'S BARELY ANY OF "ME" LEFT.
YOU DUMPED CLOSE TO ALL OF MY MEMORIES.
EVERYTHING EXCEPT THE ONES I SHARED WITH YOU. AND THE FEW YOU PEEKED AT AND COMMITTED TO YOUR MEMORY.
"I COOKED YOUR FAVORITE BREAKFAST, PETEY-- WHEATCAKES."
"DON'T FATTEN HIM UP TOO MUCH, DEAR. I CAN HARDLY OUTWRESTLE HIM NOW."

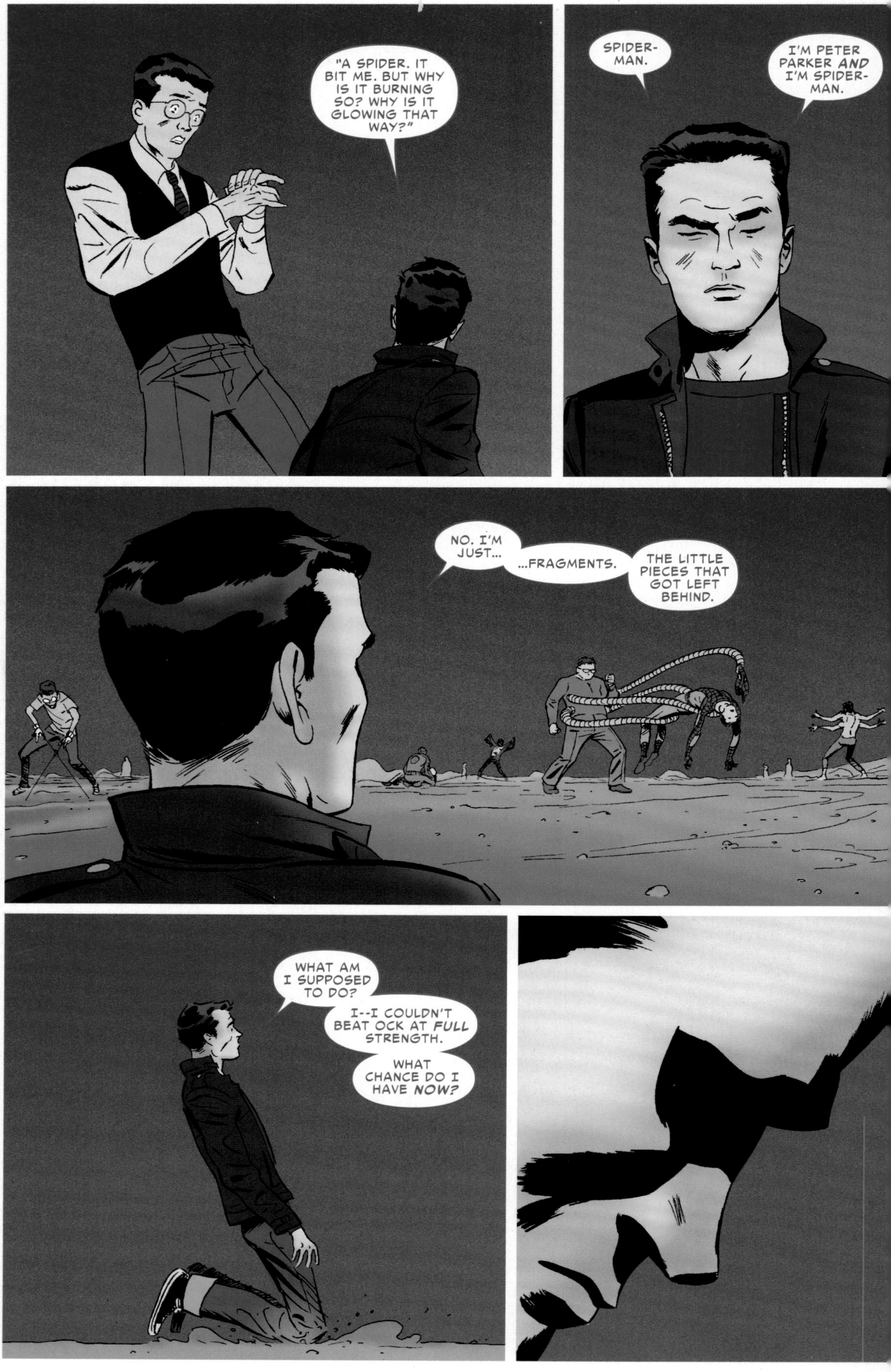
"A SPIDER. IT BIT ME. BUT WHY IS IT BURNING SO? WHY IS IT GLOWING THAT WAY?"
SPIDER-MAN.
I'M PETER PARKER AND I'M SPIDER-MAN.
NO. I'M JUST...
...FRAGMENTS.
THE LITTLE PIECES THAT GOT LEFT BEHIND.
WHAT AM I SUPPOSED TO DO?
I--I COULDN'T BEAT OCK AT FULL STRENGTH.
WHAT CHANCE DO I HAVE NOW?

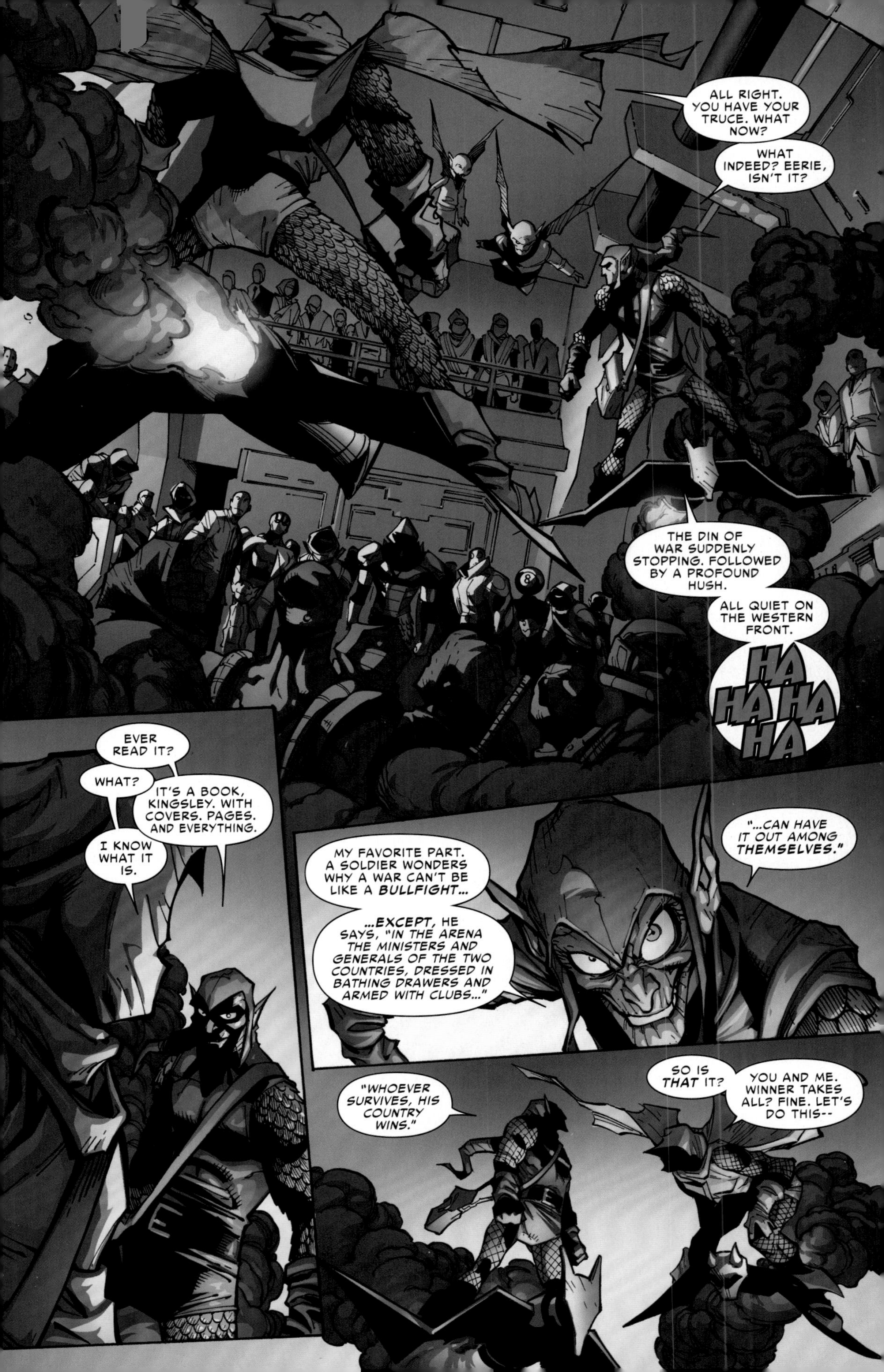
ALL RIGHT. YOU HAVE YOUR TRUCE. WHAT NOW?
WHAT INDEED? EERIE, ISN'T IT?
THE DIN OF WAR SUDDENLY STOPPING. FOLLOWED BY A PROFOUND HUSH.
ALL QUIET ON THE WESTERN FRONT.
HA HA HA HA
EVER READ IT?
WHAT?
IT'S A BOOK, KINGSLEY. WITH COVERS. PAGES. AND EVERYTHING.
I KNOW WHAT IT IS.
MY FAVORITE PART. A SOLDIER WONDERS WHY A WAR CAN'T BE LIKE A BULLFIGHT...
...EXCEPT, HE SAYS, "IN THE ARENA THE MINISTERS AND GENERALS OF THE TWO COUNTRIES, DRESSED IN BATHING DRAWERS AND ARMED WITH CLUBS..."
"...CAN HAVE IT OUT AMONG THEMSELVES."
"WHOEVER SURVIVES, HIS COUNTRY WINS."
SO IS THAT IT?
YOU AND ME. WINNER TAKES ALL? FINE. LET'S DO THIS--

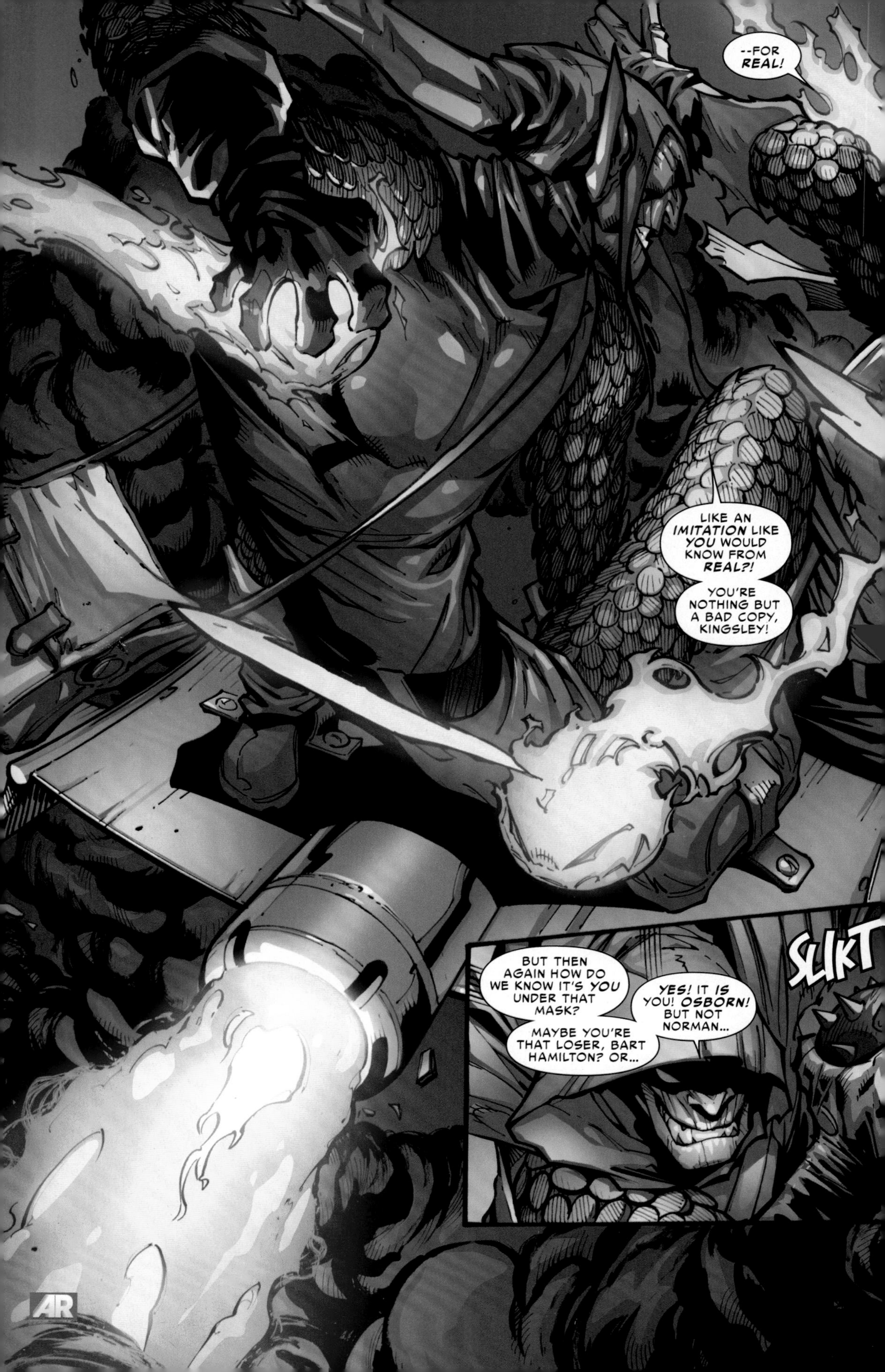
--FOR REAL!
LIKE AN IMITATION LIKE YOU WOULD KNOW FROM REAL?!
YOU'RE NOTHING BUT A BAD COPY, KINGSLEY!
SLIKT
BUT THEN AGAIN HOW DO WE KNOW IT'S YOU UNDER THAT MASK?
MAYBE YOU'RE THAT LOSER, BART HAMILTON? OR...
YES! IT IS YOU! OSBORN! BUT NOT NORMAN...

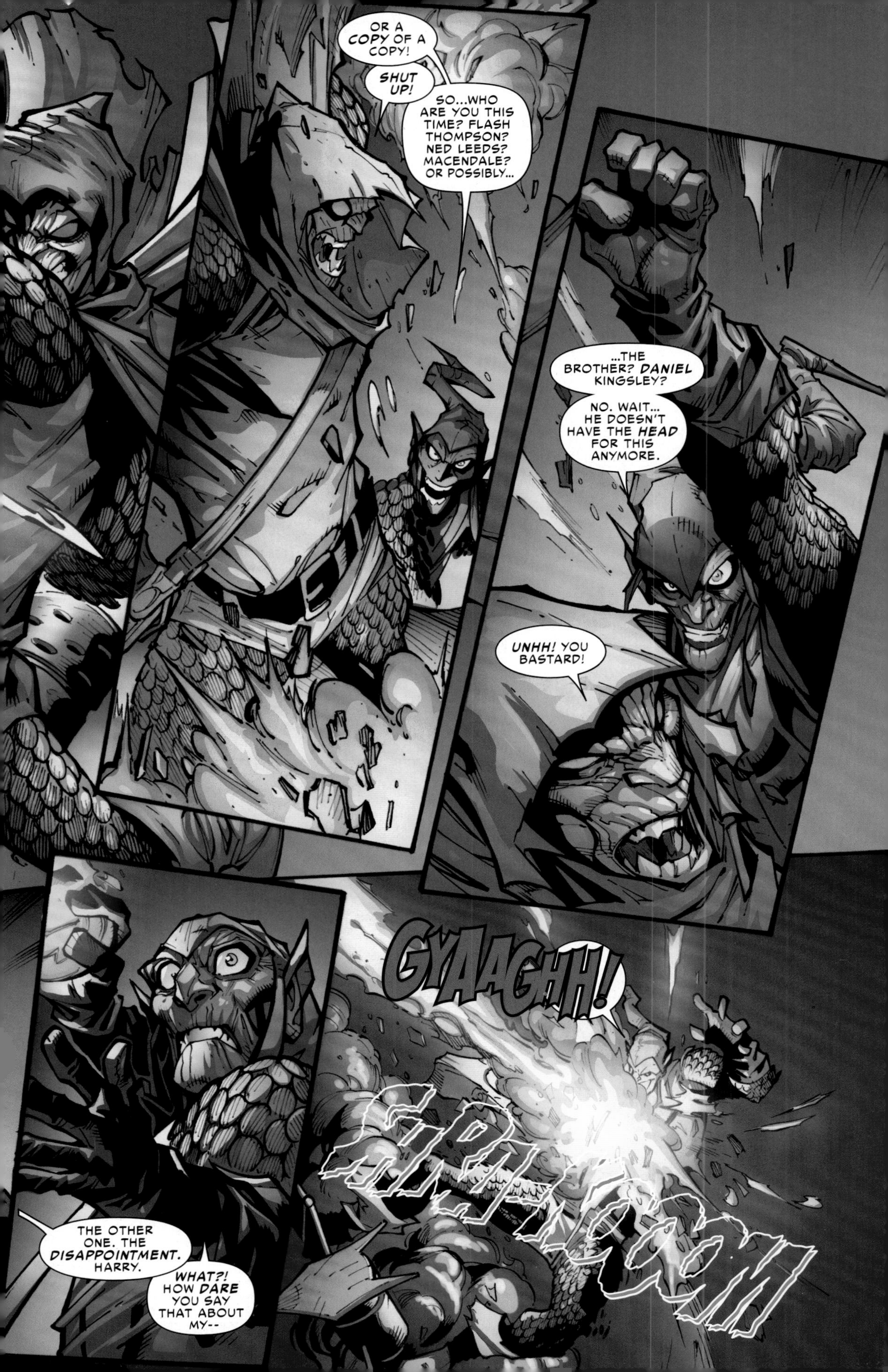
OR A COPY OF A COPY!
SHUT UP!
SO...WHO ARE YOU THIS TIME? FLASH THOMPSON? NED LEEDS? MACENDALE? OR POSSIBLY...
...THE BROTHER? DANIEL KINGSLEY?
NO. WAIT... HE DOESN'T HAVE THE HEAD FOR THIS ANYMORE.
UNHH! YOU BASTARD!
THE OTHER ONE. THE DISAPPOINTMENT. HARRY.
WHAT?! HOW DARE YOU SAY THAT ABOUT MY--
GYAAGHH!

Avengers Tower.

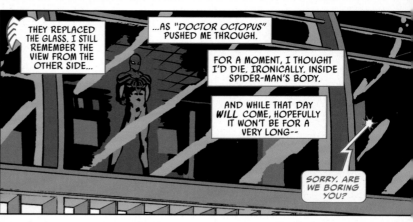

THEY REPLACED THE GLASS. I STILL REMEMBER THE VIEW FROM THE OTHER SIDE...

...AS "DOCTOR OCTOPUS" PUSHED ME THROUGH.

FOR A MOMENT, I THOUGHT I'D DIE. IRONICALLY. INSIDE SPIDER-MAN'S BODY.

AND WHILE THAT DAY *WILL* COME, HOPEFULLY IT WON'T BE FOR A VERY LONG--

SORRY. ARE WE BORING YOU?

WHAT?

WITH ALL THE CHARGES WE'RE RAISING...

...FOR DRUMMING YOU OUT OF THE AVENGERS.

NO. PLEASE CONTINUE. YOU HAVE MY WELL-DESERVE ATTENTION.

SINCE RETURNING TO EARTH, I'VE GONE THROUGH ALL OF THE TOWER'S SECURITY FOOTAGE...

...AND FOUND THIS. EVIDENCE OF YOU SECRETLY DELETING YOUR MEDICAL SCANS.

CARE TO EXPLAIN WHY YOU'D DO THAT?

SIMPLE. UNDER ENOUGH SCRUTINY, THOSE SCANS COULD REVEAL...

...MY SECRET IDENTITY.

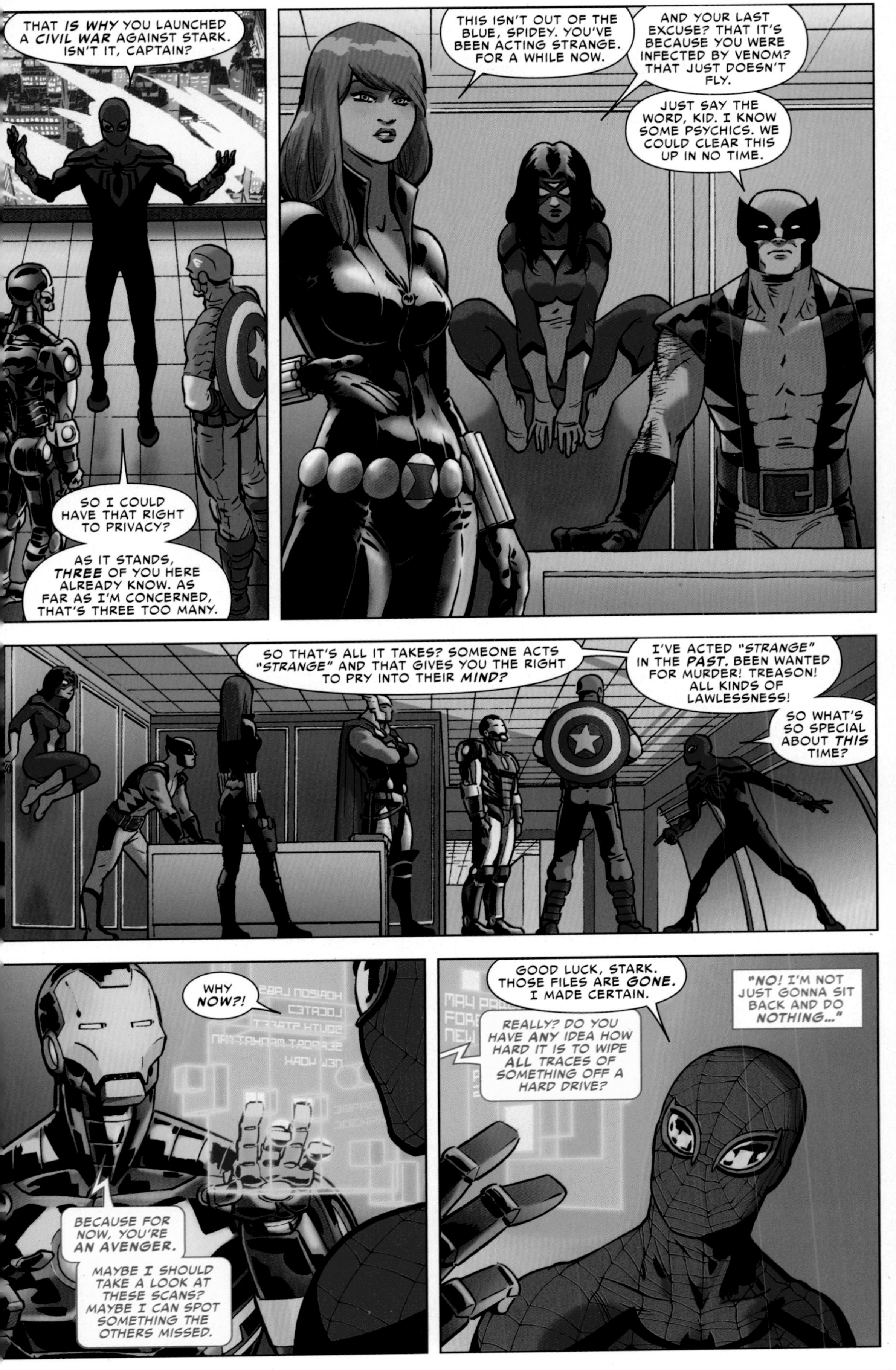

THAT IS WHY YOU LAUNCHED A CIVIL WAR AGAINST STARK. ISN'T IT, CAPTAIN?
SO I COULD HAVE THAT RIGHT TO PRIVACY?
AS IT STANDS, THREE OF YOU HERE ALREADY KNOW. AS FAR AS I'M CONCERNED, THAT'S THREE TOO MANY.
THIS ISN'T OUT OF THE BLUE, SPIDEY. YOU'VE BEEN ACTING STRANGE. FOR A WHILE NOW.
AND YOUR LAST EXCUSE? THAT IT'S BECAUSE YOU WERE INFECTED BY VENOM? THAT JUST DOESN'T FLY.
JUST SAY THE WORD, KID. I KNOW SOME PSYCHICS. WE COULD CLEAR THIS UP IN NO TIME.
SO THAT'S ALL IT TAKES? SOMEONE ACTS "STRANGE" AND THAT GIVES YOU THE RIGHT TO PRY INTO THEIR MIND?
I'VE ACTED "STRANGE" IN THE PAST. BEEN WANTED FOR MURDER! TREASON! ALL KINDS OF LAWLESSNESS!
SO WHAT'S SO SPECIAL ABOUT THIS TIME?
WHY NOW?!
BECAUSE FOR NOW, YOU'RE AN AVENGER.
MAYBE I SHOULD TAKE A LOOK AT THESE SCANS? MAYBE I CAN SPOT SOMETHING THE OTHERS MISSED.
GOOD LUCK, STARK. THOSE FILES ARE GONE. I MADE CERTAIN.
REALLY? DO YOU HAVE ANY IDEA HOW HARD IT IS TO WIPE ALL TRACES OF SOMETHING OFF A HARD DRIVE?
"NO! I'M NOT JUST GONNA SIT BACK AND DO NOTHING..."

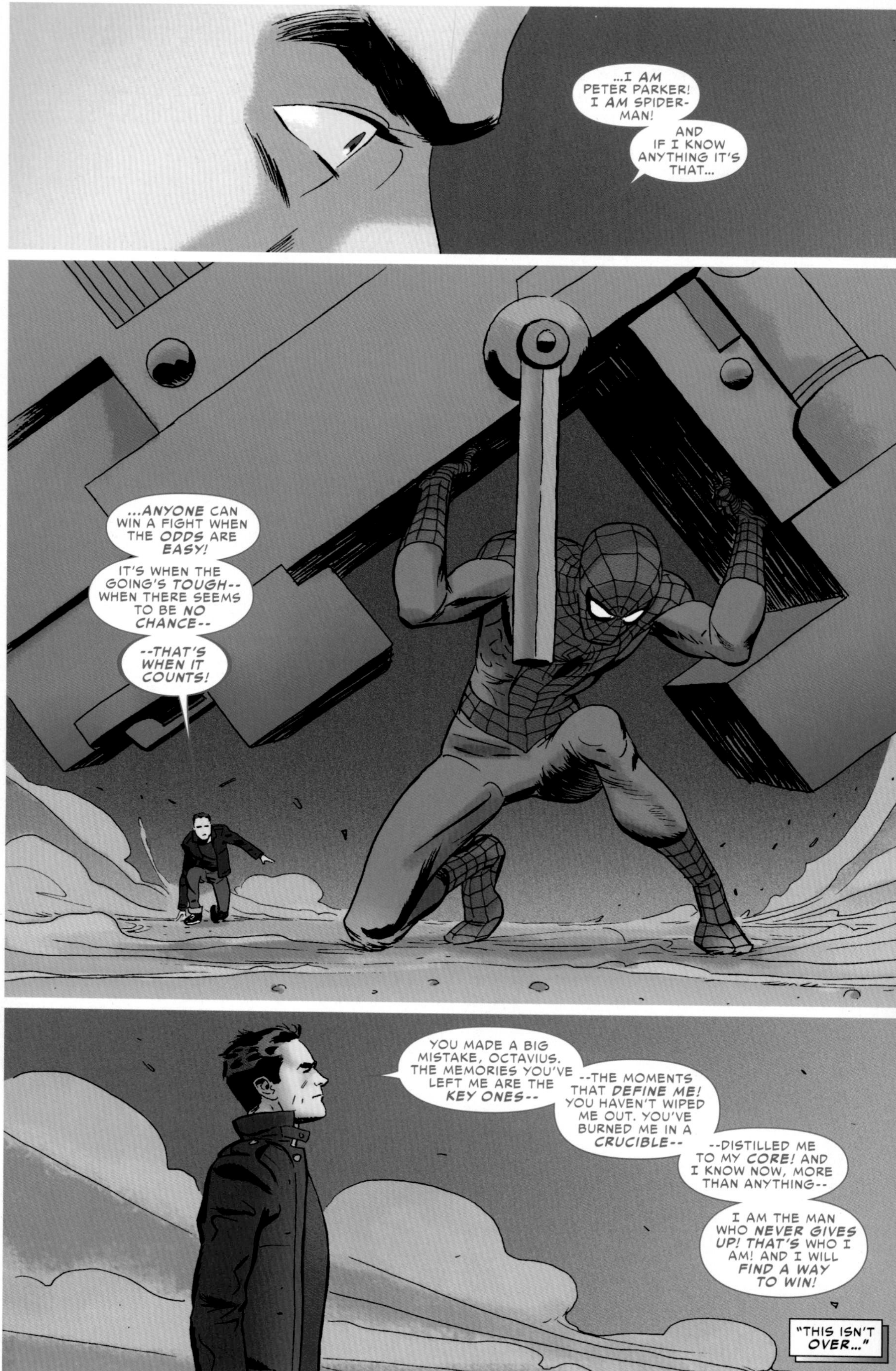
...I AM PETER PARKER! I AM SPIDER-MAN!
AND IF I KNOW ANYTHING IT'S THAT...
...ANYONE CAN WIN A FIGHT WHEN THE ODDS ARE EASY!
IT'S WHEN THE GOING'S TOUGH-- WHEN THERE SEEMS TO BE NO CHANCE--
--THAT'S WHEN IT COUNTS!
YOU MADE A BIG MISTAKE, OCTAVIUS. THE MEMORIES YOU'VE LEFT ME ARE THE KEY ONES--
--THE MOMENTS THAT DEFINE ME! YOU HAVEN'T WIPED ME OUT. YOU'VE BURNED ME IN A CRUCIBLE--
--DISTILLED ME TO MY CORE! AND I KNOW NOW, MORE THAN ANYTHING--
I AM THE MAN WHO NEVER GIVES UP! THAT'S WHO I AM! AND I WILL FIND A WAY TO WIN!
"THIS ISN'T OVER..."

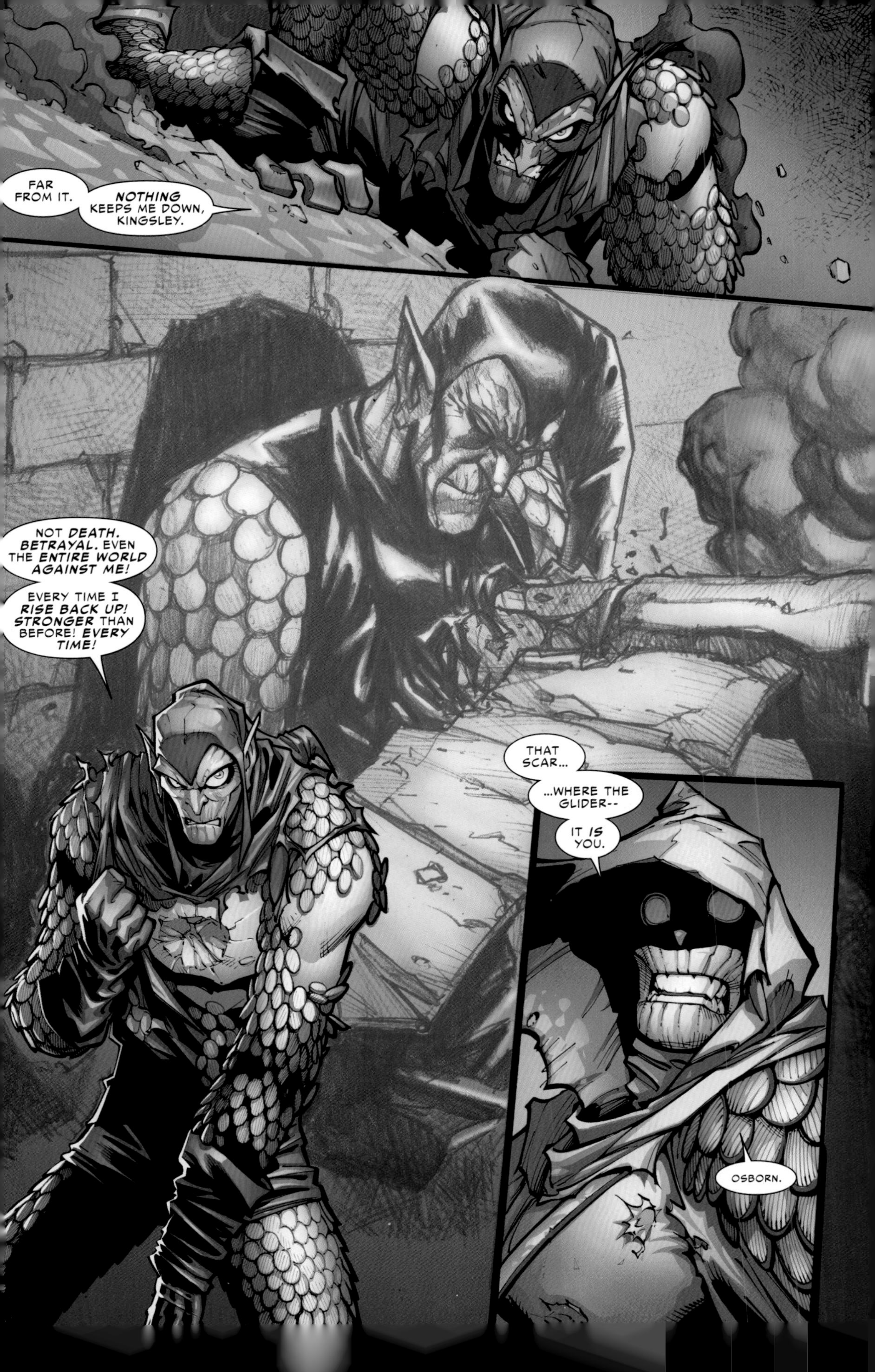
FAR FROM IT.
NOTHING KEEPS ME DOWN, KINGSLEY.
NOT *DEATH*. *BETRAYAL*. EVEN THE *ENTIRE WORLD AGAINST ME!*
EVERY TIME I *RISE BACK UP! STRONGER* THAN BEFORE! *EVERY TIME!*
THAT SCAR...
...WHERE THE GLIDER--
IT *IS* YOU.
OSBORN.

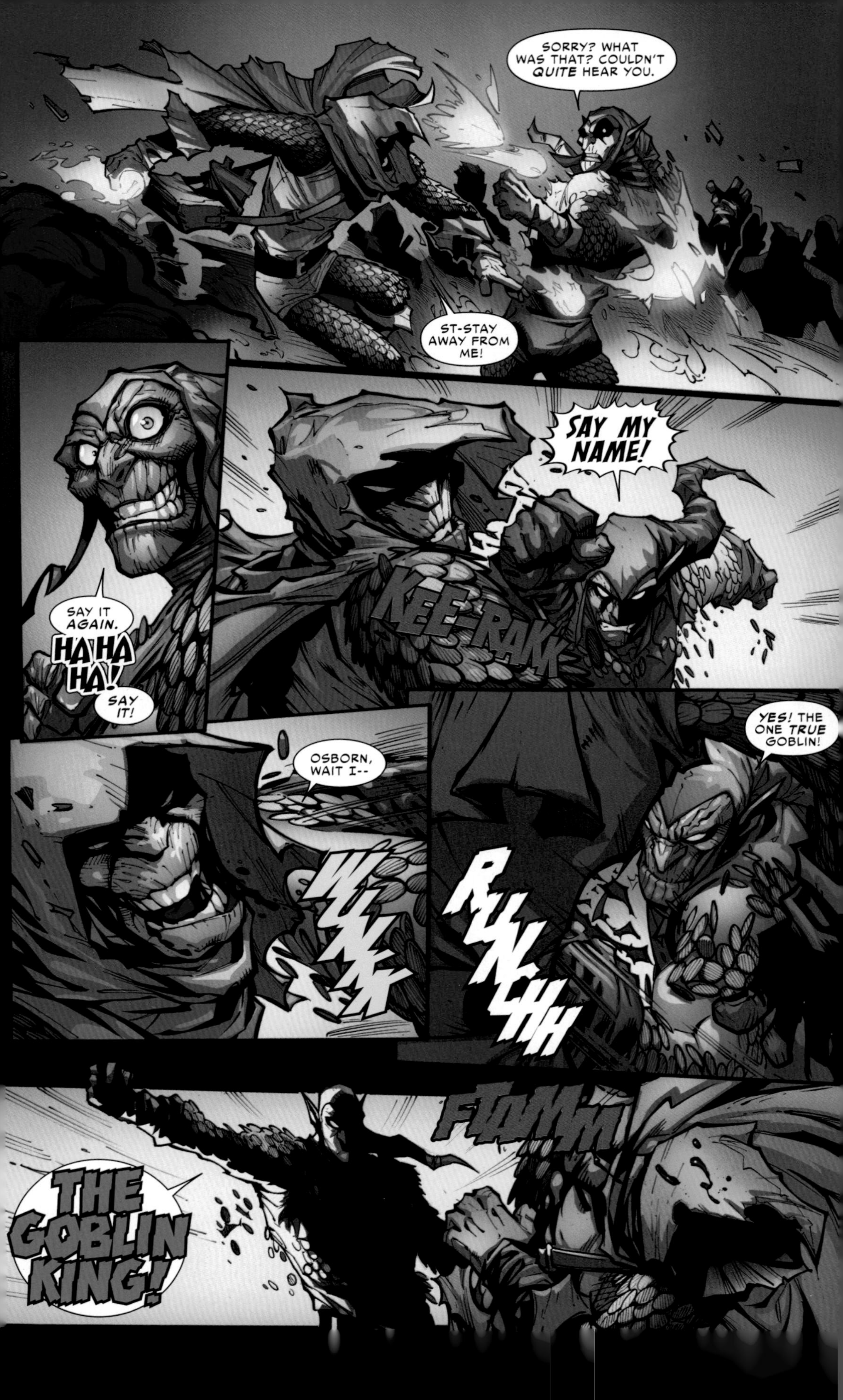
SORRY? WHAT WAS THAT? COULDN'T QUITE HEAR YOU.
ST-STAY AWAY FROM ME!
SAY IT AGAIN. HA HA HA! SAY IT!
SAY MY NAME!
KEE-RAKK
OSBORN, WAIT I--
WUNK
YES! THE ONE TRUE GOBLIN!
RUNCHH
FTOOMM
THE GOBLIN KING!

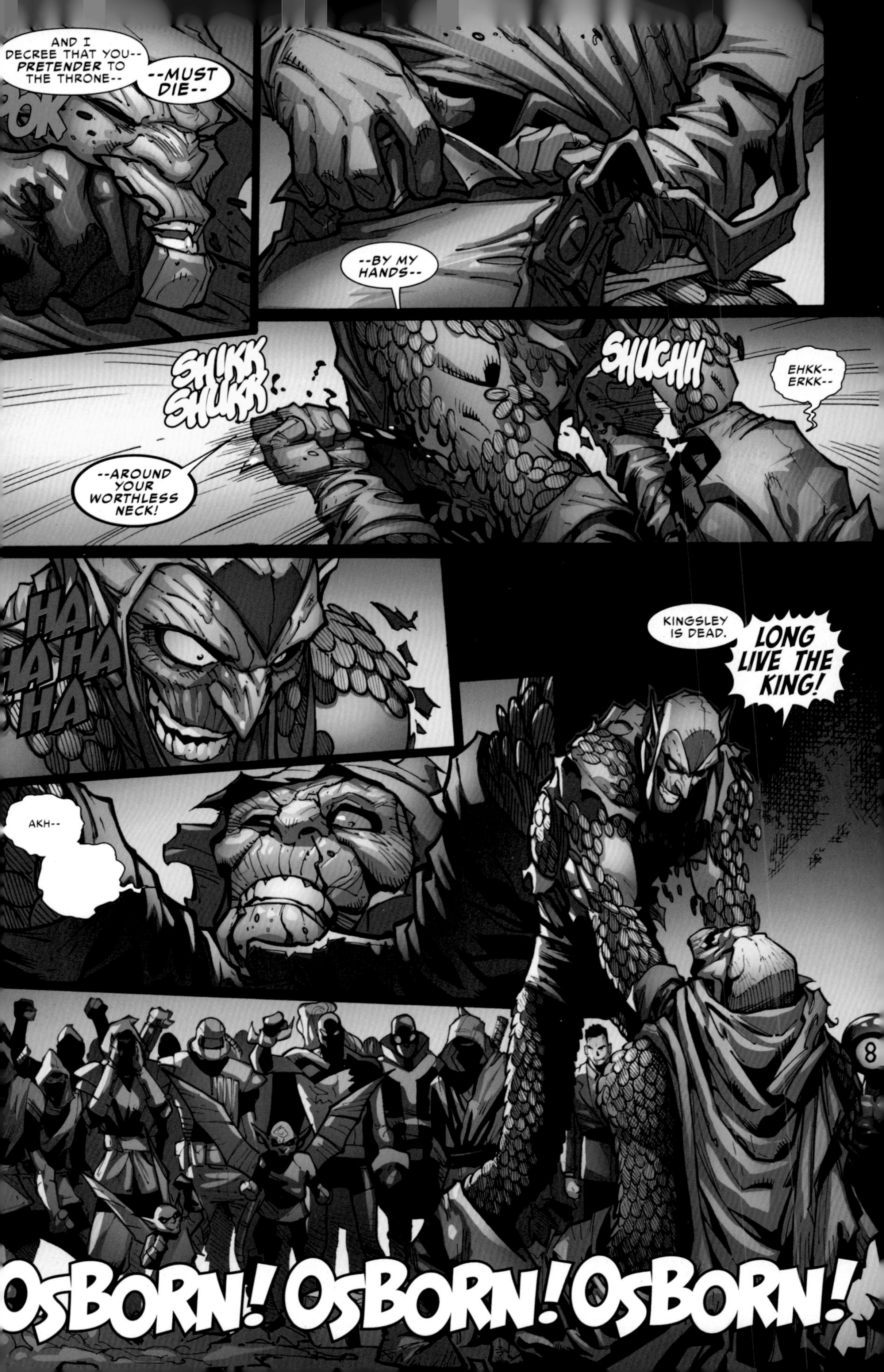
AND I DECREE THAT YOU-- PRETENDER TO THE THRONE--
--MUST DIE--
--BY MY HANDS--
SHIKK SHUKK
SHUCHH
EHKK-- ERKK--
--AROUND YOUR WORTHLESS NECK!
HA HA HA HA HA
KINGSLEY IS DEAD.
LONG LIVE THE KING!
AKH--
OSBORN! OSBORN! OSBORN!

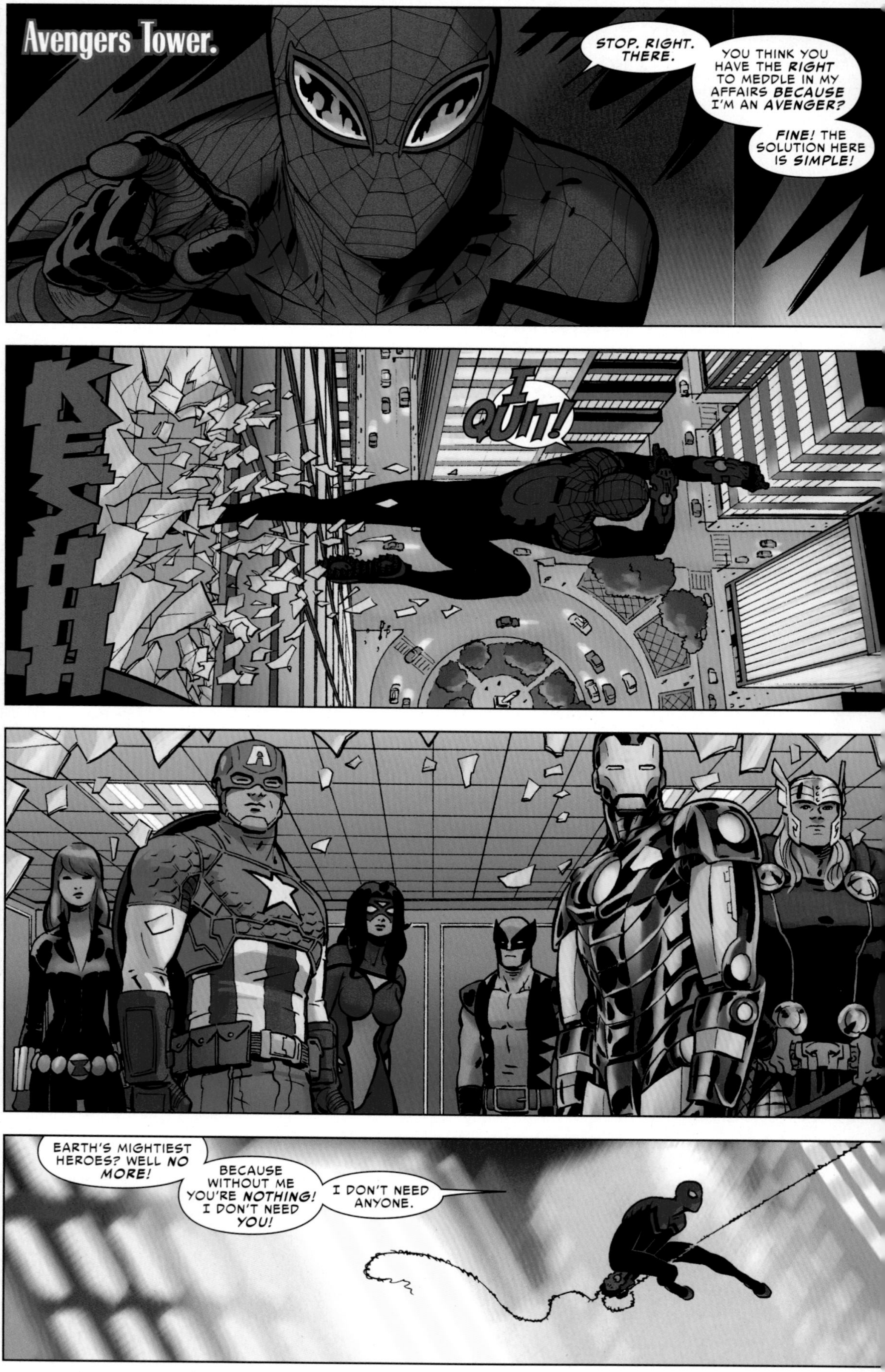
Avengers Tower.
STOP. RIGHT. THERE.
YOU THINK YOU HAVE THE RIGHT TO MEDDLE IN MY AFFAIRS BECAUSE I'M AN AVENGER?
FINE! THE SOLUTION HERE IS SIMPLE!
I QUIT!
EARTH'S MIGHTIEST HEROES? WELL NO MORE!
BECAUSE WITHOUT ME YOU'RE NOTHING! I DON'T NEED YOU!
I DON'T NEED ANYONE.

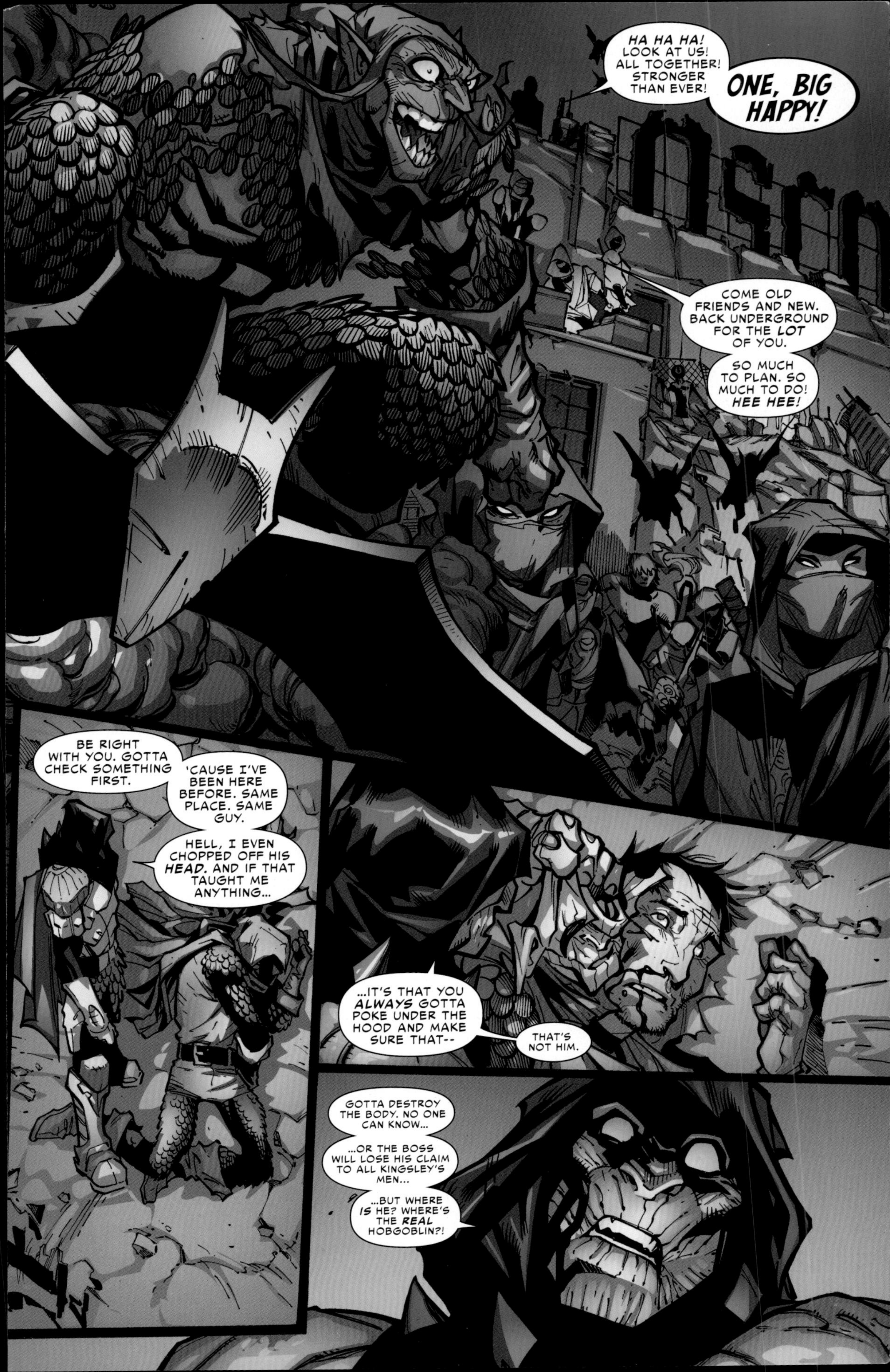
HA HA HA! LOOK AT US! ALL TOGETHER! STRONGER THAN EVER!
ONE, BIG HAPPY!
COME OLD FRIENDS AND NEW. BACK UNDERGROUND FOR THE LOT OF YOU.
SO MUCH TO PLAN. SO MUCH TO DO! HEE HEE!
BE RIGHT WITH YOU. GOTTA CHECK SOMETHING FIRST.
'CAUSE I'VE BEEN HERE BEFORE. SAME PLACE. SAME GUY.
HELL, I EVEN CHOPPED OFF HIS HEAD. AND IF THAT TAUGHT ME ANYTHING...
...IT'S THAT YOU ALWAYS GOTTA POKE UNDER THE HOOD AND MAKE SURE THAT--
THAT'S NOT HIM.
GOTTA DESTROY THE BODY. NO ONE CAN KNOW...
...OR THE BOSS WILL LOSE HIS CLAIM TO ALL KINGSLEY'S MEN...
...BUT WHERE IS HE? WHERE'S THE REAL HOBGOBLIN?!

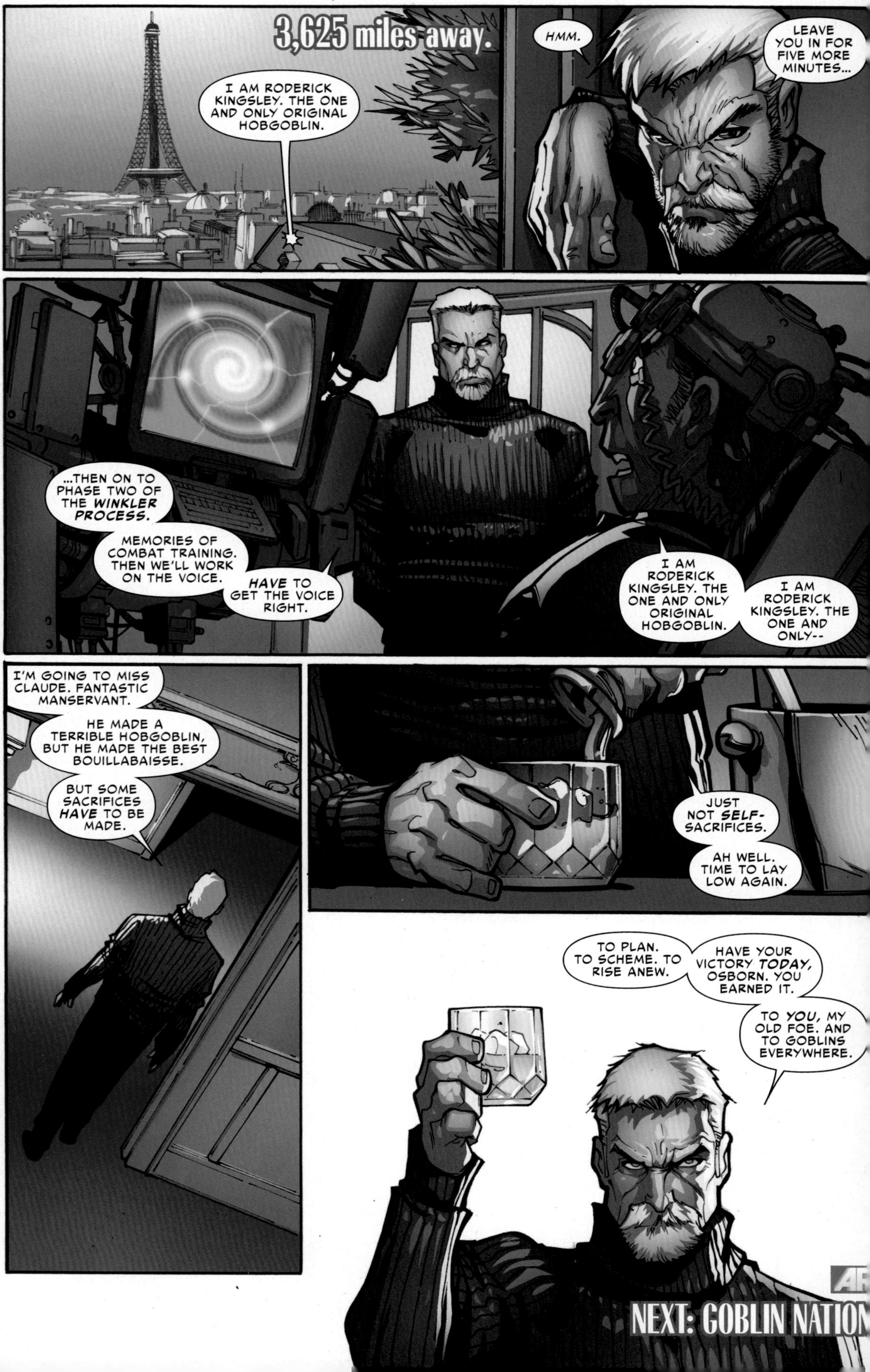
3,625 miles away.
I AM RODERICK KINGSLEY. THE ONE AND ONLY ORIGINAL HOBGOBLIN.
HMM.
LEAVE YOU IN FOR FIVE MORE MINUTES...
...THEN ON TO PHASE TWO OF THE WINKLER PROCESS.
MEMORIES OF COMBAT TRAINING. THEN WE'LL WORK ON THE VOICE.
HAVE TO GET THE VOICE RIGHT.
I AM RODERICK KINGSLEY. THE ONE AND ONLY ORIGINAL HOBGOBLIN.
I AM RODERICK KINGSLEY. THE ONE AND ONLY--
I'M GOING TO MISS CLAUDE. FANTASTIC MANSERVANT.
HE MADE A TERRIBLE HOBGOBLIN, BUT HE MADE THE BEST BOUILLABAISSE.
BUT SOME SACRIFICES HAVE TO BE MADE.
JUST NOT SELF-SACRIFICES.
AH WELL. TIME TO LAY LOW AGAIN.
TO PLAN. TO SCHEME. TO RISE ANEW.
HAVE YOUR VICTORY TODAY, OSBORN. YOU EARNED IT.
TO YOU, MY OLD FOE. AND TO GOBLINS EVERYWHERE.
NEXT: GOBLIN NATION

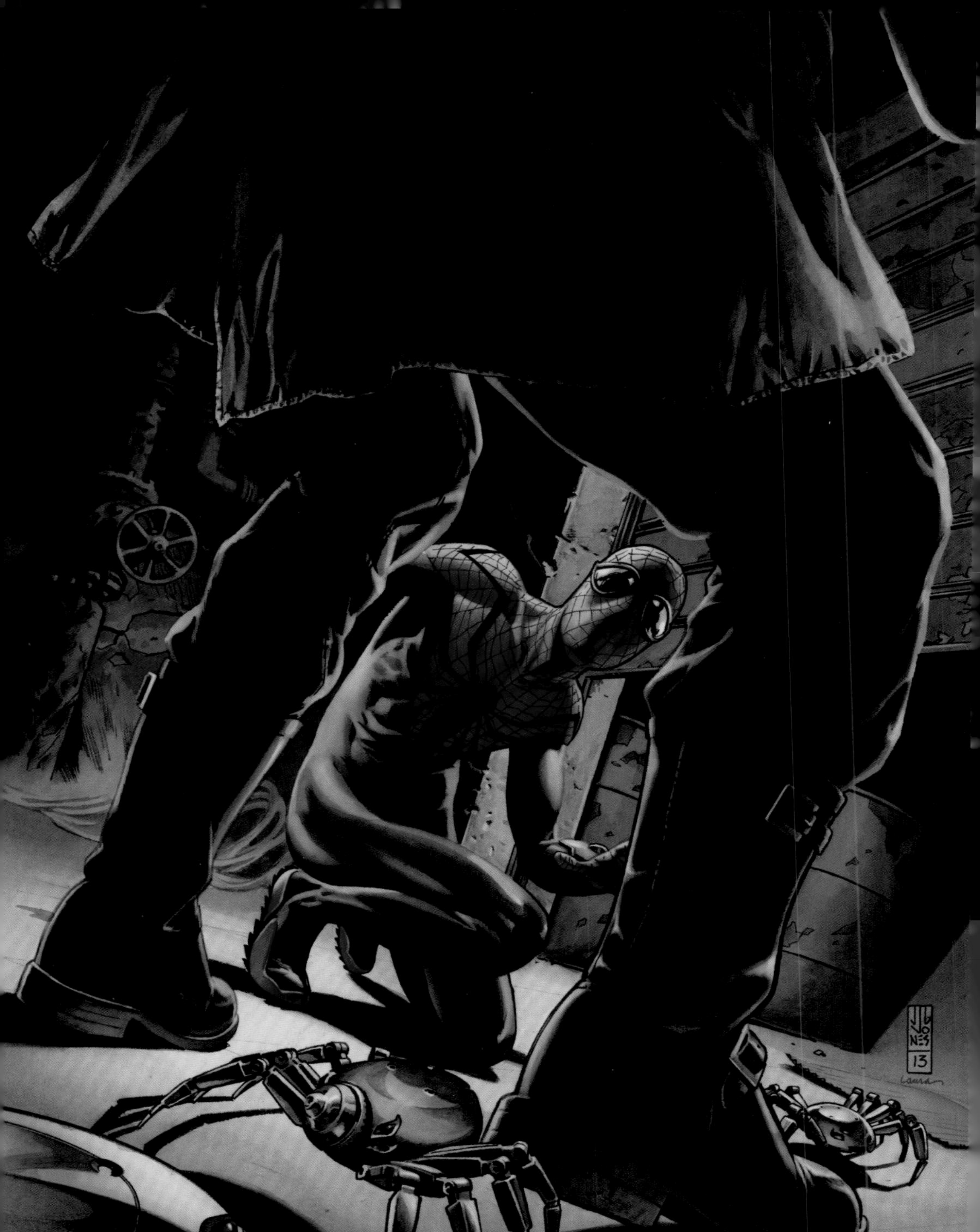

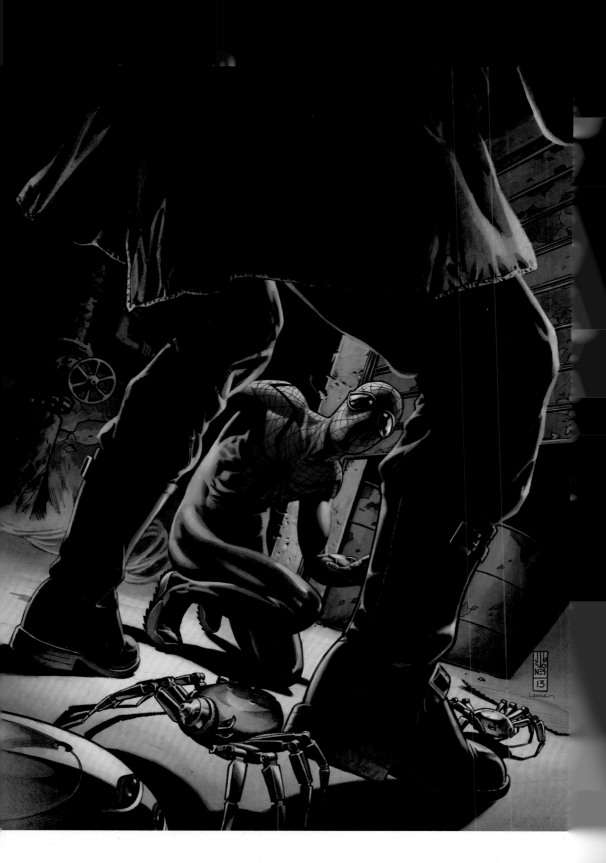

SUPERIOR SPIDER-MAN ANNUAL 1

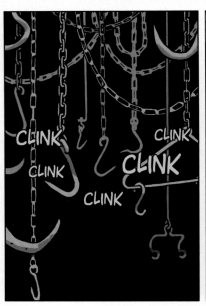

CLINK
CLINK
CLINK
CLINK
CLINK

SO YOU PROBABLY KNOW THE *KINGPIN* WAS WORKING WITH NINJAS LATELY. BUT HE KEPT SOME OF THE GUYS FROM THE OLD DAYS AROUND. LIKE ME.

YOU CAN'T SEND FREAKIN' *NINJAS* TO NEGOTIATE WITH THE *CHICAGO OUTFIT,* KNOW WHAT I'M SAYIN'?

DARK IN HERE.

ANYWAY, A WHILE BACK, MR. FISK GOT SOME DIRT ON *SPIDER-MAN.* Y'KNOW ALL THE TECH HE USES? WEB-SHOOTERS, GOGGLES, THOSE CREEPY ROBOT BUGS?

SOME TEST TUBE JOCKEY NAMED *PETER PARKER* MAKES IT ALL FOR 'IM. AND THAT'S *LEGIT,* 'CAUSE WHEN WE SNATCHED THE KID, SPIDEY CAME RUNNIN'.

NOW, I'M NO SNITCH, OKAY? I'M ONLY TELLIN' YOU 'CAUSE SINCE THE SPIDER WHACKED MR. FISK, I'M OUT OF A JOB.

AND I REMEMBER YOU FROM THE OLD DAYS. TOP-NOTCH BUTTON MAN. YOU DID NICE WORK FOR *THE HOOD.*

SO I KNOW YOU CAN USE THIS, AND YOU'RE GOOD FOR THE DOUGH, WHICH *I* CAN MOST DEFINITELY USE--

HUH?

NEWSPAPER?

REGRETTABLY, I FIND MYSELF UNEMPLOYED AS WELL.

HARD TIMES FOR US ALL.

NO! *WAIT!*

LINK
CLINK
CLINK
CLIN
INK

SHR?TCH

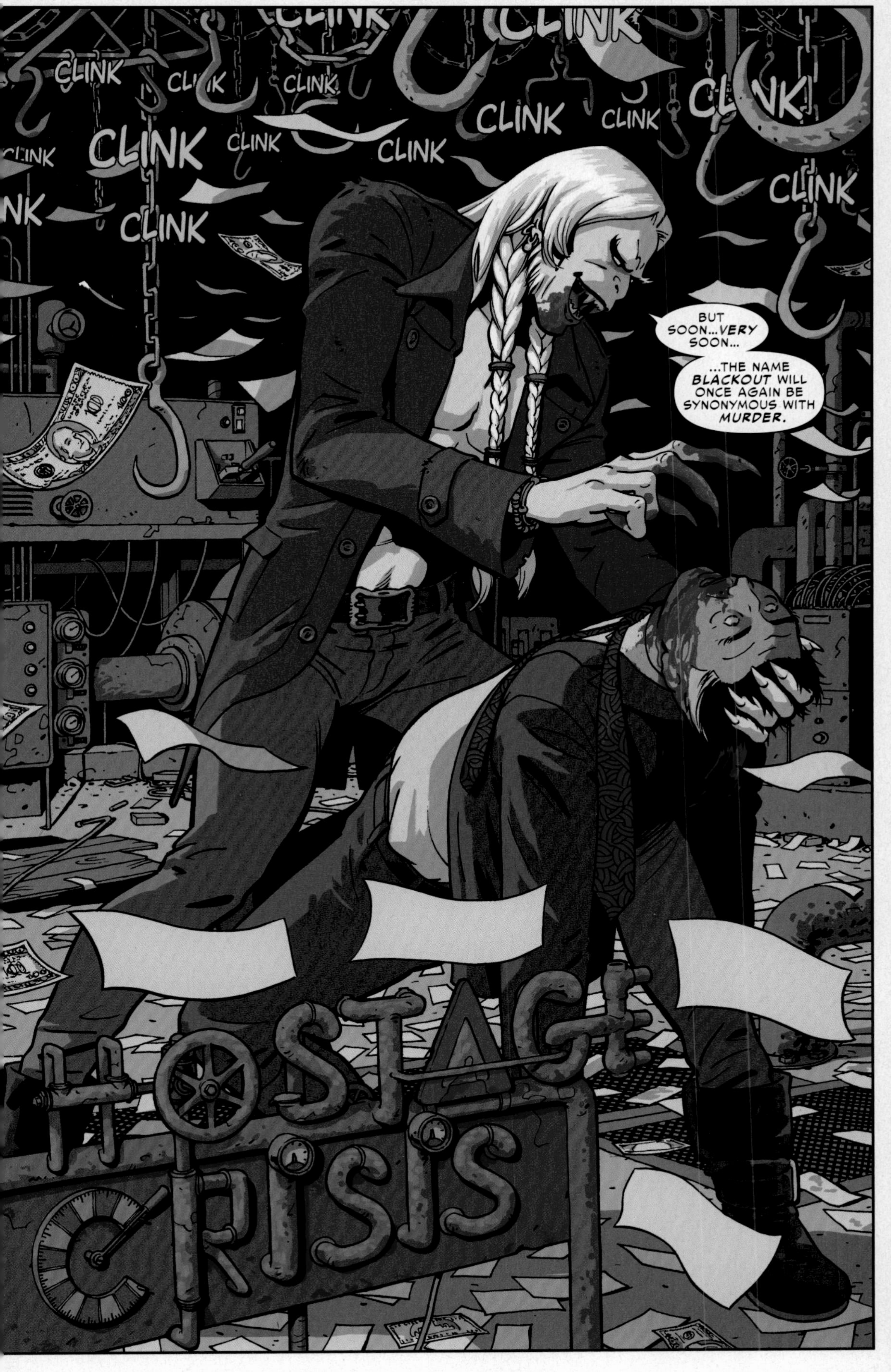
CLINK CLINK CLINK CLINK CLINK CLINK CLINK CLINK CLINK CLINK CLINK CLINK CLINK CLINK
BUT SOON...VERY SOON...
...THE NAME BLACKOUT WILL ONCE AGAIN BE SYNONYMOUS WITH MURDER.
HOSTAGE CRISIS

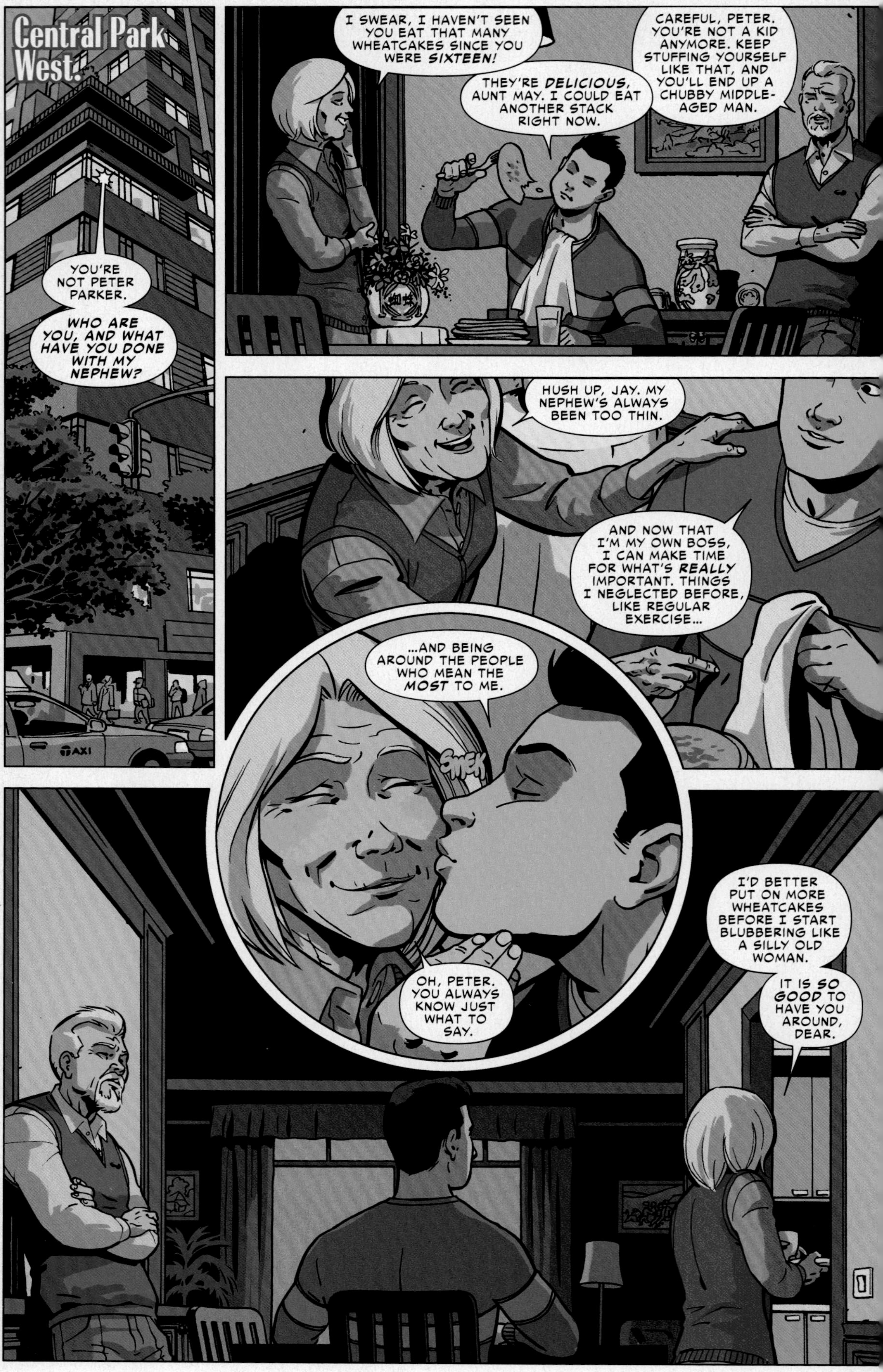
Central Park West!
YOU'RE NOT PETER PARKER.
WHO ARE YOU, AND WHAT HAVE YOU DONE WITH MY NEPHEW?
I SWEAR, I HAVEN'T SEEN YOU EAT THAT MANY WHEATCAKES SINCE YOU WERE SIXTEEN!
THEY'RE DELICIOUS, AUNT MAY. I COULD EAT ANOTHER STACK RIGHT NOW.
CAREFUL, PETER. YOU'RE NOT A KID ANYMORE. KEEP STUFFING YOURSELF LIKE THAT, AND YOU'LL END UP A CHUBBY MIDDLE-AGED MAN.
HUSH UP, JAY. MY NEPHEW'S ALWAYS BEEN TOO THIN.
AND NOW THAT I'M MY OWN BOSS, I CAN MAKE TIME FOR WHAT'S REALLY IMPORTANT. THINGS I NEGLECTED BEFORE, LIKE REGULAR EXERCISE...
...AND BEING AROUND THE PEOPLE WHO MEAN THE MOST TO ME.
SMEK
OH, PETER. YOU ALWAYS KNOW JUST WHAT TO SAY.
I'D BETTER PUT ON MORE WHEATCAKES BEFORE I START BLUBBERING LIKE A SILLY OLD WOMAN.
IT IS SO GOOD TO HAVE YOU AROUND, DEAR.

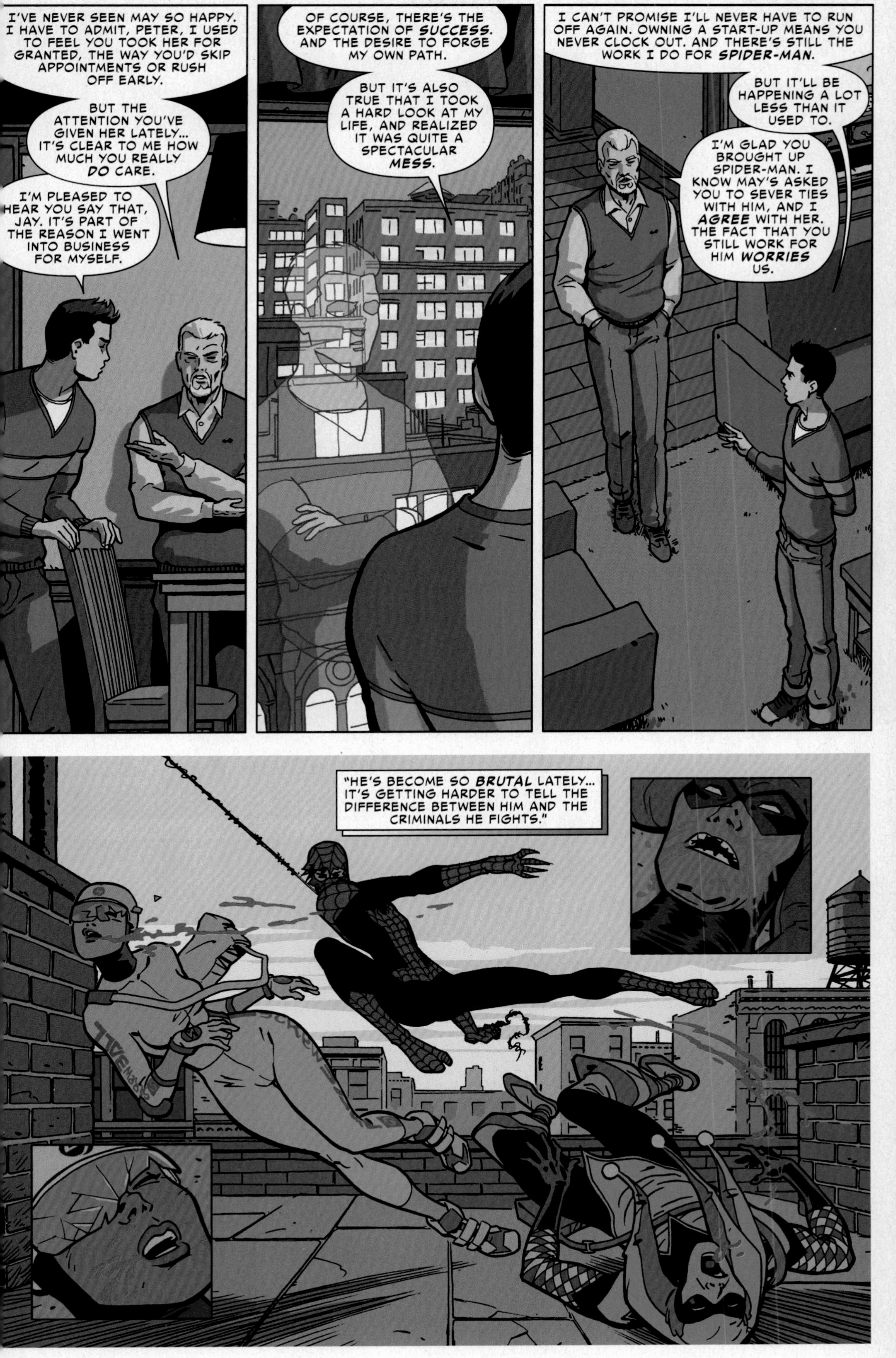
I'VE NEVER SEEN MAY SO HAPPY. I HAVE TO ADMIT, PETER, I USED TO FEEL YOU TOOK HER FOR GRANTED, THE WAY YOU'D SKIP APPOINTMENTS OR RUSH OFF EARLY.
BUT THE ATTENTION YOU'VE GIVEN HER LATELY... IT'S CLEAR TO ME HOW MUCH YOU REALLY DO CARE.
I'M PLEASED TO HEAR YOU SAY THAT, JAY. IT'S PART OF THE REASON I WENT INTO BUSINESS FOR MYSELF.
OF COURSE, THERE'S THE EXPECTATION OF SUCCESS. AND THE DESIRE TO FORGE MY OWN PATH.
BUT IT'S ALSO TRUE THAT I TOOK A HARD LOOK AT MY LIFE, AND REALIZED IT WAS QUITE A SPECTACULAR MESS.
I CAN'T PROMISE I'LL NEVER HAVE TO RUN OFF AGAIN. OWNING A START-UP MEANS YOU NEVER CLOCK OUT. AND THERE'S STILL THE WORK I DO FOR SPIDER-MAN.
BUT IT'LL BE HAPPENING A LOT LESS THAN IT USED TO.
I'M GLAD YOU BROUGHT UP SPIDER-MAN. I KNOW MAY'S ASKED YOU TO SEVER TIES WITH HIM, AND I AGREE WITH HER. THE FACT THAT YOU STILL WORK FOR HIM WORRIES US.
"HE'S BECOME SO BRUTAL LATELY... IT'S GETTING HARDER TO TELL THE DIFFERENCE BETWEEN HIM AND THE CRIMINALS HE FIGHTS."

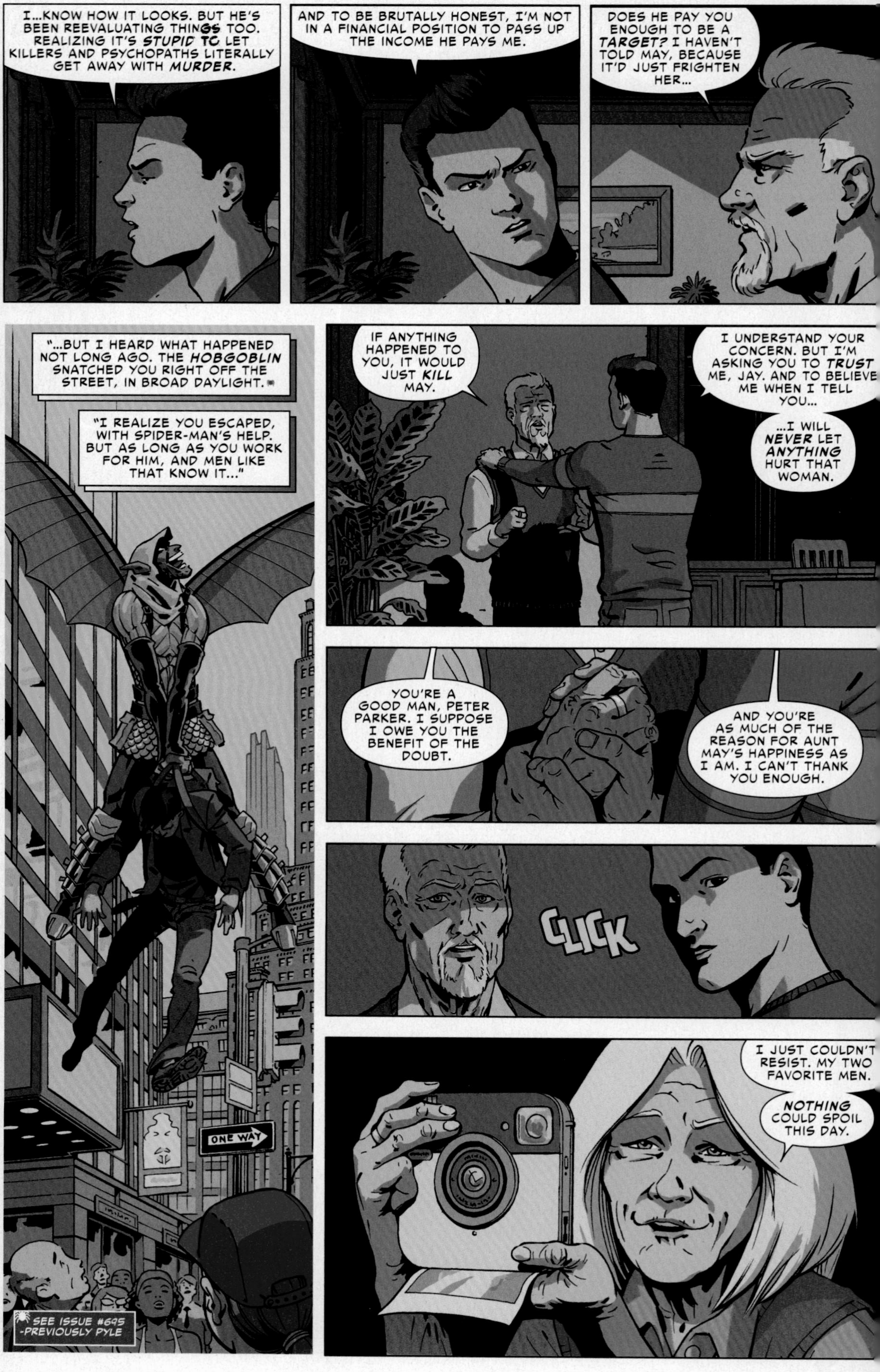
I...KNOW HOW IT LOOKS. BUT HE'S BEEN REEVALUATING THINGS TOO. REALIZING IT'S STUPID TO LET KILLERS AND PSYCHOPATHS LITERALLY GET AWAY WITH MURDER.
AND TO BE BRUTALLY HONEST, I'M NOT IN A FINANCIAL POSITION TO PASS UP THE INCOME HE PAYS ME.
DOES HE PAY YOU ENOUGH TO BE A TARGET? I HAVEN'T TOLD MAY, BECAUSE IT'D JUST FRIGHTEN HER...
"...BUT I HEARD WHAT HAPPENED NOT LONG AGO. THE HOBGOBLIN SNATCHED YOU RIGHT OFF THE STREET, IN BROAD DAYLIGHT.
"I REALIZE YOU ESCAPED, WITH SPIDER-MAN'S HELP. BUT AS LONG AS YOU WORK FOR HIM, AND MEN LIKE THAT KNOW IT..."
ONE WAY
SEE ISSUE #695 -PREVIOUSLY PYLE
IF ANYTHING HAPPENED TO YOU, IT WOULD JUST KILL MAY.
I UNDERSTAND YOUR CONCERN. BUT I'M ASKING YOU TO TRUST ME, JAY. AND TO BELIEVE ME WHEN I TELL YOU...
...I WILL NEVER LET ANYTHING HURT THAT WOMAN.
YOU'RE A GOOD MAN, PETER PARKER. I SUPPOSE I OWE YOU THE BENEFIT OF THE DOUBT.
AND YOU'RE AS MUCH OF THE REASON FOR AUNT MAY'S HAPPINESS AS I AM. I CAN'T THANK YOU ENOUGH.
CLICK
I JUST COULDN'T RESIST. MY TWO FAVORITE MEN.
NOTHING COULD SPOIL THIS DAY.

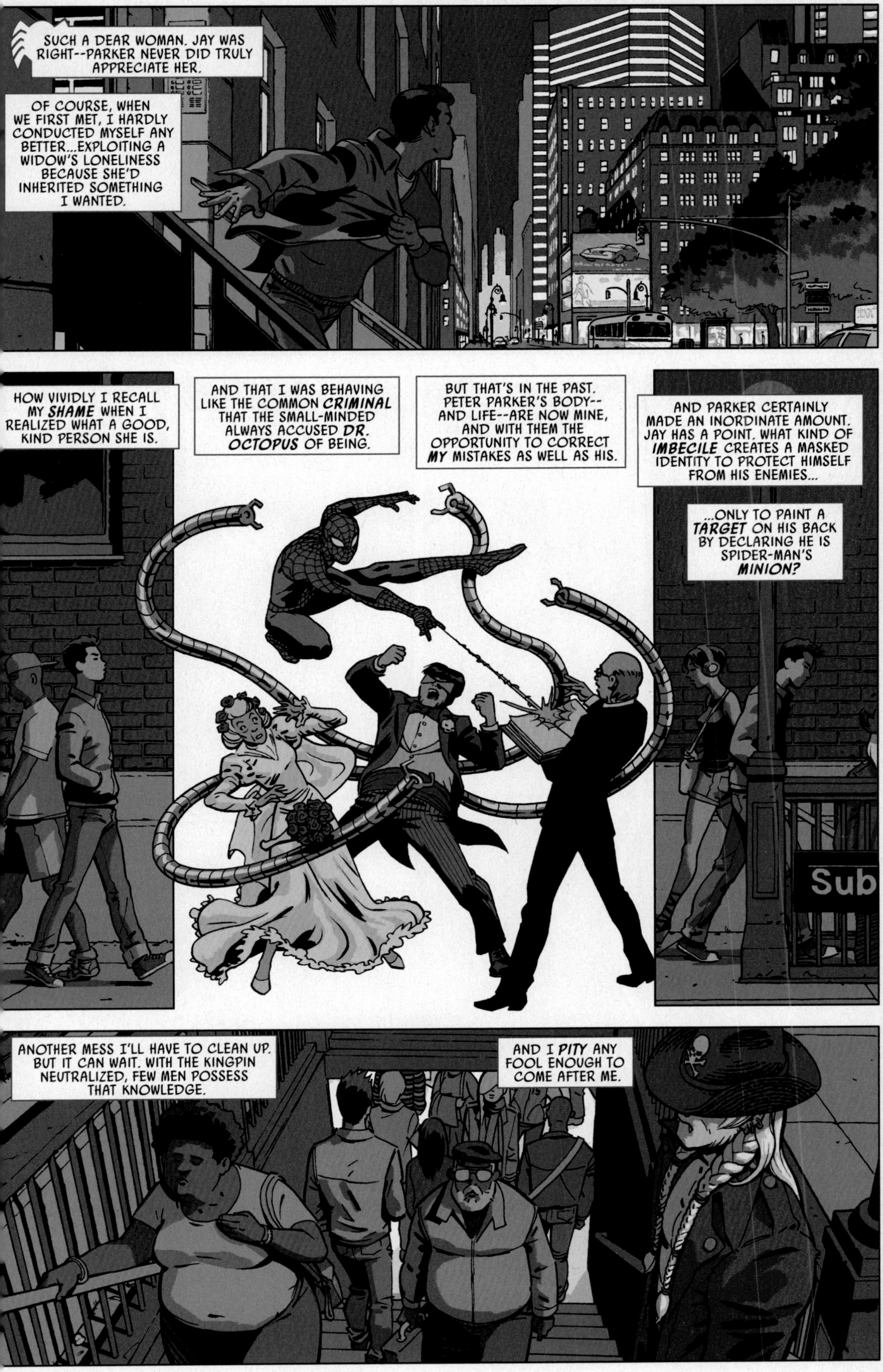
SUCH A DEAR WOMAN. JAY WAS RIGHT--PARKER NEVER DID TRULY APPRECIATE HER.
OF COURSE, WHEN WE FIRST MET, I HARDLY CONDUCTED MYSELF ANY BETTER...EXPLOITING A WIDOW'S LONELINESS BECAUSE SHE'D INHERITED SOMETHING I WANTED.
HOW VIVIDLY I RECALL MY SHAME WHEN I REALIZED WHAT A GOOD, KIND PERSON SHE IS.
AND THAT I WAS BEHAVING LIKE THE COMMON CRIMINAL THAT THE SMALL-MINDED ALWAYS ACCUSED DR. OCTOPUS OF BEING.
BUT THAT'S IN THE PAST. PETER PARKER'S BODY--AND LIFE--ARE NOW MINE, AND WITH THEM THE OPPORTUNITY TO CORRECT MY MISTAKES AS WELL AS HIS.
AND PARKER CERTAINLY MADE AN INORDINATE AMOUNT. JAY HAS A POINT. WHAT KIND OF IMBECILE CREATES A MASKED IDENTITY TO PROTECT HIMSELF FROM HIS ENEMIES...
...ONLY TO PAINT A TARGET ON HIS BACK BY DECLARING HE IS SPIDER-MAN'S MINION?
Sub
ANOTHER MESS I'LL HAVE TO CLEAN UP. BUT IT CAN WAIT. WITH THE KINGPIN NEUTRALIZED, FEW MEN POSSESS THAT KNOWLEDGE.
AND I PITY ANY FOOL ENOUGH TO COME AFTER ME.

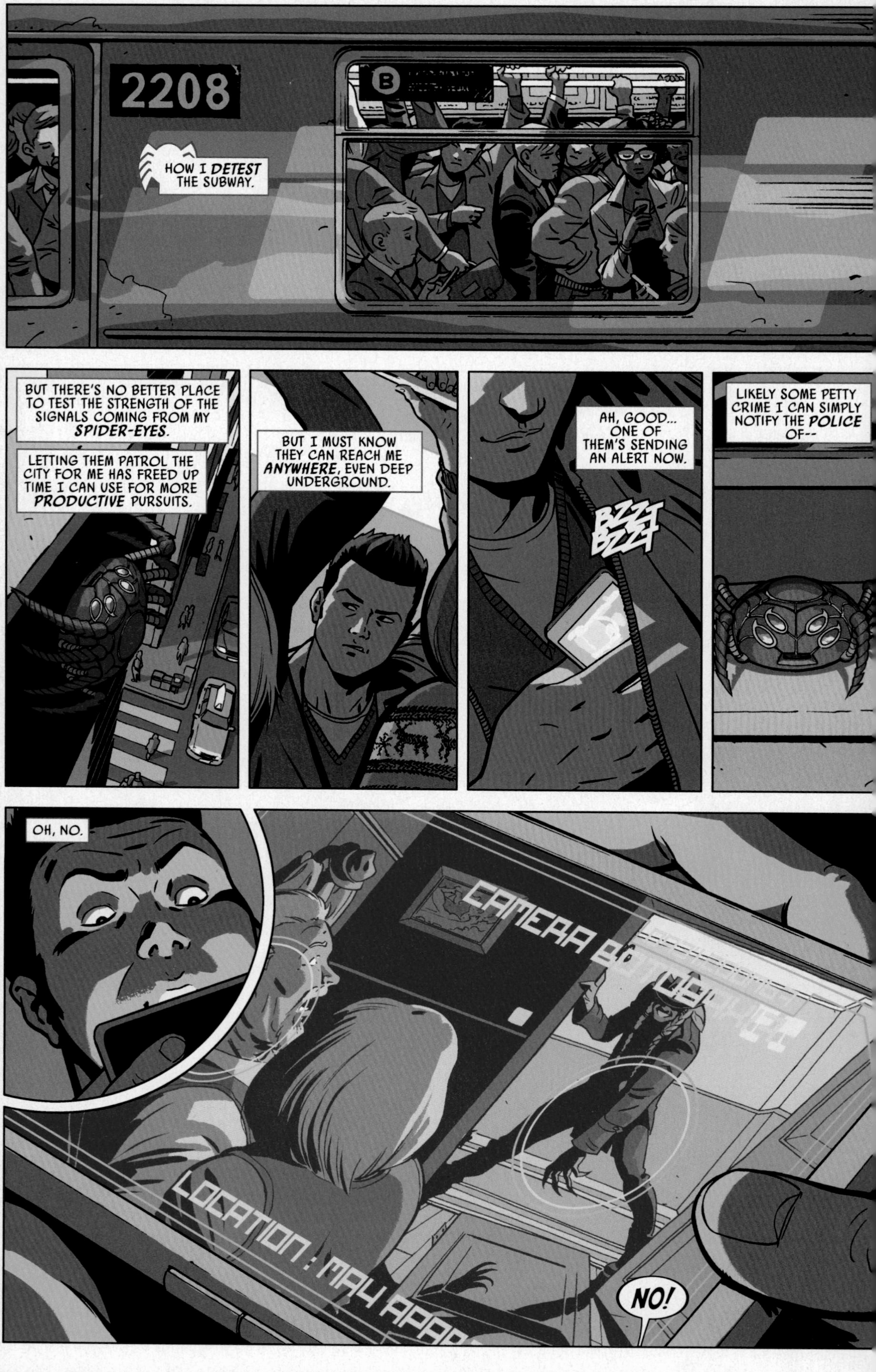
2208
HOW I DETEST THE SUBWAY.
BUT THERE'S NO BETTER PLACE TO TEST THE STRENGTH OF THE SIGNALS COMING FROM MY SPIDER-EYES.
LETTING THEM PATROL THE CITY FOR ME HAS FREED UP TIME I CAN USE FOR MORE PRODUCTIVE PURSUITS.
BUT I MUST KNOW THEY CAN REACH ME ANYWHERE, EVEN DEEP UNDERGROUND.
AH, GOOD... ONE OF THEM'S SENDING AN ALERT NOW.
BZZT BZZT
LIKELY SOME PETTY CRIME I CAN SIMPLY NOTIFY THE POLICE OF--
OH, NO.
CAMERA
LOCATION : MAY APAR
NO!

WATCH IT!

OUT OF MY WAY, FOOLS!

I'M STILL IN MIDTOWN. I CAN MAKE IT BACK IN TIME.

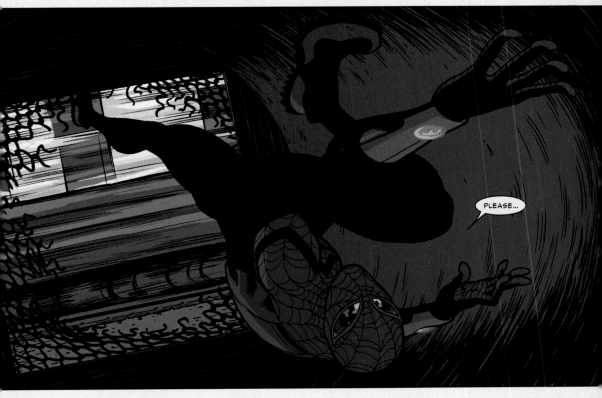

PLEASE...

JAY!

GET OUT OF HERE, MAY! I'LL HOLD HIM OFF!

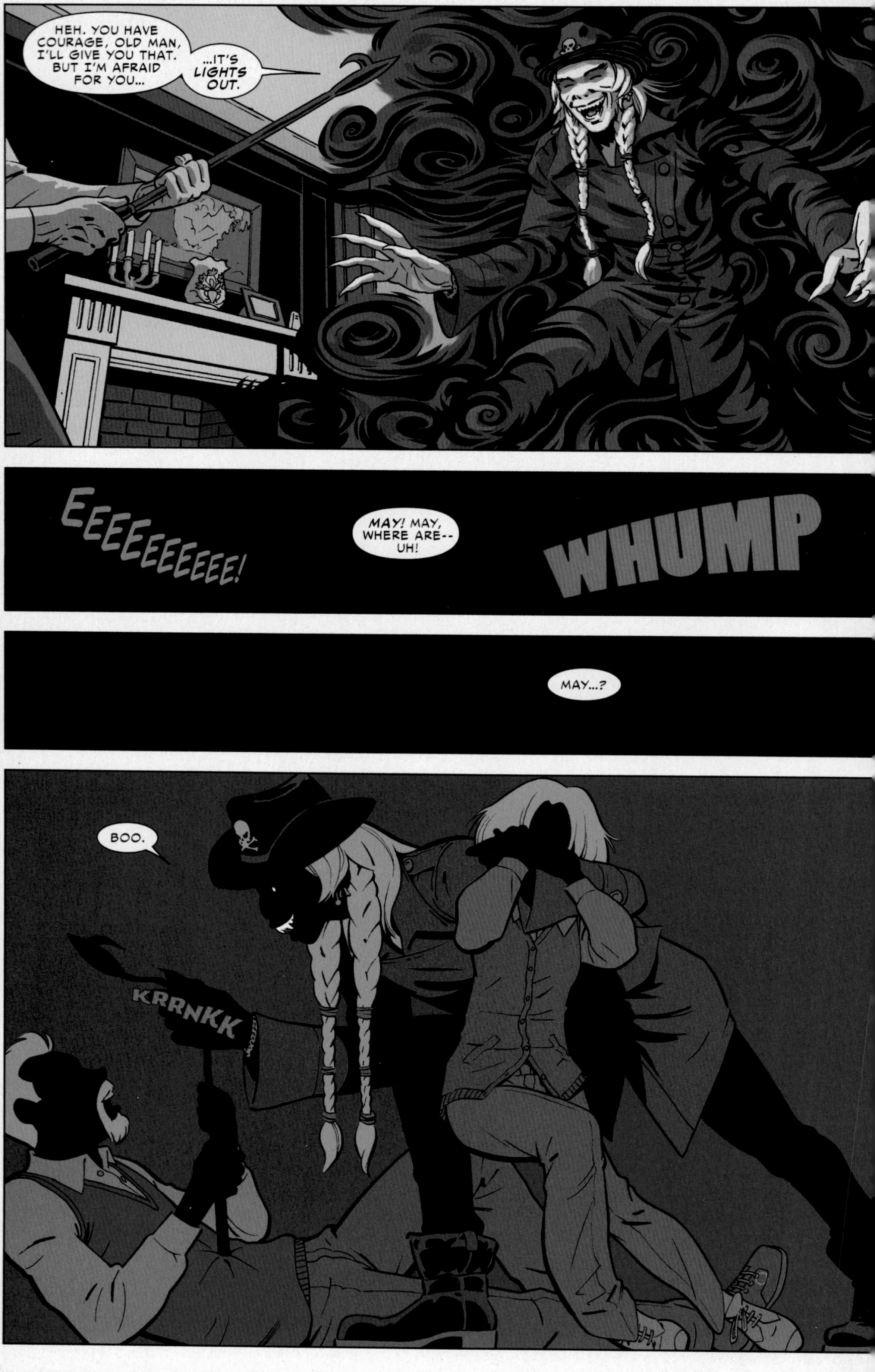
HEH. YOU HAVE COURAGE, OLD MAN, I'LL GIVE YOU THAT. BUT I'M AFRAID FOR YOU...
...IT'S LIGHTS OUT.
EEEEEEEEEEE!
MAY! MAY, WHERE ARE-- UH!
WHUMP
MAY...?
BOO.
KRRNKK

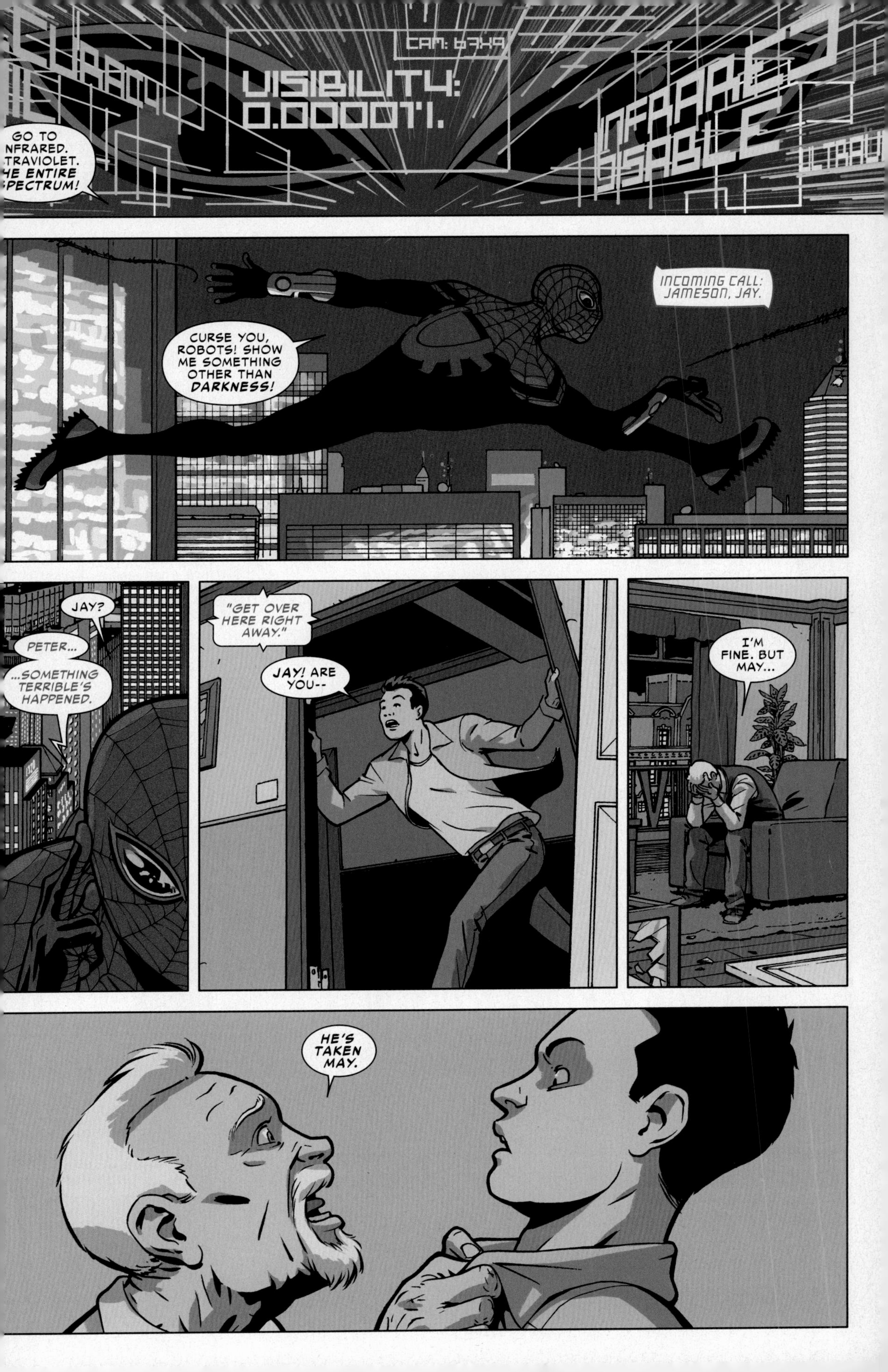
CAM: 67X9
VISIBILITY: 0.000071.
GO TO NFRARED. TRAVIOLET. HE ENTIRE SPECTRUM!
INFRARED
DISABLE
INCOMING CALL: JAMESON, JAY.
CURSE YOU, ROBOTS! SHOW ME SOMETHING OTHER THAN DARKNESS!
JAY?
PETER...
...SOMETHING TERRIBLE'S HAPPENED.
"GET OVER HERE RIGHT AWAY."
JAY! ARE YOU--
I'M FINE. BUT MAY...
HE'S TAKEN MAY.

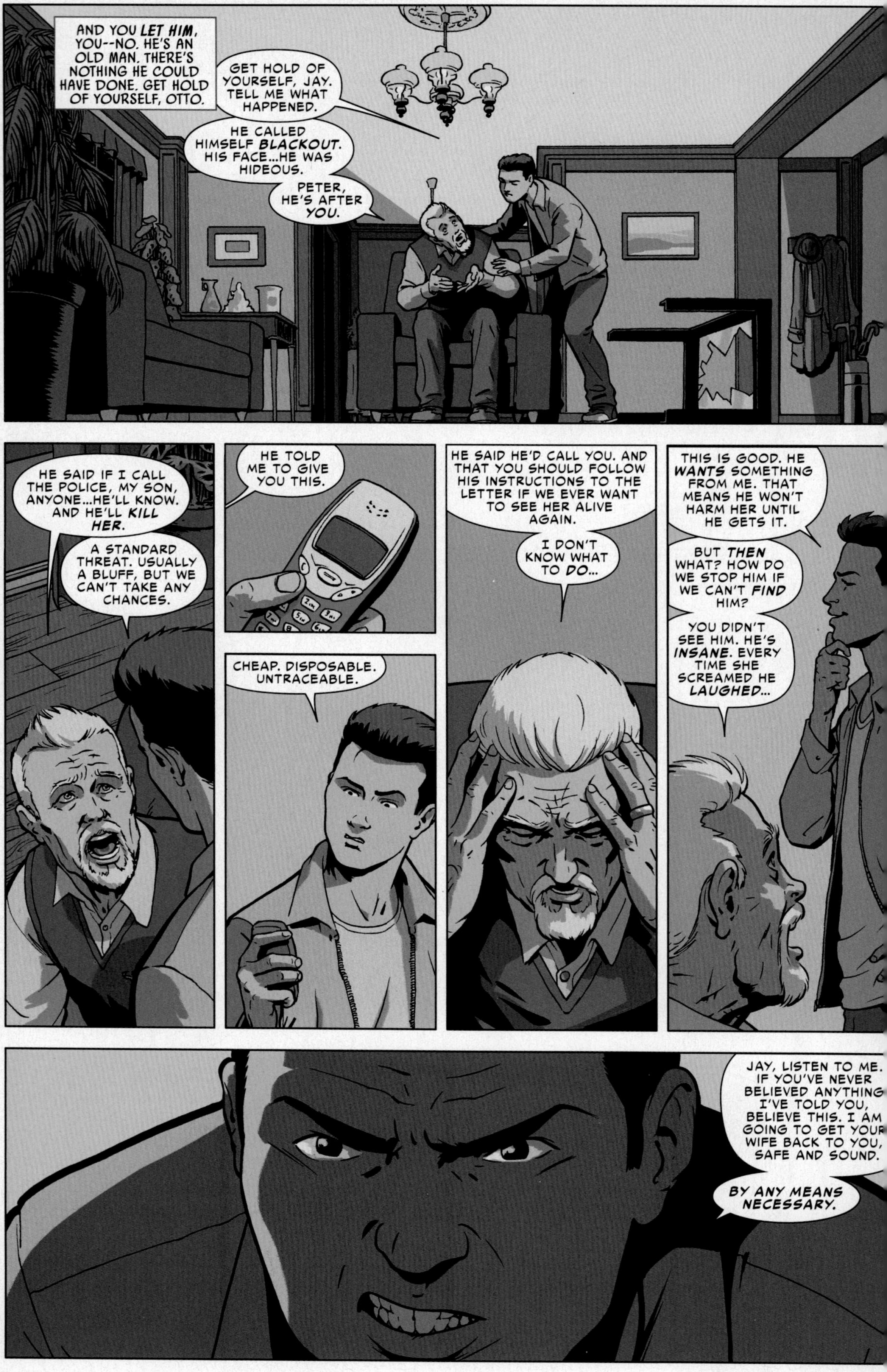
AND YOU LET HIM, YOU--NO. HE'S AN OLD MAN. THERE'S NOTHING HE COULD HAVE DONE. GET HOLD OF YOURSELF, OTTO.
GET HOLD OF YOURSELF, JAY. TELL ME WHAT HAPPENED.
HE CALLED HIMSELF BLACKOUT. HIS FACE...HE WAS HIDEOUS.
PETER, HE'S AFTER YOU.
HE SAID IF I CALL THE POLICE, MY SON, ANYONE...HE'LL KNOW. AND HE'LL KILL HER.
A STANDARD THREAT. USUALLY A BLUFF, BUT WE CAN'T TAKE ANY CHANCES.
HE TOLD ME TO GIVE YOU THIS.
CHEAP. DISPOSABLE. UNTRACEABLE.
HE SAID HE'D CALL YOU. AND THAT YOU SHOULD FOLLOW HIS INSTRUCTIONS TO THE LETTER IF WE EVER WANT TO SEE HER ALIVE AGAIN.
I DON'T KNOW WHAT TO DO...
THIS IS GOOD. HE WANTS SOMETHING FROM ME. THAT MEANS HE WON'T HARM HER UNTIL HE GETS IT.
BUT THEN WHAT? HOW DO WE STOP HIM IF WE CAN'T FIND HIM?
YOU DIDN'T SEE HIM. HE'S INSANE. EVERY TIME SHE SCREAMED HE LAUGHED...
JAY, LISTEN TO ME. IF YOU'VE NEVER BELIEVED ANYTHING I'VE TOLD YOU, BELIEVE THIS. I AM GOING TO GET YOUR WIFE BACK TO YOU, SAFE AND SOUND.
BY ANY MEANS NECESSARY.

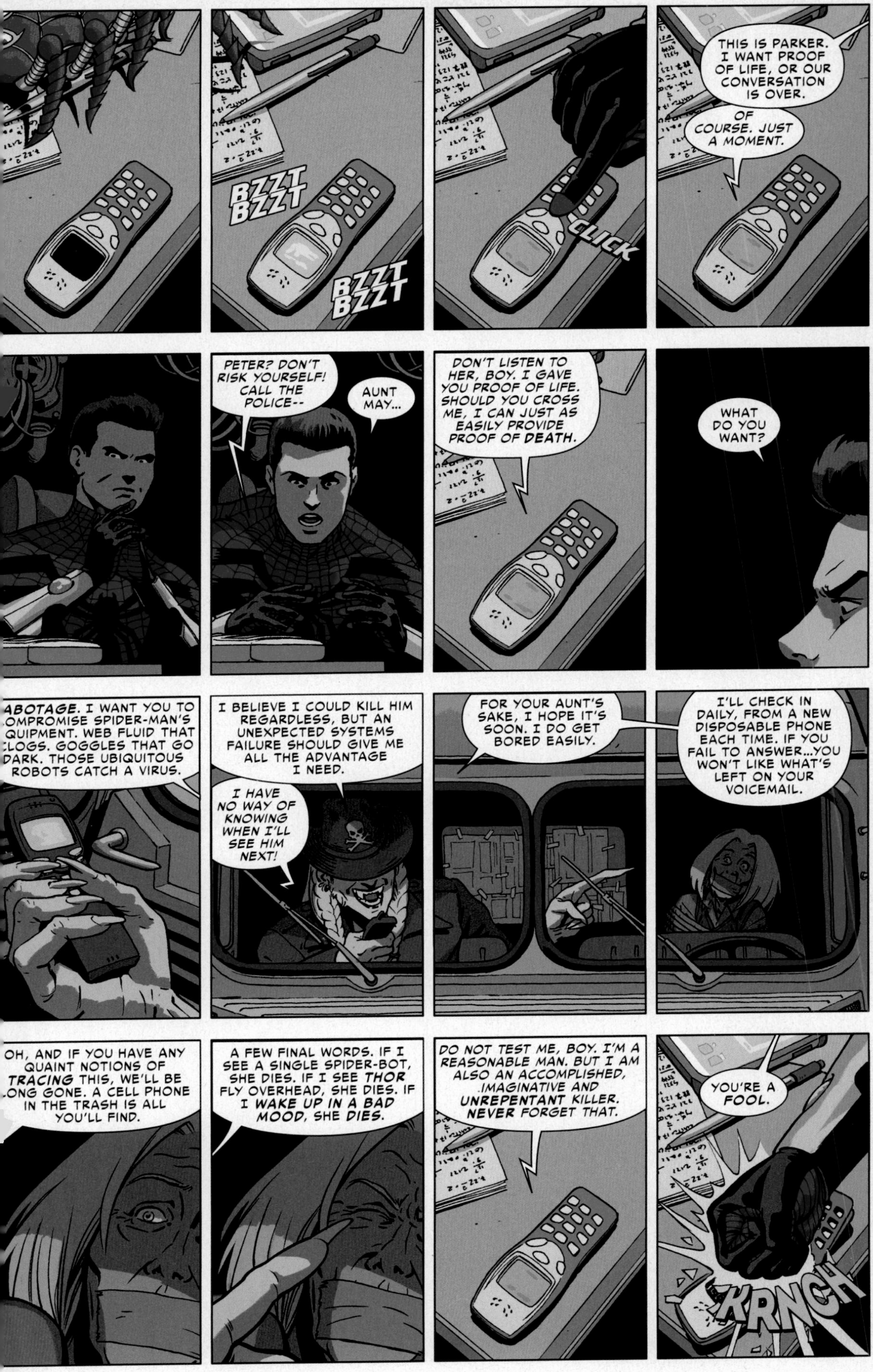
BZZT BZZT
BZZT BZZT
CLICK
THIS IS PARKER. I WANT PROOF OF LIFE, OR OUR CONVERSATION IS OVER.
OF COURSE. JUST A MOMENT.
PETER? DON'T RISK YOURSELF! CALL THE POLICE--
AUNT MAY...
DON'T LISTEN TO HER, BOY. I GAVE YOU PROOF OF LIFE. SHOULD YOU CROSS ME, I CAN JUST AS EASILY PROVIDE PROOF OF DEATH.
WHAT DO YOU WANT?
ABOTAGE. I WANT YOU TO OMPROMISE SPIDER-MAN'S QUIPMENT. WEB FLUID THAT CLOGS. GOGGLES THAT GO DARK. THOSE UBIQUITOUS ROBOTS CATCH A VIRUS.
I BELIEVE I COULD KILL HIM REGARDLESS, BUT AN UNEXPECTED SYSTEMS FAILURE SHOULD GIVE ME ALL THE ADVANTAGE I NEED.
I HAVE NO WAY OF KNOWING WHEN I'LL SEE HIM NEXT!
FOR YOUR AUNT'S SAKE, I HOPE IT'S SOON. I DO GET BORED EASILY.
I'LL CHECK IN DAILY, FROM A NEW DISPOSABLE PHONE EACH TIME. IF YOU FAIL TO ANSWER...YOU WON'T LIKE WHAT'S LEFT ON YOUR VOICEMAIL.
OH, AND IF YOU HAVE ANY QUAINT NOTIONS OF TRACING THIS, WE'LL BE LONG GONE. A CELL PHONE IN THE TRASH IS ALL YOU'LL FIND.
A FEW FINAL WORDS. IF I SEE A SINGLE SPIDER-BOT, SHE DIES. IF I SEE THOR FLY OVERHEAD, SHE DIES. IF I WAKE UP IN A BAD MOOD, SHE DIES.
DO NOT TEST ME, BOY. I'M A REASONABLE MAN. BUT I AM ALSO AN ACCOMPLISHED, IMAGINATIVE AND UNREPENTANT KILLER. NEVER FORGET THAT.
YOU'RE A FOOL.
KRNCH

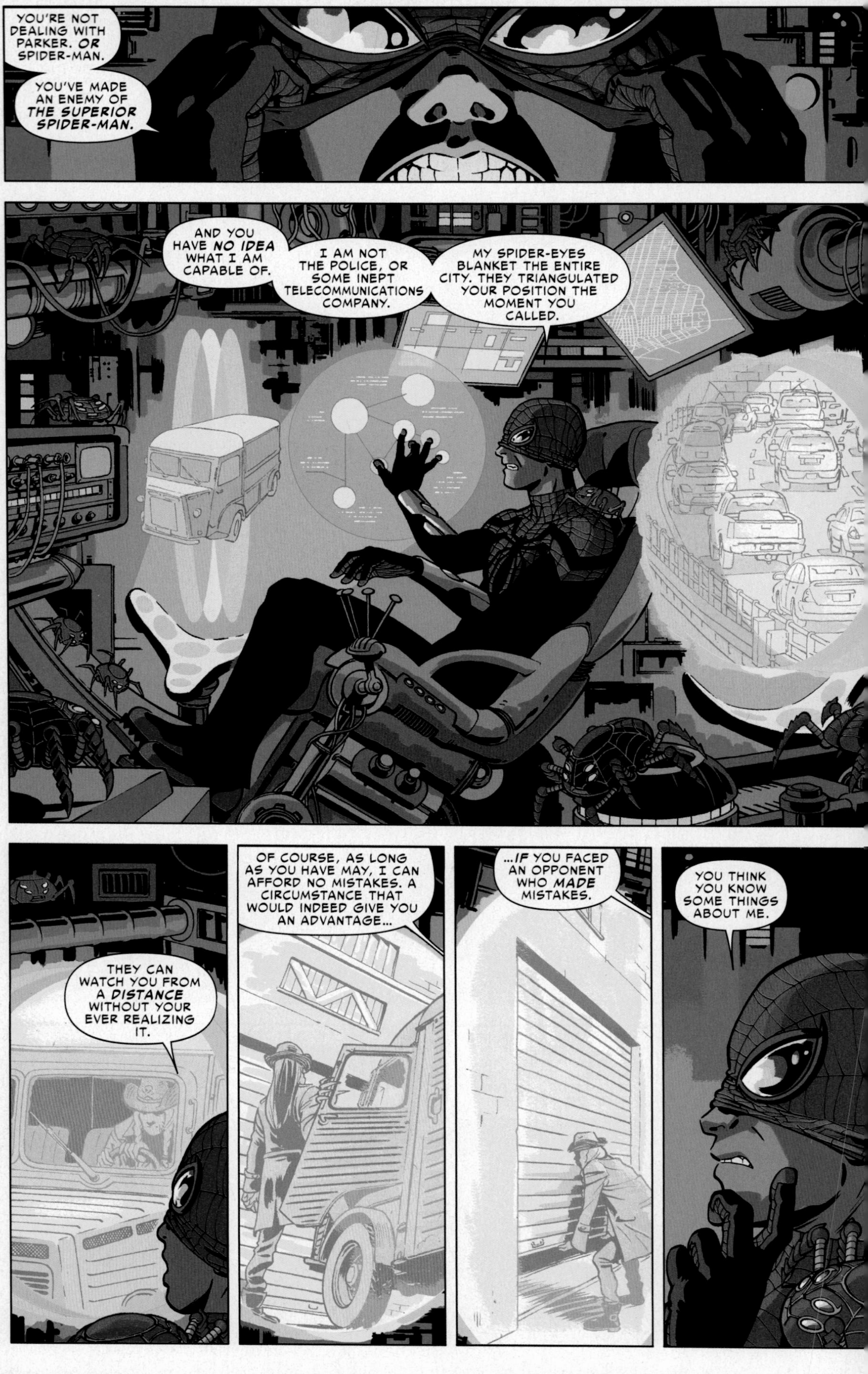
YOU'RE NOT DEALING WITH PARKER. *OR* SPIDER-MAN.
YOU'VE MADE AN ENEMY OF *THE SUPERIOR SPIDER-MAN.*
AND YOU HAVE *NO IDEA* WHAT I AM CAPABLE OF.
I AM NOT THE POLICE, OR SOME INEPT TELECOMMUNICATIONS COMPANY.
MY SPIDER-EYES BLANKET THE ENTIRE CITY. THEY TRIANGULATED YOUR POSITION THE MOMENT YOU CALLED.
THEY CAN WATCH YOU FROM A *DISTANCE* WITHOUT YOUR EVER REALIZING IT.
OF COURSE, AS LONG AS YOU HAVE MAY, I CAN AFFORD NO MISTAKES. A CIRCUMSTANCE THAT WOULD INDEED GIVE YOU AN ADVANTAGE...
...*IF* YOU FACED AN OPPONENT WHO *MADE* MISTAKES.
YOU THINK YOU KNOW SOME THINGS ABOUT ME.

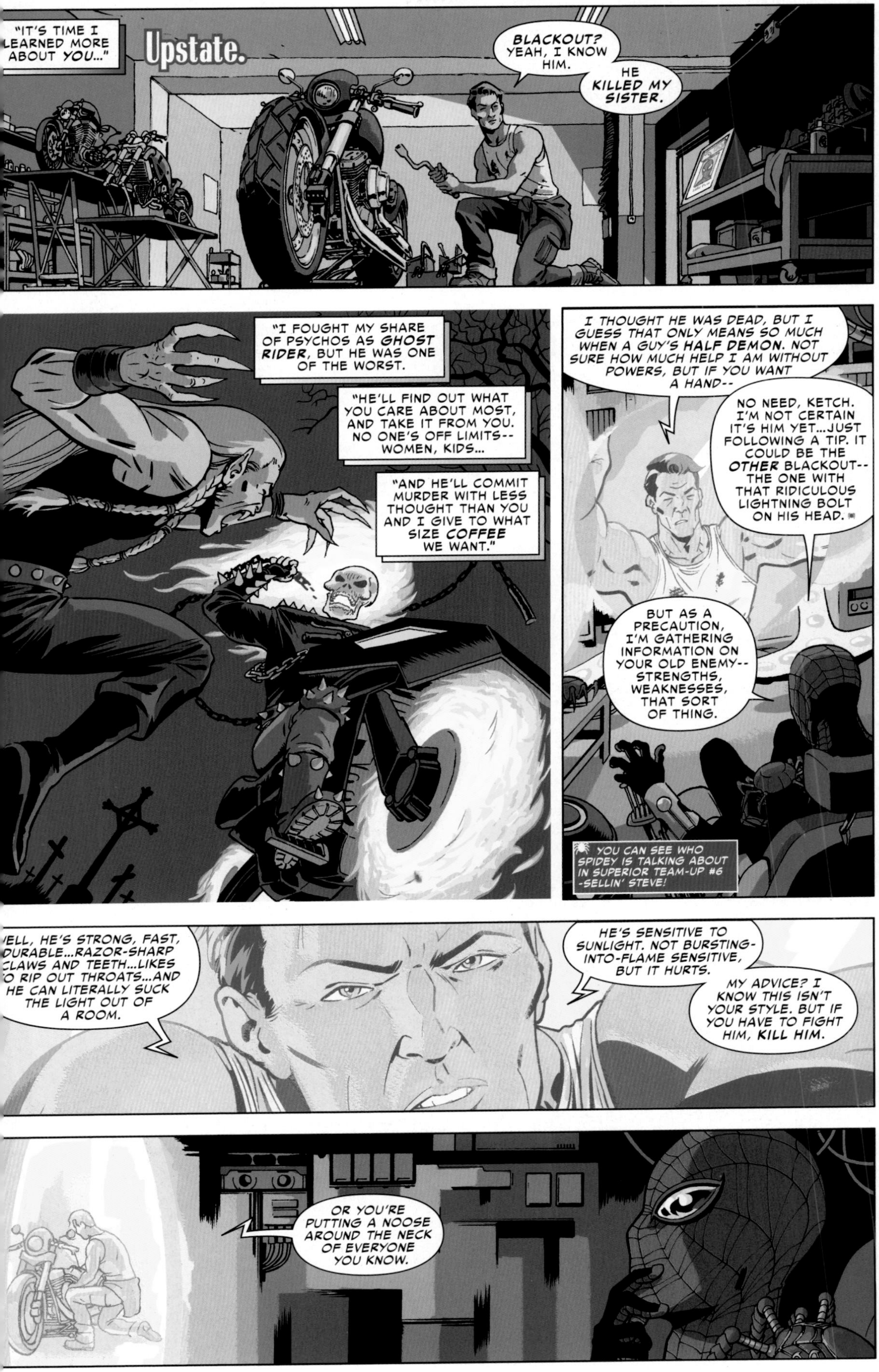
"IT'S TIME I LEARNED MORE ABOUT YOU..."
Upstate.
BLACKOUT? YEAH, I KNOW HIM.
HE KILLED MY SISTER.
"I FOUGHT MY SHARE OF PSYCHOS AS GHOST RIDER, BUT HE WAS ONE OF THE WORST.
"HE'LL FIND OUT WHAT YOU CARE ABOUT MOST, AND TAKE IT FROM YOU. NO ONE'S OFF LIMITS--WOMEN, KIDS...
"AND HE'LL COMMIT MURDER WITH LESS THOUGHT THAN YOU AND I GIVE TO WHAT SIZE COFFEE WE WANT."
I THOUGHT HE WAS DEAD, BUT I GUESS THAT ONLY MEANS SO MUCH WHEN A GUY'S HALF DEMON. NOT SURE HOW MUCH HELP I AM WITHOUT POWERS, BUT IF YOU WANT A HAND--
NO NEED, KETCH. I'M NOT CERTAIN IT'S HIM YET...JUST FOLLOWING A TIP. IT COULD BE THE OTHER BLACKOUT--THE ONE WITH THAT RIDICULOUS LIGHTNING BOLT ON HIS HEAD.
BUT AS A PRECAUTION, I'M GATHERING INFORMATION ON YOUR OLD ENEMY--STRENGTHS, WEAKNESSES, THAT SORT OF THING.
YOU CAN SEE WHO SPIDEY IS TALKING ABOUT IN SUPERIOR TEAM-UP #6 -SELLIN' STEVE!
WELL, HE'S STRONG, FAST, DURABLE...RAZOR-SHARP CLAWS AND TEETH...LIKES TO RIP OUT THROATS...AND HE CAN LITERALLY SUCK THE LIGHT OUT OF A ROOM.
HE'S SENSITIVE TO SUNLIGHT. NOT BURSTING-INTO-FLAME SENSITIVE, BUT IT HURTS.
MY ADVICE? I KNOW THIS ISN'T YOUR STYLE. BUT IF YOU HAVE TO FIGHT HIM, KILL HIM.
OR YOU'RE PUTTING A NOOSE AROUND THE NECK OF EVERYONE YOU KNOW.

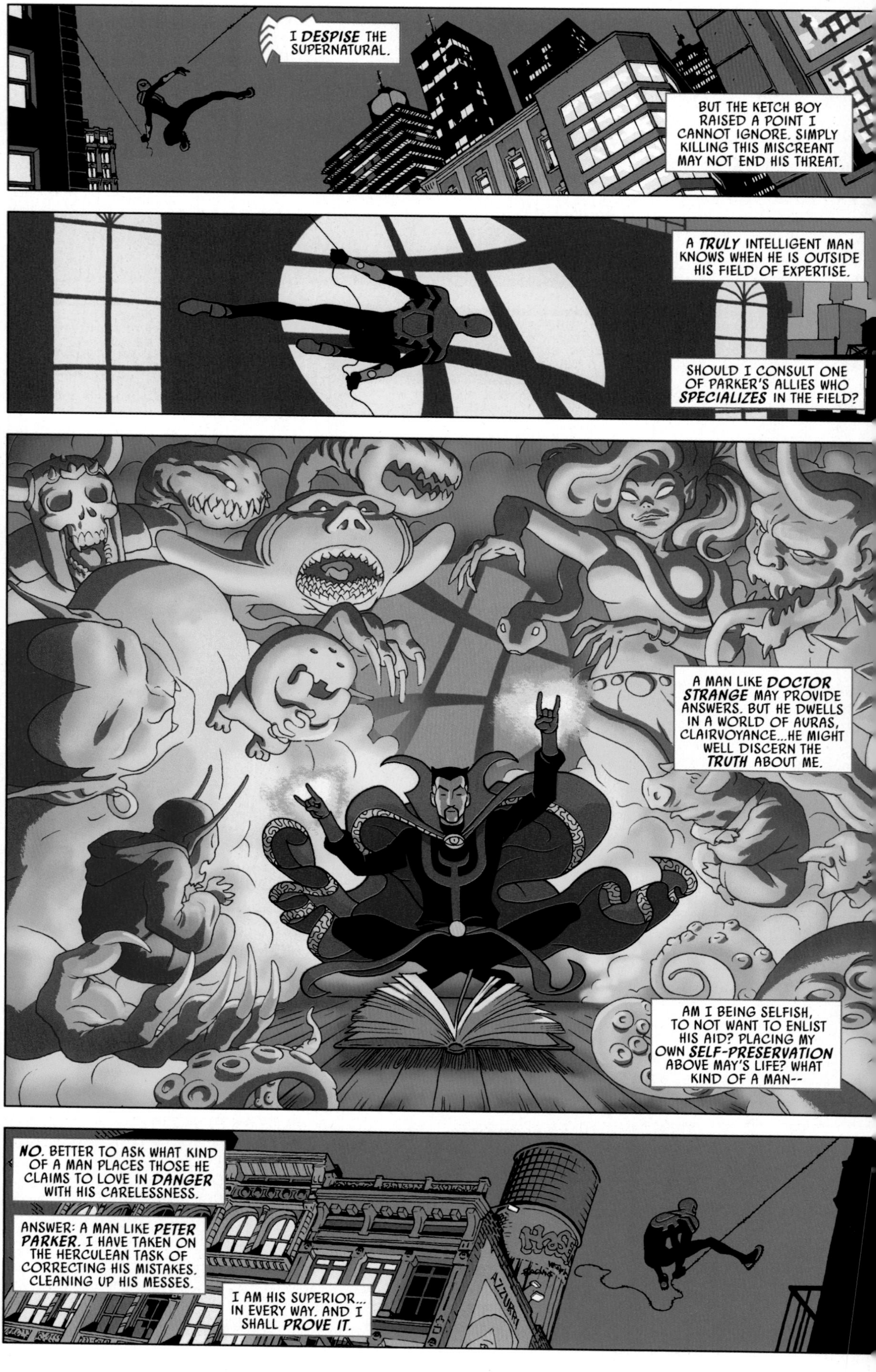
I DESPISE THE SUPERNATURAL.
BUT THE KETCH BOY RAISED A POINT I CANNOT IGNORE. SIMPLY KILLING THIS MISCREANT MAY NOT END HIS THREAT.
A TRULY INTELLIGENT MAN KNOWS WHEN HE IS OUTSIDE HIS FIELD OF EXPERTISE.
SHOULD I CONSULT ONE OF PARKER'S ALLIES WHO SPECIALIZES IN THE FIELD?
A MAN LIKE DOCTOR STRANGE MAY PROVIDE ANSWERS. BUT HE DWELLS IN A WORLD OF AURAS, CLAIRVOYANCE...HE MIGHT WELL DISCERN THE TRUTH ABOUT ME.
AM I BEING SELFISH, TO NOT WANT TO ENLIST HIS AID? PLACING MY OWN SELF-PRESERVATION ABOVE MAY'S LIFE? WHAT KIND OF A MAN--
NO. BETTER TO ASK WHAT KIND OF A MAN PLACES THOSE HE CLAIMS TO LOVE IN DANGER WITH HIS CARELESSNESS.
ANSWER: A MAN LIKE PETER PARKER. I HAVE TAKEN ON THE HERCULEAN TASK OF CORRECTING HIS MISTAKES. CLEANING UP HIS MESSES.
I AM HIS SUPERIOR... IN EVERY WAY. AND I SHALL PROVE IT.

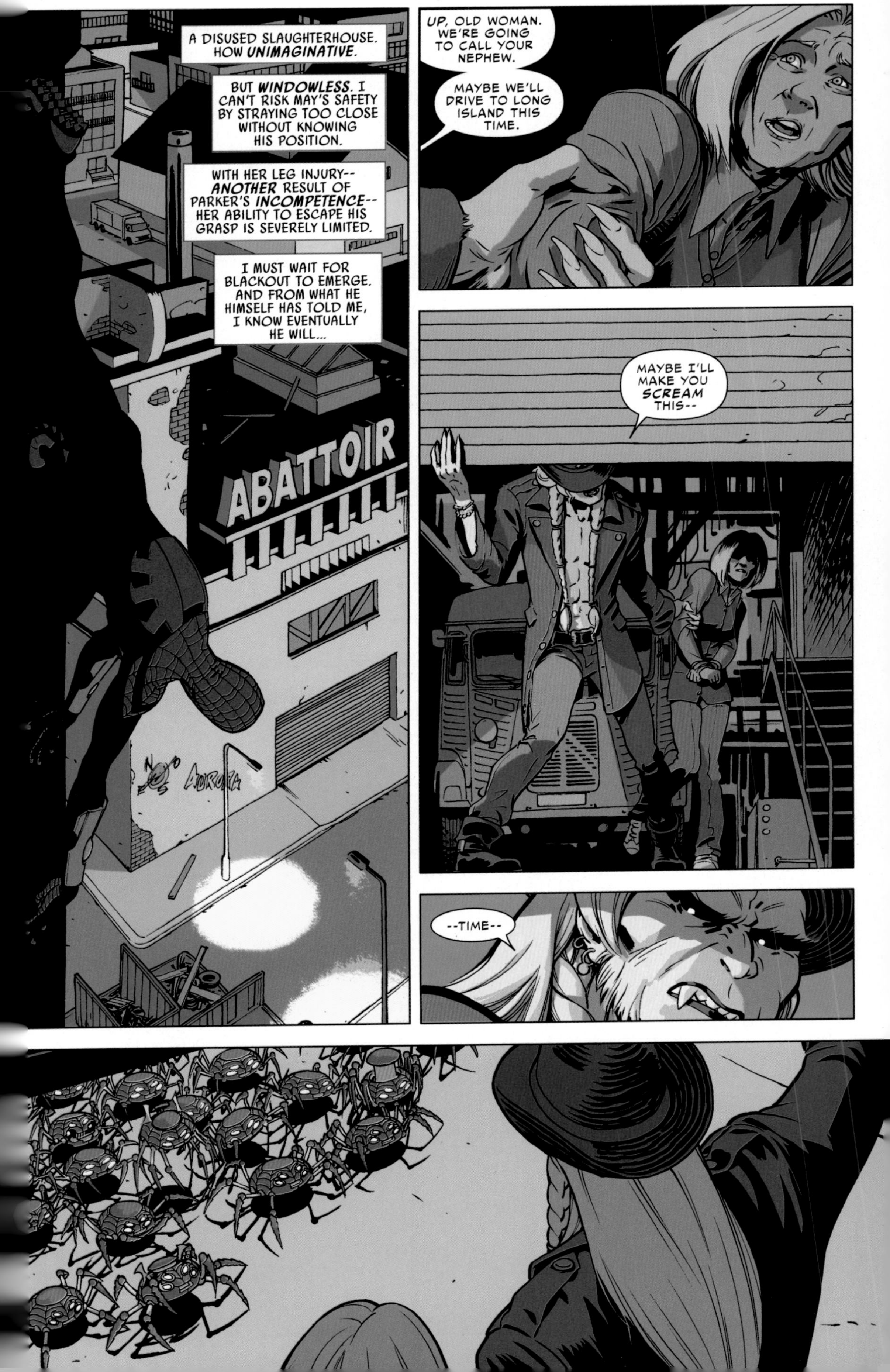
A DISUSED SLAUGHTERHOUSE. HOW UNIMAGINATIVE.
BUT WINDOWLESS. I CAN'T RISK MAY'S SAFETY BY STRAYING TOO CLOSE WITHOUT KNOWING HIS POSITION.
WITH HER LEG INJURY-- ANOTHER RESULT OF PARKER'S INCOMPETENCE-- HER ABILITY TO ESCAPE HIS GRASP IS SEVERELY LIMITED.
I MUST WAIT FOR BLACKOUT TO EMERGE. AND FROM WHAT HE HIMSELF HAS TOLD ME, I KNOW EVENTUALLY HE WILL...
ABATTOIR
UP, OLD WOMAN. WE'RE GOING TO CALL YOUR NEPHEW.
MAYBE WE'LL DRIVE TO LONG ISLAND THIS TIME.
MAYBE I'LL MAKE YOU SCREAM THIS--
--TIME--

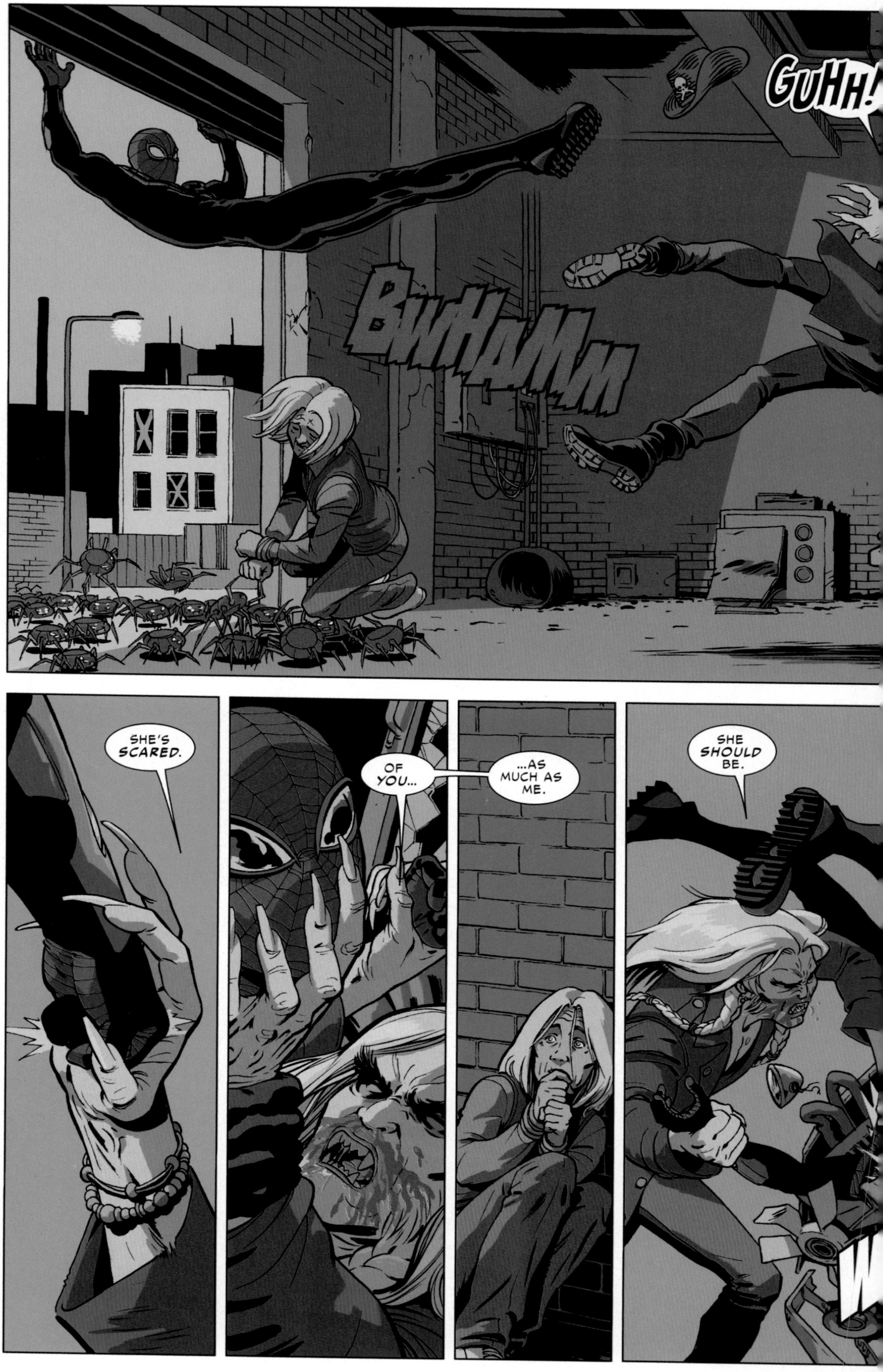
GUHH!
BWHAMM
SHE'S SCARED.
OF YOU...
...AS MUCH AS ME.
SHE SHOULD BE.

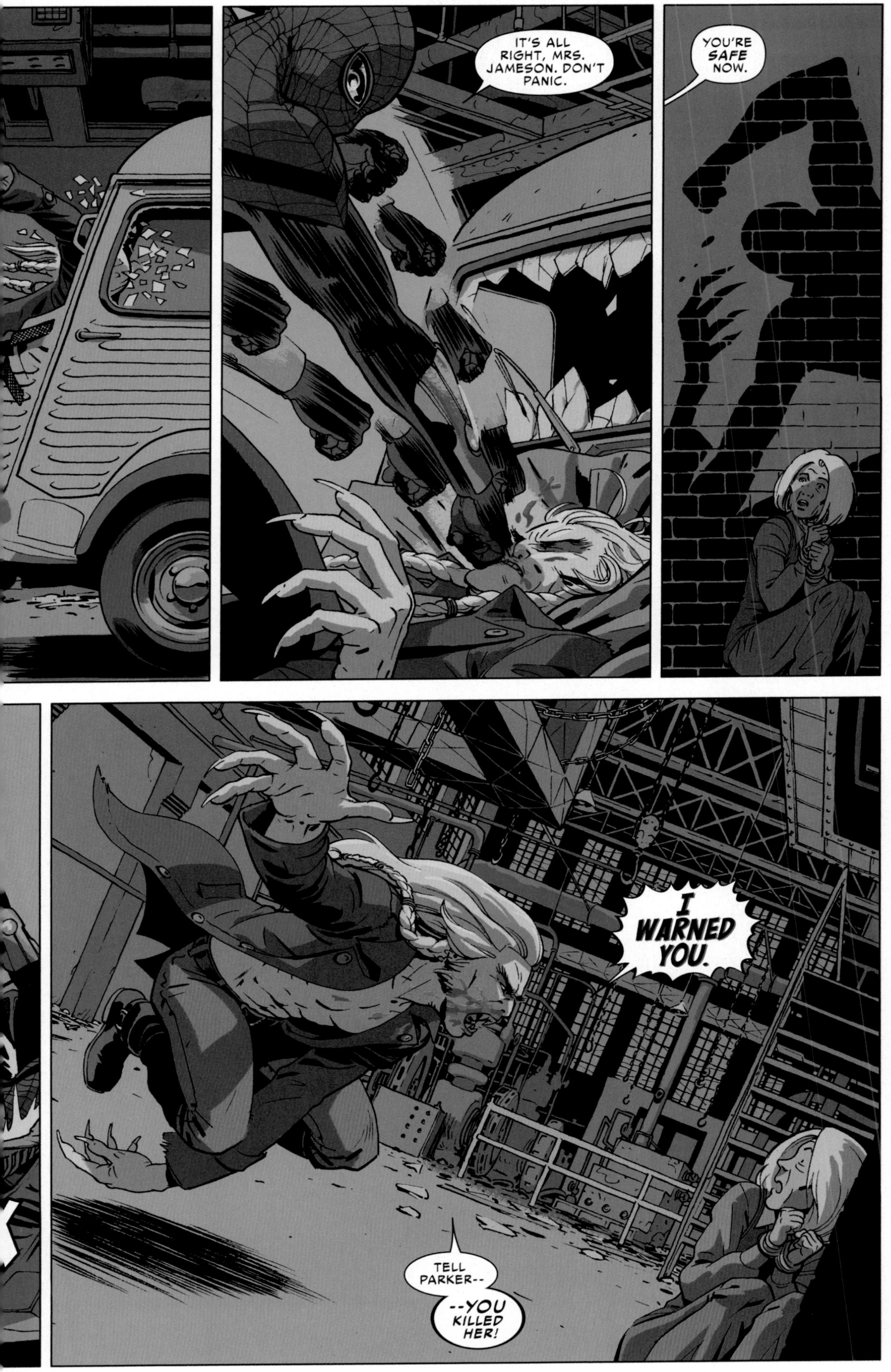
IT'S ALL RIGHT, MRS. JAMESON. DON'T PANIC.
YOU'RE SAFE NOW.
I WARNED YOU.
TELL PARKER--
--YOU KILLED HER!

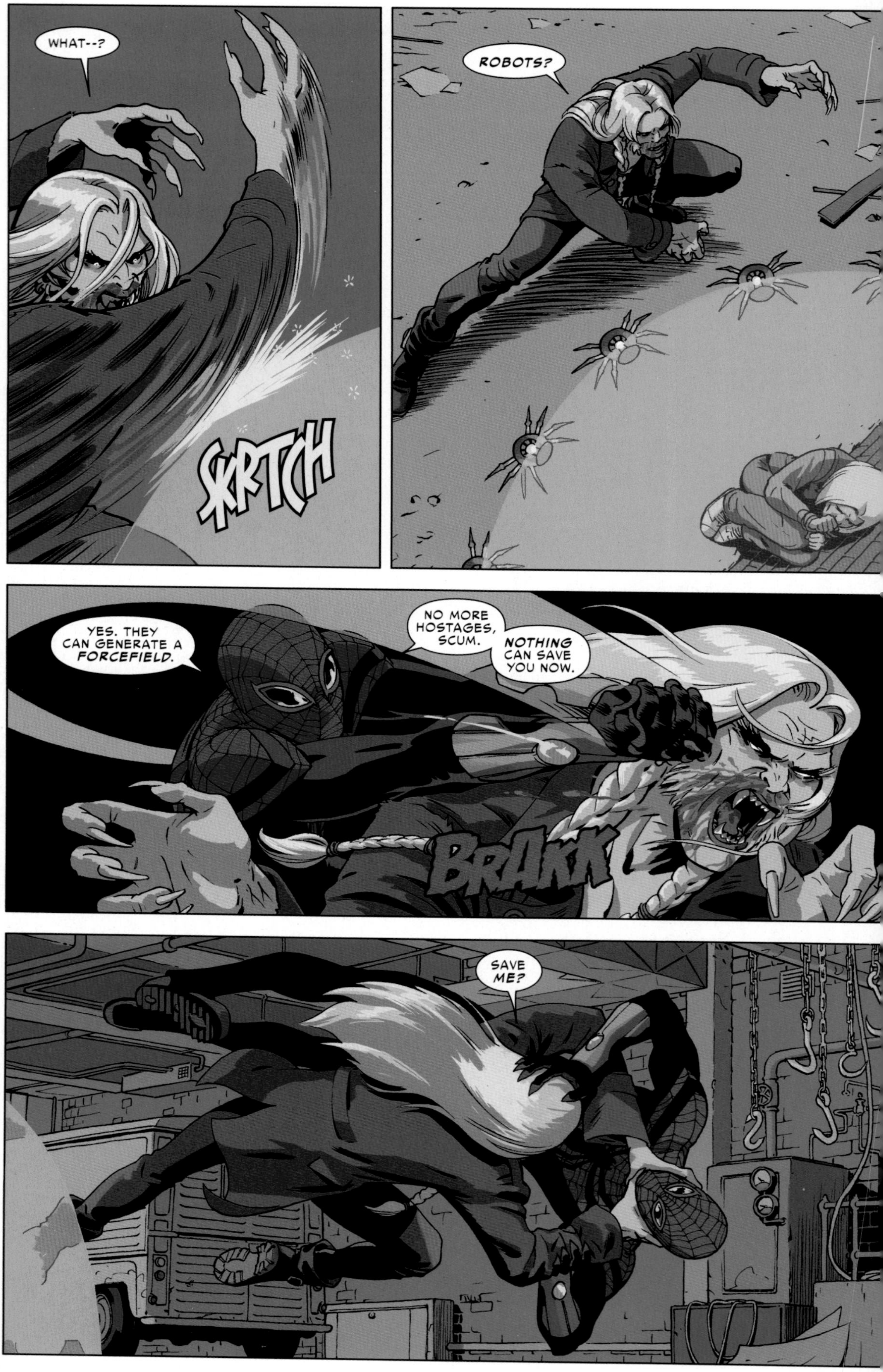
WHAT--?
SKRTCH
ROBOTS?
YES. THEY CAN GENERATE A FORCEFIELD.
NO MORE HOSTAGES, SCUM.
NOTHING CAN SAVE YOU NOW.
BRAKK
SAVE ME?

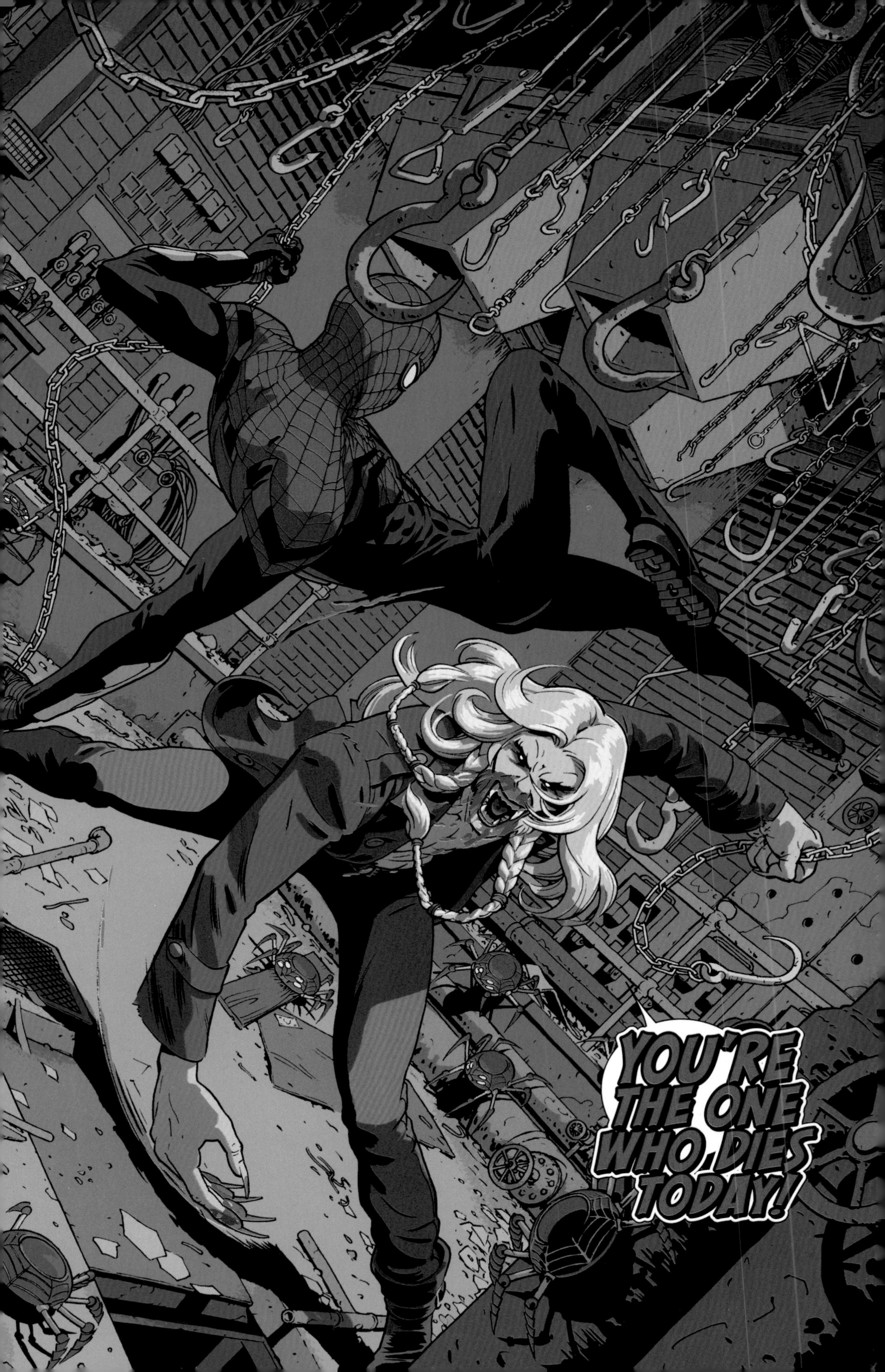
YOU'RE THE ONE WHO DIES TODAY!

KRCH

GNH!

THERE. I'M NOT SURE THE TECH YOU'VE GOT IN THOSE EYEPIECES WOULD HAVE HELPED ANYWAY...

...BUT NOW THEY'RE CLEARLY USELESS.

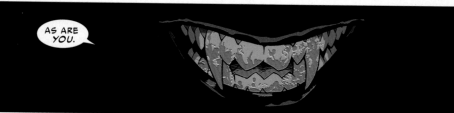

AS ARE YOU.

AH YES, YOUR DANGER SENSE. NOT BAD.

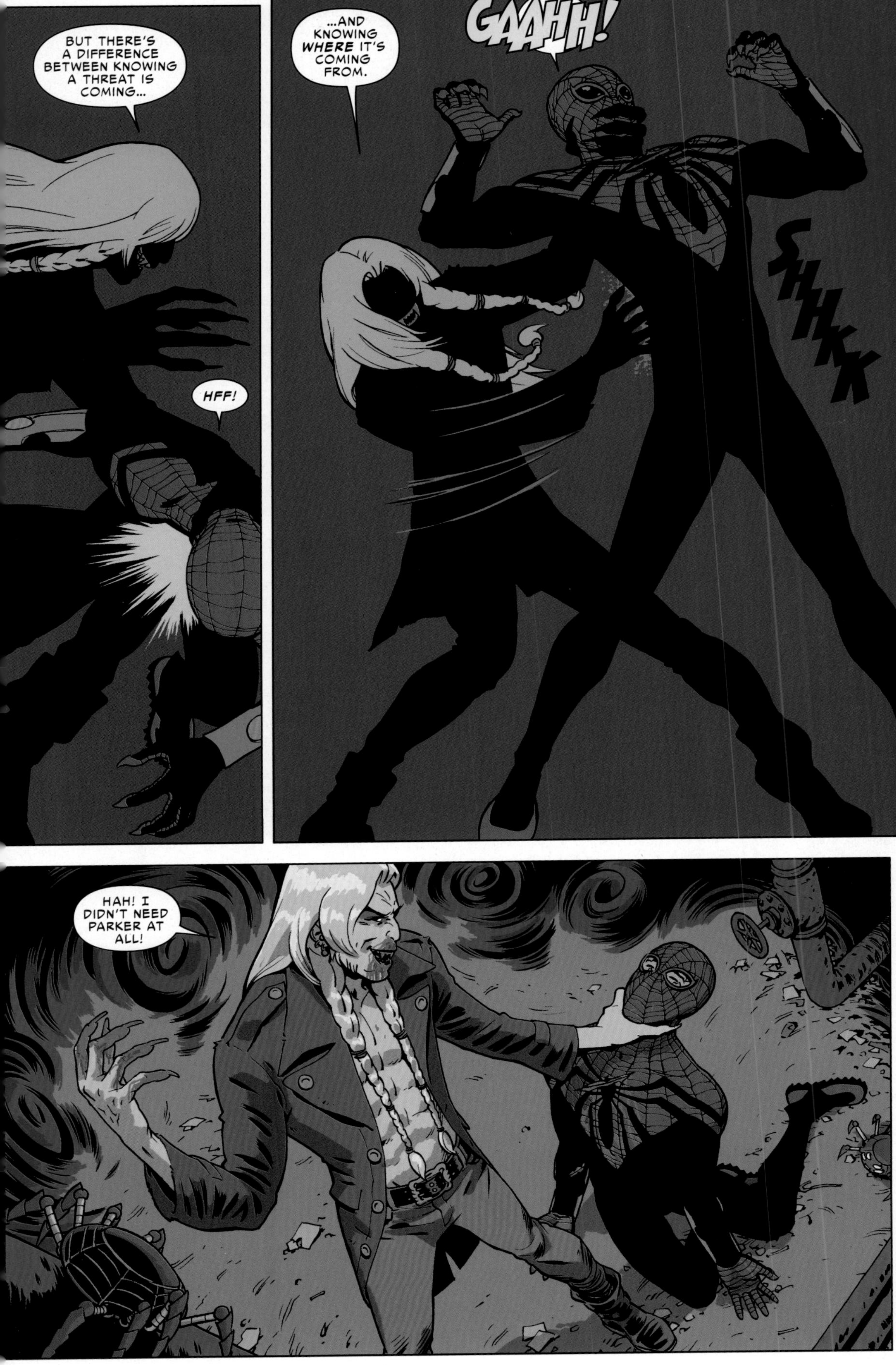
BUT THERE'S A DIFFERENCE BETWEEN KNOWING A THREAT IS COMING...
HFF!
...AND KNOWING *WHERE* IT'S COMING FROM.
GAAHH!
SHHKK
HAH! I DIDN'T NEED PARKER AT ALL!

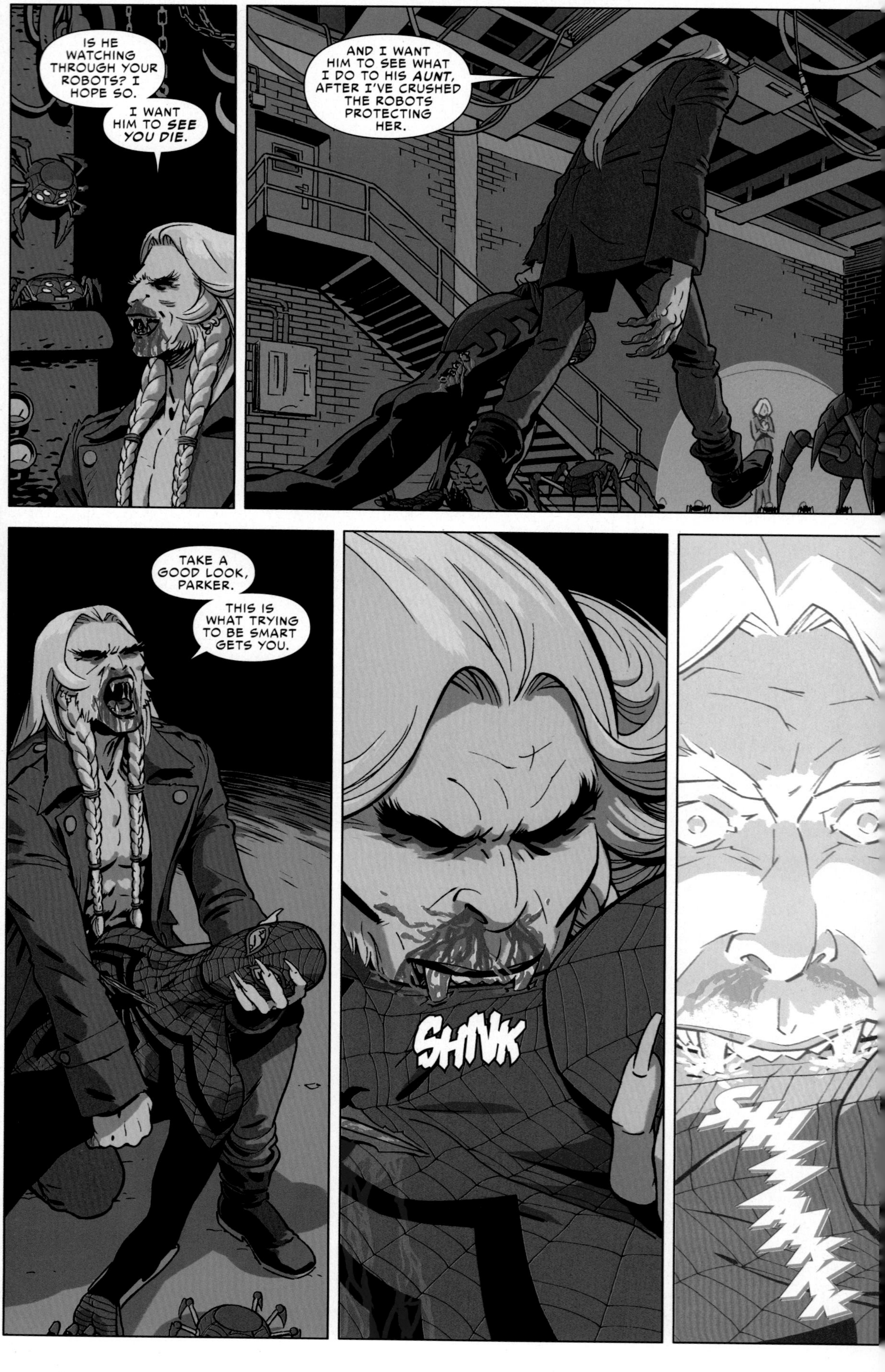
IS HE WATCHING THROUGH YOUR ROBOTS? I HOPE SO.
I WANT HIM TO SEE YOU DIE.
AND I WANT HIM TO SEE WHAT I DO TO HIS AUNT, AFTER I'VE CRUSHED THE ROBOTS PROTECTING HER.
TAKE A GOOD LOOK, PARKER.
THIS IS WHAT TRYING TO BE SMART GETS YOU.
SHINK
SHWAKKK

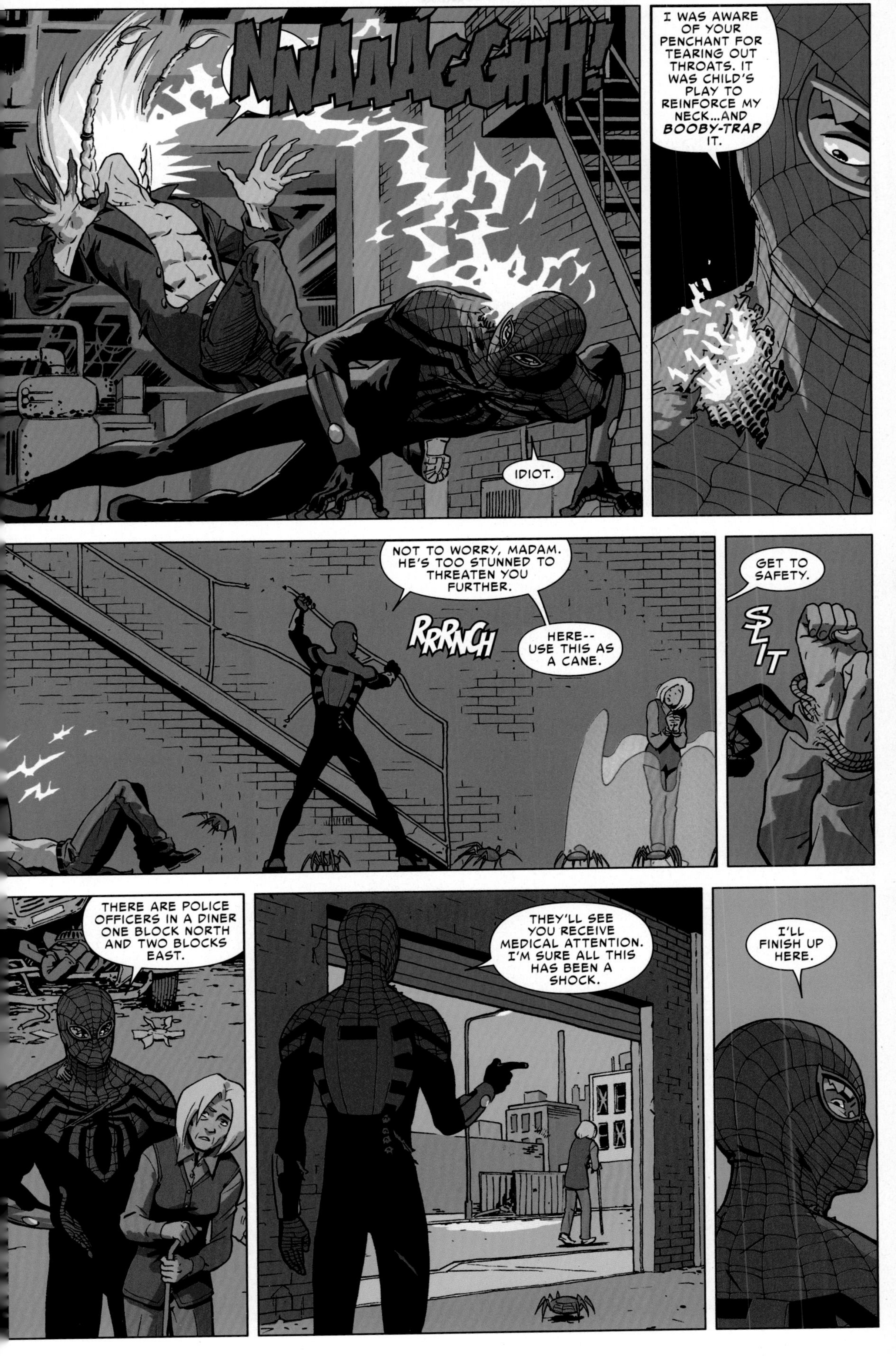
NNAAAGHH!
I WAS AWARE OF YOUR PENCHANT FOR TEARING OUT THROATS. IT WAS CHILD'S PLAY TO REINFORCE MY NECK...AND BOOBY-TRAP IT.
IDIOT.
NOT TO WORRY, MADAM. HE'S TOO STUNNED TO THREATEN YOU FURTHER.
RRRNCH
HERE-- USE THIS AS A CANE.
GET TO SAFETY.
SLIT
THERE ARE POLICE OFFICERS IN A DINER ONE BLOCK NORTH AND TWO BLOCKS EAST.
THEY'LL SEE YOU RECEIVE MEDICAL ATTENTION. I'M SURE ALL THIS HAS BEEN A SHOCK.
I'LL FINISH UP HERE.

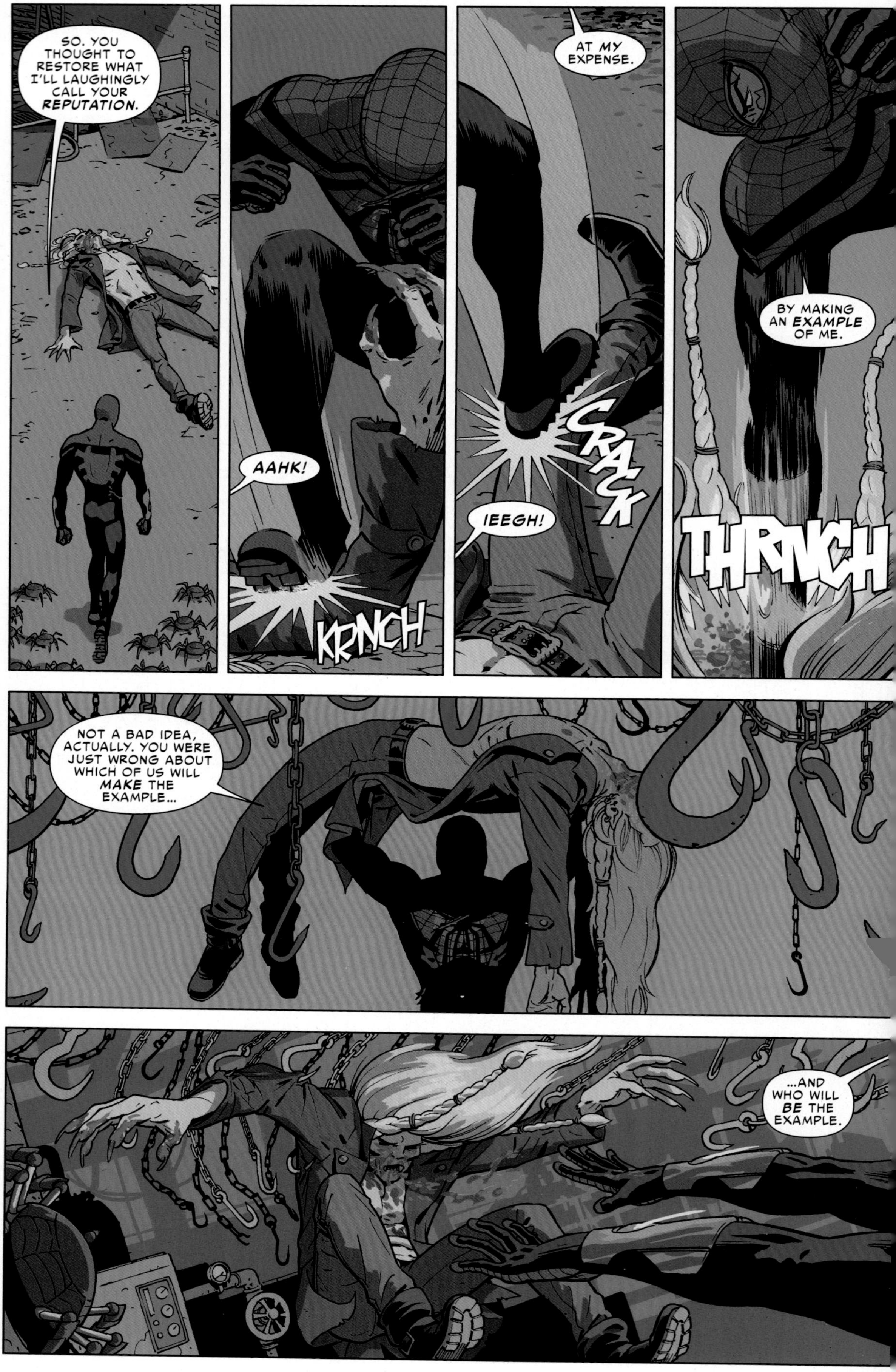
SO. YOU THOUGHT TO RESTORE WHAT I'LL LAUGHINGLY CALL YOUR REPUTATION.
AAHK!
KRNCH
AT MY EXPENSE.
CRACK
IEEGH!
BY MAKING AN EXAMPLE OF ME.
THRNCH
NOT A BAD IDEA, ACTUALLY. YOU WERE JUST WRONG ABOUT WHICH OF US WILL MAKE THE EXAMPLE...
...AND WHO WILL BE THE EXAMPLE.

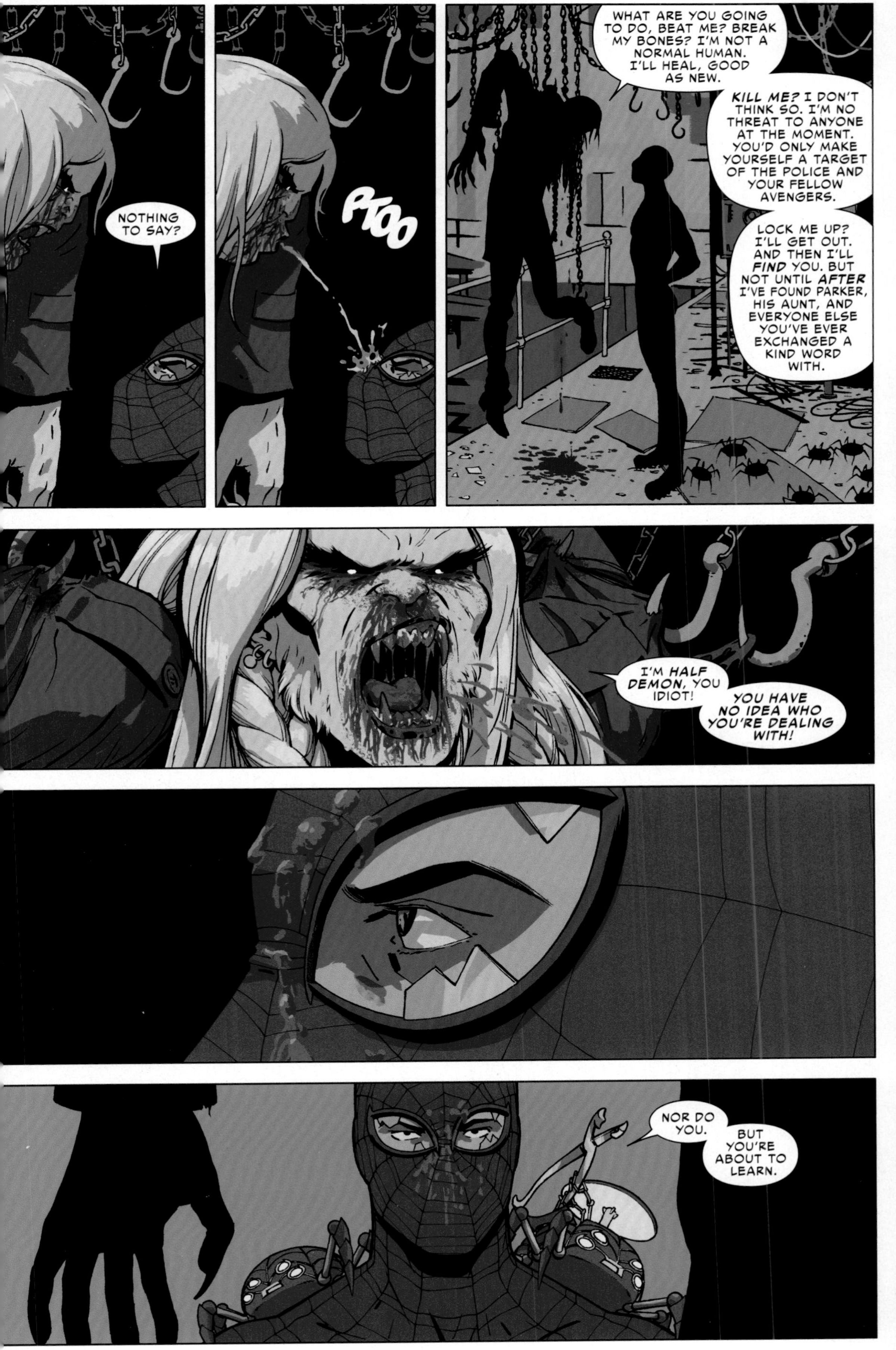

NOTHING TO SAY?
PTOO
WHAT ARE YOU GOING TO DO, BEAT ME? BREAK MY BONES? I'M NOT A NORMAL HUMAN. I'LL HEAL, GOOD AS NEW.
KILL ME? I DON'T THINK SO. I'M NO THREAT TO ANYONE AT THE MOMENT. YOU'D ONLY MAKE YOURSELF A TARGET OF THE POLICE AND YOUR FELLOW AVENGERS.
LOCK ME UP? I'LL GET OUT. AND THEN I'LL FIND YOU. BUT NOT UNTIL AFTER I'VE FOUND PARKER, HIS AUNT, AND EVERYONE ELSE YOU'VE EVER EXCHANGED A KIND WORD WITH.
I'M HALF DEMON, YOU IDIOT!
YOU HAVE NO IDEA WHO YOU'RE DEALING WITH!
NOR DO YOU.
BUT YOU'RE ABOUT TO LEARN.

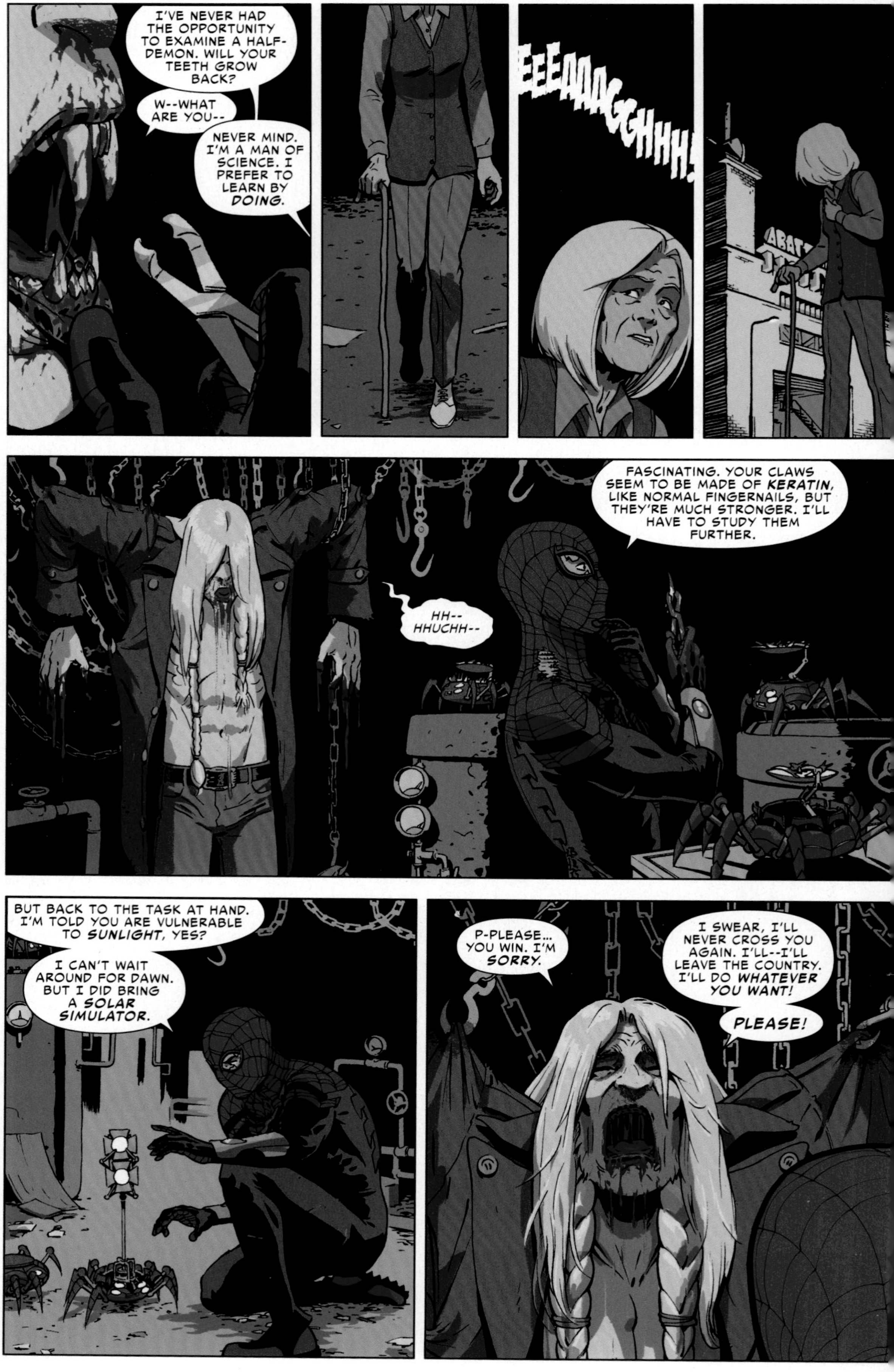
I'VE NEVER HAD THE OPPORTUNITY TO EXAMINE A HALF-DEMON. WILL YOUR TEETH GROW BACK?
W--WHAT ARE YOU--
NEVER MIND. I'M A MAN OF SCIENCE. I PREFER TO LEARN BY DOING.
EEEAAAGGHHHH!
FASCINATING. YOUR CLAWS SEEM TO BE MADE OF KERATIN, LIKE NORMAL FINGERNAILS, BUT THEY'RE MUCH STRONGER. I'LL HAVE TO STUDY THEM FURTHER.
HH-- HHUCHH--
BUT BACK TO THE TASK AT HAND. I'M TOLD YOU ARE VULNERABLE TO SUNLIGHT, YES?
I CAN'T WAIT AROUND FOR DAWN. BUT I DID BRING A SOLAR SIMULATOR.
P-PLEASE... YOU WIN. I'M SORRY.
I SWEAR, I'LL NEVER CROSS YOU AGAIN. I'LL--I'LL LEAVE THE COUNTRY. I'LL DO WHATEVER YOU WANT!
PLEASE!

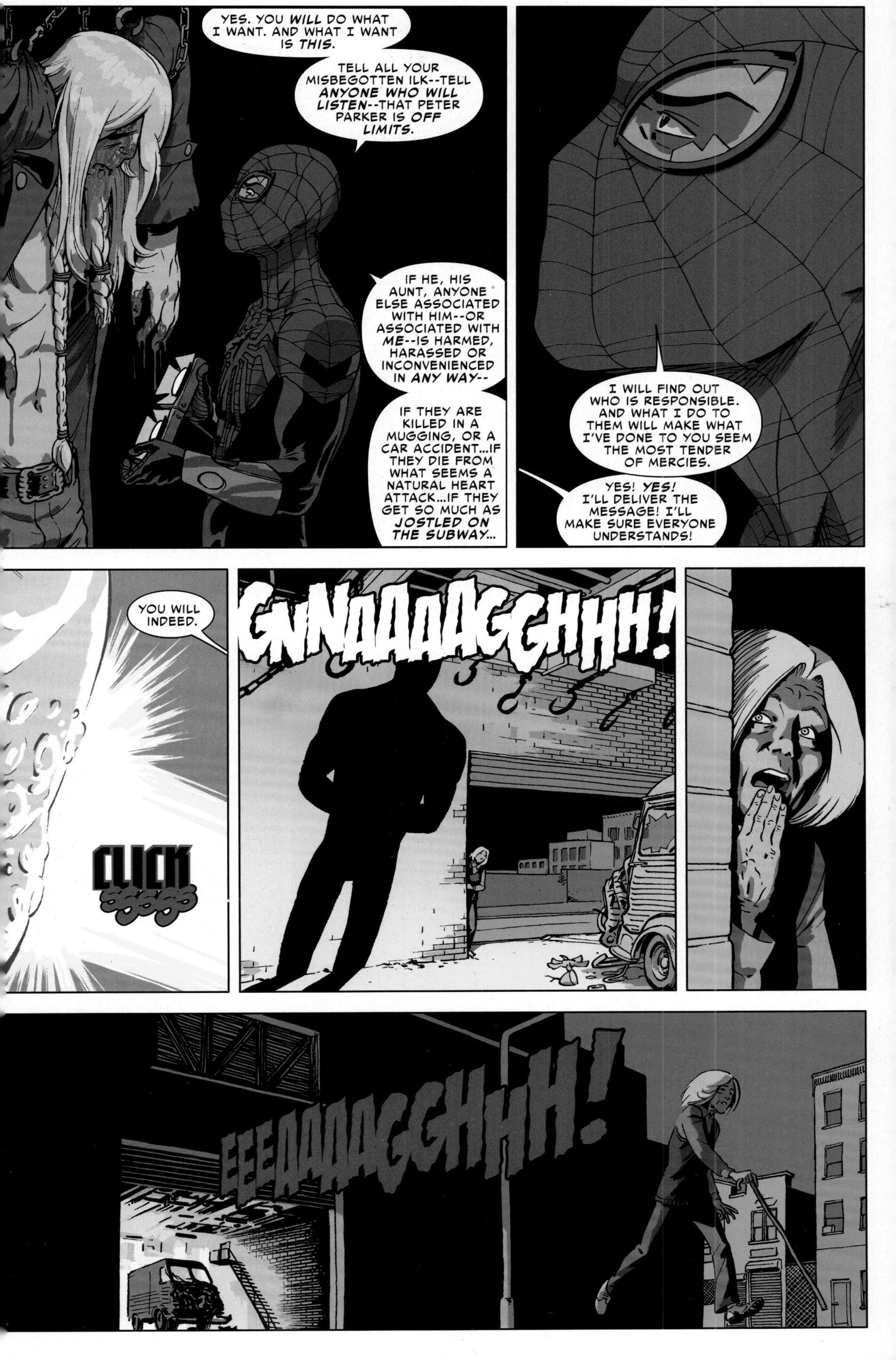
YES. YOU WILL DO WHAT I WANT. AND WHAT I WANT IS THIS.
TELL ALL YOUR MISBEGOTTEN ILK--TELL ANYONE WHO WILL LISTEN--THAT PETER PARKER IS OFF LIMITS.
IF HE, HIS AUNT, ANYONE ELSE ASSOCIATED WITH HIM--OR ASSOCIATED WITH ME--IS HARMED, HARASSED OR INCONVENIENCED IN ANY WAY--
IF THEY ARE KILLED IN A MUGGING, OR A CAR ACCIDENT...IF THEY DIE FROM WHAT SEEMS A NATURAL HEART ATTACK...IF THEY GET SO MUCH AS JOSTLED ON THE SUBWAY...
I WILL FIND OUT WHO IS RESPONSIBLE. AND WHAT I DO TO THEM WILL MAKE WHAT I'VE DONE TO YOU SEEM THE MOST TENDER OF MERCIES.
YES! YES! I'LL DELIVER THE MESSAGE! I'LL MAKE SURE EVERYONE UNDERSTANDS!
YOU WILL INDEED.
CLICK
SSSSS
GNAAAAAGGHHH!
EEEAAAAGGHHH!

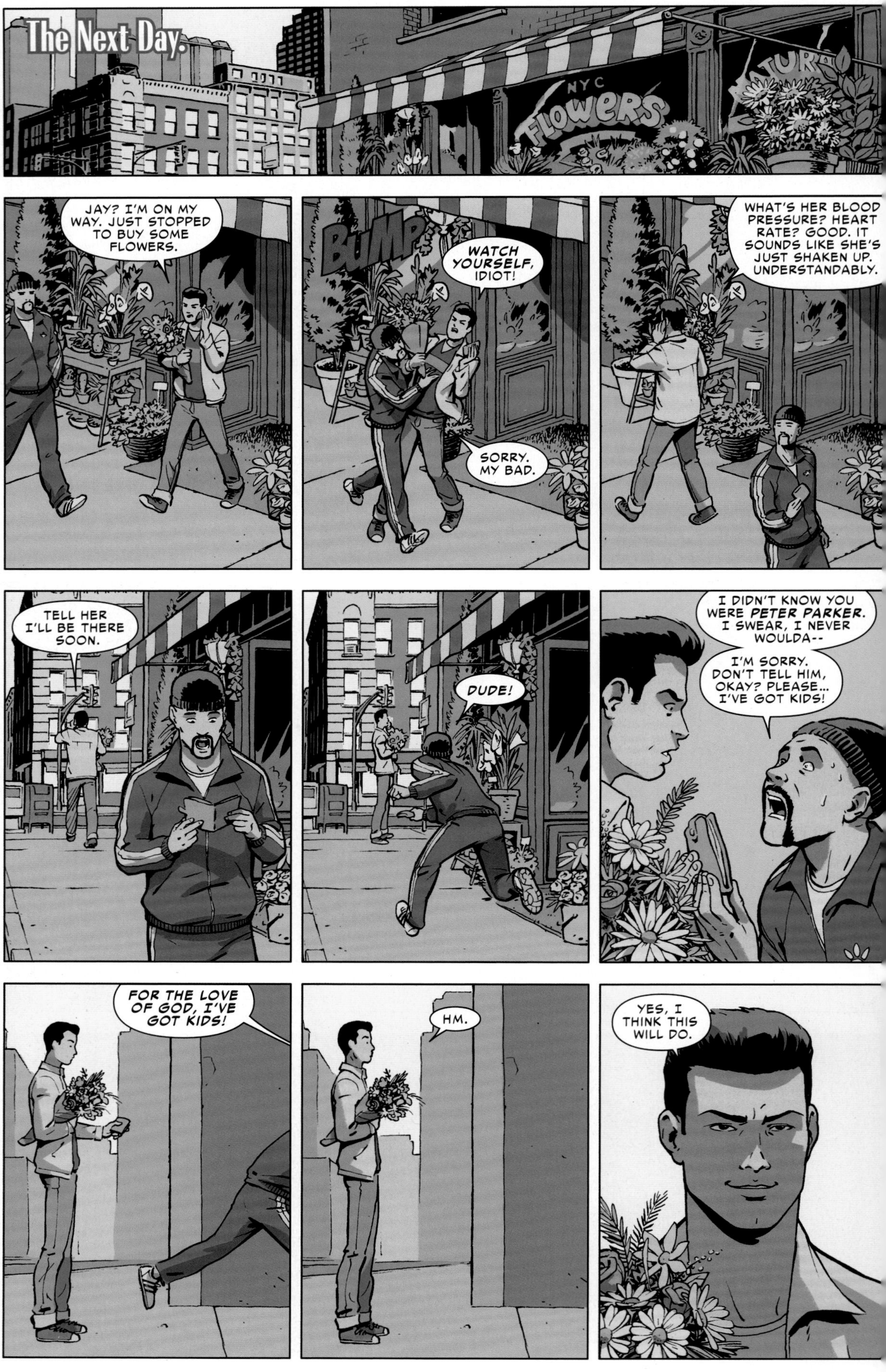
The Next Day.
NYC FLOWERS
JAY? I'M ON MY WAY. JUST STOPPED TO BUY SOME FLOWERS.
BUMP
WATCH YOURSELF, IDIOT!
SORRY. MY BAD.
WHAT'S HER BLOOD PRESSURE? HEART RATE? GOOD. IT SOUNDS LIKE SHE'S JUST SHAKEN UP. UNDERSTANDABLY.
TELL HER I'LL BE THERE SOON.
DUDE!
I DIDN'T KNOW YOU WERE PETER PARKER. I SWEAR, I NEVER WOULDA--
I'M SORRY. DON'T TELL HIM, OKAY? PLEASE... I'VE GOT KIDS!
FOR THE LOVE OF GOD, I'VE GOT KIDS!
HM.
YES, I THINK THIS WILL DO.

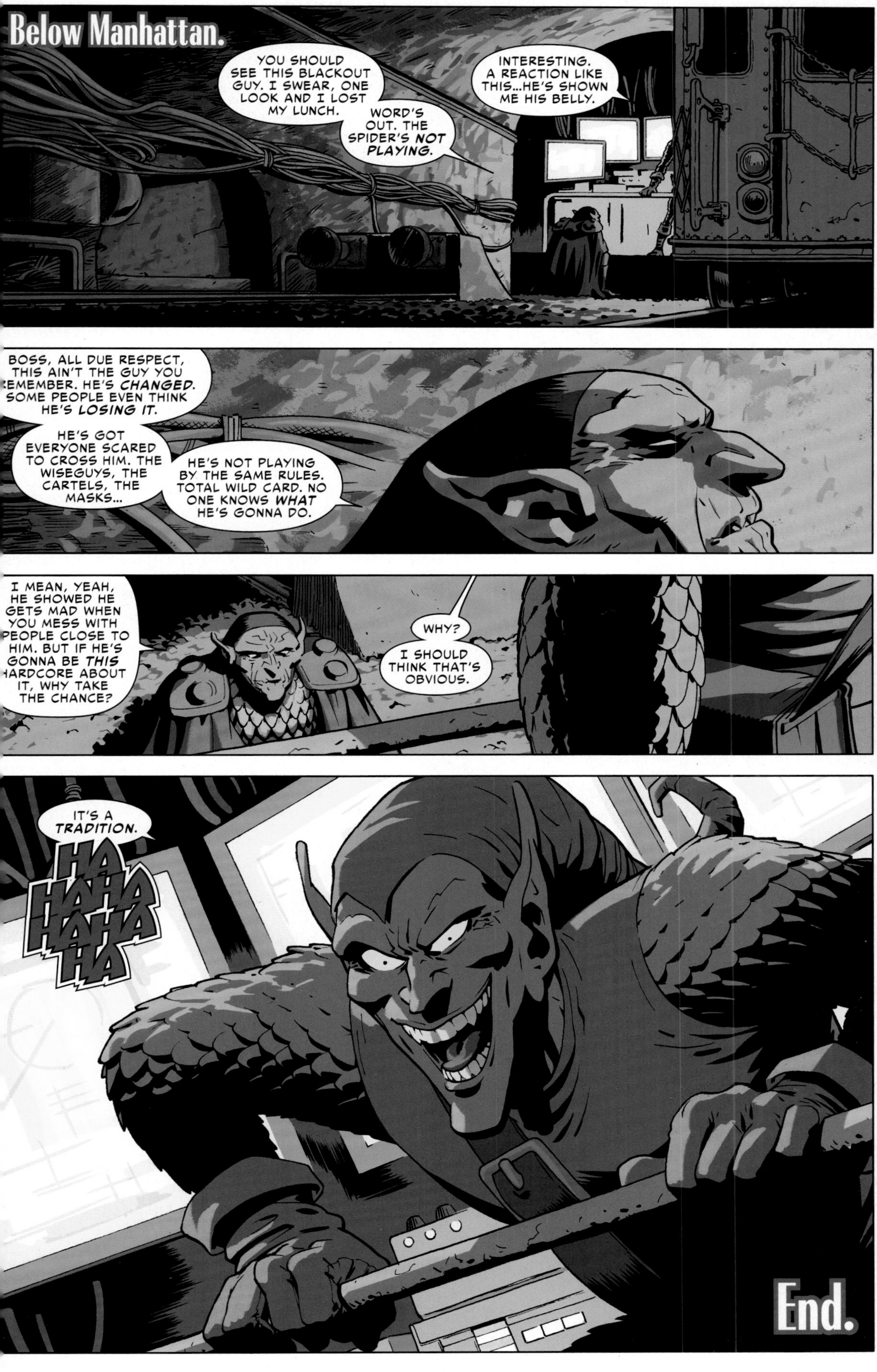
Below Manhattan.
YOU SHOULD SEE THIS BLACKOUT GUY. I SWEAR, ONE LOOK AND I LOST MY LUNCH.
WORD'S OUT. THE SPIDER'S NOT PLAYING.
INTERESTING. A REACTION LIKE THIS...HE'S SHOWN ME HIS BELLY.
BOSS, ALL DUE RESPECT, THIS AIN'T THE GUY YOU REMEMBER. HE'S CHANGED. SOME PEOPLE EVEN THINK HE'S LOSING IT.
HE'S GOT EVERYONE SCARED TO CROSS HIM. THE WISEGUYS, THE CARTELS, THE MASKS...
HE'S NOT PLAYING BY THE SAME RULES. TOTAL WILD CARD. NO ONE KNOWS WHAT HE'S GONNA DO.
I MEAN, YEAH, HE SHOWED HE GETS MAD WHEN YOU MESS WITH PEOPLE CLOSE TO HIM. BUT IF HE'S GONNA BE THIS HARDCORE ABOUT IT, WHY TAKE THE CHANCE?
WHY?
I SHOULD THINK THAT'S OBVIOUS.
IT'S A TRADITION.
HA HAHA HAHA HA
End.

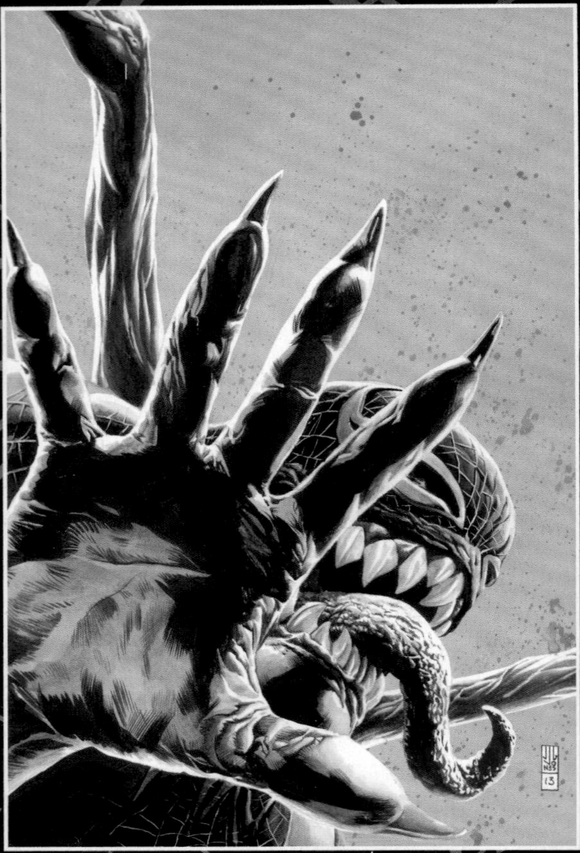

#25 VARIANT
BY J.G. JONES

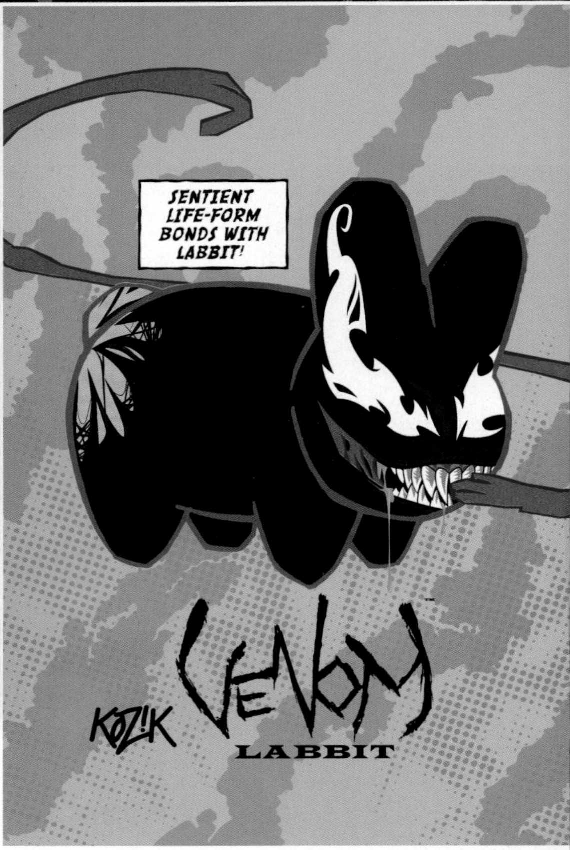
SENTIENT LIFE-FORM BONDS WITH LABBIT!
KOZIK
VENOM
LABBIT

#25 LABBIT HASTINGS VARIANT
BY KOZIK

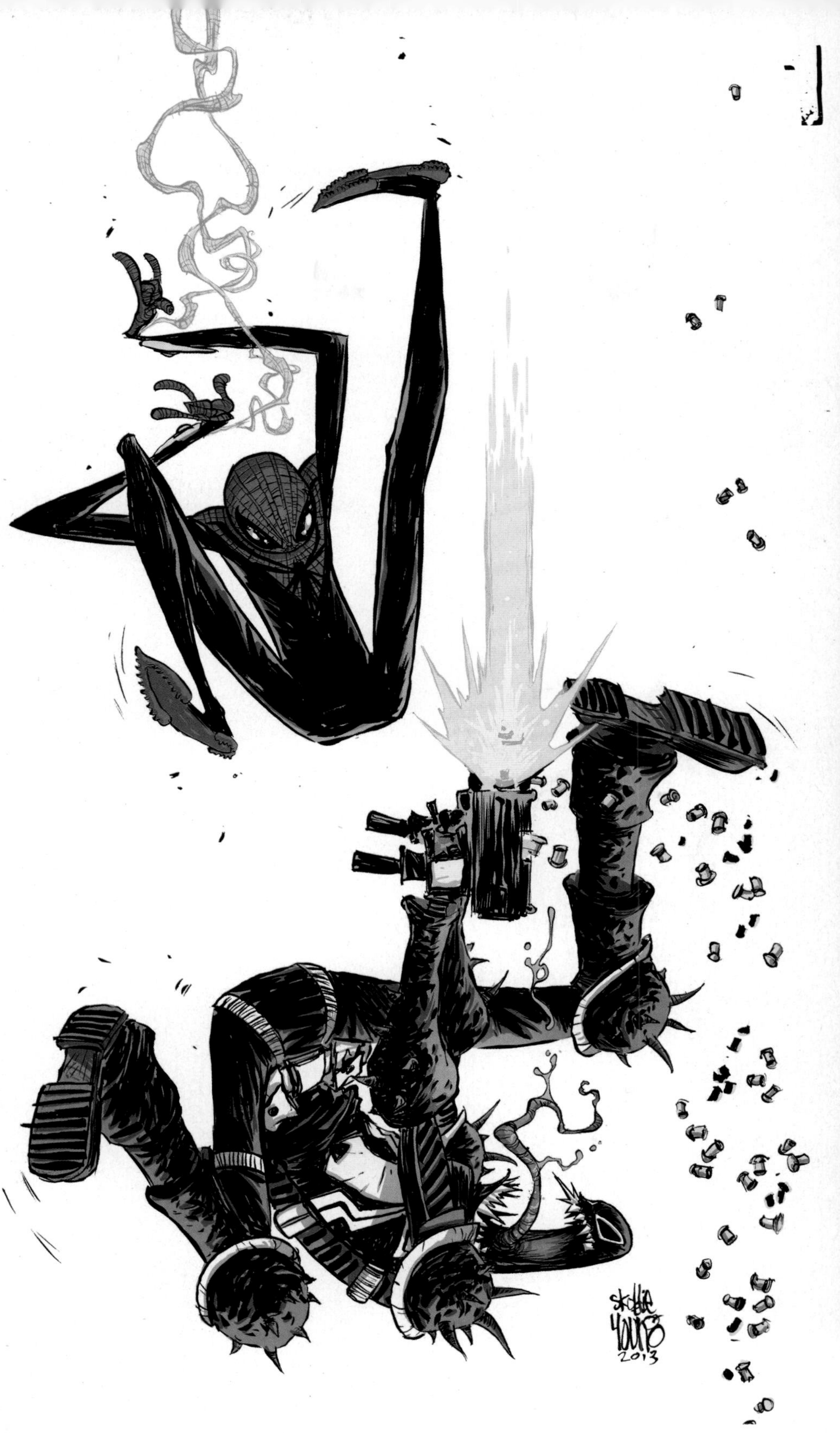
skottie young 2013

#23 VARIANT
BY SKOTTIE YOUNG

TO ACCESS THE FREE *MARVEL AUGMENTED REALITY APP* THAT ENHANCES AND CHANGES THE WAY YOU EXPERIENCE COMICS

1. Download the app for free via marvel.com/ARapp

2. Launch the app on your camera-enabled Apple iOS® or Android™ device*

3. Hold your mobile device's camera over any cover or panel with the **AR** graphic

4. Sit back and see the future of comics in action!

*Available on most camera-enabled Apple iOS® and Android™ devices. Content subject to change and availability.

THE SUPERIOR SPIDER-MAN

AR INDEX